D1339725

THE IRISH TRANSPORT AND GENERAL WORKERS' UNION

The Formative Years: 1909-1923

C. DESMOND GREAVES

THE IRISH TRANSPORT AND GENERAL WORKERS' UNION

The Formative Years 1909-1923

GILL AND MACMILLAN

First published 1982 by
Gill and Macmillan Ltd
Goldenbridge
Dublin 8
with associated companies in
London, New York, Delhi, Hong Kong,
Johannesburg, Lagos, Melbourne,
Singapore, Tokyo

7171 1199 7(p)
7171 1253 5(h)

Origination by Healyset, Dublin
Printed by Criterion Press Ltd, Dublin
Bound by John F. Newman and Son Ltd, Dublin

Contents

Preface

This volume has been prepared with the average trade union activist in mind. An attempt has been made to use common or ordinary language and to avoid the jargon of sociology or neo-Marxism. For the same reason the text has not been overburdened with references, which, however useful to the specialist, can interrupt the attention of most readers. At the same time there should be enough documentation to set the professional Labour historian on the track of what he wants.

Apart from the trade unionist and the historian, it is hoped that the general reader may find much to attract him in a story described by Sidney and Beatrice Webb as 'an epic in itself', the rise of a great organisation of the common people in an epoch of social unrest, world conflict and national revolution.

The union's first General Secretary was James Larkin, and the new style of trade unionism it introduced was given the name of Larkinism. It was a product of its time, theoretically an amalgam of syndicalism, socialism and social democracy, best described perhaps by the union's Acting General Secretary, James Connolly:

> I believe that the development of fighting spirit is of more importance than the creation of the theoretically perfect organisation.

In 1914 Larkin left for the USA. Connolly took over, only to pay the supreme penalty in 1916. Yet from the ruins of Liberty Hall sprang an organisation able to defend working-class interests and provide muscle for the national struggle. Its early leaders can be justly described as giants.

Trade union history is sometimes rated dull by non-specialists. Yet the period covered by this history was packed with rich incident and excitement. If the account makes dull reading, it can only be the fault of the author.

But unfortunately exciting times are not good for archives. Most of the union's records were seized and pulped in 1916. In repeated raids on Liberty Hall, minutes, accounts, correspondence and lists were destroyed. The earliest Executive minutes available are those of July 1921. There is thus no continuous record to work from. The story must be pieced together. Its reconstruction might have been impossible but for the salvage operation mounted by William O'Brien. He dreamed of writing the history of the movement. He will be remembered as the man who made its writing possible.

As well as the O'Brien Papers, officials of the National Library of Ireland kindly placed at my disposal the contents of three large boxes. These were uncatalogued but included copies of some of the reports made by the union to the Registrar of Friendly Societies which could not be traced by the government department. There was also a mass of uncatalogued material in the basement of Liberty Hall which included some of the papers of the late Mr Cathal O'Shannon. I acknowledge with gratitude the assistance of Mr Peter Rigney of the Irish Labour History Society in bringing this material to some rough semblance of order.

The absence of EC minutes is not quite so great a handicap as might appear, owing to the fact that national decisions were recorded in the minutes of the Dublin No. 1 branch from 1914 to 1918, and that these minutes are extremely full. Annual Reports were first issued in 1918. Day-to-day events are recorded in a succession of Labour papers, all funded by the union in whole or in part: the *Irish Worker, Workers' Republic, Voice of Labour* and *Watchword of Labour*. The first three were suppressed, but the gap can sometimes be filled from files of the Dublin *Saturday Post*. Other useful sources are the annual reports of the Irish Trade Union Congress and the minutes of the Dublin and Belfast Trades Councils. For the history of branches, minute books have survived only in the case of Dublin No. 1 and Cork city. For the rest one is dependent on national and local newspapers, from which it proved possible to date most of the reminiscences of old members.

My thanks are due to the branch secretaries who filled in questionnaires and sent newspaper articles and memoranda, and to the old members introduced to me by local officials, especially in Cork, Galway and Sligo. I must also express my appreciation of the time given me by former officials Mr William McMullen and Mr Peadar O'Donnell, and also by the late Mr Roderic Connolly. It is impossible to exaggerate the help given by officials of the National Library of Ireland, and especially by Mr Dónall Ó Luanaigh with his vast knowledge of the manuscript collection.

Within the union I must thank especially Mr Daltún Ó Ceallaigh and the officials and staff at Palmerston Road and Liberty Hall, who located and translocated a fair avoirdupois of documents. Finally I must offer my thanks to the General Officers and Executive of the union, for help and encouragement and the finance that helped to fund the research, and above all to the General Secretary, Mr Michael Mullen, whose idea the project was. None of these is in any way responsible for the conclusions I have drawn, the emphases I have given, or any errors committed. I have tried to tell the story of the union from the union's own standpoint without, I hope, infringing historical authenticity.

Regarding nomenclature, I have usually given place-names in their modern form, but when this principle would result in a glaring anachronism I have used the old form. In the matter of personal names, that in general use is employed except where it might lead to an error of identification.

C. Desmond Greaves
January 1982

Introduction

> Successful revolutions are not the product of our brains but of ripe material conditions.
>
> JAMES CONNOLLY

The importance of the 1890s – the skilled trades – rural workers – the urban 'unskilled' – infrastructure workers – struggles of 1890-91 – 'Parliament of Labour' – Connolly's ISRP – eclipse of the infrastructure unions – Taff Vale decision – politicisation – 1906 election – NUDL returns to Ireland

The social needs to which the Irish Transport and General Workers' Union responded had existed long before its foundation in 1909. The 'new unionism' made its début in England in 1889 when the 'unskilled' workers claimed their place in the sun. It is sometimes implied that there was no contemporary development in Ireland, that the 'new unionism' came to Ireland twenty years late. This is not in fact the case. The 'new unionism' came to Ireland in 1890, but its career was cut short by factors peculiar to Ireland, in particular the structure of the labour market. The methods adopted by the employers in crushing it resembled those used against the ITGWU two decades later. Tried and trusted though they were, in the replay they led to a different outcome.

The 1890s were remarkable times in Ireland, a period of seed-sowing from which many modern institutions sprang. The process which converted Irish Labour into a powerful third estate began with the establishment of the Irish Trade Union Congress in 1894. James Connolly founded the Irish Socialist Republican Party in 1896. Both of these important events, from which so much history was to flow, were delayed results of the great mass struggles of 1890. The 'unskilled' arose. They were put down again. But the working class as a whole absorbed the experience and added new weapons to its defences. Perhaps the most important result was the beginning of a long process of assimilation between skilled and 'unskilled' labour. This was, of course, encouraged by economic factors. The steady internationalisation of the market reduced the security of skilled trades serving a restricted area. The minutes of the Dublin Trades Council reveal a crescendo of protest against importations. Its Janus-like stance was summarised in the slogan 'For working class and Irish industries'.[1]

The gulf that divided the privileged and unprivileged sections of the working class in the early 1890s is not easy to visualise today. The tradesmen had been organised, legally or illegally, for over a century, at least in Dublin and Cork. Their craft loyalties had been confirmed in repeated confrontations with the employers, to whom they were bound, nevertheless, by a limited community of interest. As a result of their success in regulating, to a certain extent, the supply of labour, they had won a position of tolerable comfort, given the expectations of the time. A tradesman might earn more than twice the wage of an 'unskilled' labourer. He formed, indeed, part of a worker aristocracy, his coronet a bowler hat, his ceremonial address 'Mister'. This can be read in the studious respectability of the photographs that adorn the first reports of the Irish TUC. It is possible that Parnell had these workers in mind when, towards the end of 1889, before the storm had broken, he asked Michael Davitt: 'What is trade unionism but a landlordism of Labour?'[2]

The attitude of the skilled worker to the 'unskilled' was as ambivalent as his attitude to the employer. With him a common interest in local industry was qualified by a competition for its proceeds. Skilled and 'unskilled' had a common interest in maximising the wages fund, but the trades had definite opinions upon how it was to be divided. Organisations of the 'unskilled' were willingly recognised when, at intervals, they arose, but no effort was made to attract labourers into societies run by the tradesmen. The trades represented order. Chaos might not be completely devoid of form, but it remained chaos. The slow modification of this point of view after 1890 was of great importance.

The reservoir from which 'unskilled' labour was replenished was, of course, the land. The gradations between traditional subsistence farming and fully capitalist agriculture, employing permanent wage-earners, were innumerable. Wage labour was most prevalent in the economically advanced dairying districts of the south-east and south. In the west wage labour was largely seasonal or migratory. The permanent farm labourer had no intense impulsion to leave the land.[3] The impoverished small farmer often had every reason to do so. It was he who threatened the livelihood of the city labourer, though decreasingly as his dream of returning to a farm of his own slowly evaporated, and with it his instinctive individualism. Once fully acclimatised to city life, he could become the staunchest of trade unionists. He came as a cuckoo, but remained as a wren.

The largest division of the 'unskilled' urban workers consisted of those in domestic service. They were not even considered for organisation. Another large section comprised those who assisted skilled tradesmen, for example bricklayers' labourers. There was a substantial 'unskilled' labour force in the manufacturing industries, but the mode of presentation of census information does not enable us to estimate its size. On the other hand, the census reports distinguish 'persons engaged on railways, roads, rivers, seas, storage, conveying messages, etc.' In 1891 these numbered 38,231. Together with the gas workers and the suppliers of other essential services, they operated the infrastructure required even for purely mercantile activities. Their numbers were stable, their power, when they could exercise it, formidable. A strike in a factory harmed one employer. A strike in a trade restricted one commodity or service. A strike by dockers, coal porters or gas workers affected a wide range of economic activity. These workers formed the backbone of the 'new unionism' in both Britain and Ireland. Their weakness was that they were vulnerable to incomers and their organisations tended to be temporary, springing up during a boom and dying down with the ensuing slump.

The Dublin dockers had been organised during the prosperous early 1870s, but the Quay Labourers' Union, which took part in the O'Connell commemoration in 1875, does not appear to have survived the slump of 1879 which gave rise to the first mass unemployed movement. There was organisation among coal porters in 1880. This seems to have collapsed during the severe and prolonged slump of 1884-87. There was a marked improvement in 1888, and the next two years were exceptionally prosperous. The boom originated in Britain, and the effects were first felt there. The Webbs speak of a 'wave of trade unionism, comparable in extent with those of 1833-34 and 1873-74'.[4] In one year 200,000 members accrued to the unions. The Amalgamated Society of Railway Servants and the National Amalgamated Sailors' and Firemen's Union grew substantially. Several new unions were formed. The National Union of Gasworkers and General Labourers (NUGGL), founded in May 1889, won the eight-hour day without a stoppage. The dockers of the west coast formed the National Union of Dock Labourers, with headquarters in Glasgow. All these unions were interested in Ireland. They combined with native Irish organisations, for example Davitt's Democratic Labour League and the Dublin (later Irish) United Labourers' Union, to produce a wave of trade unionism in Ireland comparable with that of 1870-72.

The 'new unionism' was much discussed in Dublin by Adolphus Shields and his fellow-socialists. There is good evidence that members of the Dublin Socialist Union approached the National Union of Gasworkers and General Labourers with the suggestion that they should start organising in Ireland. They appointed as their Irish organiser Michael Canty, a Cork man. In March 1890 he achieved considerable success with the striking bricklayers' labourers, and began to recruit coal porters and quay labourers. At a mass meeting in Phoenix Park, with Engels's friend J. A. Poole in the chair, Edward Aveling, Canty and Shields supported a resolution which recognised 'the imperative necessity of the working class combining nationally and internationally in order to obtain the due share of the wealth it creates'.[5]

The Gasworkers' Union spread rapidly. In a series of strikes and lock-outs which led to scuffles with blacklegs and police on the quays the coal porters won concessions from all but one of their employers, McCormick, who carried on his business with the aid of countrymen and army reservists. Branches were established in Cork, Belfast and Limerick. At the end of the year there were forty-five branches, and the union claimed to have won wage increases of from 10 to 40 per cent for over 14,000 members.[6]

The organising of the railwaymen by the ASRS organiser William Foreman was actively supported by Michael

Davitt. The result was the 'greatest railway strike ever in Ireland'.[7] Settled satisfactorily, as it was thought, it broke out again on the issue of dismissal of blacklegs. An uneasy guerrilla war ensued in which summonses were issued against singalmen who left their boxes unattended, but again a settlement was reached with the DSER and GSWR. The Limerick and Waterford railway strike which began just before Christmas 1890, when the docks were black with policemen, had a different outcome. The company dismissed the strikers, and they were never re-employed. This was a blow to the ASRS, but the organisation survived in Dublin, where Foreman was instrumental in setting up the Tramway Servants' Union. The management flatly refused to entertain any communication with them.

The fiercest battles were reserved for the NUDL. During the early months of 1890 its Glasgow headquarters were fully occupied with Liverpool. But once organisation in that city was secure, the secretary, Edward MacHugh, turned his attention to Belfast, where he engaged Michael McKeown as Irish organiser. The Belfast dock strike began in July. Organisation spread to Drogheda and Newry, then to Dublin. Ships diverted from one port to another were 'blacked'. The NUDL established branches in Limerick, Cork, and in Galway, where there was a stoppage.

The great struggles on the docks of the south of Ireland merged with strikes by seamen, in some cases the dockers coming out in sympathy. The seamen's union, the NUSF, formed branches in Arklow, Wexford, Youghal and Cork. In the last city seamen who left the *Lee* were summarily clapped into jail. The result was the extension of the strike to the docks. McKeown was sent from Belfast, and the dispute lasted three months. Within days the dockers of Limerick came out, followed by the Waterford men, of whom a number were charged with conspiracy. In December 1890, therefore, the docks at Cork, Limerick and Waterford were either at a standstill or being worked by blacklegs, while the situation at Limerick was compounded by the railway strike and a strike in Cleeve's condensed milk factory. In most of these stuggles the issue was that of wages.

Strikes were not confined to the infrastucture workers. McKeown organised Pierce's foundry in Wexford. The owner dismissed all trade unionists and worked his plant with the aid of blacklegs. Tailors struck in Derry, where their secretary, James McCarron, was bundled incontinently into jail. Sligo tailors fared somewhat better. Their strike was settled, but it was immediately followed by a dock strike which lasted several months.

Throughout the year Michael Davitt was setting up organisations in the rural areas, which, though not trade unions in the strict sense of the word, catered for wage-earners while dealing mainly with issues of benefits in kind, housing, potato plots, etc. The United Labourers pushed their organisation through the small towns of Co. Dublin and Co. Kildare. The Belfast Trades Council drew up a scheme for organising women workers which ultimately saw fruit in Miss Mary Galway's Textile Operatives' Union, founded in 1893. The Council also founded the Flaxroughers' Union.

The year 1890 was thus one of feverish activity, and it must be appreciated that many of those who were active at this time were young enough to take part again when the next 'wave of trade unionism' appeared. As has been indicated, the decline of business activity and increase in the level of unemployment favoured an employers' offensive; and though there were further struggles in 1891, there were serious defeats.

Nevertheless the experiences of this period of storm and stress became embodied in organisational form. The Gasworkers' Union, one would think almost certainly under the influence of the Avelings and J. A. Poole, conceived the notion of a 'Parliament of Labour' in Ireland. Three DSU members together with Fred J. Allan, the well-known IRB man, attended at the Dublin Trades Council to ask support for a conference on 14 March 1891 which was to be addressed by C. S. Parnell, now separated from the majority of his party and in tacit alliance with the Fenians. The Trades Council was unsympathetic. It had taken up a neutral position on the Parnell split. But the meeting took place, and the Irish Labour League was formally established. Although a member of the Waterford Typographical Association 'who happened to be in town' was present, the 'aristocrats of Labour were conspicuous by their absence'.[8] Even the NUDL was anxious to dissociate itself. The Trades Council agreed, however, to taking part in the May Day demonstration organised on the initiative of the DSU. This was addressed by Shields, Aveling and Poole, together with three representatives of the Dublin Trades Council. One of these, John Simmons, had been its secretary since a few months after its foundation. With him were William Field, who became prominent as a Labour-oriented Nationalist MP, and the railwaymen's organiser William Foreman.

The example of the Labour League, which never took root, led the Trades Council to call a conference on 19 July 1891 which was attended by delegates from Cork, Galway, Wexford, Newry, Drogheda, Clonmel and Mountrath. No permanent organisation was established, and little could have been achieved in the economically bleak years of 1892 and 1893. But in 1894 the Dublin Trades Council, in consultation with Belfast and other Trades Councils, convened the first Irish Trade Union Congress. Forty-eight delegates represented skilled tradesmen, six the infrastructure workers, and four rural 'Land and Labour' Associations. The Gasworkers' Union had fallen apart in Dublin. Canty represented the coal labourers. The dockers' and tramwaymen's unions and the United Labourers of Ireland had survived, but not for long. By the end of the century neither the NUDL, the Tramway Servants' Union, nor the four Land and Labour Associations were to be found in the Congress lists. The evidence is that the NUDL was defunct, while the TSU may have preserved a tenuous existence.

After the collapse of the Irish Labour League the alliance of socialists and 'unskilled' workers – and indeed the embryonic 'Labour/Republican unity' later advocated by Connolly – that characterised the 'new unionism' came to a temporary end. A Dublin branch of the English Independent Labour Party was established, and there was much confusion over tactics. At the same time there was increasing interest, and when the group round Shields learned that James Connolly, now back in Edinburgh, was seeking an appointment as a socialist organiser they invited him to Dublin in the spring of 1896. He persuaded them to establish a new working-class party, simultaneously socialist and nationalist, called the Irish Socialist Republican Party. Connolly was a man of powerful scientific intellect, immense energy and perseverance, and total dedication to the cause he had espoused. He was an avowed Marxist. In face of poverty, disappointment and neglect, he kept up a propaganda by means of public speaking, pamphleteering and the publication of the periodical *Workers' Republic* – issued 'whenever it was strong enough to get out'. Among his early converts were Tom Lyng and the youngest of the O'Brien brothers, William, who achieved fame as a trade union leader. Adolphus Shields continued his Labour activities but does not appear to have embraced all Connolly's doctrines. Likewise E. W. Stewart, prominent as a trade unionist, drifted towards the Irish Parliamentary Party. Canty, who was moving in the same direction, remained aloof from the ISRP. Connolly represented the United Labourers on the Trades Council.

It is doubtful whether many of Connolly's followers achieved a thorough grasp of his philosophy, and perhaps he cannot be totally acquitted of the charge of dogmatism. But some of them understood some of it. After he left for the USA in 1903 he still dominated Dublin socialism. A visitor to the socialist premises remarked: 'One name and one presence pervades the little room: Connolly away in the States.'[9] Socialist ideas appealed to no considerable proportion of the working class, but were a leavening influence even as a butt of opposition.

The early years of the twentieth century were uneventful in comparison with the 1890s. The South African War distracted attention from Labour issues. An attempt to re-establish the NUDL in Dublin is of interest only because William O'Brien and nineteen-year-old Thomas Foran attended the meeting. One of the most potent influences keeping Labour quiescent was the Taff Vale decision in 1901, which extended the doctrine of corporate responsibility to trade unions. These became responsible for the torts of all persons who might reasonably be considered to be their agents.

The Webbs estimated that the Taff Vale decision cost the trade union movement as much as £200,000 in the period during which it applied. The gain to employers and the loss to wage-earners cannot, of course, be quantified. Suffice it to say that while the price of foodstuffs rose by about 2 per cent between 1900 and 1906, there was a reduction in the general level of wages. The number of strikes fell by a half, and of 135 claims for benefit admitted by the General Federation of Trade Unions, no fewer than 130 arose from efforts by employers to encroach on recognised standards.[10]

The result was the politicisation of the working class which contributed to the landslide victory of the Liberals in 1906 and the return of twenty-nine Labour members to the British parliament. The Trades Disputes Act, which became law in 1906, restored to trade unions their traditional immunities. The year 1906 was moreover relatively prosperous. The time seemed propitious for recovering lost ground. The NUDL, its headquarters now in Liverpool, first set about reorganising the Scottish ports. James Larkin, the official who was entrusted with this, was then sent to Belfast.

Larkin had been born on 28 January 1874 at 41 Combermere Street, Toxteth. His parents, James Larkin and Mary Ann McNulty, had not long emigrated from Ireland. The Liverpool dockland was a hotbed of Fenianism, and it would have been hard for Larkin to escape the nationalist influence.[11] He was sixteen when the great dock strike paralysed the port, and he may well have been involved in it. He joined the Independent Labour Party soon after it was established, and ultimately became an official of the dockers' union and acted as election agent for its General Secretary, James Sexton.

Since the NUDL records were subsequently sold to a rag-and-bone merchant, the reasons for sending Larkin to Belfast must remain obscure.[12] He was a born organiser. His oratory was both imaginative and down to earth, but typical of the ILP, which favoured an emotional, even sentimental, style of propaganda, very different from Connolly's science militant. He was a trifle egotistical and undoubtedly ambitious. Sexton may have felt that he was better out of Liverpool. The Labour Representation Committee, forerunner of the Labour Party, was holding its conference in Belfast at the beginning of 1907, and a number of trade unions were availing of the interest in Labour questions thereby aroused. It was therefore natural to send an organiser. The fact dwarfed all possible reasons. Larkin was sent.

1

Larkin's Irish Breakaway

> The *first* act of resistance is always, and must be ever premature, imprudent, and dangerous.
>
> FINTAN LALOR

Belfast transport strikes – employers' ultimatum – police mutiny – army excesses – a 'yellow' union – Larkin in Dublin – overruled by Sexton – Waterford – Cork – dismissal – an Irish union

On 26 January 1907 James Larkin, newly appointed Irish organiser of the National Union of Dock Labourers, called on Thomas Johnson of the Belfast Trades Council to inform him that that day he was taking up his duties. He had known Johnson in Liverpool in the early days of the ILP, and he stayed with his old colleague while he sought accommodation.[1] 1907

Belfast was a tough assignment. It was a city which had grown rapidly. It had few of the traditional trades of Dublin. Its local market had long been wide open to importations. There were other respects in which it differed from Dublin: in the large scale of its staple industries, engineering and textiles, and in the accentuation of the distinction between craft and 'unskilled' workers by their standing on the two sides of a religious divide.

Even among the skilled workers there were divisions. The engineering trades were based on the shipyards. Their members belonged to English unions and had long enjoyed comparability with English and Scottish workers. They did not even think it worth their while to affiliate to the Belfast Trades Council, still less to the Irish TUC. The textile workers were in a less favoured position. Those with special skills might get their price for them; those without were at the mercy of the employers. Children twelve years of age worked as 'half-timers' in the mills, often receiving only 4s for 34 hours of monotonous toil in saturated air at 70°F. James Connolly

1907 thought that this system explained the widespread illiteracy in Belfast.[2] There were all kinds of abuses. Women whose weekly wage was only 4s 6d were sometimes illegally 'fined' the whole amount and sent home penniless at the end of a week's work.

Larkin had, however, one unusual advantage. Religious sectarianism, which had been deliberately fostered by employers so as to keep the working class divided, was at a low ebb. The general disgust with the Conservative administration at Westminster had led to a revival of Liberalism. The doctrines of Lindsay Crawford, who had helped to found the Independent Orange Order in 1903, had led to his dismissal from the *Irish Protestant*, but at the end of 1906 he became editor of the newly established Liberal *Ulster Guardian*. In its columns he continued to encourage the reconciliation of the estranged religious communities. He preached a moderate nationalism stopping short of Home Rule, which was in any case not an issue, for the Liberals had undertaken not to introduce a third bill in the 1906 parliament.

Larkin moved warily at first. He sought out Michael McKeown, who was now a Nationalist councillor, and the old organiser became secretary of the new branch. Some conception of the situation on Belfast docks can be derived from the evidence given before the Departmental Committee on the Checking of Piecework Prices (Cd 4380), which was published in 1909. Larkin described the system as 'chaotic'. There was no regular rate. Stevedores paid whatever they could persuade men to accept. It might be 2d for shovelling a ton of ore. There were no means of checking weights, and workers were defenceless against illegal deductions. In 1890 Bruce Wallace had been sued for libel after giving undue publicity to complaints that it was better to be paid 6s on the quay than 9s in the public house. Things had not changed, and Larkin, who was a strong advocate of temperance, was disgusted that it should still be thought prudent to 'treat' the ganger.

Within three weeks Larkin had 400 members in Belfast and shortly afterwards a branch in Derry. By April he could claim a total of 4,000 members and had opened three offices. The cross-channel dockers, who were Protestants, had their rooms at 11 Victoria Street; the Catholic deep-sea dockers

were at 41 Bridge End. Three delegates were appointed: 1907
Thomas Cupples, John Quinn and John Davidson. The branch affiliated to the Trades Council on 9 April and was represented by Larkin, Quinn, Savage, Morrow and Davidson. From these names alone it is clear that Larkin had organised both Catholics and Protestants.

* * *

On 26 April trouble began. The NUDL men at Kelly's coal quay struck in protest against the dismissal of a man who had joined the union. Kelly unloaded the ship with the aid of carters and refused to negotiate. Larkin had not wished to fight on the issue of dismissal or the closed shop. He was aware that Kelly was a contractor to a number of public boards and ought to have been observing a fair-wage agreement. He gave an optimistic report to the Trades Council on 2 May. What he did not know was that on the previous day the directors of the Belfast Steamship Company had made arrangements with the Shipping Federation for the supply of blacklegs on request and were now sitting back waiting for trouble. It came on 6 May when, to Larkin's dismay, a number of dockers employed by this company refused to work with two men who would not join the union. He had a second struggle on his hands before he had decided the first.

Larkin instructed the BSC strikers to return to work at once. He visited the company office to apologise on their behalf. The company officials showed not the slightest interest. When the men reported for work on the morning of 8 May they were told that none of them were required. The s.s. *Caloric* berthed at Donegall Quay. It was found she had on board fifty blacklegs from Liverpool. The company proposed to employ these in unloading s.s. *Optic*, but the men on the *Heroic* (constant men, unlike the casuals who had been locked out) took sympathetic action. The company had to send for more blacklegs. A hundred arrived next day from Hull and Glasgow. Two of Larkin's sections were involved in a quarrel not of his seeking. But constant workers had struck in sympathy with casual men, a remarkable thing in itself.

The dispute at Kellys was resolved in a spectactular manner.

1907 On Thursday 9 May s.s. *Balmerino* tied up. The strikers, supported by all available casual workers, assembled in such force that the non-union men working on the quayside were completely overwhelmed. The ship was then boarded, and after a fusillade of missiles had driven them from the hold the 'free labourers' were escorted down the gangways by the union men. After another attempt to unload the vessel was foiled in the same manner the company capitulated. Wages were increased, overtime rates were agreed, meal-times were fixed, and the union was recognised.

The effect of these developments was felt across the river, where the dockers succeeded in preventing the company from sailing the *Caloric* into York Dock. There were clashes between dockers and police. Arson was suspected when a fire in one of the Princess Dock sheds was discovered just in time to save the building from destruction. The harbour police were reinforced by members of the RIC. There was now a stalemate which lasted several months.

The blacklegs were housed on board ship for their own safety and to protect them from persuasion. On 31 May a number of them ventured ashore and were refreshing themselves in the Stag's Head, Waring Street, when they were discovered and ejected by striking dockers. An altercation followed. One of the blacklegs, a man named Bamber, drew a knife. Larkin struck him with a stone, but failed to disarm him. Bamber stabbed several strikers before being overpowered. Both he and Larkin were arrested and charged with assault and battery. The blackleg was acquitted. Larkin secured the transfer of his trial to Dublin on the ground that he could not hope for a fair hearing in Tory Belfast. When at length the case was heard the prosecution chose not to call Bamber as a witness. The jury disagreed, and the matter was allowed to drop.

A fortnight went by during which the Belfast Steamship Company conducted its business successfully if expensively with the aid of blacklegs. Larkin felt he had no choice but to extend the strike if he was not to give in. Accordingly the union served on all shipping firms notice, to expire on 21 June, that, failing wage increases and recognition of the right to organise, strike action would be taken. Work ceased on 26 June. That day the carters struck in sympathy along the

entire water-front. On 29 June the employers founded their 1907
'Protection Association', and by a coincidence which few found remarkable 500 soldiers of the Sussex Regiment appeared in the city to relieve the police.

On the evening of Thursday 2 July Larkin told a mass meeting at the Custom House steps that he was resigning his leadership of the strike and handing over to a Protestant, Councillor Alexander Boyd, a member of the official Orange Order. His reason for withdrawing to the rank and file was the approach of the notorious 'twalfth' of July.

The decision, which was not in fact carried out, throws light on Larkin's personal temperament and the circumstances in which the struggle was being conducted. Larkin was a vigorous, rumbustious organiser, but he had begun his work circumspectly enough. He had tried to hold back his followers while he used legal means to compel those who broke their fair-wage agreements to observe them. Granted that his supporters fired the first shot, the employers were ready for instant war. The industrial war was accompanied by a propaganda war in which Larkin was vilified in every possible way. On the one hand, he was the English agitator. On the other, he was a 'papist'. A study of his behaviour through the years suggests that there was a sensitive, vulnerable streak in his nature. He could be hurt. He kept going by dramatising himself. He caused much mystification on those occasions when he abruptly changed roles, often on the spur of the moment. He was volatile, enthusiastic, gregarious and full of exuberant idealism. But his upbringing in the slums of Liverpool had not been such as would stiffen to complete self-confidence his undoubtedly creative spirit.

As to surrounding circumstances, the fact that Larkin could propose to hand over the leadership to an official of another trade union shows how little the strike belonged to the NUDL. Not one penny in strike pay had yet come from the head office. The struggle was largely financed by the exertions of the Belfast Trades Council and donations from other trade unions in Britain and Ireland.

The soldiers cordoned off the quays. Pickets could no longer make contact with those they wished to dissuade from blacklegging. Larkin printed copies of the Trades Disputes Act and on one occasion induced a detective inspector to

1907 allow a deputation to speak to the scabs. This was before the lawyers had got busy. Larkin himself unwittingly facilitated their work by claiming the right to address a meeting at Dufferin Dock, which was the property of the Harbour Commissioners. The resulting case was heard in Dublin early in 1908. The first dent was made in the 1906 act when it was held that a picket had no right to enter private property in the course of his duties. This might mean that he must not stand on a pavement.

William McMullen in his detailed memoir of the 1907 stoppage[3] establishes that the story that Larkin brought Catholics and Protestants together in a united demonstration on 12 July is a myth. Larkin was not in Belfast on that day. The absence of the usual sectarian troubles arose from the fact that the Orangemen were split and that one section, under Lindsay Crawford, was wholeheartedly for the workers.

The employers none the less chose the weekend of 12 July to declare a general lock-out, accompanying it with a manifesto which Professor Emmet Larkin has described as a 'remarkable piece of arrogance'.[4] They declared that 'No person representing any union or combination will, after this date, be recognised by us.' They reserved the right to employ or dismiss whom they chose on whatever terms they chose. In the event of any section going on strike without giving three days' notice they undertook that they would 'immediately lock out' all their men. They added for good measure that work would not be resumed on Monday 13 July unless the men unanimously accepted their terms – that is to say signed the appropriate document.

On 18 July Larkin visited Dublin. His purpose was to raise funds, but also to explore the possibility of establishing a Dublin branch of the NUDL. The Dublin Trades Council had already declared support for Belfast at its meeting of 10 June and had appealed for financial aid. The secretary was still John Simmons, but there had been a subtle transformation in the position of the craftsmen. The bargaining power of the trades had declined. There were complaints that some employers received their deputations 'quite curtly'. The Drapers' Assistants' struggle against the medieval 'living-in' system had made little headway. The printers had had to remove the important *Irish Independent* from their list of fair employers.

There was not yet any inkling of the immense potential of 1907
the infrastructure workers as the demand for fuel and transport steadily rose. But the old craft aloofness had gone.

Highly encouraged by his reception in Dublin, Larkin returned to Belfast to a dramatic dénouement. There had been talk of discontent among the police. They had long considered themselves underpaid, and now they were being called on to put in long hours week after week under difficult conditions for no extra money. Rumours of possible strike action had been current for some time and had been referred to by Larkin on 16 July. Now a series of minor insubordinations began, culminating in a full-scale mutiny on 24 July. There is no need to assume that the police had 'gone over to Larkin'. Sexton's statement that he addressed them in their own barracks is unsupported. But the result was instantaneous. Representatives of the General Federation of Trade Unions who had been in Belfast since 20 July patched up an agreement under which 1,000 coal workers resumed work. Sexton put in an appearance at these negotiations, and it would seem most likely that it was at this point that he agreed to pay strike benefit. Apart from anything else, it gave him command of the situation.

Following the police mutiny a military force 5,000 strong was brought into Belfast and encamped in Ormeau Park. One policeman was dismissed, six others suspended, and 150 rusticated. Under cover of the police mutiny the authorities assembled the forces that were going to destroy working-class unity by reviving religious sectarianism. In the midst of the excitement Larkin paid a flying visit to Dublin and established a branch of the NUDL at a meeting at the Trades Hall on 4 August.

The police in general observed the provisions of the Trades Disputes Act. Not so the soldiers. If a picket took hold of a horse's bridle while he spoke to the driver, he was clubbed to the ground. Worse still, making use of incidents which should have been left to the police, they concentrated on the Falls Road. They placed cordons on main roads and pickets on side streets. Workers were needlessly halted. The people were provoked into throwing stones. Soldiers then disgraced themselves by joining in the same sport. As a result of these needlessly fomented riots, respectable Protestant citizens,

1907 always ready to anticipate a Catholic insurrection in which everybody worth more than five shillings would have his throat cut, shuddered and told their children: 'The Fenians are at it again.' Larkin organised a mass meeting which was addressed by Lindsay Crawford, Alexander Boyd and the Hibernian Joseph Devlin. The demonstration of working-class unity merely stimulated the troops to fresh exertions. Next evening, 12 August, the military fired on a crowd in the Falls Road, and a boy and girl were shot dead. When an inquest was ultimately held Major Thackeray admitted that he had stationed troops where there was no disturbance, and his soldiers blandly admitted that they had entered workers' houses, sometimes smashing six doors and all the windows with their rifle butts.

At this point the London government decided matters had gone far enough and sent conciliators from the Board of Trade. The carters' strike was settled on 15 August. Both Larkin and Sexton took part in the discussions. The employers conceded an increase in wages, but insisted that the men should accept loads from non-union men. On 28 August men who worked the coal and iron-ore boats negotiated an improved wage scale, again with agreement to work with non-union men. Finally, on 4 September the dockers who had been locked out by the Belfast Steamship Company were allowed back on promising in future 'to work harmoniously with any fellow-employees'. If this is what Sexton meant by a 'settlement', his speech at the British TUC may explain his motives. After describing in glowing terms the unity achieved between Catholics and Protestants he told Congress that the strike had been costing the NUDL £3,000 a week.

Larkin was deeply dissatisfied at Sexton's negotiation of what he regarded as a capitulation, and he made himself unpopular by saying so. But he returned to his organising, and on 27 September he and Michael McKeown addressed a meeting at Newry. The chairman was James Fearon, whom Larkin had known in Scotland and who now became secretary of the Newry branch.

But the Belfast employers had further schemes in hand. The sinister implications of their insistence on the 'open shop' became speedily evident with the appearance on the quays of a new organisation. At first it was thought to be an offshoot of one of the British general workers' unions; this, however, was denied. It was called the 'Belfast Coalworkers' and Carters' Benefit Society', and its distinguishing mark was that no Catholic could be admitted into membership. On 28 October the NUDL delegate Davidson noticed two members of this society working a ship chartered by Messrs Wright. Some of its members then appeared at Kellys. In neither case would the employers dismiss them. The NUDL men had, as they thought, agreed to work with non-unionists, but they had not bargained for members of a sectarian company union. Three hundred of them ceased work, and Larkin supported them. 1907

On 20 November the newly organised Newry dockers refused to unload three Belfast steamers. In consequence shipping was diverted to the quiet port of Warrenpoint. But here, as in Newry, the local people resented the appearance of blacklegs, and there were disturbances. Fearon proved an able and conscientious secretary. On 28 November, in the midst of the turmoil, he established a section of the union in Dundalk and at about the same time organised Newry gasworks.

The dock employers did not this time import Shipping Federation blacklegs; Professor Larkin suggests that this was on account of the expense.[5] They now had available members of the 'yellow' union and a supply of unemployed men. By the end of 1907 these were readily available. They also sent out for countrymen and army reservists.

Sexton arrived on 26 November. He took the conduct of the dispute out of Larkin's hands. The two men were now scarcely on speaking terms. He instructed the men to return to work at once, and before boarding the Liverpool boat he assured them that a satisfactory arrangement had been reached. Next morning the men found that he had failed to come to any arrangement at all. Larkin was sick with a sense of shame and betrayal. Presumably with Sexton's agreement, he transferred his activities to Dublin, where he represented the NUDL on the Trades Council for the first time on 9 December. The Newry strike dragged on until just after Christmas, but ended in ignominious defeat.

1908 During the next few months Larkin was heavily committed. Once a week he attended the Dock Labour Commission's sitting in London. His wife and family were still in Liverpool. Events took place which, though of small moment in themselves, helped to shape his intentions. On 10 February he lost his appeal against the fine of 20s imposed on him in connection with the meetings at Dufferin Dock. The King's Bench in Dublin held that the Trades Disputes Act could not supersede local by-laws in matters not set out in it, and did not authorise pickets to trespass. The union gave no financial assistance to Larkin in this case; possibly he had entered the appeal against advice. He was saddled with a bill of costs which he characteristically ignored. But the Belfast Harbour Commissioners were not satisfied with gaining their point. The wanted their pound of flesh.

Early in 1908 Joseph Harris appeared on the Dublin scene as organiser for the Workers' Union. This was not, as R. M. Fox suggests, a 'bogus union';[6] it was a small general labourers' union founded by Tom Mann in 1898 to cater for what the Webbs called 'nondescript and semi-skilled workers of all sorts'.[7] Like those of the NUDL, its leaders grew interested in the possibilities of recruitment in Ireland as a result of the Labour conference in Belfast. Harris was a Dublin man, but had been for a time working in Belfast, where he represented the upholsterers on the Trades Council. He incurred the ire of the redoubtable Miss Galway when he tried to organise textile workers, and the Trades Council refused to accept the WU affiliation.

He then transferred his efforts to the capital, but here, according to William O'Brien, he found that there was no enthusiasm for joining a cross-channel organisation. On 6 March he was discussing with O'Brien the feasibility of setting up an Irish-based union for general workers. The discussions were widened to include P. T. Daly and John Farren. Daly and Harris approached the Builders' Labourers on 6 May. O'Brien had expected Larkin's support; but however dissatisfied he was with the NUDL, Larkin objected to 'splitting the workers on the industrial front'. The subject was ventilated in the Sinn Féin press, and there were awkward questions at the Trades Council. The Workers' Union's affiliation was delayed until October. Harris was no judge of his lieutenants, and the union was viewed with suspicion. The question of an Irish union catering for general workers had, however, been raised. 1908

Early in June Larkin attended the Annual Meeting of the Irish Trade Union Congress in Belfast and was elected to the Parliamentary Committee. Some have expressed surprise that in the first rules of the ITGWU support is expressed for the principle of compulsory arbitration. This was, however, ITUC policy 'reaffirmed' at Belfast. It was suggested that parliament should legislate for the submission of industrial disputes to a conciliation board before any strike or lock-out could take place. The proposal was later dropped. At this stage both William O'Brien, at his first Congress, and Larkin seem to have been on excellent terms with E. W. Stewart, who had been treasurer of the Congress since 1904.

By July the Dublin branch of the NUDL had about 2,700 members. These used to turn up for work wearing their union badges. Some of the employers objected. Larkin must have known that this issue had played an important part in the Liverpool dock strike of 1890 and that the men had ultimately agreed not to display them. Perhaps he had in mind trading off the badge issue against the removal of other grievances. But the employers flatly refused to negotiate with the union. They were, they said, prepared to listen to grievances, but only to men who approached them as individuals. There were dismissals which contributed to a rising tide of discontent. On 9 July the coal merchants paid off 400 men. At a meeting at Beresford Place, with T. C. Harrington, MP, and the veteran William Field beside him, Larkin gave an assurance that they did not seek to impose a 'closed shop'.

At this point the Board of Trade intervened. The employers agreed to take back the dismissed men pending negotiations. This was an important new departure. The centre of gravity of the working class had shifted. The interests of the capitalist class as a whole were beginning to come into conflict with the private ownership of an infrastructure upon which all were dependent.

Sexton arrived in Dublin on 18 July, and a conference was held on 30 July. The employers declined to sit with Larkin. The negotiations proceeded without him. They agreed to recognise the union, but insisted that in future they must deal

1908 directly with Sexton. This placed Larkin in an impossible position. In 1907 Belfast employers had refused to meet him; now the same thing was happening in Dublin. It was complained of Larkin in later years that he 'personalised everything'. Perhaps it was as a result of these experiences that he acquired the habit. At the meeting on 7 August at which Sexton explained the settlement Larkin took the chair, but sat through the entire proceedings, the picture of sullen resentment, saying scarcely a word. Sexton evoked no enthusiasm. He had been born in Newcastle, of Irish parents. But for the limitations of his working-class background he might have spent his days writing novels and plays. The trade union movement was his road of escape from the drabness of life, whereas to Larkin it had become a fiery crusade. The dockers felt that the man for them was the man the employers refused to meet.

Larkin had responsibility without authority. There is evidence that as early as March 1908, possibly when the discussions with Harris had been taking place, he had contemplated breaking away from Sexton. Now he must have feared that since the General Secretary was now compelled to bark himself, he might be looking round for a new dog. In the middle of August there seemed a possibility of setting up a branch in Cork. Larkin dispatched Fearon there, under what arrangement is not clear, but hardly on the union payroll. It was subsequently charged against Larkin that instead of applying to Liverpool for membership cards he obtained them from Newry. But the Newry branch had collapsed at the beginning of the year, and it is possible that Fearon had the cards in his possession and simply took them with him. Fearon was not long in establishing the Cork branch, and a membership of 1,800 has been claimed for it. If this figure is not exaggerated (and nothing is so consistently exaggerated as membership), it would be thought that the Newry cards would hardly be sufficient.

The Executive cannot have been unaware of Larkin's activities in Cork, for they paid his expenses when he attended a preliminary meeting. But they now insisted on his asking permission before undertaking journeys. The position is a familiar one when an executive is out of favour. He cannot be summarily dismissed, but he is on his way out. Two expense

accounts were disallowed, and when on 11 October Larkin 1908
notified Sexton of his intention of visiting Cork, head office refused to sanction the journey.

Nevertheless Larkin went to Waterford on 15 October. His meeting was held in the City Hall and was preceded by a torchlight procession accompanied by two fife and drum bands. The object was to organise the 'tonnage men', the casual dock workers who were at that time paid 4½d for discharging a ton of coal. The chairman was Daniel Hyland, City High Sheriff, and the speakers were Larkin and Fearon, the latter being described as secretary of the Cork branch. Shortly after Larkin began to speak a barrage of interruptions began, and fighting broke out. The disturbance was organised by a man called Cullen, at that time the leading stevedore in the port, and one in a position to dispense Dutch courage in the public house he owned. After the police had restored order about 400 men joined the union, and the Waterford branch was launched.

The interrupters had concentrated on one thing – that Larkin was setting up an *English* union. But after defending the flag Larkin could not get his expenses. It is impossible to unravel the tangle of charge and counter-charge which followed Larkin's final breach with Sexton. That Larkin was unable to give a satisfactory account of his financial transactions during the last months of 1908 was subsequently attested in court. But what can a man do when he is unable to collect 'out-of-pocket expenses'? He may well think that he will get them how he can.

On 9 November Fearon brought out 200 coal workers. The Shipping Federation dispatched 150 blacklegs from London and Liverpool. These arrived by train on the 10th. On the 11th Larkin was in Cork, and the City of Cork Steampacket Company's dockers ceased work. It was pointed out that eighteen years had gone by since the Cork dockers had preferred a wage claim. When Larkin returned to Dublin Fearon conducted the campaign with great vigour if not always with discretion.

On 17 November the Dublin carters struck and appointed a committee consisting of Thomas Foran, Michael McCarthy, John Purcell, Thomas Greene and Patrick Dobbins. Larkin was in Derry, and under instructions to proceed to Aberdeen.

1908 His status had been reduced to that of a wandering trouble-shooter. He received a telegram from Greene urging him to return to Dublin. According to O'Brien, he had arranged for this, though it is difficult to account for O'Brien's suggestion that this had been his plan from as far back as August.[8] He came at once and at a meeting in the Trades Hall learned that violence had already begun. A lorry had been thrown into the Liffey. Larkin wired Sexton and received in response the terse message 'Stew in your own juice.'

Sexton called a special meeting of his Executive, and on 28 November Larkin was informed that the General Secretary had been given authority to suspend him at any time. In the meantime Larkin had won the support of the Trades Council despite the fact, which he explained to them, that he had not the backing of his Executive. The men on the Grand Canal had come out, and 242 maltsters had joined the union.

On 29 November Larkin told a public meeting at Beresford Place that the union leaders refused to accept responsibility for the Dublin strike. A meeting of the Executive was taking place in Liverpool. Larkin held a meeting of the Dublin branch committee at 11 p.m. that night. Next evening he told a meeting that 'he understood there was to be a great movement set on foot to create a Labour Union for all Ireland. That could mean that Ireland would eventually get into touch with the Labour movement all over the world.'[9] Larkin's suspension was notified to all branches on 7 December.

The Dublin carters had chosen the best time for their strike. Christmas was less than a month away, and their services were in demand. By 1 December ten firms had conceded the union's claim. On the 6th William Partridge, at that time an engineering worker of considerable influence in Labour circles, suggested inviting the Lord Mayor and the two archbishops to mediate. On the 7th Larkin was called to Cork. There the strike was settled through the good offices of Father O'Leary, the men winning substantial concessions.

The settlement in Cork strengthened Larkin's hand in Dublin. On 15 December the Shipping Federation offered a thousand blacklegs. They would have to be paid wages and expenses, fed and housed. This time the offer was not taken up. The Chamber of Commerce called for intervention by the Lord Lieutenant. Individual merchants lodged complaints with

Winston Churchill at the Board of Trade. The strike was 1908
settled on 19 December when the two sides agreed to accept arbitration. Meanwhile Arthur Griffith's newspaper *Sinn Féin* denounced the evils brought on Ireland by the 'English' trade union. One of the strike committee, Dobbins, on a visit to Dundalk, read an attack on himself in the local paper.[10] It was written by a supporter of Griffith, P. J. McCall, who challenged him to 'start an Irish union'.

With the strike for the moment out of the way, Larkin called a meeting of the 'Irish Executive' of the NUDL, though there is no evidence that such a body had any official existence. The meeting was held on 28 December in the Trades Hall, Capel Street, and was attended by representatives from Belfast, Cork, Dublin, Dundalk and Waterford. That Michael McKeown represented Belfast is known. Probably Dobbins represented Dundalk. Whether Fearon represented Cork is uncertain; on 28 December he was in the magistrate's court charged with endeavouring to intimidate Sir Alfred Dobbin, a director of the City of Cork Steampacket Company, by picketing a music-hall in which he had an interest.

It was decided at this meeting that an Irish union would be launched. On 4 January 1909 William O'Brien wrote in his diary: 'Irish Transport and General Workers' Union founded officially from this date.'[11]

2

Foundation and Consolidation

A fig for those by law protected!
  Liberty's a glorious feast!
Courts for cowards were erected,
  Churches built to please the priest.
ROBERT BURNS

Name of the union – Larkin bankrupt – split in Belfast – Sexton's writ – Osborne decision –first rules – Labour war in Cork – defeat – Larkin arrested – court action – Dundalk TUC

1909 It is often suggested that the ITGWU was first called the Irish Transport Workers' Union, that it at first catered for transport workers only, and that the word 'general' was added when it was decided to admit fresh classes of workers. The truth is that its official title was Irish Transport and General Workers' Union from the start.

In William O'Brien's memoirs, dictated many years afterwards, he gives an account which is borne out by surviving evidence.[1] Hearing that an Irish Transport Workers' Union was to be founded, he approached Larkin with the suggestion that it should be open to general workers. Larkin explained that he hoped to bring in the railwaymen, who would not wish to be classed with general workers. O'Brien threw grave doubt on the feasibility of such a plan. When he saw the name of the union he understood that his suggestion had been adopted. But if this is correct, it is necessary to inquire why the title ITWU came to be so widely used. The obvious conclusion is that Larkin founded the new union without too clear a conception of what it was going to do.

The original rules contain the full title Irish Transport and General Workers' Union. But this is less significant than its appearance in O'Brien's diary entry for 4 January 1909. The date on which the rules were printed is not known, but it must have been after they were registered. On 4 September

1909 in Cork city Mr D. O'Connell Miley testified on oath 1909
that he was the Registrar of Friendly Societies and that on 6 May of the same year he had registered the Irish Transport and General Workers' Union. He added that papers in his possession contained a statement that the union began to function on 4 January 1909. James Larkin signed the certificate as secretary. Now the rules as printed purport to hold force 'on and from January 1st, 1909' – that is to say from before the union existed. The probable explanation is that it was desired to create a legal fiction that the ITGWU was a continuation of the NUDL and thus entitled to collect arrears.

According to the *Evening Telegraph*, on 6 February 1909 'James Larkin of 13 Benedict's Gardens, Drumcondra, Dublin, gentleman' was adjudged bankrupt as a result of his inability to pay the costs of the Belfast Harbour Commissioners following their successful suit against him. The same newspaper on 26 February reported his examination before Mr Justice Boyd. In the headline the initials ITWU are used, but in the report it is stated that when asked his profession Larkin said he was a member of the Irish Transport and General Workers' Union. The two statements made on oath corroborate O'Brien.

But the press was almost unanimous in using the shorter title. The *Irish Nation* of 2 January 1909, reporting the meeting of 28 December, announced the foundation of the Irish Transport Workers' Union. It is probably safe to assume therefore that that was the title adopted at the meeting. This assumption is borne out by the *Dundalk Democrat* of 2 January, in which Dobbins described himself as the Dundalk secretary of the ITWU. On 9 January the *Evening Telegraph* referred to the ITWU. For several days the *Irish News* reported the activities of the 'Irish Transit Workers' Union', and one number of the *Dundalk Democrat* referred to the 'Irish Transport Workers' Association'. The Cork *Weekly Examiner* of 30 January reported Larkin as speaking of the ITWU, and there can be no doubt that this title was in very wide use.

What the evidence points to is that Larkin had been telling the world that he was going to organise an Irish Transport Workers' Union. At some point between 28 December and 4 January he changed his mind. O'Brien provides the explanation. But perhaps he had no objection to the use of the term Transport Union for the time being, until he was sure that he

1909 could not bring in the railwaymen.

Precisely what happened on 4 January is not certain. The earliest surviving Dublin roll book, that for 1915, sets against the name of each member the date on which he joined the union. The earliest date in the register is 4 January 1909, and it is set against about a hundred names. This roll book will be discussed in a later chapter, but using the rough multiplier there suggested to allow for membership wastage, it may be guessed that about 1,200 members enrolled on that first day, possibly more. In the bankruptcy proceedings reference was made to a debt for badges but not for cards. Perhaps therefore the men enrolled and received a badge. Now all union badges of the early years bear the initials ITWU, and it may be concluded that they were ordered before the decision to adopt the full title ITGWU. But the rules, printed after their registration, contain the correct name. The retention of the abbreviated initials until the 'rationalisation' of the union in 1918 is probably to be explained by inertia.

The first rules of the ITGWU carry a preface which bears all the marks of Larkin's handiwork. But while it refers to 'unskilled' workers, it does not once refer to 'transport workers'. It is therefore reasonable to assume that the rules date from the period immediately preceding their registration and to defer examining them until certain intervening events have been explained.

* * *

There is a possibility that Sexton was resigned to the loss of his Irish branches. They had not proved gold-mines. He complained bitterly of Larkin's insubordination during the Belfast dispute. To accusations of too strict control from Liverpool he replied that if it had been suggested to him that the Irish desired an independent union, he would willingly have helped them to set it up. He seems to have left the Dublin headquarters at 10 Beresford Place in Larkin's possession. He was brought into the fray because of rivalries in the north.

Immediately the new organisation was announced Alexander Boyd fiercely attacked Larkin. This meant that the Belfast dockers were now to be divided along sectarian lines, for

Michael McKeown, a strong nationalist, did not hesitate to support Larkin. He brought Larkin to a meeting in Belfast on 8 January. Larkin complained that he was not validly suspended, and this claim was supported by Andrew Quinlan (whose name is given thus in the *Irish News* but as Quinn in the *Evening Telegraph*), who testified that though a delegate to the Executive, he had never heard Larkin's suspension discussed. All this seems to imply is that he was not present at the Special Executive. 1909

The chairman of the meeting was James Flanagan. A Mr Hopkins from Dublin is also reported as speaking. This may have been William Hopkins. At the conclusion of the meeting, on the motion of P. Brady, seconded by W. Curley, it was resolved:

> That this meeting, composed of the dockers of Belfast, renew our confidence in Mr James Larkin, and we, one and all, join the Irish Transport Workers' Union, and will have no other union than this one.

It was further resolved not to recognise the badge of the NUDL.

On 12 January Larkin was called to Dundalk. There a number of NUDL men were also members of an older-established Labourers' Society, concerned mostly with sick benefit. The NUDL had refused to recognise the Labourers' card on the docks. The Labourers contended that the reason they had raised no objection to the establishment of the NUDL in Dundalk was its undertaking not to enforce a closed shop against them. But the NUDL had broken this agreement in October 1908. The foundation of the ITGWU afforded an opportunity to work off resentments, and Dobbins was refused a hearing. Larkin, on the other hand, flatly denied the compact. Though he failed to satisfy the Labourers, he kept his own members, some of whom moved 'that the Dundalk branch of the National Dockers' Union now becomes a branch of the Irish Transport Workers' Union'. At this meeting Larkin invited the men in the railway workshops to come into the new organisation. He added that it would not be confined to Ireland but 'affiliated with England and Scotland'.

On 12 January Sexton addressed a meeting in Belfast. The

1909 chairman was Alexander Boyd, who took it upon himself to interfere in the affairs of unions of which he was not a member. Sexton was thus persuaded to fight for a British presence in alliance with Orangeism. If he had understood the fateful consequences of this action, he might well have preferred to allow Larkin to keep all the members. Boyd had great difficulty in making himself heard against the protests of what he called a 'noisy minority'. When Sexton rose a man approached the platform and handed him an envelope. Lest the significance of the incident should be lost he said: 'This is a challenge from Mr Larkin to meet you tomorrow night.' Sexton said afterwards that Larkin knew well that he would be in Derry on that night. But now it could be stated that Larkin had asked for a meeting and had been refused. As the disorder increased, John Quinn, the deep-sea dockers' delegate, moved 'that the dockers of Belfast no longer recognise the National Union of Dock Labourers while James Sexton is General Secretary'. Edward Magee seconded. But in the uproar that followed it was impossible to discuss the motion, much less put it to the meeting, even if the chairman had been willing. The meeting broke up in confusion in which the platform received a hail of discarded NUDL badges and one bottle. In Derry, on the other hand, Sexton had no difficulty in keeping his members.

While Sexton was in Derry, Larkin was answering him in Belfast. Patrick Dobbins presided. He explained that he had been 'deputed by the Dundalk branch to substantiate Larkin in whatever he would say'. James Flanagan told the audience that he had called to Alexander Boyd's house with a letter inviting him to attend but that the door had been slammed in his face. Apparently Sexton had insinuated that Father O'Leary had denied Larkin's part in the settlement of the strike in Cork.

Father O'Leary had indeed criticised press reports of the settlement, but he had not found fault with Larkin. With characteristic showmanship Larkin announced that he had telegraphed Father O'Leary and expected a reply any minute. It arrived while he was still speaking. It bore testimony to Larkin's assistance and added: 'Your prudence, firmness and tact at and before conference secured satisfactory settlement.' There was loud cheering as the telegram was handed to reporters. At this meeting Larkin declared that there was 'going to be only one Union in Ireland, and that would be the Irish Transport Workers' Union, and soon they would have Scottish and English Transport Unions'. If this was not bluster, it meant that he was going to challenge Sexton on his home ground. Sexton certainly thought that Larkin's ambition was to become General Secretary of the NUDL, and indeed on more than once occasion he spoke of challenging Sexton in Liverpool. But from the way his statements contradicted each other it would seem likely that he had no strategy mapped out in advance. He was smarting with a sense of grievance. While he was capable of prudence and tact, he was incapable of seeing Sexton's point of view. 1909

On the next evening, 14 January, Sexton met the cross-channel dockers. Only three of Larkin's supporters attended. Two were forcibly ejected, and the third beat a discreet retreat. The gravamen of Sexton's complaint was that Larkin had refused to accept his directions during the negotiating of the Belfast settlement and had made public statements criticising him. Sexton won unanimous support, and the meeting passed a resolution urging him to 'take the necessary steps to recover the union's property'. The Belfast dockers were now divided along sectarian lines.

On 15 January Sexton's writ was served on Michael McKeown. It demanded the return of books and furniture belonging to the NUDL. A week later McKeown agreed to give up the books, and the court suggested that the parties might come to an accommodation over the other property. A solution had thus been reached in the north. It was partition. Nor could the two sides leave each other alone. On 13 February Michael McKeown addressed a letter to the Parliamentary Committee of the ITUC (to which the ITGWU was not yet affiliated) complaining that members of the NUDL were 'blacklegging on the members of the former union'. He also suggested, somewhat precipitately, that the Congress should set up a sub-committee to inquire into the inter-union dispute. There had been complaints that the ITUC had not been consulted about the establishment of the new union. The issues in Belfast were referred to the Belfast Trades Council, whose minutes do not disclose any discussion of them. Possibly the Executive or officers decided

1909 there were enough hot potatoes in the city. But one consequence of McKeown's initiative was that, against Larkin's protests, it was decided not to invite the Transport Union to the next Annual Meeting of the ITUC.

* * *

Meanwhile Larkin was consolidating in the south. On 23 January he addressed a meeting in Cork city. The president of the Trades Council, who presided, was loud in his praises, describing him as a 'worthy organiser and gallant leader' whose efforts on the quays of Cork had been attended with great success. The Transport Union was, he explained, simply the NUDL under another name. On a show of hands the members decided to join the new union. The regularity of Larkin's proceedings in Cork was later challenged in court. The jungle law of the long-shore industry, of course, bore no relation to the formal niceties of the civil process. Fearon and his colleagues were subjected to abuse and threats, as the court cases they won showed. But they could offer violence themselves, as was shown by the cases they lost. One witness explained his vote at the founding meeting quite simply. He thought that if he did not put up his hand then, he might never do so again. An important factor peculiar to Cork which undoubtedly made matters difficult was that since the union was not in a position to pay him a salary, Fearon worked as a stevedore. Men may have felt that by leaving the NUDL they were safeguarding their employment.

Larkin returned to Dublin on 24 January. At the conclusion of a meeting he was approached by Joseph Harris with a suggestion that the Irish branches of the Workers' Union should break away from their English headquarters and merge with the Transport Union. But Harris wanted a share in the management. Larkin replied that he would 'sink or swim alone'. Pointing out that he had 'sacrificed £4 7s 6d a week in order to stand by the Dublin men', he said that he intended to organise the transport workers in every part of Ireland before asking any man to sacrifice his position. When he reached his first goal he would 'ask a bit of others to make it a general workers' union'. He said much the same to O'Brien on 29 March.

This repulse seems to have originated the hostility between Larkin and Harris. Another factor was Harris's appointment of P. J. McIntyre to the secretaryship of the Dublin branch. McIntyre was expelled from the Independent Labour Party, in which Larkin was all-powerful, in mid-February. He was widely regarded in socialist circles as a political undesirable. In 1904 he had been expelled from membership of the Socialist Party of Ireland only six weeks after he had joined it. His first attack on Larkin was published in *Sinn Féin* on 25 March. 1909

During the winter and spring of 1909 Larkin acted with caution. There were sporadic partial strikes of dockers and carters. The arbitrators of the December dispute had left some issues uncertain. But he had learned from Belfast not to engage all his forces. An important factor in his success was the support of the Dublin Trades Council. Not only did it at once accept the affiliation of the new union, but on 1 March it elected Larkin to its Executive. He gained 37 votes, following close behind John Farren with 40 and P. T. Daly with 45. There was a strong 'left-wing' current arising from the terrible distress among the unemployed. William O'Brien, the principal representative of this tendency, gained 26 votes in the election for the Executive despite having been a member of the Council for only six months. He was able to persuade the Council to revive the practice of holding a demonstration in Phoenix Park on May Day, and a committee was appointed.

The Trades Council's most spectacular effort at this period was the organisation of the unemployed. At the meeting on 1 March a deputation which included the socialist Hoskins suggested a demonstration of protest. It was decided, however, to attempt the task of registering those without work, and a bureau was opened at the Trades Hall. On the first day 1,000 men and women registered. After five days the names of 2,520 men and 373 women had been recorded. It was alleged that employers were refusing jobs to Dublin workers and bringing in country people at low wages. Larkin and M. J. O'Lehane were deputed to take the matter up with the Lord Lieutenant, while another deputation was to seek a hearing at the Corporation.

At this point another future enemy of Larkin took up his

1909 position. E. W. Stewart sarcastically 'congratulated the socialist element on their success'.[2] Stewart was secretary of the 'Right to Work Committee', whose tendency was in accordance with the politics of the United Irish League. As had happened in the past, the growing activity of the Labour movement gave rise to the demand for a Labour newspaper. Already Cork Trades Council was publishing a journal. On 26 March the Council elected a committee to examine the project. It consisted of Simmons, O'Lehane, Farren and Larkin. Following the Council's representations to the Lord Mayor a citizens' meeting was held at the Mansion House on 16 April. On that day M. J. O'Lehane told the annual conference of the Drapers' Assistants that at last the hated 'living-in' system was in decline.

The Dublin May Day demonstration was highly successful, even though some felt that Larkin 'monopolised' the audience. As a direct consequence, the very next day the Irish Socialist Society decided to reorganise as a political party. In Waterford too a May Day demonstration was held, on the initiative of the railwaymen. They invited Larkin, who sent them a message: 'Labour must rule.'[3]

* * *

How much these developments influenced the rules of the ITGWU which Larkin registered on 6 May is, of course, a matter of conjecture. The general tenour of the lengthy preamble seems to belong to the hopeful days of May 1909 rather than to the gloom of December 1908. Larkin presents first the fundamental decision to be made by trade unionism in Ireland. Is it to be Irish or British? 'Are we going to continue the policy of grafting ourselves on the English Trades Union movement, losing our own identity as a nation in the great world of organised labour?' This is precisely the question Connolly had put to the former 'Progressists' and Independent Labour Party men thirteen years previously. And Larkin gives the same answer: 'We say emphatically, No.'

The document then refers to the problems of Irish industry, its modest scale, the influx of foreign capitalists and the high degree of organisation which enables their class to 'monopolise the political power'. It refers to the presence of 800,000 'so-called unskilled' workers in Ireland, of which only 50,000 were then organised. It declares: 1909

> The Irish Transport and General Workers' Union offer to you a medium whereby you may combine with your fellows to adjust wages, and regulate hours and conditions of labour, wherever and whenever possible and desirable by negotiation, arbitration, or, if the conditions demand it, by withholding our labour until amelioration is granted.

Political recognition is also demanded. The immediate programme lists an eight-hour day, provision of work for all unemployed persons, pensions for all workers at sixty, compulsory arbitration courts, adult suffrage (that is, votes for women) and the nationalisation of all means of transport. The manifesto ends with a brave display of Labour sunburstery:

> By the advocacy of such principles and the carrying out of such a policy, we believe we shall be ultimately enabled to obliterate poverty, and help to realise the glorious time spoken of and sung by the Thinkers, Prophets, and the Poets, when all children, all women, and all men shall have their full share of the essentials of life; when men shall work and rejoice in the deeds of their hand, and thereby become entitled to the fulness of the earth and the abundance thereof.

Now of course, the rules which follow may have been drafted in January. The preamble, however, is an invitation to join a general workers' union, and the numbers quoted imply that Larkin's eye was already on the agricultural labourers. The tendency is, moreover, broadly socialistic. Even if there is no declaration that 'Labour must rule', the ultimate objective of the union is defined as an 'Industrial Commonwealth', that is to say a radical restructuring of society along proletarian lines.[4] The rules give no clue as to how this is to be achieved, but it is significant that they contain no provision for political action.

This omission may not, however, imply an acceptance of pure syndicalism. It may have a legal explanation. The British TUC had been founded to co-ordinate the political rather than the industrial activities of the separate unions. For this

1909 reason it was governed not by an Executive but by a Parliamentary Committee. The Irish TUC followed the same practice. When the agitation against the Taff Vale judgment resulted in a flood of Labour members into the House of Commons, and these insisted on the Trades Disputes Act, employers began to look askance at the political activities of the unions and to look around for fresh weapons.

On 22 July 1908 a member of the Amalgamated Society of Railway Servants called N. V. Osborne took proceedings against his own union for the purpose of restraining them from spending money on political objects. The result was a lengthy legal battle in which the issue was argued in one court after another, the humble Mr Osborne having seemingly inexhaustible funds, until the House of Lords gave final judgment on 21 December 1909. The process was followed anxiously by trade unionists, and the Dublin Trades Council discussed its progress on 26 April 1909, when things were going badly for the ASRS. It would be understandable at this time if Larkin drafted the rules of the union with the Osborne case in mind. The result of the decision in favour of Osborne was another period of parliamentary agitation which ended with the passing of the Trade Union Act of 1913. On the other hand, the constitution of the ITGWU did not provide for a political fund until 1923.

In general tenour the rules seem more the work of a pragmatist than a syndicalist. There is no reference to 'one big union', though it is stated that the principle that sectional trade unionism is useless for unskilled workers under modern conditions 'also applies to skilled workers'. Larkin had a vision of an emancipated working class, but like most members of the Independent Labour Party, he was not interested in social theory and thought it sufficient to sketch the glorious prospect.

* * *

It is possible that once the rules had been registered Larkin overestimated the security of his position. He took no care to avoid making enemies. At the Trades Council on 10 May he questioned the validity of Stewart's credentials and suggested that the National Amalgamated Union of Shop Assistants, Warehousemen and Clerks (NAUSAWC) was not a *bona fide* trade union. He moved the suspension of standing orders so that McIntyre's press campaign against him could be discussed. O'Brien, who had been supporting him, began to fear that his bitterness against McIntyre, who was not worth his resentment, would harm relations with the Workers' Union. 1909

The Irish TUC met at Limerick on 30 May. On the way to Kingsbridge Larkin told O'Brien that the previous evening he had been expelled from the organisation on the motion of E. W. Stewart. An attempt was nevertheless made to have the ITGWU (which throughout the report is referred to as the ITWU) affiliated and Larkin seated. The Standing Orders Committee received a deputation which consisted of representatives of its branches in Dublin, Cork, Dundalk and Waterford. The result was a recommendation adopted by three votes to two that the ITGWU should be accepted. The members of the Standing Orders Committee included Larkin's supporters, Patrick Lynch of the Cork Tailors and P. T. Daly of the Dublin Trades Council. Of the other three, Cassidy of the Derry Typographical Association and Cronin of the Limerick Carpenters would know little about Larkin. McConnell of the Belfast Bakers is his most likely third supporter.

The NUDL sent representatives from Derry and Drogheda, but nobody from Belfast. It has been said that the branch there did not survive the turmoil of the split. But Sexton was present in person. Larkin could see, if he wished, two other enemies, Joseph Harris and E. W. Stewart. The chairman, Alderman Michael Egan of Cork, ruled out of order the recommendation of the Standing Orders Committee on the ground that the subject of the Transport Union would arise in the discussion of the report of the Parliamentary Committee. His ruling was upheld, though not without opposition. At the appropriate time P. T. Daly moved the deletion of the paragraph headed 'Dock Labourers' Dispute'. The discussion was so protracted that it was necessary to move the closure. It was enlivened, moreover, by Larkin's interruptions from the gallery. Larkin's principal opponents were E. W. Stewart, George Greig and James McCarron, who in a verbal brush with Canty accused him of wishing to drive the English unions out of Congress. Perhaps the general opinion of the

1909 meeting was most succinctly expressed by John Murphy, a Belfast printer, who said that Mr Larkin was a great organiser 'but he must be boss, or all the fat would be in the fire'. Daly's motion was lost by 49 votes to 39. There was thus considerable sympathy for Larkin, and when D. R. Campbell proposed that the matter be referred to a committee which would report at the next Congress, Harris seconded and there was agreement without a division. In the new Parliamentary Committee Larkin's opponents were supreme. Stewart was elected chairman.

Harris's support for Campbell cannot be taken as evidence of a change of heart. He announced his intention of proceeding to Cork and organising dockers and carters in competition with the ITGWU. It was a disastrous decision in which he persisted in the face of urgent warnings by the Cork delegates. It finished the career of the Workers' Union in Ireland and came near to finishing the ITGWU as well.

In order to explain the situation that unfolded it is necessary to recapitulate events in Cork. The comparative calm that prevailed in Dublin was in part the result of the pressure for arbitration exerted by the Board of Trade. But the influence of the Liberal government was not so readily exercised on the banks of the Lee. Fearon, whose somewhat cavalier methods of organising have been noted, had placed pickets on the Palace Theatre, one of whose directors employed dockers. A picket named Cody was arrested and brought before the magistrates on 2 January. The Liberal government had appointed to the bench a working-class magistrate, Alderman Kelleher. The prosecutor, Dr Wynne, had been appointed by the previous Tory administration. He objected to the presence of Kelleher on the bench when Cody's case was called. The chairman, Sir Edward Fitzgerald, snapped: 'Stop there! I never heard a greater insult.' The case was dismissed. Following this incident there was a determination on the part of the Cork Unionists to put the masses in their place. Cody was brought up again on 9 January and on this occasion was not so fortunate.

On 4 February Fearon summoned a stevedore named Cahill who, he claimed, had threatened to take his life. A cross-summons by Cahill was dismissed, and he was fined 20s and costs. On 27 April there took place a pitched battle after which Fearon and another union man, Con Sullivan, were arrested and remanded on bail to the winter assizes. On 29 April the tramwaymen struck for shorter hours and higher wages. They were still organised in the National Union of Gasworkers and General Labourers. On 3 May the builders' labourers came out for a wage increase of 2s a week. They were getting 18s and on 6 May accepted an offer of 19s. The NUGGL sent over their general organiser, and the tramwaymen settled on 14 May. Two days later took place the 'first Labour Day demonstration for years'. It was addressed by Alderman Kelleher, Patrick Lynch and P. Murphy of the Trades Council, John Cummins of the Irish Land and Labour Association, and James Larkin. It would be understandable if the employers felt that if it must, as it appeared, fall to them once in each generation to defend their privileges, then there was no time to be lost. The opportunity was provided by Harris. He began organising coal porters at Morrison's Island. One of his recruits was a stevedore named Rourke. On 10 June ITGWU men demanded that Messrs Sutton should pay off Rourke and his men. Asked to await the arrival of the manager, they refused and walked off the job. The strike spread rapidly. Coal porters of the City of Cork Steampacket Company came out in sympathy, followed by the carmen and storemen of Suttons. Backed by Harris, who was still in Cork, Rourke gave as his reason for refusing to join the ITGWU that it was an 'unrecognised body'. 1909

Larkin hurried to Cork and addressed a mass meeting in Parnell Place. It may be that he was smarting after the defeat in Limerick. He seems to have forgotten the sound maxim that disputes between workers always involve an employer. He declared that the issue before the Cork dockers was independence from Britain. That was the issue between the two unions, but it was not the cause of the local dispute. For generations the employers had manhandled cargoes with the aid of plentiful cheap labour. Now that the dockers had recovered their militancy they intended to introduce machinery, perhaps nothing more than a few steam winches, but enough to cause alarm. The ITGWU men feared that Rourke intended to start the process of mechanisation with the aid of Harris's members.

According to the *Cork Examiner*, on 15 June 200 members

1909 of 'an English dock union' started work on the quay. There was no need for the Shipping Federation this time. The railway porters threatened to black parcels addressed to the City of Cork Steampacket Company. Both the general manager of the GSWR and the secretary of the ASRS hastened to Cork. They proved unable to prevent the stoppage, which began at 2 p.m. on 16 June. More English dockers arrived and finally blacklegs from the Shipping Federation. Railwaymen were brought from country stations to do the work of the porters. Father O'Leary tried to mediate. The employers declined to meet him. They were going to seize time by the forelock. They set up a new organisation, the Cork Employers' Federation Ltd, and passed the following resolution which was issued to the press on 18 June:

> That we, the employers of Cork, hereby bind ourselves and the firms we represent as follows:
> (1) To immediately dismiss any employee who shall wilfully disobey any order out of sympathy for any strike or trade dispute.
> (2) That the vacancy so caused shall be filled forthwith by local labour if procurable, failing this that the vacancy be filled from any available source.
> (3) That any such employee discharged shall not be employed by any member of the Federation.

On 18 June also Fearon and others were charged with picketing the Queen's Theatre on 30 November 1908 with a view to compelling Messrs Dobbin, Ogilvie & Co. to take David Regan and Timothy Meighan into their service. The case against them had been dismissed on 27 February, but the higher court now ruled that the magistrates were wrong.

The old familiar routine of street clashes, baton charges, arrests and fines continued day after day. Mineral-water workers, railwaymen on the Cork and Bandon Railway and flour-millers ceased work. One employer after another closed his doors against workers who refused to have dealings with the blacklegs. Father O'Leary tried to persuade Rourke's men to leave the job for a few days so that the ITGWU men could resume and matters could then be discussed in a calmer atmosphere. Harris instructed them to work on. It was then revealed that until he recruited them to the Workers' Union on 12 June they had never held union membership in their lives. The Cork Trades Council appealed to the Workers' Union to withdraw Harris from the city. 1909

Larkin was fully aware that the strike could not be won. It had been thrust upon him thanks to the nervousness of his members. He made repeated efforts for a settlement. But the employers were out for unconditional surrender. By the end of June there was hunger. School attendance fell to a half: parents refused to send their children to school without breakfast. Then dismissals in the building trade began. On 2 July the employers locked out men who refused to sign 'the document'. On 5 July the Dennys workers refused to accept 'black pigs'. They were locked out. On 7 July the employers published their terms for re-engaging locked-out workers. One of the clauses was that 'employers may adopt any conditions necessary for the conduct of particular businesses (including the use of machinery) and that the workmen shall agree to same'. A slow drift back to work set in. Railwaymen living in company houses were given notice to quit. Neighbours helped to prevent the evictions. Until 11 July the ITGWU men were receiving only 3s 6d a week. In the following week they got 1s 5d.

On 18 July Fearon was in court again, on charges arising from the riot of 27 April. After the court had considered an affidavit in which he complained that he could not hope for a fair trial in Cork under present conditions, the case was held over to the winter assizes. Already people were commenting on the strange sight of former strikers working alongside Shipping Federation blacklegs. Only the coal porters remained firm while they balloted on the employers' proposals. The vital issue of the strike came to the fore. All but one of the employers' stipulations were accepted. But only four out of 209 men were prepared to accept machinery. The strike therefore continued. On 29 July a number of women, the wives and daughters of ITGWU men, assaulted Rourke in the cattle market. Girls taking food to his men were waylaid. He and his son were stoned. Years later Larkin professed to see in all this the germ of the Citizen Army. In reality the struggle had degenerated into a faction-fight between the adherents of rival stevedores.

1909 A serious result of this demoralisation was the split in the Cork Trades Council, whose funds had been exhausted in the first weeks of the dispute. On 12 August representatives of the skilled trades met to establish their own body, the Cork District Trades Council. These included the bootmakers, bookbinders, carpenters, plasterers, shipwrights, painters, stonecutters, printers and engineers. The president was R. McNamara, who had once taken up the cudgels for Parnell, and among those present were some who 'thirty years ago formed the Cork Trades Council'. The trades complained of the frequency of strikes and expressed the opinion that 'trades bodies could best decide questions affecting trades'.[5]

The old Trades Council met on 18 August. Several of the members turned on Fearon and asked whether the ITGWU was a *bona fide* union, since it could not support its members. Fearon was reduced to explaining that the strike had not been sanctioned by the union's headquarters in Dublin. Clearly Larkin had been bitten by his own dog.

Larkin was temperamentally incapable of accepting defeat. He remained in Dublin and allowed the strike to fizzle out as it was bound to do. One of his members, Daniel Coveney, wrote to him describing the general demoralisation and accused Fearon of wrecking the union. Everybody was blaming somebody else. Coveney appealed to Larkin to return to Cork, but Larkin could not bear to fly the flag of surrender.

In Dublin he had made some slight gains. The Trades Council passed a resolution condemning the chairman of the Limerick conference for ruling out of order the recommendation of the Standing Orders Committee. The committee set up to investigate the inter-union dispute cautiously recommended the affiliation of the ITGWU. On 16 August O'Brien and Canty contrived to have the Workers' Union expelled from the Trades Council, Stewart availing himself of the opportunity to twit O'Brien and P. T. Daly on their earlier position. But two days later, as Larkin was walking home from his office, he was suddenly arrested and lodged in the Bridewell.

He was taken to Cork next day, where along with Fearon and Coveney he was accused of 'conspiracy to defraud'. The prosecution alleged that these men had collected subscriptions to the NUDL and had applied them to their own use. As we have already surmised, there was a grain of truth in this. In fact two ethics were in conflict. As Larkin saw it, the money had been used to wage war on behalf of his class. But the law took a different view: if Larkin had made up his mind earlier that he was going to break with the NUDL and had collected subscriptions for a new union – or indeed for any specifically definable legal purpose – there would have been no offence, so long as he did with the money what any responsible person would be expected to do. But the law is not so constructed as to take account of working-class realities. Larkin had collected for one thing and used the money for another. There was a case to answer. 1909

There were curious aspects of the committal proceedings. First was the fact that they were instituted so long after the offences alleged. In January 1909 one Simon Punch objected to being handed an ITGWU card in place of the NUDL one that he had surrendered. It was widely believed even among critics of Larkin that Punch was in contact with Sutton, the employer of the stevedore Rourke, and that a plot was hatched to bring Larkin to book. Some thirty dockers are said to have signed a memorial which was then taken to the police. The police did not, however, take action until August. Secondly, the Crown Solicitor, Dr Wynne, the man who had objected to the presence on the bench of the magistrate Kelleher, now objected to Sir Edward Fitzgerald 'on instructions from Dublin Castle'. Fitzgerald refused to leave the bench. Wynne then treated him with a studied insolence which aroused public suspicion, especially when it was revealed that Dr Wynne was also solicitor of the Cork Employers' Federation.[6] While the trial was proceeding the general manager of the GSWR visited Cork to present badges to the staff who had helped to break the strike. Houses were built in which those blacklegs who were married could now settle down.

A true bill was found. But it was nearly a year before Larkin stood trial. He soon recovered his spirits. When the Dublin Trades Council launched a defence fund he expressed himself confident of victory. But he avoided confrontations, even in 1910 when the trade depression began to lift. The

1909 months that followed the Cork débâcle were outwardly uneventful, but the balance was slowly tilting in his favour. The Socialist Party of Ireland was formally launched at a public meeting on 19 September. In the same week the Trades Council journal appeared for the last time, but almost immediately Connolly wrote from the USA announcing his purpose of returning to Ireland and suggesting the transfer of his own paper *The Harp* to Dublin. Stewart and Larkin were increasingly at loggerheads. On one occasion, after Larkin had denounced Stewart for attacking him in the press, Stewart declared war in unmistakable terms. Speaking with great deliberation he told the Trades Council: 'At the proper time and at the proper place I will meet and overturn this ruffian.' But he was making enemies himself, especially O'Brien and Canty.

Towards the end of November 1909 P. T. Daly severed his connection with Sinn Féin and began to gravitate towards the SPI. The ITGWU did nothing spectacular but became a recognised part of the political scene. It began to recover membership in Dublin. In Waterford the Trades Council's new secretary was a vigorous young man called Thomas Dunne. He persuaded the local ITGWU branch to affiliate. It would appear from somewhat ambiguous newspaper reports that while he did not become its secretary for a number of years, Dunne acted as ITGWU delegate of the local branch to the Trades Council. (ITGWU rules provided that tradesmen could hold simultaneous membership in their craft union.)

The conspiracy trials were due in December. Larkin secured a change of venue to Dublin and consequently a further delay. But Fearon's separate indictment was proceeded with, and he was awarded six months' hard labour. During his imprisonment he suffered a nervous breakdown and was removed to a mental institution. He was not fit to stand trial on the conspiracy charges, but later recovered, returned to Newry and remained a strong supporter of Larkin. The Cork branch of the union was, of course, annihilated, though a few individuals retained their membership.

* * *

1910 James Connolly's determination to return to Dublin was

expressed in letter after letter to William O'Brien, who at 1910 one time favoured the return for the sake of the SPI, and at another hesitated for the sake of the livelihood of Connolly and his family. In January 1910 Larkin accepted the sub-editorship of Connolly's paper *The Harp*, which was now transferred to Dublin. When Connolly failed to send copy, he turned out a February issue which O'Brien thought disappointing. He especially objected to Larkin's personal attacks on Sinn Féin leaders, though these were fully in line with the kind of treatment that Larkin was accustomed to receive from Griffith. But Griffith was not the whole of Sinn Féin. O'Brien established a committee whose object was to bring back Connolly for a lecture tour. It was hoped to find some way of retaining him permanently as organiser of the SPI.

On 5 March 1910 E. L. Richardson informed the Parliamentary Committee of the ITUC that he could no longer continue to act as secretary. The committee elected E. W. Stewart, who was now at the zenith of his political career. At the same time the Trades Council had, much to his annoyance, become uneasy about the validity of his credentials. There were rumours of business ventures. When the Trades Council met on 14 March Larkin was elected a delegate to the forthcoming ITUC meeting at Dundalk. Stewart's own union, the Shop Assistants' Union, decided to send not Stewart but a delegate from Cork.

Opening on 17 May 1910, the Dundalk meeting was a turning-point in the fortunes of the ITGWU. The union sent five delegates: Thomas Foran (General President), John O'Neill, John Bohan, William Hopkins and James Halligan. Their individual qualifications are not recorded. The Dublin branch had its headquarters in the old NUDL rooms at 10 Beresford Place. Its secretary was Thomas Greene, who had been NUDL secretary. The Congress was called to order by E. W. Stewart, who somewhat surprisingly announced that Miss Mary Galway would open the proceedings. She referred to the recent death of King Edward VII and invited delegates to support a motion of sympathy with his bereaved queen.

'Humbug!' shouted William O'Brien.

'Conduct yourself,' said Stewart. 'Respect a lady if you

1910 don't respect yourself.' This remark drew some applause.

'What about Whitehaven?' called Dawson Gordon of the Belfast flaxroughers. This was a reference to a recent colliery disaster in which many miners had lost their lives.

'That is coming later,' said McCarron of the Derry tailors.

'Oh! Any time will do for that!' interjected O'Brien.

When P. T. Daly rose to speak Miss Galway invited all those in favour of the loyal motion to stand, and she then declared the motion carried. It was an astute move, but it ensured the division of the conference from the start. Broadly speaking, there were three currents of opinion: the Unionist, which saw the United Kingdom as one country with one Labour movement; the Nationalist, which supported Redmond and regarded any independent Labour development in Ireland as a threat to his influence; and a third, consistently separatist, which aimed at a separate Labour movement in a separate Ireland. These last, together with some of the undecided, were now put on the alert. Nolan of the Dublin bookbinders explained that while personally King Edward deserved respect, he himself declined to recognise the English King so long as Ireland was denied constitutional rights. When McCarron moved the vote of sympathy with the victims of the colliery disaster (another astute move) William O'Brien proposed a collection for their families. This amounted to £4 1s 3d. McCarron was then moved to the chair.

The dispute between the ITGWU and the NUDL was discussed early in the proceedings. On its results depended the seating of the five delegates. The special committee had found that there was no justification for the breakaway 'if such secession is based upon complaints as to illegal action or improper treatment on the part of the National Union'. But on the other hand, 'As it is accepted on all sides that there is no objection to the formation and existence of an Irish Union, we are of the opinion that the Irish Transport Workers' Union is a *bona fide* Labour Union and entitled to recognition in the Trade Union movement.' The Parliamentary Committee confessed to being divided upon the recommendation of the investigatory committee and now submitted the matter for the judgment of Congress.

D. R. Campbell of the Belfast Trades Council moved that

the report of the investigatory committee should be accepted. 1910 E. W. Stewart objected. He proposed that the matter should stand over until the ownership of funds in dispute between the two unions had been decided by criminal proceedings now pending. This blatant felon-setting did not improve Stewart's popularity. Canty urged the affiliation of the Transport Union and added that his experiences of English organisations was that when Irish branches were in a hole they would leave them there. This remark was greeted with applause. M. J. O'Lehane said that fellow trade unionists must be considered innocent until proved guilty. The chairman, whom time had somewhat transfigured from the young militant of 1890, suggested that the special committee had exceeded its terms of reference in making a recommendation to Congress. After the Derry and Drogheda NUDL delegates had moved the deletion of the acceptance paragraph Congress adjourned so that the delegates could be conducted round MacArdle's brewery.

When Congress reassembled next morning Larkin and his five delegates were still outside. The Standing Orders Committee stressed the need for expedition. The early adjournment on the previous day had not been in accordance with their recommendations. It was proposed to proceed with non-contentious business. At this point Larkin drew attention to his existence, and Nolan pointed out that Larkin had been sent as delegate of the Dublin Trades Council, not of the ITGWU. Delegates grew impatient. Had the Parliamentary Committee the right to overrule Congress? When this question was answered in the negative E. J. O'Neill of the Dublin carpenters demanded: 'Well, why not admit the men and let us get on with the business?' But still McCarron stalled. He allowed Harris to launch an attack on Larkin which covered ground outside the terms of the resolution, and protected him even when his remarks drew protests from Canty and cries of 'Shame!' It was pointed out that Harris himself had proposed forming an Irish breakaway from an English union. Patrick Lynch of the Cork Tailors, who had supported the ITGWU at Limerick, now ranged with Harris. There was laughter when his colleague, Michael Egan of the coachmakers, objected to being referred to as 'his worship from Cork'. After D. R. Campbell had replied the amendment was put to the

1910 vote and lost by 38 votes to 22. William Walker then interposed to warn the chairman against making Larkin a martyr. He proposed an amendment that the ITGWU 'be and hereby are affiliated to the ITUC'. This was seconded by the Belfast baker McConnell and carried by 42 votes to 10. M. J. O'Lehane then moved that the Transport Union delegates be admitted.

According to the report of the Congress, which was edited by P. T. Daly,

> At this point, Mr Larkin who had been in the gallery came into the body of the hall where the delegates were sitting. Speaking in a very excited manner he said he came upon the floor as a delegate. The Congress decided by a large majority that he was a delegate and he asked why he should be debarred. There were sitting in the Congress 'notorious blacklegs' and 'enemies of Trade Unionism'.

The chairman ordered him to take a seat. It was not far off lunch-time and the Parliamentary Committee would report after the recess. William Walker suggested that the Parliamentary Committee had now no existence. The chairman replied that it existed until its report was accepted. This was, however, his last quibble. Larkin and the ITGWU delegates were then seated amid applause.

It was next Stewart's turn to be discomfited. He and P. T. Daly were contending for the position of secretary. Walker suggested that Stewart was not eligible as he was not a delegate. McCarron replied that he was in the same position as a co-opted member of a corporation. Walker challenged the chairman's ruling, which was set aside by 32 votes to 20. The chairman was compelled to inform Stewart that he was no longer secretary. Daly was elected unopposed. Stewart remarked ungraciously that after the vote seating the ITGWU he had no desire for the position.

Then it was McIntyre's turn. The Standing Orders Committee reported that the credentials of one of the Workers' Union delegates had been signed by a man who had for some months past been working as a blackleg. Messrs Harris and McIntyre were requested to meet the Standing Orders Committee and account for themselves. Three trade unions, the Dublin Corporation Workers, the brushmakers and the ITGWU, complained that members of the Workers' Union were engaged in unfraternal practices. It was decided that the Parliamentary Committee would investigate, and meanwhile McIntyre agreed to withdraw. On Canty's motion Larkin was seated as delegate of the Dublin Trades Council. Whereas this was undoubtedly correct procedure, it caused a difficulty. The Transport Union, with the largest single delegation at the conference, representing 3,000 workers, a vital part of the workforce of the capital, was not represented on the Parliamentary Committee, for Larkin was moved to it as representative of the Trades Council. Owing to the rule that no organisation could have two places on the committee, O'Lehane, who gained a higher vote, took precedence. 1910

McCarron refused nomination for the Parliamentary Committee, on which he had served since 1894. In the course of his closing remarks he announced that he proposed to take no further part in the affairs of Congress. His reason was the election of P. T. Daly, 'who would not be prepared to carry out the resolutions of that Congress so far as conveying them to the British House of Commons'. Daly expostulated that the chairman was misinformed. But McCarron persisted. It is quite clear that McCarron, away in Derry, simply did not know that Daly had left Sinn Féin. He was in fact resigning for nothing.

As it happened, McCarron continued to attend Congresses as a delegate until 1917, but by this abdication he lost his authority and substantially weakened the traditionalist wing of the movement. Stewart was never seen there again and steadily moved over to the side of the employers. In the following year the Shop Assistants' Union was represented by Thomas Johnson.

The 1910 Congress did not represent a complete victory for the national element, but it disposed of their bitterest opponents. It was the decisive Congress for the ITGWU. The new chairman of the Parliamentary Committee was D. R. Campbell. He was a man of intellect and independent judgment, in politics a socialist. While P. T. Daly and M. J. O'Lehane may have lacked Campbell's grasp of principles, they supported Larkin the man. Daly was secretary, O'Lehane was treasurer. If these three pulled together, they should

1910 usually get their way. An interesting incidental is the constructive part played by Canty. He had preserved from his early experiences in the National Union of Gasworkers and General Labourers little more than a strong trade union consciousness and a belief in a Parnellian style of nationalism. There was some appropriateness in his so gracefully preparing the way for the organisation that was to succeed where his had failed.

3

Enter the Giants

Yet, Freedom! yet thy banner, torn, but flying,
Streams like a thunder-storm *against* the wind.
BYRON

Larkin in prison – Connolly returns – Larkin released – three leaders compared – the Irish Worker *– wave of strikes – Wexford – Belfast – Irish Labour Party founded*

Larkin returned to Dublin to work on the June issue of *The Harp*. In its columns he gave the political anatomy of McCarron, Harris, Stewart and McIntryre. Stewart had announced his intention of quitting the Labour movement, but Larkin could not resist the temptation of hurling a stone after his retreating figure. The four libelled gentlemen took legal advice. They wanted an apology or they would issue writs. Before they could do so Larkin was in jail, and O'Brien, who was to substitute for him, decided that the most discreet course would be to allow the paper quietly to disappear. 1910

The conspiracy trial took place before a Co. Dublin common jury. Larkin's 'peers and equals' were not to be the artisans and shopkeepers of the Liberties, but comfortable farmers mingled with the retired military men of Pembroke and Rathmines. 'I'd be as safe in Cork,' he told O'Brien. When the trial opened, Sexton and Simon Punch repeated their evidence. It was claimed that Sexton appeared under subpoena. If his memoirs are to be believed, he considered that he was performing his public duty at grave risk, for he went everywhere armed. There were twenty-four counts, and on 17 June Larkin was sentenced to twelve months' imprisonment with hard labour. The sentence caused consternation. Larkin's counsel had failed to make the point that he had gained no personal benefit. But all efforts to secure a retrial failed, and he was lodged in Mountjoy Prison. But Coveney was acquitted after Larkin had made an appeal

1910 on his behalf.

Larkin appointed P. T. Daly to take his place. Daly was an experienced trade unionist and organiser. He had an attractive personality. He spoke well on the platform, where he was witty though not profound. He was not, however, a strong character. In 1908, when he was secretary of the Supreme Council of the IRB, he had visited the USA to collect funds for that organisation. On his return he failed to pay over a sum of £300. What was worse, instead of explaining the discrepancy and asking for time in which to make it good, he waited until it was discovered. This took place in April 1910. He was not, however, immediately expelled from the organisation. It was felt that his financial troubles were to a great extent the result of neglecting his own affairs in his enthusiasm for the republican cause. One imagines that his self-esteem suffered a blow, and, as there is little charity in politics, he began to drink. It is easy to understand his devotion to Larkin, who, without knowing it, provided him with a second mission in life at the crucial moment. Daly told O'Brien that he had little confidence in his capacity to hold the union together without Larkin. But instead of concentrating on preserving the Dublin branch at all costs, he spent much of his time in Belfast, for reasons which were largely personal.

On 26 July Connolly arrived from America. William O'Brien told him that the party was doing badly and advised him to seek work as an organiser of the ITGWU. But Connolly several times refused: he had come home for the purpose of producing and disseminating socialist propaganda. He spoke at the Trades Hall on 2 August. The immense broadening of his outlook during his seven years in the USA was at once apparent. Most of the old tradesmen stayed away. But Simmons, who took the chair, commented afterwards: 'If that lecture was socialism, then I'm a socialist.'[1] Two days later he spoke at the Bricklayers' Hall. Richard O'Carroll took the chair, and P. T. Daly was in the audience.

On 7 August Connolly was in Belfast, where he set up a branch of the Socialist Party of Ireland. Among its members were D. R. Campbell, Tom Johnson, Daniel McDevitt and Bulmer Hobson. When Daly arrived Connolly spoke at one of his meetings, but no progress was reported. Connolly next

visited Cork, where a group of his old colleague Con 1910
O'Lyhane's followers still survived. He recruited Daniel Coveney, whose ordeal had not weakened his nerve, and John Dowling of Cóbh, then considered one of the leading socialists in the south.

The successful establishment of the SPI alongside the union had far-reaching consequences not only in the matter of personnel. Larkin had founded a national union, but his socialism was still cosmopolitan: his party was the English-based Independent Labour Party, of which he had founded five branches in Belfast and one in Dublin. Connolly's vision of an independent Ireland generating its own current of social change, leading to a 'Workers' Republic', gave a sense of wider purpose to the more thoughtful union members. On 16 September P. T. Daly applied for membership of the SPI. At the end of the same month Connolly became a member of the Dublin No. 1 branch of the ITGWU.

But all was not plain sailing. In his anxiety to secure meetings for Connolly, O'Brien had approached the Waterford Trades Council on behalf of a non-existent trades organisation in Dublin. Unfortunately the Council replied to the Trades Hall. Thomas Greene complained that a handbill advertising one of Connolly's meetings carried the words 'under the auspices of the Transport Union'. No authority had been given, unless, of course, Larkin had given verbal authority to some visitor to Mountjoy. The SPI held a meeting outside Greene's office in Beresford Place. There a somewhat unstable person who was not a member of the SPI mounted the rostrum and attacked the clergy because of Father Kane's Lenten lectures against socialism. A letter signed 'William Murphy' appeared in the *Evening Telegraph*. Bohan and O'Brien ascertained that it gave an address that did not exist. They speculated on the identity of the author. Could it be McIntyre, or even Greene? In essence it was an attack on alleged attempts by socialists to make use of the name of the union. At the next meeting of the Trades Council the following exchange took place:

Nolan (Bookbinders): One would think that this Mr Connolly was the devil himself.

Healy (Bottlemakers): So he is.

1910 *Nolan*: Well I have listened to Mr Connolly, and I certainly say that what he has to say won't do the workers any harm, although it may not do them any good.

In the meantime a committee of which the accountant O'Brien Hishon was secretary was campaigning for the release of Larkin. A memorial was presented to the Lord Lieutenant. It bore many distinguished names, including those of the Lords Mayor of Dublin and Cork, six Dublin and Cork MPs, and (understandably) Sir Edward Fitzgerald. The memorialists stressed that there was no evidence that Larkin had applied NUDL funds to his personal use. They appended statutory declarations by members of the November 1908 strike committee testifying to the receipt from Larkin of all the moneys in question.

Too much need not be made of this. The declarations were not made until 8 August 1910, nearly two years after the event. No accounts were produced. Affidavits were not sworn. In one case, it has been pointed out, the money was supposedly received two days before the strike had begun. But obviously what was meant by the phrase 'own use' depended on who you were. To the Crown Solicitor the starting of an Irish union with funds collected for an English one was an act of personal caprice which was perverse into the bargain. To Larkin it was part of a battle in a holy cause in which he himself figured as knight-errant. The ordinary man, for his part, knew that the enemies of the Crown were often the friends of the people; and as for the question of the funds, he was inclined to shrug the matter off with 'Didn't they get enough out of us, anyway?'

Larkin was released on 1 October. The authorities might have been willing to make a martyr of him provided he remained in jail. By letting him out after two months they made him a hero. His release was celebrated by a torchlight procession and a mass meeting in Beresford Place. People who had previously taken no interest in the Labour movement attended, partly out of curiosity. Countess Markiewicz cycled into town and was accommodated with a chair on the brake. She was invited to speak and declared, Larkin dissenting, that all Ireland's troubles were due to the English connection. In one sense the Countess was right, but Larkin was not thinking historically but practically.[2]

Larkin's release was a turning-point. The fortunes of the union dramatically improved. This is shown by the 1915 roll book. Against the name of every 1915 member of Dublin No. 1 branch is set the date on which he first joined the union. The number who joined in 1909 was 160. To these can be added 120 who joined in 1910, giving a total of 280 for the two years. Obviously the disruption of 1913 and the war of 1914 had drastically thinned the ranks of the original membership. One estimate of the strength of the No. 1 branch in 1910 is 2,700. If the count was made on 31 December, this would suggest a multiplier of 2,700 divided by 280, or roughly 10. But fewer discrepancies arise if we use 12. On this basis the influx into the branch in 1910 was about 1,440, who for the most part joined in the second part of the year. To this total must be added the members of the James Street and High Street branches. That these were gaining members is evidenced by the complaints of 'poaching' referred to the Executive of the Trades Council, the usual arbiter in demarcation disputes. Although painters and lamplighters were recruited, the backbone of the union remained the casual dockers and the regular men of the Burns and Laird Lines, City of Dublin Steampacket Company, T. & C. Martin, Brooks Thomas, Tedcastles and the Dublin and Wicklow Manure Company.

* * *

Of the state of the movement in general something can be learned from the diaries of William O'Brien and his correspondence with Connolly, now spending much of his time in Belfast. Trade was still depressed. There was much indignation when Redmond's party refused to insist on the application to Ireland of the act for the 'feeding of necessitous schoolchildren'. The parliamentarians expected to be in the saddle and did not wish to be burdened with such expensive fripperies. Larkin denounced their preference for a low-wage economy and blamed low wage levels for the sluggishness of trade. The fear that he was going to make Home Rule too expensive was the fundamental motivation of the extraordinary campaign of vilification waged against Larkin, which may have caused

1910 the hypertrophy of some aspects of his character.

In considering the interrelations of the three main personalities in the movement perhaps we can turn to the 'Father of Medicine', old Hippocrates. It was he who first distinguished the type of man he called 'choleric', and in his description we can recognise Larkin. He could display immense energy, almost superhuman dynamism. Yet he could be plunged into profound gloom and depression. Indeed he himself complained of having to fight depression. He appears to have been depressed by his experience of prison, even though the 'hard labour' was the lightest that could be found. To be deprived of spontaneous action was a torture to him. It threw him into a self-pitying mood, and this could be broken by sudden explosions of resentment. Thus on one occasion when his views were challenged he so completely lost his temper at an SPI meeting that O'Brien threatened to leave the chair.

O'Brien was the complete opposite, very much the 'phlegmatic' man, never excessively enthusiastic, indeed constantly countering Connolly's optimism and warning of dangers ahead. He was unable to inspire people, but his own complete reliability helped to keep them going. His diary records hard bargaining with the 'sanguine' Connolly over the question of what salary the SPI could afford to pay. Connolly could always see the opportunities. But he was never cast down when they failed to become realities, for by then he could see fresh opportunities. He had an ever-active imagination tuned to the unfolding of possibilities. O'Brien, on the other hand, recognised the difficulties and did not hope for too much.

Towards Larkin, Connolly had mixed feelings. He respected him for his ability to personify the Labour movement. Not since O'Connell had any man possessed such a gift of moving the masses. He had a vivid turn of speech with just that touch of the gutter that makes the small man not merely hate, but despise the great. But his self-centredness, increased by the denunciations heaped upon him, was irritating to Connolly. Larkin could be hurt. It was as if he had to stifle his self-critical ability. Connolly once described him to O'Brien as an 'undisciplined overgrown schoolboy'.

Round these three men the affairs of the Irish Labour movement revolved in the period of storm and stress which

came with the long-awaited trade revival in the spring of 1911 1910
and which pushed the struggles of 1889 out of memory.

Connolly had settled in Belfast in March,[3] in time to be 1911
present at the election of Michael McKeown as delegate to the Galway meeting of the ITUC.[4] That Connolly would have liked to attend himself there is no doubt. He cannot have doubted McKeown's eligibility, but seems to have suspected that a Nationalist councillor would be cool towards political Labour.

Redmond's supporters were at this time trying to reduce Labour representation on public boards, and on his first appearance as ITGWU delegate to the Dublin Trades Council on 27 March Thomas Foran moved a resolution protesting at the reduction of the Council's representation on the Board of the Richmond Asylum. Delegates of the union also protested when the Dublin Chamber of Commerce resisted the extension of the Factories and Workshops Amendment Act to Ireland.

* * *

On 27 May Larkin published the first number of the *Irish Worker and People's Advocate*.[5] Its appearance coincided with Greene's candidature for Dock ward in the Poor Law elections. There has never been any publication to resemble it. It was full of passionate invective against the abuses endured by the workers of Ireland. It was also conducted without the slightest consideration for the law of libel. That it frequently hit the nail on the head is shown by the very small number of actions taken against it.

The wholesalers refused to handle it. Newsboys collected it from the printer, and a few sympathetic newsagents retailed it. Otherwise it was obtainable only at Beresford Place. There is no need to accept the high circulation claimed, namely 94,994 in September 1911. The total population of Dublin was little over 300,000, and in any case Larkin could never have known his circulation so accurately. The most reasonable estimate is based on a claim made in October, which indicates that the printer's capacity was limited to 20,000. This was, of course, a huge circulation. That of *Sinn Féin* fluctuated between 2,000 and 5,000. Assuming that Dublin contained

1911 about 50,000 'adult males', something like a third of these must have bought the paper, which one can therefore safely assume was read or discussed by the entire working class of the city. This was something unprecedented in any city in the world.

On Whit Sunday 1911 members of the union went on a day excursion to Cork. Special trams were engaged to take members from O'Connell Street to Kingsbridge, and special trains took them to Cork. They were accompanied by the union's fife and drum band and the O'Connell Pipe Band. After hearing a short Mass said by Father O'Leary they listened to a distinctly longer speech by Larkin and then set off on excursions to Cóbh, Crosshaven or Blarney. A special article in the *Irish Worker* warned them of the evils of intemperance. P. T. Daly remained in Cork as 'southern organiser'.

Next day, 5 June, the ITUC met in Galway. The union was represented by delegates from three Dublin branches and one from Belfast. Dublin No. 1 sent Larkin, Foran and the dockers' delegate Laurence Redmond. Dublin No. 2 sent James Halligan, and No. 3 John Bohan. Only Larkin spoke in the debates. The conference was uneventful but carried forward the tendencies shown at Dundalk. Harris was compelled to repudiate McIntyre, who had offered cheap labour to a coal merchant. His explanation was not accepted, and the Workers' Union was disaffiliated. Larkin, O'Brien and the bricklayer Richard O'Carroll were elected to the Parliamentary Committee. P. T. Daly and D. R. Campbell retained their positions. The other members were George Greig and Mary Galway. With the votes of M. J. O'Lehane and O'Carroll secure for most purposes, those who were moving in the direction of a separate Irish national Labour movement were now in command.

Larkin was losing interest in the British ILP and no longer kept close contact with William Walker. The demand for an independent Irish Labour Party was becoming insistent. At this congress the ITGWU paid £5 8s 8d in affiliation fees, the next highest contribution being the £3 10s paid by the Postmen's Federation. The advance of the 'left' was steady and relentless. When Simmons fell sick the Trades Council chose William O'Brien as their temporary secretary.

* * *

In the middle of 1911 a spring that had long been winding into an ever-tightening coil suddenly snapped. At last there was a concerted effort to break the power of the Shipping Federation, whose blacklegs had denied port workers the slightest advance in living standards during twenty years. Preparation had been made. In November 1908 a Transport Workers' Federation had been set up. Its proposals for a national conciliation machinery were ignored by the Shipping Federation. A wage claim by the National Sailors' and Firemen's Union was treated similarly. The federated unions set up a network of local strike committees, the most important of which were in London and Liverpool.

Early in June it was decided to call a simultaneous strike in all ports. This was the only way to paralyse the Shipping Federation. The employers and their agents could comb the doss-houses for scabs, but they could not transport them. The Irish ports were involved. But the National Sailors' and Firemen's Union had only 400 members in Dublin and no organisation either there or elsewhere. They appointed the ITGWU their agent in Ireland, and on occasion NSFU members were paid strike benefit from ITGWU funds. William O'Brien recorded his recollection that Larkin telephoned him on 12 or 13 June asking for Connolly's address. The new responsibility could not be discharged without a full-time official in Belfast. Larkin wired Connolly appointing him northern organiser, and the stoppage began on 14 June.

Three days after the strike began a group of Dublin businessmen met to discuss the advisability of forming an employers' association for the purpose of fighting the unions. Among them was the city's most powerful employer, William Martin Murphy, proprietor of the *Irish Independent*, principal shareholder in the tramway company, a man with interests in three continents, and a supporter of the Healeyite wing of the Irish Parliamentary Party. At a further meeting on 30 June the Employers' Federation was brought formally into being, and copies of the articles of association of its predecessor in Cork were circulated by way of encouragement.

The ITGWU was mainly concerned to prevent blacklegging. Articles were published in the *Irish Worker*. The Glasgow

1911 NSFU wired that a ship had sailed for Dublin with a scab crew. Dockers refused to unload her. In this way the seamen's strike led to sporadic stoppages on the docks. In Liverpool the non-Federation transatlantic shipping lines with their vast but vulnerable profits capitulated after a week. The Federation firms, smaller but more numerous and employing half the labour force, were not so easily persuaded. Tom Mann, chairman of the strike committee, fearing the possibility that they might keep going with the aid of local blacklegs, appealed to all transport workers to refuse facilities to companies who were members of the Federation. Larkin published his appeal in the *Irish Worker* of 1 July. The Irish companies mentioned included the Belfast Steamship Company, the City of Dublin Steampacket Company and Tedcastles.

The strike of the shore workers destroyed the power of the Shipping Federation almost, as Tom Mann put it, 'within a few days'.[6] But the strike continued. The dockers and carters had preferred their own demands, and the seamen refused to resume until these were met. In Ireland, however, the companies refused to give in, so that here the strike continued for a different reason. On 13 July the Employers' Federation met under the chairmanship of Mr Samuel McCormick, who must have looked back nostaligically on defeats he had inflicted twenty years ago, and discussed a general lock-out. Eight hundred men were indeed locked out. But at this point the Castle intervened, and on the 14th Larkin, McKeown and Tom Mann, who had arrived in Dublin that morning, met the Under-Secretary for Ireland, explained the demands of the seamen and expressed the willingness of the men to resume work. The employers were persuaded to accept the NSFU terms, and all workers in a position to do so went back. Thus it came about that what was a continuous struggle in Liverpool was divided into two phases in Dublin. In Belfast, however, the Head Line stood out, and the struggle went on.

The state to which the unfortunate deep-sea dockers had been reduced as a result of the weakness of the union in Belfast was described by Connolly in the *Irish Worker*, and he is worth quoting:

> In order to extract the last ounce of energy from their 1911 bodies a system of bonuses was introduced among grain labourers. Every gang turning out more than 120 tons of grain received as a bonus the magnificent sum of 6d per man. This, taking 100 tons as an average day's work, meant that for one-fifth of a day's work extra crowded in the ten hours, they received one-tenth of a day's pay. This in itself was bad enough, but in actual practice it worked out even more mischievously. By tips to winchmen, firemen and others the pace was kept up upon the unfortunate fillers and carriers; curses, obscene epithets, and even physical violence were frequently used to supplement the usual fear of dismissal, while the tallymen and checkers were forbidden to reveal the actual tonnages being done until the end of the day's toil. As a result of this systematic slave-driving the work was driven higher and higher, until 160, 180 and 200 tons as a day's work ceased to excite any comment or to be considered in any way remarkable. . . .
>
> All day long in the suffocating heat of a ship's hold the men toiled barefooted and half naked, choked with dust: while the tubs rushed up and down over their heads with such rapidity as to strain every muscle to the breaking point in the endeavour to keep them going, and with such insane recklessness as to be a perpetual menace to life and limb. Add to this inferno of industrial slavery that the men could not even retire to attend to the wants of nature unless they paid a substitute to take their place: that a visit to a w.c. or a drinking fountain often entailed dismissal . . . and the reader will have some conception of the depths of degradation to which our unfortunate Belfast brothers were reduced.[7]

The Belfast branch seems to have been revived by McKeown, who took out fresh membership in August 1910. He had little success in recruiting, one presumes through the lack of an issue. The 1915 roll book shows that only 11 who joined before 22 July 1911 were still members in that year. Connolly began a campaign of outdoor propaganda. The roll book indicates 20 new members on 22 July, 12 the following week. Using a multiplier of 5, this implies large recruiting meetings

1911 at which 160 enrolled. Some of these, for example members of the Cupples family, had fought with Larkin in 1907.

The new branch was without funds, but Connolly was able to raise financial support through street collections and other activities. The settlement in Dublin meant that funds were available from the head office. The Belfast strike was still in progress when events in Liverpool precipitated further strife in Ireland. On 5 August railwaymen on the north docks began an unofficial strike in sympathy with the dockers and seamen. Three days later all work had stopped, and there were demands that the strike should be made official. By 13 August the city had been packed with police, for whom extra-long batons were being specially turned, infantry and cavalry were drafted in, and gunboats anchored in the Mersey. A peaceful unarmed gathering of demonstrators was charged by the police, and it was remarkable that only two were killed. The result was a complete stoppage of all transport, by rail, road and water, overhead and underground. On 15 August two workers were shot dead by soldiers.

Next day the ASRS called a rail strike covering the whole of Great Britain and Ireland. The ITGWU gave the railwaymen immediate support by refusing to handle 'black' goods. Dublin once more became the scene of clashes between strikers and blacklegs and strikers and police. Because of the disruption of railway services the Dublin timber merchants locked out their men. This was on 21 August. On the 22nd the dock strike was settled, thanks to government intervention. The rail strike was therefore also called off. The terms of the settlement were satisfactory to the men. The Belfast employers, rather than find themselves isolated, offered a compromise which Connolly accepted. This brought the grain workers an extra 3s a week and limited the load to 100 tons a day. There were gains for men working tanker and general cargo. But the Dublin timber workers, who were earning only 14s a week, refused to go back without a wage increase.

While the transport strike held public attention a wave of strikes and wage demands convulsed Dublin. Increases were won by general labourers, bill-posters, sandwichmen, millers, mineral-water workers, soap and candle makers, builders' providers, brewery workers and some categories of dockers.

During the railway strike there was a spontaneous stoppage 1911 of the newsboys, who demanded an increased commission. The police used them with extreme brutality. Larkin won their hearts by supporting them in the *Irish Worker*. Even the depressed tramwaymen began to organise.

There were simultaneous developments in Wexford. McKeown addressed a meeting there on 11 July, reminding his hearers of the time when he had stood on the same spot twenty years earlier. A branch of the union was established, and when the *Loch Etive* sailed into port with a scab crew she was duly blacked. In Waterford the ITGWU branch had not survived. The Trades Council therefore undertook the duty of preventing blacklegging, but on 8 August organised a meeting which P. T. Daly addressed and at which the branch was revived. Next day a branch was started at Kilkenny and another shortly afterwards at New Ross.

Larkin was, of course, exultant. A great victory meeting was held in Beresford Place, addressed by himself, Daly, Connolly and William Partridge. Partridge was born in Sligo and reared in the railway town of Claremorris. His father, an Englishman working on the Sligo railway branch, may possibly have emigrated to Ireland during the victimisations of the 1880s. Partridge himself settled in Dublin around the turn of the century and worked as an engineer for the GSWR at Inchicore. He was a strong trade unionist with socialist tendencies and became one of the most capable orators in Ireland.

* * *

Members of the Trades Council were full of praise for the new industrial methods, though indeed the Irish workers had used the boycott and the sympathetic strike in the past. They had always been prepared to struggle, but could do so effectively only when favourable trade conditions made their employers dependent on them. Such conditions recurred at intervals of approximately twenty years, as if the ten-year trade cycle missed a beat. The peculiarity of the 1911 boom was, as will be seen, that before its impulse was altogether spent there came the war of 1914-18 which extended boom conditions over a period of six years, long enough for con-

1911 siderable consolidation of Labour's gains.

The employers, however, did not think they would have fallen victims to the trade cycle but for the malignant personality of Larkin. He was now in the high spring of his career, bustling, businesslike and confident. He had a vision of a great bloodless revolution in which the half-starved ill-clothed denizens of the slums would win a new life that would include leisure and culture. He thought that all that was necessary was the *will*, and he made himself the embodiment of that will.

The *Irish Worker* sounded a strong national note. There was good coverage of Gaelic games. Micheál Ó Maoláin provided interesting if occasionally indiscreet Gaelic League notes. All forms of Irish culture were encouraged. Standish O'Grady contributed a serial. The paper provided expert economic information, together with lists of fair houses and trade union rates. On the other hand, the police and bureaucracy were held up to ridicule, the press to contempt. Larkin's strong point was invective. Personalities were not spared. Eloquent abuse was heaped impartially on millionaire Murphy and impecunious Griffith, whose views on trade unionism were identical with that of the 'carrion-crow' loyalists of the North. Whence came the literary skill that produced this weekly swarm of hornets? None was necessary. It was Larkin's oratory congealed in print. It came bubbling out. For Larkin believed he could see the revolution taking shape before him, with himself as its chosen instrument.

On 19 August the *Irish Worker* announced the foundation of a Women Workers' Union and appealed for recruits. Three days later something under 3,000 women employed at Jacob's biscuit factory stopped work in pursuit of a pay claim. The claim was conceded on the 27th, but the company declined to recognise the union. The Irish Women Workers' Union was launched publicly at a meeting in the Antient Concert Rooms on 5 September. It was addressed by the Countess Markiewicz, Hannah Sheehy-Skeffington, Miss (Sinéad?) O'Flanagan, Larkin and Daly. Thereafter a weekly women's column was contributed to the *Irish Worker* by Larkin's sister Delia, who appears to have acted as secretary to the new organisation.

As quickly as one strike was settled another began. Need-

less to say, all did not end in victory for the workers. On 1911
15 September the timber merchants whose goods had been blacked by the railwaymen sent a test consignment to Kingsbridge under heavy police escort. The DSER was subjected to legal proceedings from its refusal to accept 'black' timber. The intention was to serve the other companies similarly if the goods were refused. Two men who refused to touch the timber were dismissed. The result was a strike. Members of the ASRS Executive came to Dublin. The railway companies declined to meet them.

There was nothing for it but a general strike. This was called, but only in Ireland. Blacklegs were brought across the channel, but many of these, to their credit, were prevailed upon to return home. Army reservists were then brought in. The military themselves were conscripted, to load and unload at Claremorris, to fire and drive between Mallow and Tralee. Clearly the only way to prevent the government from strike-breaking in Ireland was to provide a strike nearer home and see if they could break that. The Irish had loyally obeyed a call to strike in sympathy with Liverpool dockers. Why should they, in their own difficulty, be denied a similar expression of solidarity from members of their own union? To this the Executive Committee member Williams replied inconsequently that Irish affairs were incomprehensible to Englishmen. This was to invite the question of why the ASRS took it upon themselves to organise Irish workers if they were incapable of understanding their affairs. There was only one-way solidarity. It was Sexton and the dockers in another form.

The GSWR went to the length of locking out 1,300 engineering workers at Inchicore. At this point the ITGWU threatened to withdraw all labour in the remotest degree connected with the railways. The directors then agreed to take back nine-tenths of their former staff. They failed to fulfil this undertaking, and there was severe victimisation, mostly on the GSWR (at Dublin, Mallow and Cork) but also at Amiens Street. Larkin was often accused of breaking contracts; he might with justice have argued that he had learned the business from well-placed educators. The rail strike lasted until 3 October. The timber workers held out, but were forced to admit defeat three days later.

1911 During these strikes support was forthcoming from Irish-Ireland circles. In mid-September the Parnell Gaelic Football Club expelled two members from their team for blacklegging. On 30 September Ballagh (Co. Tipperary) Irish-Ireland Society passed a resolution in favour of the railwaymen. But at the Sinn Féin conference on 1 October the resolution from Drumcondra (Seán O'Casey's branch) deploring attacks on strikers was heavily defeated.

The union was expanding not only in Dublin. On 23 August, during the rail and dock strike, the Dundalk employees of the Dundalk and Newry Steampacket Company came out for demands of their own. They wired for Larkin, and McKeown was sent from Belfast. The strike was successful, but because of the lack of local leaders McKeown remained in Dundalk until shortly before Christmas, when he claimed 1,000 members. He organised the two breweries and won a 2s a week increase. But when demands were made on the timber merchants, builders, brickworks owners and coal merchants, these formed an employers' association and refused to deal with the ITGWU. The result was a series of strikes, the flooding of the town with police, clashes between police and pickets, and the usual tally of arrests and sentences. A new and important factor in the struggles of 1911 was the sympathy of the rank and file of the national organisations. McKeown acknowledged £40 from the Operative and Labour Society. The Irish National Foresters and the Total Abstinence Society made donations. On 5 November the divisional Ancient Order of Hibernians promoted a Gaelic football match in aid of the strikers. This fraternisation possibly had a political origin: on 25 September Captain James Craig and his Unionist friends held the notorious meeting at Craigavon at which they undertook to defy parliament if it should enact Home Rule. Thanks to the unity which was achieved in Dundalk, all sections in dispute won wage increases of from 1s to 2s.

Two other branches were founded during this period, the first at Bray on 10 September. The speakers were the president and secretary of the Dublin Trades Council, Tom Lyng, and George Burke for the union. On 17 September, at a meeting presided over by the mayor, Alderman D. O'Donnell, and addressed on behalf of the union by Walter Carpenter,[8] a Sligo branch was established. The initiative had been taken 1911 by the Sligo Trades Council and its secretary, H. Hughes, a veteran of the 1880s. John Lynch became union secretary.

On 27 September began the disastrous strike of the Bridge Street Bakers against the introduction of new machinery. On the same day the Dublin Chamber of Commerce discussed the organisation of the employers in a concerted effort to smash the ITGWU at all costs. The railway strike was described as 'the beginning of social war – setting class against class – a revolution'. As the bread famine tightened and denunciations multiplied, especially in the *Irish Independent* and Griffith's *Sinn Féin*, O'Brien wrote to Connolly: 'It will take Larkin all his time to get out of the present difficulty. I fear the Wexford affair is hopeless.'[9] But, as we shall see, he was wrong.

The Wexford lock-out was the hardest fought struggle of 1911, lasting well into the following year and providing impressive evidence of the transformation that had taken place since 1890. P. T. Daly transferred his activities from Cork to Wexford shortly after McKeown's visit and organised the foundrymen at Pierces. At first it looked as if history would repeat itself. The owners locked out the entire workforce. But this time the men stood firm. The dockers then came out for an increase of wages. The employers attempted a general lock-out. Extra police were drafted into the town, and a worker, Michael Leary, was killed in a baton charge.

Messrs Pierce had expected the workers to renounce the union and go cap in hand for their jobs. When they failed to do so it was proposed to reopen the ironworks with scab labour. This was brought in during the second half of October, when Griffith was thundering against the ITGWU and inviting workers to join another union.

There was an uneventful deadlock until, at the beginning of November, a motor manufacturer named Belton and the editor of the *Wexford Record*, whose owner was connected with Pierces, ambushed P. T. Daly late at night and beat him unconscious with heavy clubs. They were interrupted by passers-by; otherwise, it was conjectured, his body might have been found next morning in the harbour. It is a revealing commentary on the state of class relations that the local infirmary refused to admit Daly and that the police refused informations when the branch secretary visited the barracks

1911 to prefer a charge. Daly, when he recovered, insisted on a prosecution, and Belton was fined 20s. This penalty for a premeditated assault, even attempted murder, contrasted glaringly with the prison sentences and hard labour meted out to the workers involved in minor and accidental scuffles — men who had made no demands but merely joined a trade union.

The new-found independence of the working class, which was to a great extent the result of the ITGWU, was providing clear evidence that alien rule was the protector of privilege against the workers, as it had been against the tenantry. It contributed to the growth of national consciousness. The Wexford struggle was remarkable for the support it won among the lower middle class. Eamonn Ceannt publicly dissociated himself from Griffith. On the motion of Seán Etchingham the Leinster Council of the GAA decided to donate to the strike fund the entire net proceeds of the hurling final between Dublin and Kilkenny. The AOH (American Alliance) donated £40. Above all, throughout the length of the stoppage Wexford shopkeepers supplemented the strike pay, which came from Dublin, with generous credit. An important memorial of the past and presage of the future was the action of Oulart Irish Trade and Labour League in voting funds. Local hurling matches were played to raise money for the same purpose. Under the impact of events in the towns the rural workers were beginning to reawaken.

In December peace returned to the quays. Casual workers' wages went up from 4d to 5d an hour. Timber merchants raised wages from 13s to 15s a week. Similar increases were granted by the local brewers. But the foundry strike went on. The company tried to persuade its old employees to return as free labourers. To carry on indefinitely with blacklegs presented difficulties, and the imported men were unpopular in the town. It was for 'persistently following' one of these that Richard Corish was arrested.

While the Wexford struggle was in progress there were further developments in Belfast. Early in September a docker named Keenan was accidently killed when a bag was released a moment too soon. He was not a member of the union but had promised to join, and as an old quay worker he was given a few days' grace. At the inquest the employers' solicitor suggested that the bag had been dropped deliberately upon a non-union man. The newspapers had a field day with this 'amazing allegation'. Connolly stopped all work on the ship affected and demanded a retraction from the merchant involved. While waiting for this merchant he was forcibly put off harbour property. He informed the police that since he could not apparently speak to his members on the quay, he would have to speak to them somewhere else. He called out all 600 men from the lower docks. Within ten minutes the quays were deserted. Within an hour he had two apologies, and next day the solicitor's withdrawal appeared in the press. Connolly then set about organising the ropeworks, and opened a sub-office at 6 Dalton Street, Ballymacarrett. 1911

The linen trade suffered a setback at the end of the summer, and mill-owners agreed to restrict output. As had happened before, each of them sought to evade his responsibility by trying to extract equal work from fewer hours. The management of York Street mills tried to achieve a higher intensity of labour by saving the time that was being lost in talking, laughing, singing or 'adjusting the hair during working hours'. The notices went up, and offenders were to be fined. On 4 October there was a spontaneous strike. Some of the girls approached Connolly for advice. He agreed to organise them and submitted a wage claim. The management replied with a lock-out. With the aid of the Belfast Trades Council street collections were taken up and 2s strike pay was provided for over 1,000 women. The new rules were withdrawn, but the wage increase was not forthcoming. Connolly advised a return to work on the old conditions and, disregarding the protests of Miss Galway, established the Irish Textile Workers' Union. Shortly afterwards he negotiated an 80-ton day for the grain workers without loss of earnings.

* * *

The year 1911 must be accounted one of the most successful in union history. When it ended branches had been established in Dublin, Dún Laoire, Bray, Wexford, Waterford, Cork, Sligo, Belfast and Dundalk. All these branches, with

1911 the exception of that in Cork, were fully functional. There were three offices in Dublin and two in Belfast. In both of these cities a start had been made in the organisation of the women. In every place in which the union was established there had been advances in wages and improvements in working conditions. The union's position in the ITUC was unchallengeable. Full support was being received from the Trades Councils of Dublin, Waterford, Sligo and Belfast. The 1915 roll book is a useful pointer to the growth of the Dublin No. 1 branch. Of the membership registered in 1915, 906 had taken out their cards in 1911. If we again use the multiplier of 12, then as many as 10,000 members must have joined. This is not impossible. The registrar's figure for the total membership of the ITGWU at the beginning of 1912 was 18,089. Of these no fewer than 13,009 were stated to have become members during 1911.

All this had been achieved in face of a boycott by the most powerful employers and a bitterly hostile press. The union had attended the unveiling of the Parnell monument in Dublin on 1 October with banner and band, and its contingent in the temperance demonstration on 4 October was, according to O'Brien, the 'talk of the town'. But the press did not trouble to record these events. Instead there was denunciation and one misrepresentation after another. According to the railwaymen, public opinion had been turned against them, thanks largely to the *Irish Independent*. This newspaper was also the most virulent against the ITGWU. Understandably some members fell by the wayside. In October Thomas Greene, who had been shaken by the allegations of socialism, resigned as secretary of No. 1 branch. His refuge appears to have been the Workers' Union. His place was taken by John O'Neill, who filled the post with credit for many years. Most important of all, the finances of the union were now secure. On Christmas Day the union provided a substantial breakfast at the Trades Hall for eighty sandwichmen and gave 500 children dinner and toys. The separatist *Enniscorthy Echo* noted that the 'good deeds of this Trade Union' found little appreciation in the Dublin press.

1912 It would be a cynic who would suggest that these good deeds were performed in view of the municipal elections in January. But doubtless they had their effect. At the end of

January Larkin was elected to the City Council with 1,190 votes against his opponents' combined total of 464. His UIL opponent was the outgoing councillor C. L. Ryan, whose personation agent was E. W. Stewart, now a local pillar of Redmond's party. Bohan was elected with the narrow majority of 50. Foran, though defeated, polled 567 against his opponent's 725. But Larkin did not long enjoy his councillorship. Information was sworn against him by Stewart to the effect that he had accepted election while disqualified by a criminal conviction. In due course Larkin was fined £5 and the seat was declared vacant. 1912

The wave of strikes, which affected the whole of Ireland in 1911, subsided in 1912. But the earlier part of the year saw some bitter struggles. In Dundalk McKeown had established a branch of the IWWU. Work for women was scarce in the town, and Vincent Carroll, the tobacco manufacturer, paid his girl employees a less than munificent 4s a week. Just after Christmas they asked for 6s. Their employer offered what he said was equivalent to 5s. But on examining the complex piecework system that he proposed, they decided that it would leave them worse off. When they rejected it they were locked out, and despite the efforts of McKeown and a visit from Connolly, the employer was able to conduct his business with scab labour. The girls did not admit defeat until the end of March.

The lock-out at the Wexford ironworks continued into February. Towards the end of January P. T. Daly was arrested on a trumped-up charge of incitement to violence. In view of all the violence that had taken place, it is remarkable that he should only be heard advocating it after five months had elapsed. He was whisked away to Waterford jail, and no doubt it was hoped that the men would then abjure the union and return to work on the employers' terms. On the other hand, this very anxiety to speed matters up betrayed a desire to resume normal relations. Connolly was sent to take Daly's place. He had learned that the employers were prepared to recognise any union but the ITGWU. He therefore proposed to transfer the members to a new union, the Foundrymen's Union, providing there was no objection to its affiliating to the ITGWU. This arrangement was accepted, and Richard Corish became the secretary of the new organisation.

1912 On 20 February Connolly, Peter O'Connor, secretary of the Wexford Branch, and Michael O'Connor, the railway worker who was now acting as secretary of the Waterford branch, visited New Ross. The branch had collapsed. P. J. McIntyre had paid a visit and had succeeded in suborning its secretary. When a strike took place he had refused to produce the books. Peter O'Connor therefore refused to hand over strike pay. Meetings were held and the branch re-established. P. T. Daly was awarded a month's imprisonment on 4 March and was released on 2 April. Meanwhile on 1 March Waterford gas workers won an advance of 2d an hour. The deep-sea dockers of Belfast won 6d a day. It was during this period that a more commodious Dublin head office became necessary. The union took over the old Northumberland Hotel at 18 Beresford Place, a building with Young Ireland associations. The transfer was made during the week ending 24 February 1912, and the new premises quickly received the title Liberty Hall.[10]

The National Insurance Act came into force early in 1912, and in connection with its recognition as an Approved Society, the union published a list of its branches in the *Irish Worker* of 6 April. There were four in Dublin and eleven others.[11] A branch in Cork city bore the title 'Storemen and Carmen's Union'. It is to be presumed that Daly had succeeded in organising certain grades but that it was not judged opportune to defy the employers then. Thus at the 1913 meeting of the ITUC Lynch attended for the Cork Storemen and Carmen. But in the following year Coveney attended quite openly as delegate of the Cork branch of the ITGWU.

* * *

The annual excursion in 1912 was to Wexford. The numbers were smaller than those of 1911. Larkin believed that this was because of certain counter-attractions in Enniscorthy. But it may be also that the trade boom had slackened. There was much distress in Dublin, Belfast and Waterford, and the employed worker was inclined to husband his resources. The date was 26 May, and next day the ITUC was to meet at Clonmel. Larkin made a speech which might be interpreted as marking his conversion to the 'one big union'.

He said:

> Tomorrow we are going to advocate one society for Ireland for skilled and unskilled workers, so that when a skilled man is struck at, out comes every unskilled man, and when an unskilled worker is struck at, he will be supported by the skilled tradesman.[12]

It seems likely that the proposed new departure was an indication of Connolly's growing influence in the union. During his stay in America he had broken with the more rigid and dogmatic principles of 'syndicalism', but was still to some extent influenced by them. Syndicalism was, of course, never a comprehensive system logically worked out. Its exponents differed widely among themselves. A common proposition was that of industrial unionism: workers were to be organised primarily by industries and only secondarily by trades. That Connolly was pressing for the setting up of an Irish Labour Party indicates that he had abandoned the notion that trade unions should 'build up an industrial republic within the shell of the political state, in order that when that industrial republic is fully organised, it may crack the shell of the political state and step into its place in the scheme of the universe'.[13]

At one time he had even gone so far as to say that 'Under a Social Democratic form of society the administration of affairs will be in the hands of the representatives of the various industries of the nation.'[14] While he no longer worked to that principle, syndicalist thinking nevertheless remained an influence throughout the Labour movement – a circumstance which explains decisions taken at various times. There was confusion as to the role of the industrial and the political in the transformation of society.

At Clonmel Connolly on behalf of the ITGWU proposed the historic resolution which resulted in the formation of the Irish Labour Party. He moved:

> That the independent representation of Labour upon all public boards be, and is hereby, included amongst the objects of this Congress.[15]

Connolly pointed out that the establishment of Home Rule would inevitably lead to the disruption of existing parties.

1912 The motion was carried by 49 votes to 18, a measure of the bitter resentment against the policy of Redmond's party, who were now obstructing the extension to Ireland of the medical benefits of the Insurance Act.

After this political declaration of independence on the part of Irish Labour Larkin moved his resolution:

> That in the opinion of this Congress it is essential that a closer union should exist between the various trades and labour bodies in Ireland, and for this purpose the Parliamentary Committee be instructed to draw up a constitution upon which an Irish Federation of Trades should be based, such constitution to be submitted to the Trades Unions of the country without delay.[16]

Bennett of the NSFU seconded, and Connolly supported the motion; but it was rejected by 28 votes to 23. Apart from his own union, Larkin drew support from the socialists and Trades Council delegates. But there was considerable opposition from cross-channel and craft unions. Even William O'Brien was hesitant and sought unsuccessfully to move an amendment.

The passing of Connolly's resolution had less immediate historical effect than the rejection of Larkin's. For Home Rule did not come, whereas the employers' onslaught did. It is not possible to say precisely what Larkin had in mind. But if the Parliamentary Committee had drawn up a plan, it is doubtful whether it would have gone beyond the provision of a central fund to be available to any union under attack. This would have been of immense value in the struggles that were soon to take place.

A third resolution with far-reaching implications was passed. It began:

> The Congress urges that Labour unrest can only be ended by the abolition of the capitalist system of wealth-production with its inherent injustice and poverty.[17]

The immediate measures proposed were in accordance with tradition: the 48-hour week and a minimum wage. J. D. Clarkson has suggested that these demands 'were to be merely incidental to the high aim of overthrowing autocracy in industry to make way for the Co-operative Commonwealth, the Workers' Republic'.[18] In view of the failure of Larkin's resolution, this would probably be to go too far. 1912

Larkin was elected chairman of the Parliamentary Committee, with William O'Brien as vice-chairman. Daly and Campbell held their positions. All the officials were avowed socialists. The remainder of the committee (Thomas MacPartlin, Richard O'Carroll, Thomas McConnell and M. J. O'Lehane) were, if not active propagandists of socialism, at the very least advanced Labour men. The sole exception was Miss Galway, who retained her position for another year. She had been quite unsuccessful in persuading Congress to censure the ITGWU for founding the Textile Workers' Union. In most things she would be in a minority of one.

4

Home Rule is Cheap Rule

Of every £2 supposed to be spent on the Government of Ireland, nearly one-half is pocketed by an employé of the bureaucracy.

JOHN REDMOND (Drumkeering, 1907)

Labour and Home Rule – Sligo – vilifying Larkin – Connolly in Belfast – shipping agreement – proposed conciliation board – Cork branch revived – rural workers – organising tramwaymen

1912 The Clonmel conference showed that a transformation had overtaken the Irish Labour movement in two decades. It was now separated not only from the British Labour Party but also from the official Nationalists. There was a growing appreciation of the fact that the leaders of Redmond's party hankered after government on the cheap, just as its industrial supporters favoured cheap labour.

In 1891 Parnell had shown himself the first Irish statesman to recognise the key importance of the working class. In calling on the workers to save the nation he anticipated Connolly. But there was no question as to who would lead the nation. That would be the Irish Parliamentary Party, which Parnell hoped to reconstitute and revitalise. During the period when Home Rule was in abeyance trade unions could support the parliamentarians, who were pressing the nationalist demand, while taking their grievances to Labour men who had been elected Nationalist MPs, men such as William Field and J. P. Nannetti, who represented the old trade unionism.

The return in 1910 of a Liberal government dependent on the Irish Party for its majority, brought Home Rule within sight once again. But 1911 saw the outbreak of the 'great unrest'. If the Labour Party were not to replace the Liberal as the main opposition party, concessions must be made. These concessions took the form of a programme of social legislation. 1912

There was every reason to suppose that the government, as part of the Home Rule 'package deal', would insist that Ireland accepted financial responsibility for land purchase. Redmond's party had no mind for accepting in addition the cost of a programme of social legislation. Redmond therefore consistently opposed the extension of the English legislation to Ireland. The result was the alienation of Irish Labour and the movement towards an independent party. If the British had been prepared to foot the bill for buying out the landlords – and after all it was their ancestors who had installed them – the course of history might have been different. The manufacturers of the Belfast area, for one thing, might have continued to support Home Rule. But, and this is the essence of it, the Liberals were supporting Home Rule only because their majority depended on it. The result of their opportunism was to force Redmond into two unwanted confrontations, one with Labour, the other with the Ulster Unionists. And because the country districts were the only areas where the parliamentarians believed themselves to be safe, efforts were made to introduce gerrymandering provisions into the electoral clauses of the bill. Important urban areas such as Wexford, Dundalk and Sligo were to be merged with surrounding rural areas. The result was the further antagonising of Labour.

Trade unionists who had grown up in the Parnell era had to make a choice between severing their connection with Redmond or seeing their influence in the Labour movement dwindle to vanishing-point. Stewart had gone in 1911. Canty remained in the movement, but Larkin suspected him of sympathy with Stewart and tried to infiltrate his union and install P. T. Daly. Michael McKeown, indeed, stood as a Labour candidate in the Belfast municipal elections, but lost his seat. Of those who supported the parliamentarians more indirectly, by urging support for the British Labour Party, William Walker accepted a government appointment and left politics in 1912. McCarron continued to resist. His argument against an Irish Labour Party was that 'the working man has no country'. He thought this an argument for belonging to the British Labour Party rather than the Irish.

There were also developments within the Irish Parliament-

1912 ary Party. The leading Northern Nationalist, Joseph Devlin, MP, began to use religious sectarianism as a means of holding working-class support. For this purpose he led a breakaway from the Ancient Order of Hibernians called the Board of Erin. He thereby played into the hands of the Unionists by helping them to hold the Protestant workers of Belfast. In Munster and south Leinster the revival of Land and Labour Associations was favoured. This was to take up the tradition of the Land League from which Redmond's party had originally been derived. On New Year's Day 1912 a convention of these organisations met at Portlaoise under the presidency of J. J. Shee, an opponent of the Hibernians. Branches were revived throughout Limerick and North Cork. They took up the cudgels for the labourer. Their main demand was for the 'second half-acre' – that is to say for land, not for wage increases. But they could not remain totally indifferent when the cost of living had risen by 15 per cent since 1902. In February 1912 they joined with the Limerick branch of the National Asylum Workers' Union in promoting a wage claim.

Finally it is necessary to note the state of relations between British and Irish Labour. Corresponding to the industrial differences that have been mentioned was Labour politicians' habit of supporting the Irish Party in opposition to ameliorative legislation in Ireland. To put the matter crudely, their influence with their constituents depended on their securing favours the Liberals alone were in a position to bestow. The Irish Party was keeping the Liberals in office and must therefore not be offended. The result was Irish disillusionment with British Labour.

* * *

The last substantial strike of the 'great unrest' began at Sligo during the first week of June 1912. It started when workers refused to dig coal in a hold fifteen feet deep for 5½d an hour. They demanded 6d. P. T. Daly was sent. While in charge of the dock strike he took the opportunity to organise storemen and warehousemen, and there were one or two small stoppages in the town. Workers in the grain boats at Strandhill then came out for their own demands.

Michael McKeown relieved Daly on 15 June. He organised 1912
the men on the Liverpool boats, as well as a number of carmen and corporation workers. The coal workers won a complete victory on 22 June. As a result of the membership gained, the branch was enabled to lease new premises. This building was occupied on 2 July and was given the name Liberty Hall.

An important aspect of the victory in Sligo was that the workers won the right to elect stevedores. In Dublin the stevedores' alliance was sought by other means. On 10 June 1912 they were called to a meeting at Liberty Hall. Larkin suggested to them that they might feel disposed to set up an organisation of their own and offered to draft some rules for them to consider. The Stevedores' Association was formed on 20 June, and Larkin at once negotiated with it an increase in the size of gangs as a means of reducing unemployment. A new price-list was agreed. The stevedores thus became independent of the employers, but since the union possessed the industrial power which would secure them in an emergency, they became to that extent dependent on the union. Larkin won a bloodless victory.

Despite the general industrial peace, broken only by the efforts of the IWWU to organise Keogh's sack factory and a number of laundries, the nationalist newspapers kept up a continuous press campaign against Larkin. The *Evening Telegraph* published McIntyre's squibs, however offensive or absurd. For example, it was alleged that Larkin's son was a leader in the imperial Boy Scouts. But young James was only seven years old and attending Pearse's Irish-Ireland school, St Enda's. Larkin was not too tongue-tied to retaliate. He sent a reporter in disguise to the doss-house in which McIntyre worked as a general factotum. His description was not complimentary. A constantly intensifying war of words raged for two years.

McIntyre and Stewart were joined by Thomas Greene and William Richardson, who had also gone over from Labour to the UIL. An individual who attracted consistent abuse in the *Irish Worker* was one John Saturnus Kelly, a city councillor who had organised a bogus union among the railwaymen. Larkin constantly alleged corruption in the Corporation, but libel suits were markedly few.

1912 As Larkin became the target of ever-increasing attack he came to expect compensation from his own supporters. He grew hypersensitive. When his ruling as chairman of the Parliamentary Committee was challenged he refused to act and offered his resignation. At the inaugural meeting of the Irish Labour Party on 16 September he made a very negative speech for which he afterwards apologised on grounds of ill-health.

Two Labour men, Michael Brohoon and William Partridge, contested municipal by-elections on 1 October. Both were strong candidates. On 7 August Partridge had been dismissed from the Inchicore engineering works with a week's salary in lieu of notice. His offences were two. One was making a collection for the benefit of the victims of the Belfast pogrom of the preceding month. The other was that of objecting to the bringing in of unqualified Protestants to do the work of qualified Catholics who were then dismissed. The press campaign against what was now being called 'Larkinism' must have contributed to the defeat of the two candidates. In a letter he sent to Connolly on election day O'Brien wrote:

> William Richardson with the aid of the *Telegraph* and the *Irish Independent* works the anti-Larkin, anti-Socialist racket for all it is worth.[1]

At the beginning of December a curious lawsuit opened before Chief Baron Palles and a jury. It is usually known as *Long v. Larkin*. A stevedore called Long had refused to join the Stevedores' Association. He was told that unless he did so he would not get men to work for him because of the stevedores' agreement with Larkin. When he engaged thirty-three ITGWU members to unload a ship's cargo the men were called out after one hour's work. Long instituted civil proceedings against Larkin, alleging conspiracy to injure him in his business. Two union officials, Redmond and Hopkins, were joined, as well as three stevedores, Newan, Donohoe and another Long. The jury found that the dispute was not between Long and his workmen, but between Long and the Stevedores' Association; there was no trade dispute, and Long should be awarded £275 damages. The defendants appealed, and some years later this decision was upheld by the House of Lords. Larkin believed that Long was an agent of the Shipping Federation and that the decision was political. He spoke of the 'perverse verdict of an employers' jury'. 1912

The press made the most of the opportunity to represent Larkin as a dictator interfering with the course of normal trade. He, in return, drenched the offending sheets in invective and ridicule. The Unionist *Evening Mail* he called 'the G-man's pinkeen, the porter-stained Mail', while its principal rival was called the 'Evening Trolley-wobble'. His readers were delighted by his exuberance and effrontery. O'Connell vanquished the widow Moriarty with a show of Euclid; all the parallelograms in the world would not discomfit Larkin. Yet in all his picturesque vituperation there is no doubt about his burning indignation against the corruption, greed and hypocrisy of those who batten on the people. A typical example is his denunciation of the Redmondite Councillor Michael Swaine:

> This foul, parasitic growth, along with three others of the same character as himself, left the alleged workingmen's club on Wellington Quay, drunk as usual, paraded up Parliament Street, past the House of Corruption, Cork Hill, and then when Micky and his pals scrambled along as far as Christchurch Place, Micky took the chair, called the meeting to order in his usual gentlemanly manner and Chesterfieldian language, and splattered out 'Let's all go down to that — Irwin's house and serenade the —.' And no sooner said than acted upon, and then for forty minutes Micky and his satellites howled and shouted foul and lewd sounds under Thomas Irwin's (the Labour candidate for Wood Quay) window. This is one of the City fathers, Micky Swaine, who goes to a race meeting, to use his own words, without a tosser, and can bring back £200. What a combination we have gathered under the alleged branch of the UIL, Wood Quay, – Micky Swaine, president; P. J. McIntyre, proselyte keeper of a doss-house, vice-president; and J. S. Kelly, blackmailer and rogue, secretary. What a combination! – The three graces.[2]

The union continued to make progress. The possession of commodious premises at Liberty Hall made possible a wide range of activities. Soon after the hall was opened a room was

1912 provided for the band. A weekly Irish class, a choir and a dramatic society were started. In late June a room was provided for the weekly meetings of the engineering machinists' section, which united men from the Port and Docks Engineering Department, Ross & Walpole and other concerns. A section was opened for warehousemen, vanmen, monocasters, stone-polishers, and rotary hands. Now at last Thoms, Helys and Easons were organised. The scanty data in the 1915 roll book suggest that these may be the first *sections* (as opposed to branches) officially established in the union.

A new branch was established at Inchicore which met at the Emmet Temperance Hall. Here also there were Irish classes and a great variety of social activities. Partridge was brought back from rural exile and installed there. In normal office hours he worked for the Insurance Section of the union. He was one of its most dedicated workers, available at any time, writing, speaking, organising. He contributed copiously to the *Irish Worker*, but his real strength was his oratory, for which he had an ideal voice, strong, flexible and resonant.

There was also progress in Belfast, where Connolly answered the state of sectarian division in the musical scene by organising the 'Non-Sectarian Labour Band', composed of members of several trade unions. This headed the demonstration held in July 1912 for the purpose of recruiting to the Irish Textile Workers' Union, of which Winifred Carney was secretary, Ellen Gordon delegate, and Connolly himself organiser. Later Thomas Johnson's wife, Marie, worked in a part-time capacity. The famous manifesto *To the Linen Slaves of Belfast* was issued in November.[3] There was little progress on the docks. The Catholics of the deep-sea docks were organised, but under the prevailing conditions of bigotry and sectarianism it was not possible to approach the Protestants.

The union grew less rapidly in 1912. There was a mild recession, and meetings of the unemployed were held. Larkin had been compelled to ask the stevedores for work not wages. The deduction from the 1915 roll book is that about 1,680 new members joined. Other sources suggest a figure nearer 1,000, bringing the grand total to about 24,000. Claims to higher figures seem to bear the mark of exagger-

ation. Indeed, if allowance is made for losses, a fairer estimate 1912
might be 20,000 to 22,000.

* * *

New rules, necessitated by the Insurance Act, were registered on 10 October 1912.[4] These rules differ little from those of 1909. The reference to compulsory arbitration is deleted. At Clonmel M. J. O'Lehane had advocated the establishment of arbitration courts, but it was no longer believed that arbitration should be compulsory. It may be that there was hesitation over putting fresh powers in the hands of Redmond's party. A demand for land division was also dropped.

The rules provided for a General Executive Committee composed of one delegate each from Munster and Connacht, two from Ulster and four from Leinster, together with the two general officers. Under rule this Executive ought to have been elected in November 1912 so that it could take office on 1 January. It has been suggested that it seldom if ever met. There is, however, evidence of its election. In the *Irish Worker* of 4 January 1913 it is stated that Michael McKeown was one of its members. We can guess that the other Ulster member was Connolly and that the Connacht member would be John Lynch.

Members of the ITGWU were candidates in the municipal 1913
elections of January 1913. In Belfast McKeown lost his seat, and both Connolly and D. R. Campbell were defeated. The docker Brohoon and Partridge were returned in Dublin, though three other Labour candidates were defeated. In Wexford Richard Corish and in Sligo John Lynch were successful.

It was alleged that the UIL not only falsified voters' rolls, but used this falsification to facilitate impersonation. There were many publicans among the Hibernians, and Larkin suggested that what they possessed in plenty they dispensed freely. The comparatively poor showing of the Labour candidates must be viewed in conjunction with these practices and the continuous press campaign. At the same time a transition was beginning. Leaders of industrial struggles were providing a new type of public representative.

1913 It was Partridge's opinion that the coming of Larkin had, for the first time, given the common people *hope*. This must be set against all the fallibilities and extravagances of his character. The working class began to believe that the pyramid of exploitation, injustice, robbery and jobbery, whose top was festooned with viceregal prerogatives, police commissioners' powers, and the rights and responsibilities of landlord, presslord and employer, could be rocked by a well-coordinated jerk from those who rested on its bottom stones. The irreverent tone of the *Irish Worker*, mocking every pretension of the ruling class, exposing the thief in striped trousers and boiled shirt, was admirably adapted to this end. The feeling was created that something could be *done*.

The employers' contention was that the ITGWU was a wanton disturber of the natural order of things. Arnold Wright, their paid apologist, compounding inaccuracies with the expertise of a high-class chef, paints a picture of mounting aggression which led the inconceivably long-suffering employers to screw up their courage and cry 'enough'.[5] For example, it is stated that there were more than thirty strikes in eight months. But industrial unrest is measured not only by the number of disputes but also by their magnitude – and anyway there had been periods in 1911 when there were thirty strikes in eight *days*. The recession of 1912 was overcome in 1913, and the prosperity was greater even than that of 1911. And yet the union for the most part contented itself with holding what had been won.[6] It could not be held responsible for the prolonged struggles of the silkweavers and coachmakers; but its support for these workers seriously alarmed the employers. In the case of the coachmakers the ITGWU 'took over the labourers and kept them out until the coachmakers won'.[7] The significant fact was not that the union was spoiling for a fight, but that when a fight did take place it was liable to be extended according to the principle of the 'sympathetic strike'.

Apart from two instances, one in Dublin, the other in Sligo, ITGWU actions in 1913 were of modest dimensions. The Dublin strike involved the City of Dublin Steampacket Company. The dispute arose out of the 1911 settlement. The ship-owners had agreed to base the wage rates of Dublin seamen on the principle of parity with Liverpool. The wages of dockers and carters were to be governed by a conciliation board representing the two sides of industry. Parity did not materialise despite many requests from the NSFU. Nor was the conciliation board established. Its formation was prevented by the obstruction of one firm, the City of Dublin Steam-packet Company. This company ignored the union's complaints and would not even discuss them. After five men who had agreed to join the union were instructed by management not to do so, the men ceased work on 30 January 1913, the employer inserting in the press the piteous lamentation that since the supply of blacklegs had apparently dried up, they were no longer in a position to maintain their services.

The justice of the union case is supported by ample evidence covering the previous eighteen months. Yet even so distinguished an academic historian as Professor Larkin seems to take for granted that the union was the aggressor. His explanation of the dispute is that the company 'was a good choice for a stand-up fight'.[8] Why should the union wish for a 'stand-up fight' and peer around for an eligible enemy? To fix upon the union a reputation for reckless bellicosity was part of the tactics of those who, anxious to weaken the working class for political as well as industrial reasons, were justifying their own intended aggression in advance.

The strike dragged on for several months. During this time Larkin is depicted as establishing his reign of terror over one brow-beaten employer after another. Actually he was anxious and depressed. The campaign of vilification never abated. That the *Irish Worker* never muted its confident tone is hardly relevant: a general must hearten his troops. But on 22 March O'Brien wrote to Connolly:

> Things are in a very bad way still. We requested Larkin to reconsider his decision to resign the chairmanship [of the Parliamentary Committee] but he flatly declines to do so and moreover he states that he will not even be a delegate to the Congress.[9]

The letter goes on to explain that McCarron was organising 'all the old gang from all parts of the country' to recapture control of the ITUC at its meeting in Cork, where 'Campbell, Daly, Larkin and myself are at all costs to be removed from

1913 the PC'. Then comes the description of Larkin:

> The fight here grows keener against Larkin and his union every day. The misrepresentation in the press is cruel and has a very bad effect on his members, I greatly fear. Scarce a day passes but the *Independent* contains an attack of some kind, and the *Telegraph*, which up to nine months ago was not so bad, is even worse, because it has ten times the influence of Murphy's rag. How it will all end 'tis hard to say. Larkin is looking and feeling bad lately and if the strain is not eased soon I fear he will break down mentally and physically. He must be made of iron to stand it so long. He is despondent too, which is most unusual with him, and he told me a week ago, and a number of us last night, that if this fight with the City of Dublin was over he would resign and leave the country altogether.

Yet at a meeting in Smithfield on the day this letter was written Larkin seemed bursting with vitality. Whatever his deficiencies, like Hercules he drew fresh strength from contact with the ground.

The trouble in Sligo began on 8 March. The branch secretary wrote to the *Irish Worker* complaining of the fantastic inaccuracy of *Irish Independent* reporting. It seems that Martin Moffat, a local seaman on board the steamship *Sligo*, inquired about 'cattle money', the extra payment made to seamen for attending to cattle during a voyage. He was told this would not be paid. He replied that the crew was too small and reported to John Lynch, president of the local ITGWU branch and delegate for the NSFU. The donkeyman turned off his engine, and the men went ashore. They were arrested for disobeying a lawful order, and most of them were sentenced to two weeks' hard labour, later reduced to seven days. The Shipping Federation was able to supply blacklegs. But at this point the ITGWU men refused to load the vessel. Scab dockers arrived on the next boat from Liverpool. P. T. Daly was sent from Liberty Hall, and J. H. Bennett of the NSFU came from Belfast.

Over the next three weeks the strike extended. Troops and police poured into the town. The old familiar scenes took place. Strikers fought scabs, and police fought strikers. Stones were thrown, not by strikers but by 'irresponsible youths'.

Plate-glass windows were shattered. Clerks carrying parcels to the post office were attacked, the shipping company's clerks incurring special attention. Coal workers struck. During a fracas in the Liverpool shed a blackleg named Garvey struck a union member, Dunbar, on the head with a shovel. The injury proved fatal.

Sligo was the comparatively small capital of the most industrialised county in Connacht. Its inhabitants comprised the descendants not only of town workers and the local small farmers, but also of coal-miners and iron workers, together with a few incomers from west Ulster. Some of the local landlords, moreover, had dabbled in industry. Such a population was almost unanimously in favour of the workers, and great meetings were held at the Town Hall with the support of the mayor. One such meeting, on 20 April, was said to have been the biggest in Sligo for fifty years. Before agreeing to mediation in Sligo it was able to send congratulations to Dublin on the settlement of the dispute with the City of Dublin Steampacket Company. By 26 May the major shipping companies had signed agreements which gave the Dublin men the rates they had asked for. Conciliation machinery was agreed upon and what was in effect a 'cooling-off' period. There is no evidence of 'bloody-mindedness' on the part of the union.

The desire to negotiate an agreement is the probable explanation of Larkin's 'open letter to the people' on 'how to stop strikes'. This was published in the *Irish Worker* on 26 April. Larkin proposed that the Board of Trade should operate conciliation machinery in each of the four main divisions of industry. Boards composed of equal numbers of employers and trade unionists should examine all disputes. If 80 per cent of the workers in an undertaking became members of a trade union, then the union should have the right to insist that all others should join.

These proposals were not taken up. But it is further evidence that Larkin was not seeking a permanent state of strife. He wished through organisation to bring about improved conditions, but thereafter to regulate industrial relations on the basis of agreements.

The settlement of the dispute with the City of Dublin Steampacket Company relieved the pressure on Larkin, and

1913 he did not carry out his threat to leave the country or stay away from the ITUC. But he appeared to his friends exhausted and unwell. This situation continued until O'Brien finally persuaded him to see a doctor.[10] The diagnosis was nervous debility caused by overwork. Thereafter his health improved. Despite press reports that 'Larkin dare not set foot in Cork', he arrived there on 12 May, ready to face the 'old gang'. As O'Brien had anticipated, McCarron and his friends mustered all their forces. But their attack was mismanaged. McIntyre, joined by a Cork man called Dennehy, who was probably ill-informed on ITUC matters, accompanied an attack on Larkin with one on the Congress. This irritated delegates who differed from Larkin in policy but felt able to do any criticising that was necessary themselves. The ITGWU was represented by thirteen delegates. These included Larkin, Connolly and P. T. Daly.[11]

The position of Daly seems curious. He had been elected secretary of Congress while a delegate of the Dublin Trades Council, E. W. Stewart being ousted because he was not a delegate. Yet, unless the record is defective, Daly had held the post on this basis for two years. Now he appeared for Sligo, where, despite the fact that he had been leading a strike there on nomination day, his membership can have been no more than nominal. The IWWU sent Delia Larkin from Dublin and Ellen Gordon from Belfast. The two women's union had thus merged. The Cork Storemen and Carmen were represented by Daniel Lynch, and Richard Corish represented the Foundrymen.

Congress closed on 13 May, but a number of delegates remained in Cork. An attempt was to be made to reconstitute the Cork branch of the union. There were difficulties. The Corporation refused to allow Larkin the use of the City Hall. He was accommodated by the Builders' Labourers. In Daunt Square and at Cóbh open-air meetings were addressed by James Connolly, Ellen Gordon, Thomas Lawlor, William Partridge and William O'Brien. When the others returned to Dublin Partridge remained in Cork, and it was he who officially reopened the branch and found offices at 4 Merchants' Quay. His general advertisement for members appeared in the *Irish Worker* of 25 May. He had attended the conference as delegate of the Dublin No. 2 branch of the Amalgamated Society of Engineers. He was working for the ITGWU but remained an engineer at heart.

Partridge soon returned to Dublin. He was required for the massive Labour Day demonstration in Phoenix Park. This took place on 25 May but might scarcely have taken place at all for the coverage it received in the press. He was replaced in Cork by Peter Larkin, James's brother, who was assisted by John Dowling, P. T. Daly and Con O'Lyhane, home for a few weeks' holiday. Open-air meetings were held on the quays. By the middle of June there were 900 members. A print section was organised. When Ben Tillett attended the Conference of the General Federation of Trade Unions, held in Cork in July 1913, the English dockers' leader spoke at a public meeting in favour of the ITGWU and urged all present to join.

The Storemen and Carmen's union decided to merge, and the re-established Cork branch became No. 20. Its members were gratified and amused to note that as soon as the existence of the organisation was announced in the press the City of Cork Steampacket Company gave their workers a voluntary increase of 2s a week. The Clyde Shipping Company and Messrs Sutton speedily followed suit.

While these events were proceeding in the south the union was organising the farm workers of Co. Dublin. It is possible that Peter Larkin's arrival may have prompted this initiative. A somewhat similar agitation was under way in Lancashire, where the Clarion Cycling Clubs made propaganda forays into the countryside every weekend. The Lancashire farm workers were paid 18s a week. They demanded £1 and a half-holiday each Saturday. The corresponding Dublin demand arose when, as a result of the application of the Shop Hours Act, the Smithfield hay and straw markets were transferred from Saturday to Friday. The County Dublin Farmers' Association resisted the change as long as possible, but finally submitted. Here was the opportunity for the farm workers to claim Saturday afternoon for themselves.

The *Irish Worker* of 25 June urged city workers to spend the long summer evenings in the rural areas and to explain to the farm workers the benefits of organisation. Some meetings were addressed by Peter Larkin. He was a political leader in his own right, though he lacked his brother's charisma. He

1913 struck O'Brien as a 'typical Socialist Labour Party' member. He had indeed represented the Liverpool dockers at the 1910 syndicalist conference in Manchester. He was well read in Irish history. At one meeting he quoted Davitt's *Fall of Feudalism in Ireland*, but added the extraordinary statement that it was 'banned in Ireland'. This suggests a trace of anti-clericalism.

The first meeting of the campaign was held at Baldoyle on Sunday 8 June. This was three weeks before the Lancashire strike. The average Co. Dublin farm worker took home 14s a week. The union called for a substantial increase. It also asked for an improvement in the deplorable standards of housing and for the half-day holdiay. The campaign attracted members of other unions, and the speakers included the two Larkins, Partridge, MacPartlin and Thomas Lawlor. Meetings were held at Swords, Clondalkin, Lucan and Blanchardstown. On Saturday and Sunday, 26 and 27 July, representatives attended in these towns 'to solicit members for the Farm Labourers' Section of the ITGWU'. The farm workers flocked in. The Farmers' Association judged it wise to negotiate. No agreement was reached. A strike was called at the beginning of the harvest, and on 17 August the farmers agreed to pay 17s for a 66-hour week, with special rates in proportion. Micheál Ó Maoláin was appointed North Co. Dublin organiser.[12]

The campaign of the ITGWU among the rural workers of Co. Dublin is of great historical importance. For one thing, the union now occupied a high proportion of the ground held by the Gasworkers' Union in 1890, at least in the south of Ireland. For another, the organised strength of the city workers was deployed in support of the farm workers.

In August 1913 the ITGWU decided to insist that only union men should cart produce to the city markets. A man called Donovan sent a load of hay to Smithfield, where it was sold to a Mr Clerkin of 7 Tara Street. Donovan's man, Thomas Daly, was not a member of the union. The delegate, J. J. Nolan, told Clerkin that if he accepted hay from Daly, all his men would come out. He refused the load. Donovan tried unsuccessfully to sell it elsewhere and was compelled to take it back. Such experiences brought the farmers to the negotiating table. But later, when the union was embroiled in the city, they did not hesitate to break their agreement.

What might perhaps be called the 'old' Transport Union reached the zenith of its influence in the summer of 1913. It is not easy to form a reliable estimate of membership. The 1915 roll book lists 346 members who first joined in 1913, 298 of them before 15 August. If we ignore the later part of the year, when many more must have left than joined, we can guess that perhaps 3,600 additional members were gained in Dublin. If we take into account Cork and the smaller branches, the total membership cannot have been far short of 30,000. This figure was indeed claimed by officials other than the General Secretary.

It is impossible to read the *Irish Worker* or the reminiscences of people who were active at the time, without being impressed by the spring-like quality of the political atmosphere. There was a sense of adventure, of novelty and of historical purpose. The age of the common man was at hand if only he would seize his opportunity. Larkin had recovered his spirits and was indeed showing an optimism bordering upon euphoria. It was as if he had continually to reassure himself. He swung between doubt and certainty, each larger than the reality demanded. At a Trades Council meeting he declared that Dublin was the best organised city in the world. This was possibly true: the same assertion had been made ninety years previously.[13] But Larkin did not look at Dublin and try to divine its secret; he looked at himself. He had done 'one man's part' in bringing this happy position about.

The *Telegraph* and *Independent* continued their attacks. As well as replying to them in the *Irish Worker*, Larkin permitted the publication of praise of himself which most editors would be at pains to avoid. He was referred to as 'the Chief' and 'the one and only Jim Larkin'. He would urge his followers to support worthy causes in such terms as 'Jim Larkin wants every reader to support . . . the fête to be held at Jones Road.' 'Jim Larkin and his trusty lieutenants' were engaged in their worthy activities. Notices were signed 'By order, Jim Larkin'. Connolly hated what he called 'all this playing to one man', and towards the end of July 1913 he wrote to O'Brien complaining of Larkin's thirst for admiration.[14]

1913 The industrial war which now broke out dwarfed all its predecessors. Its deep political springs have been indicated. The immediate occasion was an attempt to organise the tramwaymen which showed every prospect of success. Apart from the more isolated rural workers, these now formed about the only important industrial section which had not progressed beyond the standards of 1890. There had been many attempts to organise them, for example in 1903. The management made a principle of refusing to recognise a trade union, and workers who gave voice to grievances were either dismissed or promoted, according to circumstances.

The ITGWU made its first appeal to the tramwaymen during the great struggles of August 1911. One of the difficulties was that the men worked 365 days a year. They had no time off. Carriage-cleaners received 19s for working seven nights a week from 10 p.m. to 9 a.m. They were thus paid 3d an hour. Sixpence a week was deducted for membership of 'the Society'; this was a device for paying workers compensation for accidents out of their own money. A man could be summarily dismissed if an inspector found one uncollected fare in a car designed to carry fifty people but packed with a hundred. Correspondents described the work as 'continuous torture' and suggested that if a meeting were called at midnight, it would be well attended.

The secret of William Martin Murphy's power was his system of reserve staff. Each applicant for employment had his name placed on a waiting list. When he reached the head of the list he was called to work. He might secure temporary work, replacing a man who had fallen sick, or permanent work, replacing one dismissed. At any time he could be subjected to a fine for some petty misdemeanour, and if he ventured to demur, he could, according to the gravity of his offence, either go back on the waiting list or lose his employment altogether. Murphy had invented a system of self-regulating scabbery.

Larkin seems to have been prompted to a speedy attack on Murphy's citadel by the circulation of rumours that, in order to forestall the ITGWU, a 'scab union' was to be invited to organise all tramwaymen. It is a fair guess that this would be the society conducted by John Saturnus Kelly. A meeting was called at Liberty Hall at midnight on Saturday 28 June 1913. The appeal singled out especially conductors, motormen, permanent-way maintenance men and power-house men. The result may have been indecisive, for a further meeting was called at midnight on 12 July. This time brakes were provided to carry men back to Dalkey, Palmerston Park, Terenure, Inchicore and Clontarf. In the advertisement for this meeting the power-house workers were mentioned first. Yet another meeting was held on 29 July. The advertisement explained that its business was 'important to power-house men'. The interested observer (and no doubt Murphy himself) would remark that Larkin was paying strong court to those workers who could by throwing a switch immobilise every tram in Dublin.

Already dismissals of suspected ringleaders had begun. Murphy entertained some of the men to Oxo, Bovril and sandwiches in the small hours at the Antient Concert Rooms. He denounced the ITGWU while giving the most solemn assurances that he had no objection to a 'respectable' trade union. Larkin, he declared, was shortly to meet his Waterloo. Larkin replied that Murphy would be dispatched to his St Helena. The degree to which class struggle had become a personal struggle is illustrated by passages from Larkin's editorial:

> William Martin Murphy, the only public man in Ireland who has been publicly branded as a damned liar . . . you have been driven from public life as a toady, a renegade, an untruthful and dishonest politician, a false friend, a sweating employer, a weak-kneed tyrant. . . . Larkin is prepared to meet you face to face on any platform and prove you are a poltroon, liar and sweater . . . and that your only god is profit.[15]

It has been urged in Murphy's defence that the last statement was untrue. The *Freeman's Journal* assured the public that 'The making of profit had never been his leading idea. . . . To him and many others . . . the game of business . . . was more fascinating than any form of sport.' But for those whose livelihoods were dependent on him it was small consolation to be told that if they were overworked or underpaid, this was all part of the game. It is no relief to

1913 a hunted fox that nobody wants him for dinner. The union was asserting the principle that workers would allow no man to play with their lives.

5

War on the Workers

It is not they – it is you who are blind Samsons pulling down the pillars of the social order.

GEORGE RUSSELL

Independent *lock-out – tramway strike – baton charge in O'Connell Street – general lock-out – leaders in jail – food-ships – Askwith inquiry – children to England – arming blacklegs – British TUC – 'yellow' press – disengagement*

The point at issue in the great industrial upheaval that now 1913
rocked Dublin for six months was a simple one. It was the right of a worker to join the trade union of his choice. Whatever the remoter calculations of those who assailed this right, that is the ground they chose. The workers in the *Irish Independent* and the tramway system had a perfect legal right to join the ITGWU. William Martin Murphy told them in effect: 'Exercise that right, and I will exercise my right of dismissing you.' When rights are equal, force alone decides.

Neither the tramwaymen nor the men in the dispatch department of the *Independent* had preferred any demands. They had combined with a view to this, it is true. But Murphy did not wait to find out whether the demands would be reasonable or not. The fact of organisation was enough for him. On Friday 15 August he walked into the dispatch department and ordered the staff to leave the union or face dismissal. Some forty were immediately paid off. The newsboys then refused to sell the *Evening Herald*; they had idolised Larkin since he supported them in 1911, and some of them had joined the republican Fianna Éireann. Next day vanmen of Easons blacked the *Independent*. They were locked out. Scab drivers were brought in, and scuffles broke out. On Sunday 17 August Murphy tackled the tramwaymen and dismissed 200 who refused to leave the union.

On Thursday 21 August the tramway parcels service was

1913 suspended. There had been objections to carrying the *Independent* and *Herald*, and Murphy thought it would be better that no newspapers should be distributed than that he should carry bundles for his competitors. The union demanded the reinstatement of the locked-out workers, in default of which strike action would be taken. But Murphy had made his dispositions. On Tuesday 19 August he had paid a personal visit to Dublin Castle. The results were speedily visible. The Dublin Metropolitan Police were reinforced by members of the Royal Irish Constabulary. This was a sure sign of trouble. Next day special constables were sworn in, and reserves of RIC men were stationed at Dún Laoire. The government had placed the machinery of the state at the disposal of one wealthy citizen.[1] It was in justification of this class discrimination that Murphy's apologists tried to brand Larkin as the aggressor. He had indeed used immoderate and ill-advised language; but he had not only remained within the law, he had protested against an action which no union executive in the world would hesitate to answer with an official strike. The Trades Council had fully endorsed the union's position at its meeting on 18 August.

The organised tramwaymen met at Liberty Hall in the small hours of Sunday 24 August. They had all received a circular from the company demanding an undertaking that if the union called a strike, they would continue to work. Once again the employer was the aggressor. And a decision had to be made at once. Larkin was empowered to call them out at his discretion. No firm date was agreed. To one member who asked when the trams would be halted Larkin replied: 'When they will no longer move.'[2] That is to say that he was hoping for action by the power-house workers to whom he had been paying court. These were the hardest to replace, and if they had come out, all the trams in Dublin would have come to a simultaneous stop.

The power-house men did not respond. Rather than wait for another meeting, it was decided to approach the men *en route*. Newspapers noted great activity by union officials during Monday. They were seen stopping trams and holding brief conferences. At 10 a.m. on Tuesday 26 August a large number of tramwaymen switched off their motors, threw their coats over their arms, and left the trams where they stood. Some of them were later prosecuted for this. The strike was almost complete. But the company quickly mustered sufficient reserve workers and blacklegs to maintain an 'emergency service'. The old familiar situation arose. Strikers expostulated with blacklegs. There was scuffling and stone-throwing, leading to police intervention with the usual train of arrests, prosecutions, fines and imprisonment. The glass windows of the trams were soon falling in tinkling cascades. So much damage was done in one day that it was decided not to attempt to maintain the emergency service after dusk.

On the 27th a great open-air meeting was held outside Liberty Hall. William O'Brien took the chair, and there was much fiery talk, especially from Larkin and Partridge. All day long there had been violent clashes and tempers were thoroughly roused. Carson had been urging his Ulster Volunteers to refuse to pay taxes in the event of Home Rule being enacted, and if necessary to resist collection by force. On that very day the *Belfast Telegraph* reported that he had been invited to lunch with the Kaiser. Larkin asked why, if it was in order for Carson and his friends to resist in arms the edict of the imperial parliament, it was not in order for union men to arm against the Dublin police who were attacking them.

There was no official explanation, but on the morning of Thursday 28 August five men were arrested in their homes and taken to Mountjoy. They were Larkin, Partridge, O'Brien, P. T. Daly and Thomas Lawlor. The charges were seditious libel and conspiracy. O'Brien contrived to have a telegram sent to Connolly in Belfast. He arrived in Dublin to find them all free men. They had given an undertaking to be of good behaviour and had arranged what they hoped would be an even bigger meeting for Friday evening.

Larkin had announced a mass demonstration in O'Connell Street on the following Sunday. This was prohibited at the instance of a magistrate, E. G. Swifte, who was himself a shareholder of the tramway company.[3] There was intense excitement when Larkin, speaking like Parnell from an open window, declared that he would hold the meeting 'dead or alive'. In a spectacular gesture he set fire to the magistrate's proclamation. Connolly, in more circumspect but equally unmistakable language, also urged that the ban

1913 should be defied. Next day he and Partridge were arrested. A special court was held. Refusing to give bail, Connolly was sentenced to three months' imprisonment. There was a warrant out for the arrest of Larkin, but he had escaped in a taxi from the rear of Liberty Hall and was hiding in Rathmines, where Countess Markiewicz improvised a party so as to put the police off the scent. They made no attempt to search. They had plenty to occupy them. There were savage attacks on strikers in what is now Pearse Street, and a riot at Ringsend where spectators objected to a scab who was playing in a football team.

William O'Brien was in a difficult position. Connolly was in jail and Larkin in hiding. When O'Brien reached Liberty Hall in the evening police were making baton charges in Beresford Place and its vicinity. In one of these a young man called James Nolan was killed. Another, James Byrne, was so severely injured that he died in hospital. Foran had received a message from Larkin indicating that he intended to persist with the meeting. But nobody could suggest a means of secretly transporting him from Rathmines and holding a meeting without making overt preparations. O'Brien tried to negotiate a change of venue. When he failed in this he decided to transfer the meeting to Croydon Park, the recreation centre at Fairview which the union had acquired at the beginning of the month and had opened with a 'temperance fête' on bank holiday. He notified the *Sunday Freeman* of the change. But in the meantime Larkin had solved the translocation problem and had sent the *Freeman* a letter for its stop-press edition.[4]

Next morning workers assembled at Liberty Hall, and most of them moved off in the direction of Croydon Park. Presumably the police saw them go. While it is true that they had reason to anticipate the appearance of Larkin in O'Connell Street, they must have known that there could be no meeting in the accepted sense of the word. There was no platform, no audience. Nevertheless huge forces were stationed in all the side-streets attached to the main thoroughfare. There can only be one conclusion. If the slightest excuse were to be given, the police were to be allowed to vent their spleen on harmless by-standers and crowds coming out of Mass at the Pro-Cathedral. A gigantic act of mass intimidation had been planned. It was later revealed that all troops were confined to barracks in full uniform throughout Saturday and Sunday. If O'Brien had not transferred the meeting to Croydon Park, something like civil war might have broken out. 1913

On Saturday evening rooms were booked at the Imperial Hotel, where Clerys now stands, in the names of Mr Donnelly and his niece. The visitors drove up at 10 a.m., and porters carried in their copious luggage. Donnelly was in fact Larkin, disguised with a false beard and wearing Count Markiewicz's frock coat. He was assigned room 13, while his 'niece', Miss Gifford, had no. 24. They retired to their rooms. But at midday Larkin came down to the smoke-room and stepped out on to the balcony facing O'Connell Street. He shouted 'I'm Larkin' and began to speak.

He was arrested in less than a minute, and that should have been enough. It was not, however, enough for the police. They seem to have acted on the assumption that a person addressed is thereby joined in a common purpose with his addresser. His voice instantaneously converted passers-by into conspirators. The police drew their batons, poured out of the side-streets and mercilessly set about the people. They ran in pursuit of those who managed to escape, following them into the narrow streets on the east side. Baton charges were made in the tenement areas. People tried to halt the invaders by dropping coal, even showering cups and saucers from the windows. Doors were broken down. Private apartments were forcibly entered. In one room, whose sole occupants were Mrs Cummins and her week-old child, they dragged the woman out of bed and gave the baby a black eye. Michael Whelan had his arm broken in two places when he tried to stop a policeman from kicking children. According to Partridge, who described their behaviour at the British TUC in Manchester, many to them were the worse for drink, and this opinion was reported in newspapers throughout Europe.[5]

The *Daily Sketch* reported that 460 people were injured and 210 arrested. The Dublin *Saturday Post*, a county not a city paper, reported that over 600 people were taken to hospital. Some of the victims swore informations against individual policemen, alleging assault and malicious damage.

1913 No action was taken, and the result of the official inquiry was universally described as 'whitewash'.

There was, of course, an immediate and intense public reaction. The authorities had bungled hopelessly. They had earned the hatred of ordinary people and disgraced themselves before the world. But the men whose heads were to have been broken as a preliminary to long terms of imprisonment were safe and well at Croydon Park and in a position to reply to an atrocity that could not be repeated. Partridge, MacPartlin and Lawlor left for Manchester, where the British TUC was meeting. There Larkin's old enemy James Sexton proposed a motion demanding freedom of assembly in Dublin. Congress agreed to send a delegation. Keir Hardie came at once. After addressing the Trades Council and visiting Connolly in jail he left for Belfast, where the Trades Council gave immediate support. Resolutions of protest against the pogrom poured in from all sides. The *Labour Leader* questioned the legality of Connolly's imprisonment. Four Dublin MPs demanded an inquiry. The Trades Council established a strike fund in Dublin and issued an appeal for donations.

Other employers followed Murphy's example. Jacobs locked out all members of the ITGWU. In this establishment the 'no talking, no singing' rule was enforced, and notices on the walls prohibited the wearing of trade union badges in the factory. They had tolerated the organisation of their factory workers solely because of the Transport Union's control of the carting industry. A strike took place on 30 August when men working a lift refused to handle flour that had arrived under police protection. The reaction of the management was to close the factory. The 'black' flour had come from Lucan flour mills, where W. E. Shackleton, a former luminary of Sinn Féin, always to the fore in keeping the lower orders low, locked out his entire workforce because he understood some of them had joined the ITGWU. At the same time surrounding farmers tore up the agreements they had so recently signed. Members of the Women Workers' Union were locked out at Patersons (matches), Clarkes (cardboard boxes), Somersets (linen embroidery) and the Savoy Company (confectionery).

While Larkin and Connolly were in jail day-to-day decisions

were taken by the committee of No. 1 branch, whose secretary John O'Neill issued an appeal for funds. At Foran's suggestion it was decided that all finances should be handled by the lock-out committee of the Trades Council. 1913

On 2 September the coal merchants locked out their men. On the evening of that day a tenement building at 66 Church Street collapsed in a heap of rubble. It had housed twenty-six people, of whom five died and many others were badly injured. The hero of the incident was Eugene Salmon, who saved several of his sisters but lost his own life while trying to extricate the last. He was aged seventeen and was one of the workers locked out of Jacobs.

The Employers' Federation met on the 3rd. Murphy had, as he thought, set a good example, and others had followed him. He suggested that now was the time to enforce a general lock-out. No fewer than 404 employers supported him. They undertook to dismiss any worker who declined to sign a document renouncing the ITGWU or, in the case of non-members, undertaking not to join it. Each employer agreed to deposit in a bank account a sum proportional to the number of his employees, to be forfeited if he broke his undertaking. Two days later, when Arthur Henderson brought over the British delegation, he found the employers in an intransigent mood and the men's leaders behind bars. Little progress was made. On 7 September Connolly, determined not to remain passively incarcerated while momentous events proceeded outside, went on hunger-strike.

Two days later the master builders locked out their labourers. These men were not members of the Transport Union but of their own society. There was no justification for asking from them a pledge not to join the ITGWU. They had no wish to join it, but were understandably unwilling to admit their employers' right to decide what union they might or might not join. Afterwards the employers' motive became known. It was to deprive of their livings a section of workers who might be sympathetic to those already locked out and contribute to their strike fund. That was the meaning of class war.

On 11 September 1,000 carters who had refused to handle black goods were locked out. Farmers in Co. Dublin began dismissing union members. This action provoked strikes.

1913 On 9 September the Farmers' Association declared a general lock-out between the city and Donabate, the harvest having been for the most part saved. At Finglas a boy of seventeen was shot in a riot resulting from a publican's serving a herd who had not stopped work. Arnotts locked out their porters on 18 September. The timber and cement industries came to a standstill on the 22nd. By now 20,000 workers were idle.

Both Larkin and Connolly regained their liberty before the lock-out was complete. Larkin successfully appealed against the refusal of bail and was released on 12 September. He left at once to fulfil engagements in Liverpool and Manchester. The following morning a deputation waiting on the Lord Lieutenant; it consisted of William O'Brien, P. T. Daly, Francis Sheehy-Skeffington and Eamon Martin of the Fianna Éireann. Its members impressed on an already very apprehensive man the incalculable consequences that would follow upon the possible death of Connolly. Connolly's wife was staying with Martin and his sister. That evening the viceregal car drew up at their door, bringing a release order addressed to the governor of Mountjoy. Lillie Connolly, Ina and Eamon Martin then went for Connolly in a taxi and took him to Countess Markiewicz's house.[6] After a few days he went to Belfast to recuperate. He was seemingly none the worse.

The Labour/separatist alliance was strongly in evidence. On 14 September an *aeriocht* was organised under the auspices of the football league, the Colmcille Branch of the Gaelic League and a number of teams. It took place at Towerfield, Dolphin's Barn. There were games, music and dancing. Three Transport Union bands played selections, those of the No. 1, Inchicore and Sligo branches. The appearance of the Sligo men may be connected with the fact that this was the only provincial town affected by the Dublin stoppage. On 23 August Brewsters, the newsagents, had responded to events at Easons by locking out those of their employees who were members of the ITGWU. Seán Connolly's impersonation of the 'flat-footed bobby' is said to have been received with great delight. The purpose of this event was to provide for the dependants of the two men, Byrne and Nolan, killed by the police.

Larkin arrived back in Dublin on 15 September. Next day he received a wire from P. T. Daly in London to the effect that the British TUC had voted £5,000, and issued an appeal for collections. William O'Brien recorded that at his suggestion Larkin proposed that assistance should be given not in cash but in kind. He gave no reason for what may have been an error. Though there was something spectacular in breaching the blockade of a beleaguered city, the course adopted left the small shopkeepers of Dublin in a precarious position which aid in cash would have made safer, thus isolating the employers. 1913

Larkin visited the Aldwych offices of the TUC on 23 September, later going to Manchester, where the Co-operative Wholesale Society was loading s.s. *Hare*. From Manchester he wired O'Neill that the foodship would tie up in Dublin on Saturday 27 September.

The aim of the British TUC did not exactly coincide with that of the union. The British wanted to settle, the Irish to win. What was required from England was action, not sympathy. But if there were to be industrial action in England, the TUC officials would have to give up their role of mediators and accept that of combatants. The arch-opponent of such action was the railwaymen's leader, J. H. Thomas.

Nevertheless there was industrial action. Following Larkin's visit three men at the LNWR goods station in Victoria Street, Liverpool, ceased work. They were sent home. Immediately the entire workforce followed them. The strike spread to the Canada and Alexandra Docks. Soon there were 1,500 railwaymen out. On the following day the number had risen to 2,000. The strike spread to Birmingham, then to Crewe, Derby and Gloucester. Ramsay MacDonald, who, in the words of the moderate *Daily Sketch*, 'conducted the Labour Party as though it were a wing of the Liberal Party', spoke and wrote continuously against 'syndicalism' and the 'sympathetic strike'. J. H. Thomas thought he had reduced his critics' position to absurdity when he argued that if the principle of the sympathetic strike were to be accepted, the railwaymen would never be at work.

Some recent writers have dismissed the notion of action in Britain in support of Irish trade unionism as utopian. But the answer to this opinion lies in the issue of the Dublin lock-out. That issue was the continued existence of a demo-

1913 cratic Labour movement. Nobody would expect the railwaymen to strike every time the candlestick-makers demanded a wage increase. But if those railwaymen were to be locked out if they refused to handle a 'black' candlestick, then they too had rights to fight for. J. H. Thomas was not only opposing international solidarity (which, admittedly, demands more than usual political awareness), he was depriving his own members of a weapon. There was no question of closing the railways. If the English leaders had had the vision to take the simple step of refusing to handle 'tainted goods', not only would the Dublin employers have been defeated, but they themselves would have been immeasurably strengthened. They lacked that vision, and by the time the first foodship arrived the sympathetic strike movement had petered out. The Dublin workers asked for action; they received charity.

* * *

The first phase of the struggle ended at this point. The relentless and implacable way the employers moved into action, with the assistance of the forces of the state, generated among the masses a mood of fierce determination to resist that bordered on exaltation. 'Defeat, bah!' wrote Connolly. 'How can such people be defeated?' But such flashes of euphoria were interspersed with spells of soberer judgment. In the same article, 'Glorious Dublin', Connolly complained of British Labour politicians 'who play the enemy's game'.[7] Such trade union leaders as J. H. Thomas not only opposed sympathetic action by their members, but, when they were victimised for it, actually co-operated with the employers against them. Nor did the wider political implications of the lock-out escape attention. Home Rule was expected. The existence of a strong Irish Labour movement was a distasteful prospect to those who thought themselves its natural beneficiaries. Hilaire Belloc's *New Witness* wrote: 'The AOH felt itself endangered by Larkinism,' adding, after the arrests: 'Larkin was prosecuted at the instance of a Nationalist politician.' The Board of Erin had replied to the Unionist sectarianisation of the Protestant workers by attempting to sectarianise the Catholics. And now, while Carson and his followers were setting up what they called a provisional government and allotting ministries, the enemy to be fought to the last was the working class of Dublin.

If it had to be charity, then its arrival was not too soon. By 27 September some workers had only missed one pay packet; others had been out for six weeks. The basement of Liberty Hall was now reconverted to its old use. Delia Larkin and Countess Markiewicz supervised the operation of soup kitchens, and thousands of women and children were invited to take their meals at the hall. Clothes and underwear which had been given were distributed to those who needed them.

On 29 September a Board of Trade inquiry into the dispute opened, with Sir George Askwith in the chair. Murphy represented the employers, and Harry Gosling of the National Transport Workers' Federation, the workers. The employers' case was presented by T. M. Healy. He described the situation in Dublin in words reminiscent of the Board of the Green Cloth, the committee for regulating the woollen trade in the 1820s, which the Webbs, believing it to be a committee of trades, described as ruthlessly enforcing its by-laws until its 'dictates became the terror of the employers'.[8] Healy declared that the Transport Union had imposed 'the most finished system of tyranny that was ever started in any country'. His main complaint was against the use of the sympathetic strike. Both Larkin and Connolly stated that they were prepared to limit its use, and at one point it seemed that a settlement might be possible. A scheme was proposed under which, in return for reinstatement and withdrawal of 'the document', the union would renounce the use of the sympathetic strike against any employer prepared to submit to Board of Trade conciliation, and no strike or lock-out would take place until conciliation had been attempted. But both to the British trade unionists and to the Board of Trade the employers returned the same reply. They would not accept reinstatement. They were obdurate.

Their obstinacy provoked a public outcry. The London *Times* sharply criticised it in an editorial. The *Irish Times*, a moderate Unionist paper, then as now very much the organ of the professional classes, who tried to preserve some semblance of balance in their judgments, on 7 October published George Russell's famous open letter to the employers. He told them:

1913

> Your insolence and ignorance of the rights conceded to workers universally in the modern world were incredible, and as great as your inhumanity. If you had between you collectively a portion of human soul as large as a threepenny bit, you would have sat night and day with the representatives of Labour, trying this or that solution of the trouble, mindful of the women and children, who at least were innocent of wrong against you. But no! You reminded Labour you could always have your three square meals a day while it went hungry. You went into conference again with representatives of the State, because dull as you are, you know public opinion would not stand your holding out. You chose as your spokesman the bitterest tongue that ever wagged in this island, and then when an award was made by men who had an experience in industrial matters a thousand times transcending yours, who have settled disputes in industries so great that the sum of your petty enterprises would not equal them, you withdraw again, and will not agree to accept their solution, and fall back again on your devilish policy of starvation.[9]

The employers were unmoved. They now suggested the removal of Larkin and the appointment of officials approved by the Board of Trade. Early in October began the eviction of workers who had been unable to pay their rent.

Since there was total deadlock in Dublin, Larkin spent as much time as possible addressing meetings in England, where he consistently reiterated the need for industrial action. He won support. He collected funds. But the Labour leaders would not budge. The British TUC had decided its policy. The press began speculating about its motives. These were, stated simply, that British Labour was dependent on the Liberal government for reforms to satisfy its members, while the Liberal government was dependent for its majority on Redmond. The *Morning Post* reminded readers that William Martin Murphy was not a Unionist. This was a shrewd hint to Tory supporters that the continuance of the dispute might not work against their interests.

A stagnant situation was the worst possible for a man of Larkin's temperament. To him action was the breath of life. In the early days of the lock-out he was as one filled with a sense of divine mission. On 14 September he had declared in Manchester: 'I care for no man or men. I have got a divine mission, I believe, to make men and women discontented.' But the comfortable bosses of Britain's big unions were not likely candidates for the barricades. The mission began to turn sour. At a Daily Herald League meeting at the Memorial Hall, Farringdon Road, he attacked them bitterly. They were, of course, unmoved. He had provided them with reasons for continuing their policy that were different from the real ones: they could now talk about Larkin's unreasonableness. 1913

Perhaps it was his mounting impatience that led him to countenance a scheme proposed by Mrs Dora Montefiore. This was to save Dublin children from the hardships of the lock-out by taking them to England to be cared for in the homes of sympathisers. That Larkin could agree to this proposition illustrates another facet of his character. His mind was large and imaginative, but it was artistic rather than scientific. A man of more logical bent would have seen at a glance that taking the children to England was simply another form of charity, a foodship in reverse, while what Larkin wanted was industrial action. He was acting contrary to his own purpose.

Mrs Montefiore and others were soon in Dublin. Parents prepared to send their children were easily found. But on 21 October Archbishop Walsh of Dublin described the whole plan as a blatant attempt at proselytising. He was mistaken, of course. But the proposers of the scheme were also guilty of misjudgment. Republicans and socialists in Ireland knew that despite all appearances to the contrary, there were people in England who wished the Irish nation well. But the mass of the people could not be expected to believe it until it came within their own experience. Their faith had been preserved in face of dungeon, fire and sword. Could they expect anything else now? In a word, they treated the English socialists as 'soupers'. It was most unfair, but it was very understandable.

There were wild scenes when Mrs Montefiore, Grace Neal and Delia Larkin tried to take away their small charges. Mrs Montefiore was arrested and charged with abduction. Tara Street baths, where children were being washed and reclothed before departure, were invaded and the children sent home.

1913 In Sheriff Street or Ringsend people gladly accepted the relief. But an unfortunate woman whose philanthrophy took the form of organising children's games in the area of the Liberties was attacked by a mob and the police were compelled to arrest her in order to rescue her.

On 27 October Larkin was tried on charges two months old. Essentially there was one charge: incitement. One employer asked to be excused from service in the jury because his firm was involved in the dispute and he was an interested party. Exemption was refused. Larkin was found guilty of sedition. He denied using the words alleged, but the jury believed the police. He was sentenced to seven months' imprisonment without hard labour. As previously, he appointed Connolly to take his place.

Connolly had been opposed to the sending away of the children, and on taking charge he had the scheme discontinued. But he demanded that those who objected to the feeding of the children in England must feed them in Ireland. He stopped all free dinners at Liberty Hall for one week. Charitable organisations were overwhelmed. The magnitude of the problem was brought home to them, as well as the implications of the employers' actions. Archbishop Walsh joined those calling for a settlement. While reversing Larkin's policy on the relief question, Connolly refused to take the opportunity to oust Larkin and assume sole leadership himself. To do this would have been a betrayal not only of Larkin but of the members. The affair of the children soon blew over, but under cover of the temporary furore the employers began to bring in blacklegs from England, fifty from Manchester on 29 October and a hundred from Liverpool on 5 November. To meet this challenge mass picketing was instituted. The employers then began to provide the scabs with firearms. When one of these shot a boy in the knee no attempt was made to arrest him. There were angry scenes when police tried to disperse the massed picket. Three companies of the Surrey Infantry were sent to protect scabs at Jacobs.

In these circumstances two necessities presented themselves. One was to strike at the government that was giving the employers every facility. The other was to arm the workers for their own protection. Three by-elections were pending, the first in Reading. Partridge was dispatched there with a request to all trade unionists to vote against the Liberals as a protest against the imprisonment of Larkin. When on 10 November the news came that the Liberals had been defeated at both Reading and Linlithgow, rockets were fired from the roof of Liberty Hall. The third contest was at Keighley, where there was a spectacular increase in the Labour vote. 1913

The British press acknowledged that the election results alarmed the government. It was given cause for more alarm. Great public meetings were held where men with world-famous names demanded Larkin's release. At the Albert Hall on 1 November George Bernard Shaw advised the workers of Dublin to arm. He invited the government to prosecute him for sedition, as he would then 'have an opportunity of explaining to the public exactly what he meant'. The government chose not to provide such an opportunity.

On 12 November Connolly issued a manifesto which appealed to the British workers over the heads of the trade union leaders. He called upon them to black all goods originating in Dublin. This was a serious step, and he accompanied it with another. He closed the port of Dublin 'as tight as a drum'. This action breached the agreement of 26 May, and the shipping companies protested. To Connolly it seemed that 26 May belonged to a forgotten age. He replied that circumstances were exceptional. A network of vigilance committees began to be established through Britain. A meeting of railwaymen decided not to handle tainted goods. After less than twenty-four hours Larkin was released.

He was not in good shape. He appeared at Liberty Hall in the afternoon of 13 November, but suffered from a severe reaction. He spent the rest of the day at home with a raging headache, and it was Connolly who addressed the meeting at Beresford Place. Two days previously the Industrial Peace Committee had abandoned its position of impartiality and declared that the blame for the deadlock rested on the employers. Its members reconstituted themselves as the 'Civic Committee' at a meeting held on 12 November at the rooms of R. M. Gwynn at 40 Trinity College. One of their number was Captain Jack White, a distinguished soldier, son of the hero of Ladysmith, a Co. Antrim man and a prominent

1913 Protestant advocate of Home Rule. He approached Connolly to suggest a 'drilling scheme', pointing out that people ran away from the police because they were not trained and the police were. Connolly adopted his proposal and at the meeting on the 13th announced the decision to recruit a 'citizen army' of locked-out men. Two companies were formed, and they paraded at Croydon Park on 23 November. For the first period of its existence the organisation was referred to in the press as the 'transport union citizen army'. It was an offshoot of the union, necessitated by the special conditions of the lock-out. Some writers have considered it significant that it was founded a few days before the Irish Volunteers. There is, however, no significance whatsoever in the respective dates of foundation. The two organisations were set up for entirely different purposes, and it was sheer coincidence that the dates were so close. Nobody could foresee the roles in which they would ultimately be cast.

Larkin left for England to try to extend the unofficial movement and to raise funds. The appearance of the Citizen Army perceptibly improved the manners of the police. It became customary to 'shoe a shaft' by contracting a cylinder of steel round the end of a pick-handle; the resultant weapon was longer and heavier than a policeman's baton. There were now two worlds at war in Dublin. On the one hand stood the Labour movement, the republicans, the Irish-Irelanders and the Liberal intelligentsia. On the other stood the employers, the repressive forces of the state and the leaders of the Hibernians. Devlin sent up a cry for 'Catholic unions'. Even his own rank and file did not respond. Griffith was opposed to the workers on grounds of damage to Irish industry. He could not carry the whole of his organisation with him. The ITGWU dominated the Manchester Martyrs commemoration procession. The Hibernians did not even walk.

The Parliamentary Committee of the British TUC was to meet on 19 November. Connolly joined Larkin in London on the 18th. The two men demanded a refusal to handle Dublin goods and measures to stop the flow of blacklegs across the channel. (There were still men refusing to handle Dublin goods, especially in Liverpool and South Wales.) Robert Williams of the National Transport Workers' Federation asked

at least for the calling of a Special TUC to consider the alter- 1913
natives. Next day the Albert Hall was the scene of another great meeting. Students, foiled in an attempt to plunge the auditorium into darkness, tried to create a disturbance. They were disposed of by a group of muscular stewards led by Con O'Lyhane.

The Parliamentary Committee's decision was published on 20 November. There was to be no blacking of goods and no action to halt the flow of blacklegs. There was to be a Special TUC, but not until 9 December. Those attending it would not be elected delegates but full-time officials. The *Morning Post* claimed that the delay was intended to allow time for government action. It reported without comment that in Dublin the RIC and military were not only obtaining their own supplies but drawing vehicles with heavy loads for private interests.

British newspapers commented on the way Labour spokesmen now turned against Larkin. The *Daily Citizen* openly attacked him. To add insult to injury, Havelock Wilson of the NSFU not only encouraged his members to work the steamers of the Head Line, but made statements condemning sympathetic strikes. He was moderate now. Twenty-five years had passed since the authorities had jailed him as they now jailed Larkin. But could he forget after only two years that the sympathetic strike of the ITGWU had saved his organisation in Ireland? Or that his members had lived on ITGWU strike pay? The effect of such seeming base ingratitude on one of Larkin's temperament was to make him more recklessly outspoken as he saw the cards being stacked against him.

Great sums of money were, of course, being sent to Dublin. Quite apart from the TUC, the Miners' Federation was sending £1,000 a week. Trades Councils, branches of individual unions and socialist societies were making collections. When the Trades Hall in Capel Street finally closed, many thousands of documents were destroyed, and history has not been able to record the efforts of those many obscure people in places little heard of, who understood the principles that were being upheld by the workers of Dublin. Nothing must be said that would disparage their sacrifice and dedication. But Larkin held that if the British trade union leaders accepted their responsibility, all this would become unnecessary.

1913 In Dublin there was a further attempt at conciliation, this time on the initiative of Archbishop Walsh. The two sides met on 6 December, Connolly leading for the union. Once again he agreed to restrict the use of the sympathetic strike, but once again the employers refused to yield on the question of reinstatement. At the end of an all-night sitting at the Shelbourne Hotel the conference admitted failure. It was, however, the first time that representatives of union and employer actually met face to face.

The Special Congress in London met at the Memorial Hall. Two choices were before it. The official proposal was to continue support while once again seeking a compromise. The 'rebel' proposal, as the *Daily Herald* not very diplomatically called it, was to issue an ultimatum: if the employers refused a reasonable settlement, by a date to be fixed, all goods from Dublin were to be declared black.

The chairman was J. P. Davis. Six hundred delegates attended. Arthur Henderson reported for the TUC delegation that had visited Dublin two days previously and had contrived to bring workers' and employers' representatives together for fifteen minutes. Connolly and Foran, who represented the union, felt that the future war cabinet minister was pressing them towards an unacceptable settlement. He, on the other hand, did not conceal his opinion that the Irish trade unionists were intransigent. With the parliamentarian's skill in the art of innuendo, he irritated Larkin with well-camouflaged taunts. Harry Gosling, on the other hand, concentrated his criticism on the employers. Connolly, in a sober and statesmanlike speech, pointed out that in refusing reinstatement the employers were inviting the union to accept the position that would exist if there were no union at all – that is to say, hire and fire at will. He agreed that there had been 'too much recrimination', but added that it had not been restricted to one side.

Then the bombshell exploded. One of the avowedly radical delegates, Ben Tillett, proposed a motion in two parts. The first deplored and condemned the unfair attacks upon British trade union officials. (Attacks on Irish officials were presumably less damaging.) The second expressed confidence in the gentlemen who had been 'unjustly assailed' and belief 'in their ability to negotiate an honourable settlement if assured of the effective support of all who are concerned in the Dublin dispute'. In other words, the ITGWU was to abdicate its position as principal and allow the British to reach a settlement. 1913

The wise thing for Larkin to have done would have been to concentrate on the substance and try to get the resolution withdrawn with honour or accepted without prejudice. But matters had gone too far for wisdom. 'Mr Chairman, and human beings', he began. Whether this meant that the chairman was not a human being, or that the others were not much more, it pleased nobody. He was constantly interrupted. At times the meeting was in uproar. As usual, Larkin personalised everything. He poured out his frustrations in denunciations of Havelock Wilson and J. H. Thomas. He unwittingly assisted the passage of Tillett's resolution. The 'rebel' proposal, moved by Jack Jones of the National Union of Gasworkers and General Labourers, was lost by 2,000,000 votes to 200,000. The conference then decided to hold a further meeting in Dublin in an effort to secure a settlement, and to continue financial support until the dispute was settled.

Ben Tillett was, of course, bitterly criticised for his disastrous intervention. He defended himself by saying that his sole object was to remove the disunity that was hampering the movement. But if this had been so, his resolution would have had one clause. It had two.

* * *

Connolly fully appreciated that the second stage of the struggle — deadlock — had now ended. Attempts at compromise had failed. Now the attempt to bring in powerful allies had failed. It was necessary to face the prospect of disengagement. He wrote bitterly of the London decision:

> We said that if scabs are working a ship and union men discharge it in another port so loaded, then those union men are strike-breakers, since they help the capitalist in question to carry on his business. . . . We asked for the isolation of the capitalists of Dublin, and for answer the British Labour movement proceeded calmly to isolate the working class of Dublin.[10]

1913 On the action of the National Union of Railwaymen and the National Seamen's and Firemen's Union he was scathing by simple statement of fact:

> The Seamen's and Firemen's Union men in Dublin were next ordered to man the boats of the Head Line of steamers, then being discharged by free labourers supplied by the Shipping Federation. In both Dublin and Belfast the members refused, and they were then informed that union men would be brought from Great Britain to take their places.[11]

Later he wrote:

> The Dublin fighters received their defeat, met their Waterloo at the London Conference of 9th December. At that conference the representatives of organised Labour declared that they would not counsel the use of any kind of economic force or industrial action in support of the Dublin workers, and immediately this was known, the fight was virtually lost.[12]

Larkin left London to fulfil engagements in Glasgow and Birmingham. Connolly took the train to Holyhead. J. H. Thomas's message to the men on the North Wall, that strike pay would cease and they must return to work, arrived ahead of him. Thomas had not even waited for the conference. The ITGWU advised the railwaymen to obey union instructions, for Connolly was anxious not to divide their loyalties. But the tide was turning in Dublin too. The canal workers had returned to work.

Connolly called a meeting of the ITGWU Executive for Sunday 14 December. It has been supposed that the constituted Executive Committee never met and that the union was controlled exclusively by the committee of No. 1 branch. No EC minutes have survived, but one meeting, that of 3 March 1914, is recorded in the minute book of No. 1 branch. It seems unlikely that Connolly would take responsibility for calling a meeting without Larkin's consent, and equally unlikely that the issue of the Dublin strike would be referred to a body which never met. The most likely thing is that the EC met irregularly and that the minutes were not carefully preserved. That the meeting of 14 December was of the EC seems the more likely from the fact that Ellen Gordon was in Dublin, possibly as the second member representing Ulster. 1913

At the EC meeting it was decided that all men who were able to return to work without signing 'the document' should do so at once, without prejudice to any future settlement. The City of Dublin Steampacket men were to present themselves on Tuesday 16 December. Letters were to be sent to the other shipping companies. Larkin arrived at Dún Laoire on the day of the meeting. Whether he was expected at it is not certain. Certainly he did not attend, but remained at the port, where he addressed a meeting of members. It has been suggested that he knew the decisions that would have to be taken, but could not bring himself to be a party to them. The press reported disagreements. What they were can be guessed from the fact that the EC decision was not carried out.

The British Joint Labour Board (of the TUC and Labour Party) sent their final delegation, which opened negotiations with the employers on 18 December. With the union and the Trades Council the British visitors had worked out the Labour proposals. These were that the employers should withdraw 'the document'; that the workers should abstain from sympathetic strike action pending the establishment of a wages board on 17 March; that no worker should be refused employment on the grounds of his or her association with the dispute; that no stranger should be engaged until all the old workers had been employed; and that the cases of former employees not re-employed by 1 February 1914 should be considered at a conference on 15 February. The employers once more rejected the reinstatement proposals, and the conference was a failure. That week the renegade Greene advertised the foundation of the 'Irish Dockers' and Workers' Union'.

The overall position of the union at the end of 1913 is not easy to estimate. When the 1915 roll book was compiled there remained in membership only 48 persons who had joined during the 169 days from 15 August to 31 December. In the 196 days from 1 January to 15 August there were 298 recruits. This means that the rate of recruitment during the last four and a half months dropped to one seventh of what it had been during the earlier period. There must have been some loss of membership in Dublin, if only of men who emigrated to escape starvation, but it is hard to quantify it. During the intense enthusiasm of the struggle it is not to be expected that many left. But a large membership meant a large burden rather than a large support. In Belfast much the same situation prevailed among the dockers, though the textile workers were unaffected. From the fact that a load of Guinness had to be taken from Sligo to Derry it is clear that the Sligo branch was still in control of the port and that the NSFU men were with the ITGWU. There is other evidence too that Sligo was the most flourishing branch. The total membership claimed by the union remained something over 25,000. This is a very high figure.

In the south there seems to have been some regression. Branches still existed in Cork, Waterford and Wexford, but some of the members seem to have fallen away as a consequence of the scurrilous attacks made on the leaders of the union by the two Hibernian sheets, *The Liberator* and *The Toiler*. The first issue of *The Liberator* appeared on 28 August 1913, so convenient a date for William Martin Murphy that one would think that he must have had a hand in it. The name of the editor was not made public. But the publisher was Bernard Doyle, who had issued the first *Irish Worker*. Over many years he had maintained connections with E. W. Stewart, and the fact that the names of the Labour renegade William Richardson and John Saturnus Kelly receive favourable mention confirms the Board of Erin influence. A connection with Murphy is suggested from the publication of attacks on those who wished to see a new art gallery established: it was Murphy's blocking of this project which for so many years deprived Dublin of the Lane bequest.

The tendency of *The Liberator* was Redmondite. It said little about contemporary nationalism, but published articles about 1798. Its attacks on socialism were based on total disregard for the facts. 'Quotations' from Marx and Engels were shamelessly manufactured and then impertinently fathered on Connolly and Larkin, who would never have given voice to such nonsense. Its purpose was to discredit Larkin. But it was a dull publication. It may be no coincidence that within a few days of its collapse, hoodlums broke into the shop where the *Irish Worker* was printed, scattered the type and smashed the formes. It did not, however, miss an issue. 1913

The other 'yellow' sheet was far more dangerous. Its aim was not so much to discredit Larkin as to try to break his nerve by blatant slander. *The Toiler* was first issued on 13 September. It professed respect for the employers, the clergy and E. W. Stewart, but for scarcely anybody else. Its editor was P. J. McIntyre, whose dabblings in scabbery have already received notice. He had, of course, now completely severed his connection with the trade union movement. No other editor in Ireland approached him in unscrupulous scurrility.[13] His targets were Connolly, O'Brien and above all Partridge and Larkin, all of whom had insulting names invented for them. O'Brien was 'hoofy'; Partridge was 'the dirt-bird'. But his speciality was character-assassination. His allegations were ludicrous. Larkin said his father's name was James, his grandfather's Bernard, and that the last was from Co. Armagh; and anybody who cares to examine the Liverpool census can confirm this genealogy. But McIntyre claimed that Larkin was an Orangeman and published a bogus marriage certificate which gave him the wrong wife. He further claimed that Larkin was really the son of Carey the informer, and every week he published side by side pictures of Carey and of Larkin *after he had been disguised* by Countess Markiewicz for his incursion into the Imperial Hotel. The London *Times* supported Larkin, who ignored these attacks. At the same time he could never be sure that some planted Hibernian would not interrupt a meeting with demands for his birth certificate. He complained in his speeches that he was being 'crucified'. The strain must have been almost unbearable.

It is possible that the attacks helped to bolster up support for Redmond's party in rural districts. They seem to have influenced nobody who was actually engaged in the struggle with the employers. It should be recorded, however (for it has not been) that the agricultural workers of Co. Dublin displayed a fortitude in every way comparable with that of the city people. At Lucan petty assizes on 17 November a farmer called Masterson sought possession of a cottage occupied by his employee Maher. It was admitted in court

1913 that Maher had milked the cows that morning. The Transport Union solicitor, William Smyth, asked Masterson: 'Is it because he won't sign this magic warrant that you are going to evict him?' The farmer replied: 'I can get men without a magic warrant.' Maher said he was being evicted because he would not give up Larkin's union. 'I would give up the colours first,' he added. Labourers were discharged for refusing to sign 'the document' at Blanchardstown and Swords. At Swords sixteen possession orders were granted against labourers in one day; and in the evening Joseph Early thought the time appropriate for holding a meeting for the purpose of founding a 'New Labour Union' unconnected with the ITGWU but closely connected, one may be sure, with the UIL, whose satellite bodies had halted the wages movement on the borders of Co. Meath.

* * *

While in Belfast, Connolly became convinced that there was no alternative to the policy he had suggested – disengagement. He went back to Dublin determined to persuade Larkin. On 30 December the two men issued a joint statement to dispel rumours of a split. This was a 'holding operation'. Both of them spoke at the funeral of Alice Brady on
1914 4 January 1914. The girl had been shot by the scab Traynor on 18 December and had died in hospital on 2 January. Traynor was arrested and charged with murder. The charge was then reduced to one of manslaughter. The magistrate then ruled that since he held his gun by permission of the police, there could be no case to answer. Apparently he could do what he liked with it! On such grounds a man who held dynamite under licence was free to blow up the Mansion House. Traynor walked out of court without a stain on his character.

Connolly caught cold at this funeral. To make matters worse, as he was returning to Glenalina Terrace he was kicked in the stomach by a drunken man. He was incapacitated for two weeks. The strike committee tried to reason with Larkin, but he would not admit that victory was impossible. He had put too much of himself into this struggle. But the position was becoming desperate. On 7 January the

NSFU sent seamen from Liverpool to act as scabs against their own members. On the 8th the Burns men were accepted back on the old conditions. A general meeting of all workers involved in the stoppage was held on 18 January at Croydon Park. On the 17th Larkin had been evicted for the second time. But still he hesitated. MacPartlin opened the meeting and proposed that all who could return to work without having to sign 'the document' should do so at once. Larkin arrived late. He vehemently opposed the new policy, maintaining that they could hold out for another year if necessary. According to William O'Brien, he was received in silence. Two hours later he communicated the decision of the meeting to the press. There was nothing else for it. 1914

Next morning the City of Dublin Steampacket men returned. Meetings were held in Liberty Hall to consider which firms were likely to insist on 'the document'. On 22 January Larkin and O'Brien attended a meeting of the Parliamentary Committee of the British TUC, where they were told that the future of the support fund was in question. Two days later the London building workers who had refused to sign 'the document' were locked out, as their historian R. W. Postgate puts it, by employers who fancied themselves 'already in the position of Dublin Murphy'.[14] In the following week Connolly and Larkin went to Glasgow, where the Labour Party was holding a conference. They were refused a hearing. On 1 February the Dublin builders' labourers signed 'the document'. On 10 February the British relief fund closed. The one bright spot was the decision of the Amalgamated Society of Engineers to levy their members 3d a week for the relief of Dublin.

The smaller firms readily accepted their workers back on the old terms. The coal merchants Heitons welcomed their forty employees with open arms. Indeed the foreman bought them all a drink before they started. Jacobs, on the other hand, selected those they took back carefully and submitted them to humiliating medical examinations accompanied by scornful comments. On 15 February there were still 4,000 men and 1,000 women locked out. That week there was no strike pay. They were now making the subtle but painful transition from strikers to unemployed. It became clear to most of them that the only course open was

1914 to sign 'the document' and fight again if opportunity offered. For those who could not regain their employment the winter of 1914 was a time of which perhaps the less said the better, except that their heads remained unbowed.

When the struggle was over, the union solicitor, William Smyth, presented a bill covering two years which amounted to £1,422 3s 10d, something like £80,000 in 1982 currency. Most of this expenditure resulted from the lock-out. There were forty-eight cases under the Workmen's Compensation Act, only two of them pursued during the lock-out. There were sixteen cases of wrongful dismissal. Members accused of larceny were defended, and in one case the union was prepared to sue a publican who had refused a member a drink.

When we consider the lock-out cases the magnitude of the union's effort becomes apparent. The union provided legal aid for no fewer than 400 members accused of intimidation, smashing windows of trams, throwing stones, inciting to riot, resisting arrest and assaulting the police. Many cases were taken to appeal, and though the proportion of acquittals did not reach ten per cent, it was not negligible. In the case of Frank Moss, who went on hunger-strike, the conviction was quashed on appeal. When the evictions began, sixty-three ejectment cases were fought.

Eight farmers were sued for the payment of harvest money. The thirty-eight tramwaymen who were summoned for abandoning their cars were all defended and escaped with trifling fines. Counter-charges were brought against policemen, but the magistrates usually refused to accept them. Larkin himself was evicted twice and after losing his appeal on 15 January 1914 went to live in Croydon Park.

The large-scale legal defence of members involved in industrial disputes was an ITGWU innovation. In 1890 men who were taken up had the effective status of criminals. They must stand in the dock, receive their sentences and take their medicine. Now there was a civil element in such trials. By the expenditure of many pounds out of union funds there was purchased a new outlook according to which workers were citizens. It was something of incalculable importance, and it foreshadowed the great change in the status of the worker that has marked the later years of this century.

Was the 1913-14 lock-out lost, won or drawn? It was all 1914
three. It was lost formally in the fact that the workers at length had to ask for peace on what terms they could get. It was drawn in the sense that the employers were too exhausted to make use of their victory. But it was won in a far deeper and more permanent sense. The workers acquired an entirely new sense of their own power. It had been demonstrated that though the power of the employer was still greater than theirs, already theirs was of the same order of magnitude. P. S. O'Hegarty denies Robert Lynd's claim that 1913 paved the way for 1916; but there is a sense in which Lynd was a hundred times right.

6

Down but not Out

I have known Defeat and mocked it as we ran.
RUDYARD KIPLING

Fund-raising in England – Connolly on the lock-out – threat of partition – Larkin's nervous breakdown – resignation – resignation withdrawn – world war – friction in the union – Larkin to USA – Connolly takes over – rebuilding begun

1914 Larkin spent the greater part of the winter raising funds in England. The appeal was now for relief. Larkin's campaign was directed towards the supporters of the British Socialist Party, and he made much of the 'Co-operative Commonwealth'. He was assisted by his brother Peter and Jack Carney, a Belfast man he had known in Liverpool who subsequently became his secretary. Lennon and Donegan made a more humanitarian appeal. Their 'Dublin Help Committee' was sponsored by the Lord Mayor of Liverpool. Delia Larkin spent a week in the district with her dramatic company before moving on to Oxford and London. She aroused interest but raised little money.

On 14 February 1914, while Larkin was still in England, Thomas Foran asked Connolly to come to Dublin, where he seems to have remained for about five weeks. The Head Line was the only important shipping company to maintain the lock-out. A thousand men were still idle in Belfast. If the company could be induced to accept ITGWU dockers in Dublin, it might help resolve the dispute in the north. The union had indeed offered to work a Head Line ship, but learned that stevedore Long was in charge of it. The danger was that Greene's scab union, well advertised in McIntyre's *Toiler*, should gain a foothold and the ITGWU be frozen out.

Foran explained that there were other problems too. One of them concerned relations with the NSFU. The head office of this union refused to recognise the existence of an industrial dispute. It continued to instruct its members to work the Head Line vessels. Despite the union's record of co-operation, the company decided to reintroduce the Shipping Federation ticket. On 8 March Connolly was in London, asking Ben Tillett to refuse the Head Line facilities on the Bristol Channel. A week later an official of the NSFU visited Dublin, and co-operation between the two unions was resumed. The purpose was to break the deadlock in Belfast. 1914

It was during Larkin's prolonged absence that the committee of Dublin No. 1 branch began to manage the routine affairs of the union. Their minutes, beginning at this time, have survived and provide a mass of valuable detail. It is of great interest to note the imperturbable way these ordinary men handled their business. They showed firmness, realism and resource, bringing to the conduct of the affairs of the union the qualities developed in them by their daily lives.

A special meeting was called on 27 February. Foran presided and with the secretary John O'Neill, his fellow-trustee William Fairtlough and other members of the committee[1] discussed a single item – how to curtail branch expenditure. A sub-committee was appointed. Only one immediate proposal was made when the meeting was resumed, namely to dispense with the services of the secretary of the tramwaymen's section. From this action it is to be concluded that Murphy had got his own way at least in that field. But that the union was by no means on its beam ends is shown by two small examples. A letter from the Lucan branch asked that a meeting should be arranged in the area. The flour merchant Shackleton had therefore not been so fortunate as Murphy. And a deputation from Kill o' the Grange branch requested assistance in organising a local pottery.

The committee met once a week. At most meetings members of the union presented themselves with requests for the fare that would enable them to emigrate to Glasgow. These were invariably granted. Those who claimed exceptional hardship were assisted by means of money grants. Occasionally new members were enrolled. Assistance and advice were given to other branches of the union. Differences had arisen in the Inchicore branch between Partridge and his members;

1914 a special meeting was arranged and the dispute was resolved. A half-year's rent of the Inchicore branch's headquarters at the Emmet Hall was paid out of central funds. When a deputation from the Jacobs branch reported that they had no funds to pay the rent of their premises, No. 1 branch gave them a cheque for the amount. One of the Cork branches had fallen on evil days and applied for the payment of its electric light bill. The applicant in this case was invited to appear in person. The victimisation of such groups as the casual grain porters was discussed, and the committee took whatever steps were possible to restore the position of the union. The dispute was used by some companies as an excuse for excluding dockers' delegates from harbour property. The union's tactic was to edge back to the position existing before the stoppage. The branch elected six delegates to the Irish Trade Union Congress, the 'coming of age' Congress that was to be held in Dublin.

The quiet confidence with which Foran, O'Neill and Fairtlough carried out their policy of retrenchment and reorganisation must have been a reflection of opinion on the quays. If those who had been locked out were defeated, those who had struck had lost little of the ground previously won. The core of the union was preserved intact. The burdens might be immense, but they would lighten. Finances would become easier. And Foran had a secret cause for optimism: he had salted away an emergency fund of £7,500 which was used in September to complete the purchase of Liberty Hall.

The effect of the lock-out on the workers of all industries was to strengthen their consciousness of themselves as a class. In 1910 Larkin had told O'Brien that his members would never accept the appointment of the socialist Connolly. Now Connolly was an accepted leader, in some ways more regarded even than Larkin. His ideas were now respectable. As he himself put it,

> There are times in history when we realise that it is easier to convert a multitude than it ordinarily is to convert an individual; when indeed ideas seem to seize upon the masses as contra-distinguished by [sic] ordinary times when individuals slowly seize ideas.[2]

As for Larkin himself, they did not turn against him for

not leading them to victory. As well rend the Fenians after the failure of 1867. The Dublin men thought they had been betrayed by the cross-channel leaders as they had been in 1907 and 1911. 1914

Connolly wrote many bitter words about those who had failed the test of internationalism. It is doubtful if he ever again had confidence in the British movement. In a May Day message to Glasgow he wrote:

> How can I write it when I know that in the Labour ranks on May Day processions of many of the seaport towns of Great Britain there will be represented unions that at this moment and for three months back are and have been openly and deliberately assisting the capitalist to smash a militant union and starve its members for their loyalty to working-class principles? May Day is the feast of Labour, but the betrayed Irish Transport and General Workers' Union is the Banquo's ghost that arises to disturb the feastings and feasters.[3]

'Betrayal' is a heavily loaded word, carrying associations of greed, cowardice and duplicity. In an individual it implies a recognised obligation wilfully disregarded. In an institution the case is more complicated. Connolly sought an explanation in accordance with syndicalist thinking. How, he asked, had great industrial organisations become infused with a parochial craft spirit. He began to re-examine the subject of trade union organisation and was ultimately led to recognise the limitations of syndicalism.

For the time being he concluded that the doctrine of 'tainted goods' was essential for the defence of Labour in the industrial field, and that 'the first duty of the militant worker' was to 'work for industrial unionism in some form'.[4] Later he complained that 'Into the new bottles of industrial organisation is being poured the old, cold wine of craft unionism.'[5] The only solution was the choice of officials 'from the standpoint of their responsiveness to the call for solidarity'.[6] But who will look after the keepers?

Connolly was seeking an organisational remedy for a disease which others have thought political. The old trade unionism grew up while Britain held a virtual monopoly of world trade, and its craft spirit was accompanied by much

1914 narrow nationalism. The new unionism appeared in the age of imperialism, when a few advanced countries shared the underdeveloped world among them, each envying what the others possessed. In all these countries, but especially in England, an upper stratum of the Labour movement had come to regard itself as part of the establishment. They spoke of 'our' Empire, thereby identifying themselves with the foreign policy of an employers' government. They gave their consent to a system of international plunder. Their attitude to the Irish was bound to be affected by this general outlook. In this sense the betrayal of Irish Labour was imperialist.[7]

Jacobs took back only 100 out of 672 men and boys and imposed wage reductions of from 2s to 4s a week. The women and girls on the whole fared better. For those who were unfortunate an unemployed movement was started. In connection with this a meeting in Beresford Place on 13 March was addressed by Connolly and Captain Jack White. The boom of 1913 had ended. Quite apart from the lock-out, unemployment was increasing. It was intended that at the close of the meeting the Citizen Army should march to the Mansion House, where it was proposed to present a petition to the Lord Mayor. As the Citizen Army moved off, a policeman on Butt Bridge tried to halt the procession to let a mail-van through. Precisely what happened next was disputed. It was agreed that the horse was seized by the bridle. It was also agreed that Captain White struck out with his blackthorn, but he denied attempting to strike the driver. He resisted arrest and later appeared in court with his head swathed in bandages. Those were the days, of course, when a gentleman was a gentleman. It was suggested to the Captain that there must have been a misunderstanding. The Captain agreed, in view of this, to withdraw his counter-charges against the police, while the Crown entered a *nolle prosequi*.

As a result of this contretemps, White was unable to speak on Sunday 15 March at a meeting in Swords arranged by Micheál Ó Maoláin. The original purpose of this meeting had been to establish a company of the Citizen Army. Thirty-two men with hurleys marched from Liberty Hall, the speakers preceding them on a brake. A large force of police accompanied them in hackney cars, and fifty more awaited them at Swords. Connolly's fiery speech must have corresponded to the mood of the working class, though it went somewhat beyond the rules of the union. He said that 1914

> There never were rebels in Ireland more rebellious than the members of the Transport Workers' Union. They had no respect for British laws. They claimed the right to own this country and all that was in it, and to have what they were able to produce by their own labour. No matter what was in the Home Rule Bill, they were not going to be content with it; the workers of the north were not going to have an excluded Ulster.[8]

The reintroduction of the Shipping Federation ticket by the Head Line had by now thoroughly alarmed the British unions. Connolly attended an indecisive conference of those concerned. From Cardiff, where it was held, he returned to Belfast. Now that Larkin was once again at the helm in Dublin, Connolly's presence was no longer required there.

* * *

On 19 March the Prime Minister suggested partition on the basis of county option. Carson objected to 'a sentence of death with stay of execution'. But, to the amazement and indignation of nationalist Ireland, Redmond accepted. The Unionists were speaking openly of civil war. It was 'the path of duty', said Sir James Campbell, MP, in a speech at Swansea. There were rumours that the Ulster Volunteers were preparing to seize military stores, and on 14 March Sir Arthur Paget was instructed by the War Office to provide additional protection at Armagh, Omagh, Carrickfergus and Enniskillen. Troops were to be sent from the Curragh. On 20 March Brigadier-General Gough and fifty-seven officers offered to resign their commissions, and the government immediately climbed down. It is easy to chase a cat into a dairy.

At this point it was brought home to the Labour movement that there was a real possibility of partition. The Unionists meant business. The Parliamentary Committee of the ITUC decided to hold a protest meeting in O'Connell Street on 5 April, and its manifesto, written in Larkin's

1914 characteristic style, was published in the *Irish Worker* on 28 March. It pointed out that in the discussion of the partition proposal 'the workers were the only class in the community whose interests were not consulted'. The division of Ireland was 'unthinkable'. The manifesto continued: 'If it is lawful for Carson to arm, it is lawful for us, the workers, to arm.' It was significant that this statement was signed not only by Jim Larkin, Tom Johnson, D. R. Campbell and William O'Brien, but also by W. E. Hill of the Railway Clerks' Association. As for Connolly, his opinion had already been published on 14 March:

> Such a scheme as that agreed to by Redmond and Devlin, the betrayal of the national democracy of industrial Ulster, would mean a carnival of reaction both North and South, would set back the wheels of progress, would destroy the oncoming unity of the Irish Labour movement and paralyse all advanced movements while it lasted. The vaunted saviours of the Irish race agree in front of the enemy and in the face of the world to sacrifice to the bigoted enemy the unity of the nation and along with it the lives, liberties and hopes of that portion of the nation which in the midst of the most hostile surroundings have fought to keep the faith in things national and progressive.[9]

Larkin seemed on the surface to be fighting-fit. At a union 'rally' in the Antient Concert Rooms on Monday 23 March he spoke vigorously, to a packed hall, of the need to organise agricultural workers. But on the evening of 31 March it was announced that he had agreed to stand for parliament in opposition to the Prime Minister and would shortly be leaving for East Fife. That he was still in Dublin on 29 March is known from the circumstance that he was visited on that day by Con O'Lyhane, who was toying with the idea of starting a Citizen Army in England. But on the 30th he paid a visit to London, returning on the afternoon of the 31st. When in London he used to make his headquarters the *Daily Herald* office. It is therefore to be guessed that the proposition came from George Lansbury, who does not appear to have considered the possible reaction of Larkin's colleagues.

There was consternation among officials both of the union and the ITUC. Connolly telegraphed: 'Myself and

friends implore you not to oppose Asquith. If you do you 1914
will ruin your career. Leave that to fools like Lansbury.' Tom Johnson wired to P. T. Daly: 'Unanimous agreement here madness Jim to Scotland. Hope rumour untrue.' Larkin seems to have gone to Scotland, for he wired McKeown from Glasgow on 4 April, but presumably the prospect did not attract him. He does not appear to have addressed the anti-partition meeting next day, at which the union was represented by P. T. Daly, William Partridge and Alderman John Lynch from Sligo. All the speakers were summoned for obstruction and fined 5s. When Will Thorne, the first secretary of the Gasworkers' Union, asked the Chief Secretary why the summonses had been served, in view of the fact that members of parliament had recently and frequently addressed meetings in the same place, Birrell replied that the police were anxious to test the law in order to find out whether it was legal or illegal to hold public meetings in Sackville Street (i.e. O'Connell Street, Dublin). If this had been true, the defendants should have been informed of it and no penalties should have been imposed, for the offence had been committed before the law was decided. The Chief Secretary was, of course, showing his contempt for trade unionists, British and Irish, by giving a frivolous answer. But the meeting was noteworthy for another reason. On this occasion for the first time the Citizen Army carried its flag, the famous 'Plough and the Stars', the work of Mr Megahey of the City Art Gallery.

It was now that Larkin suffered the reaction he had been trying to fight off with excessive activity. His dynamism disappeared, and he fell into listlessness and apathy. Sometimes he would not come in to Liberty Hall for several days. Usually concerned with the smallest complaint of hardship or misfortune, he now strove to avoid all contact with those who wanted their fare to Glasgow or a grant to stave off starvation. He occupied himself with plans for extending social activities at Croydon Park, but left the regular business of the union to McKeown and Foran. He rallied in May and on the 15th crossed to London for the farewell banquet to Con O'Lyhane, who was emigrating to America.

When the ITUC agenda was published it was seen that a motion condemning partition was down in the name of

1914 the ITGWU:

> That in the opinion of this Congress, any attempt to exclude any portion of Ireland from the provisions of the Home Rule bill is undesirable; that this Congress heartily endorses the manifesto issued by our Parliamentary Committee and directs the various Trades Councils in Ireland to press the matter on the Parliamentary representatives of their districts.

The ITUC met at the City Hall on 1 June.[10] Larkin was in the chair. He delivered a magnificent *ex tempore* address, which, as he put it, came from the heart. The most important business before Congress was the adoption of a constitution for the Labour Party. The ITGWU resolution on partition was moved by James Connolly and seconded by Richard Corish. It was carried by 84 votes to 2. Connolly played a considerable part in this Congress, and there seems little doubt that had it not proved his last, he would have become the recognised leader of Irish Labour. The only new delegate to distinguish himself was Denis Houston of the Belfast Trades Council.

In all but his opening speech the chairman was, as his biographer puts it, 'impossible'. His emotions were too strong for him. He interrupted, commented and took umbrage in the face of contradiction. O'Brien, in proposing the vote of thanks, said that

> He had certainly proved a remarkable chairman, a unique chairman. He had made them revise all their dictionaries, and all books written on rules of order. But they had put him in the chair, not because they thought he would be an ideal chairman, but to honour him for his work for the Trades Union Movement.

To this expression of appreciation Larkin made a curious reply:

> I am glad someone has added salt to the soup. I do not thank you for eulogy; I am more used to other sorts of flattery. I will love my enemies and beat my friends into doing things. All I think of is principle, and when I take a line of action nothing will stop me.

Before leaping to the conclusion that this was a display 1914
of vanity one should ponder the mystery of Larkin's character. Was it perhaps the very opposite of what it seemed to be – like the bluster of the small child who says: 'I am big and I am strong and I can knock the house down'? Was it a condition of his activity that he should over-compensate deep uncertainties and inhibitions? If this is so, his life had a tragic aspect. We should perhaps see him as a sensitive spirit deeply hurt by the failure of his plans, a man whose exaggerated self-assurance was required to negate and transform the doubt and immaturity within. His speeches bristled with inaccuracies. He could thrust reality unceremoniously aside. He had a vision of a world remoulded. From his own contradictory character came his capacity, absent in many men of greater intellectual attainment, to personify to the underdog the underdog transfigured, freed from the restraints imposed on his personality by his economic position. It was the softer side of Larkin that attracted the lifelong admiration of a perceptive artist like O'Casey, whose eyes began to sparkle as soon as his name was mentioned.

This view of Larkin possibly helps to explain his behaviour in the crises which followed. Differences had arisen between him and the committee of No. 1 branch. The General Secretary did not usually attend its meetings. He had done so on 26 May and sat there without saying a word. This was ominous. But the ITUC and the Poor Law elections followed immediately and engaged his attention. On 9 June the committee, in Larkin's absence, held a general discussion on 'the best possible means of getting all the branches into good working order again after the late troubles'. It was decided 'to call a meeting of all the officials of the different city and county branches for the next Sunday evening, 14th instant at 4 o'clock'.

This meeting does not appear to have taken place. A special meeting of the branch committee was called on Friday 19 June. Foran reported that on Wednesday he had received a letter from Larkin in which he tendered his resignation. He had tried to secure its withdrawal but Larkin had been determined. On the motion of Michael McCarthy it was agreed to send a deputation consisting of the whole committee to speak to him at Croydon Park. It was suggested

1914 that he should explain his reasons at a general meeting on the following Monday. But he gave no promise. On Sunday 21 June he went with the Citizen Army to Bodenstown. A mass meeting was held at Croydon Park. Corish came from Wexford, Lynch from Sligo, and Connolly from Belfast. When Larkin arrived at Kingsbridge he was met by three bands, and a huge procession escorted him through the city. He was informed that unless he undertook to attend Monday's meeting, the entire concourse would spend the night in the grounds. He then agreed to postpone his decision until Monday and referred to two grievances, one the poor results of the Poor Law elections, and the other interference from other officials of the union.

William O'Brien believed that the election results were a severe blow to Larkin and precipitated his attack of depression. But neither the *Irish Worker* nor the *Daily Herald* gave the impression that this issue figured prominently at the meeting. The issue discussed at the Antient Concert Rooms was that of interference and opposition, implying differences of opinion over how the union should be run. Larkin was anxious to develop social activities at Croydon Park. He had begun the restoration of the negelected gardens. He had plans for union medical and dental services. The committee, on the other hand, considered its first priority to be that of restoring the organisation and finances. And they had not waited for Larkin.

Larkin's biographer suggests that his self-confidence was severely shaken and that he required reassurance that he was still needed. That he was suffering from overstrain and nervous reaction can be learned from his own testimony. In the course of his speech he said: 'No one under God's sun knows what I have been through.' He explained that he was speaking under the influence of 'strong emotion and physical disabilities'; he had been 'fighting depression and physical difficulties'. And that he was under medical treatment is deducible from the fact that when on 5 July he spoke in Trafalgar Square, London, he did so 'against doctor's orders'. P. T. Daly contrasted his present physical condition with that of the vigorous young fellow who had appeared in Dublin in 1907. Connolly moved a resolution pledging support to Larkin's leadership. He thought Larkin was 'overstrung',

saw opposition where there was none, and needed a rest. 1914
He thought Larkin might yet live to thank God he had produced men capable of criticising him. The resolution was carried. Larkin withdrew his resignation, and Foran set a match to the document amid 'great scenes of enthusiasm'.

It was Connolly, as usual, who grasped the essential. Since the lock-out Larkin's lieutenants had 'grown up'. Until then trade unions catering for the infrastructure workers had always depended on a personal leader. Now for the first time the 'unskilled' workers had produced a collective leadership able to take more than routine decisions. This was the meaning of the proposal to call the conference of branch officials. That it was not called does not affect the principle. From the day the decision was taken the union's future was secure, and it became gradually clear that Murphy's strategy which appeared so successful on the surface was in reality an utter failure.

The committee handled the new situation in the most mature and diplomatic manner possible. At the meeting of 23 June they decided to ask the General Secretary what powers they possessed following the general meeting. When a deputation from the band came to suggest that its uniform should be identical with that of the Citizen Army, the matter was referred to Larkin. When the Citizen Army, in turn, requested the use of Croydon Park for a display, that was referred to the same quarter, as was a request from the women's ambulance corps. Requests for assistance from members were similarly referred. By mid-July the branch committee was taking its own decisions much as before the crisis, remitting the arrears of members who now wished to join again, taking disciplinary action against those who misbehaved in the 'House' room, and discussing measures to reduce branch expenditure.

Connolly had done his best to prevent Larkin's resignation. His gifts could still be useful to the movement. Not so O'Brien. When Connolly discussed the matter with him he was for letting Larkin go. From this point on O'Brien must be counted among his opponents. Another feud may have originated at this time. McKeown gave utterance to criticisms of P. T. Daly. Larkin dismissed him on the spot. It may be that O'Brien's opposition to Daly, which many believed

1914 largely personal, had its origin in this same stormy period. Daly lacked the gift of industry, Larkin that of prudence, and O'Brien that of forgiveness.

The union was not directly involved in the arms landing at Howth on 26 July. But when the authorities tried to intercept the Volunteers who were bringing the guns into Dublin some of them escaped into Croydon Park. That evening the Scottish Borderers fired on an unarmed crowd at Bachelor's Walk, killing three and wounding thirty-two. The incident aroused great indignation. But a week later came a far greater catastrophe. The European war broke out. Britain declared war on Germany on 4 August. The political situation was immediately transformed. Home Rule was accepted in principle but put in cold storage. Unemployment was reduced as reservists joined the colours. The employers and the government were made dependent on the workers in an entirely new way.

* * *

The *Irish Worker* carried Connolly's denunciation of the war in its issue of 8 August. His immediate concern was with the prospect of excessive exports of food from Ireland. To prevent this might require more than a transport strike, it might mean 'armed battling in the streets'.[11] He visualised two further possibilities: first the escape of Ireland from the 'brigand Empire', and second the overthrow of European capitalism. The National Executive Committee of the ITUC met on the 10th and developed at some length Connolly's call for the defence of Irish food supplies. It did not hesitate to suggest the use of arms. The war was described as 'foreign' and 'for an Empire that despises you'. The implications are therefore critical. But it falls far short of Connolly's willingness to accept German aid if this could be seen to promote Irish independence, and, as Arthur Mitchell has pointed out, it 'skirted the main issue', support for or opposition to Britain.[12]

The union does not appear to have issued a manifesto. But a public meeting under union auspices was held at Croydon Park on 11 August. William O'Brien took the chair. He expressed the view that the working class was not strong

enough to demand that the war should be stopped; instead 1914
workers should take adequate steps to protect food supplies. Larkin, on the other hand, closed some passages of rather confused eloquence with the statement that the Irish people 'should not take part in this European war. They should stand aside as an independent people.' That the members agreed was shown by the cheers that followed.

Larkin seems to have recovered his natural vigour. The outbreak of war provided the stimulus of action without which to him life was not life. He held a number of public meetings at which he eloquently denounced the war and the capitalists. But he was still unsettled. It was as if the failure to humiliate Murphy had delivered a blow to his self-esteem from which he found it hard to recover. On 18 August he wrote to P. L. Quinlan in New York that he had 'not had a holiday for years' and was 'not in love at present with the work here'. He revived an earlier project of a lecture tour in the USA.[13]

This had been first suggested to him by W. D. Heywood of the Industrial Workers of the Work when they were in Manchester on 15 November 1913. At Christmas Larkin was compelled to deny rumours that he was going at once. He wrote to Con O'Lyhane on 1 July 1914 asking him to arrange the tour. It was presumably at the meeting on 10 August that the National Executive Committee of the ITUC suggested sending to America a delegation of two, one of them Larkin, to collect funds for the newly established Labour Party. But Larkin declined to fall in with this suggestion and told O'Brien that he intended to go as a 'free lance'.

Under these conditions it was not surprising that there was fresh friction between him and the committee of No. 1 branch. This arose towards the end of August. Apparently a piano had been purchased out of union funds. It was used for the most part by Delia Larkin in her cultural work. The committee considered that she should reimburse the general fund from finance available to her. It is a fair speculation that the move came from Foran, who had a high sensitivity in monetary matters. When Delia refused to pay up the piano was locked. Delia broke open the lock. A storm in a teacup can have fateful consequences. When the committee com-

1914 plained to Larkin he refused to become involved. Possibly he did not wish to risk a passage at arms with his formidable sister. The committee met on 5 September and resolved that Miss Larkin be requested to find other premises in which to carry on the work of the IWWU. On that day Larkin returned from Cork. Once more he had been refused the City Hall, but had addressed a gathering of 6,000 in Daunt Square.

On 8 September Foran read the committee a letter from the General Secretary informing him that he was calling a general meeting on the following Sunday at which he would 'deal with the committee'. On the motion of one of its most respected members, William Fairtlough, the committee resolved that its members would resign *en bloc*. At this point the minutes cease; there is not even a note that the motion was carried. The files of the *Irish Worker* offer no clue, except that the meeting was postponed from 12 September to 27 September. Finally it was postponed to 4 October. No report was published. Presumably Larkin announced his departure for the USA, and the committee agreed to resume its work.

But now differences arose over the question of who should manage the affairs of the union while Larkin was absent. Larkin decided to make P. T. Daly Acting General Secretary and leave Connolly in charge of the Insurance Section. He telephoned to Connolly, who replied that he disliked insurance work. Connolly wired O'Brien on 5 October and in a letter posted the same day urged him to see Foran and suggest a committee meeting as soon as possible. Connolly was afraid that if Daly were head of the union, its relations with the republicans would be jeopardised. O'Brien suspected that Larkin's aim was to have the union badly managed so that he could come back and show how to put it right. His motive may have been no more devious than a desire to have a tractable man in his place who would take his advice even when offered from a distance. Connolly wrote politely declining the Insurance post. The committee met on 13 October, and Foran persuaded Larkin to appoint Connolly to the position of Acting General Secretary and Daly to the Insurance Section. The committee then voted £10 to the General Secretary's expenses.

Larkin delivered a farewell address at a carnival held at Croydon Park on 18 October. His final message to the union was published in the *Irish Worker* of 24 October. The new appointments were confirmed: Connolly became Acting General Secretary and Commandant of the Citizen Army. Larkin's last speech before he left Ireland was delivered in Cork on 22 October; this time he was given the City Hall. He sailed from Liverpool on 31 October. It was expected that he would be absent for no more than a few months; in fact he was away over eight years. He carried with him an address presented to him by the Dublin Trades Council which described his work as 'magnificent, prodigious and noble'. Reference was made to the severe strain imposed on him by the Labour war of 1913-14 which had had the effect of impairing his otherwise splendid constitution. It is no exaggeration to say that the most serious casualty of that struggle was Larkin. But the Trades Council trusted that after recuperation he would resume his labours. 1914

The *Irish Worker* of 24 October was the first to be produced by Connolly. From 14 November it carried below its title the words inscribed on the famous streamer then displayed in front of Liberty Hall: 'We serve neither King nor Kaiser, but Ireland'. Every issue carried this slogan until the paper was suppressed after the issue of 5 December. The paper lost much of its flamboyance. Within two months it had become an ordinary Labour journal, remarkable only for the high quality of Connolly's articles. Almost certainly it lost circulation.

Connolly presumably entered on his new duties on Monday 19 October. He found the union's financial position desperate and was reduced to asking provincial branches to send all their available funds to Liberty Hall. For several months the committee of No. 1 branch had not functioned properly. Larkin's demoralisation had spread. A fish goes bad from the head down. But Connolly introduced a different style of leadership. A joint meeting of the committee of No. 1 branch and the city shop stewards was held on 27 October. Connolly asked them for suggestions that would enable the committee to help them in their work. Only twelve committee members attended, but a special meeting convened for 8 November attracted eighteen. It was Connolly's aim to encourage them

1914 to shoulder responsibility for the running of the union. It was decided to circularise other unions for financial assistance, to hold section meetings, and to demand weekly reports from branches. The Aungier Street branch was to be re-organised. Micheál Ó Maoláin was instructed to call together the members of North Co. Dublin; it is not certain whether he did so. E. O'Dwyer was appointed county organiser a week later. It may be at this time that Ó Maoláin was transferred to the Insurance Section, where he would work closely with P. T. Daly. It was also decided to abandon Christmas charities.

The affairs of the union showed a marked turn for the better during the autumn of 1914. The position of No. 1 branch had never been seriously endangered. Steps were taken to assist Inchicore, Aungier Street and Thomas Street and to deal with the indiscipline of Sligo, which was remiss in sending returns. Efforts were made to affiliate a branch in Limerick, and the committee of No. 1 branch began to be accepted as a national standing committee.

It is only fair to note that a certain improvement had already taken place before Larkin left. The 1915 roll book shows that the turning-point was September. The union began to make recruits. During the first eight months of 1914 the recruitment rate was about 7 per week; during the last four months it was 14.

On 5 December the *Irish Worker* appeared with large blank spaces. The printer had been threatened by the authorities. A few days later his premises were raided and his machine put out of action. By a strange coincidence *The Toiler*, after recording with delight the suppression of the republican press, voluntarily ceased publication with the issue of 19 December. McIntyre's printer was William Hastings of the *Western News*, Ballinasloe. McIntyre owed him £180 when the paper discontinued. Hastings pressed for payment, but for a long time McIntyre made no move. Finally he sent Hastings the following telegram, which is completely characteristic: 'I have dished you with the advertisers, and you can use your advertisement forms for other purposes.' Hastings wired back: 'If advertisers are afraid of a blackmailer I have no doubt of your success.' Hastings then revealed that 'Some parties sent him to ask me to print *The Toiler* and gave money to pay for it.'[14] It requires little imagination to guess who those parties were.

7

Ordeal by Debt

The greatest of evils, and the worst of crimes, is poverty.
GEORGE BERNARD SHAW

Union finances – staff wages – union conference – Executive elected – Kerry organised – Delia Larkin leaves – strike against shipping firms – membership increases – wages movement

The year 1915 formed, with the early part of 1916, one of 1915
the most difficult periods of union history. The inspiration of the great lock-out had departed, but its debts had not. Over £1,000 was due to the solicitor William Smyth. There was a mortgage on Liberty Hall, and smaller accounts arising from the lock-out continued to come in long after it was over.

In order to understand the extent of the difficulties Connolly had to contend with, it is useful to estimate the financial position. There were two current accounts with the Hibernian Bank. The No. 2 account, belonging to the Approved Society, need not concern us, except that on the society's payroll were a number of people who were active in the affairs of the union, for example Thomas Foran, P. T. Daly, William Partridge, Micheál Ó Maoláin and Delia Larkin. A single account was used for the general fund and for the finances of Dublin No. 1 branch. The accounts must have been kept in such a way that they could be distinguished, for there are references in the minutes to transfers. Under rule a General Treasurer should have been elected. In practice Foran was in charge of finance. The property of the union was vested in three trustees, who could refuse to sign cheques for purposes contrary to rule, but not for purposes in accordance with rule. All cheques required the signature of the General Secretary, together with those of the three trustees or one trustee and the General President. John O'Neill, secretary of No. 1 branch,

1915 was a trustee, and it was he who arranged payments, no doubt securing counter-signatures according to the availability of those empowered to sign.

The total assets of the No. 1 branch were available to the general fund, and in practice all payments were sanctioned by the committee of that branch. What we will now try to estimate are, firstly, what was the balance in the general fund on 1 January 1915, and secondly, what was the income and expenditure for that year. No accounts have survived, and it is therefore impossible to give definitive answers to these questions. But intelligent guesswork applied to surviving evidence makes possible a rough picture of the situation that had to be faced. From this it will be possible to see why there were no spectacular developments.

In April 1916 the balance at the bank was withdrawn for safe keeping. It amounted to £100. At the end of November 1913 a sum of £7,500, mostly in notes of high denomination, was held in the safe at Liberty Hall. During December £1,800 was expended in strike pay. A further £1,600 was expended in the early months of 1914, and £600 was paid in legal fees. The sum of £5,000 was paid for Liberty Hall, the purchase being completed in October 1914 after O'Brien's brother Daniel had inspected the building. A mortgage was raised to the amount of £2,000, repayable to the Northern Bank. There were thus no reserves left. The £7,500 was exhausted.

If we now turn to regular income and expenditure, a sum of £4,100 was placed on deposit in April 1914. One would expect something under £100 interest to accrue before the capital was expended. There was at the end of September 1914 a balance at the bank of £447, which was relodged on deposit. It is clear that the union treasury was being depleted at an average rate of £20 a month. In view of the aftermath of the lock-out and the presumable transfer of Connolly's salary from Belfast (where he retained his membership) to the general account, it would seem unlikely that there could be much more than £300 at the end of the year. Moreover, during the last week in December there was a sudden lock-out at the City of Dublin Steampacket Company. This involved 150 men. If anything was left in the fund at the beginning of January 1915, it can only have been a small iron reserve not to be touched short of a catastrophe. If some of the commitments affecting 1915 had already been accepted, it may be that the fund was exhausted.

Let us now examine these commitments so as to estimate what Connolly had to raise. The largest item was the payment of £40 a month to Smyth & Son, solicitors. There was £10 a month mortgage repayment, and £20 a month rent of Croydon Park. The sum of £25 was paid to St Vincent's Hospital, in return for which the union could claim 365 bed-days a year. A donation of 5 guineas was made to the League for the Blind. There were small amounts paid to the Athletic Club and the union's band. *Ex gratia* payments included £20 to Peter Larkin's wife when her husband was arrested under DORA, £60 for medical fees for Larkin in America, and £40 to enable his wife to visit him. During the time she was in Ireland she was paid 50s a week.

It is difficult to compute the wages bill for Liberty Hall. It is not certain how many people were employed. Among those who appear to have been on the payroll, judging from the minutes of No. 1 branch, were Connolly, John O'Neill, two outside delegates (Laurence Redmond and John Nolan) and for a time a building section delegate. A caretaker was employed and a 'billiard-marker'. Allowing an average wage of 30s a week, the fully attested workforce would demand £12 a week, and it is hard to believe there were not also typists and other assistants. Joseph Metcalfe is listed as the assistant secretary. It is not clear whether he was paid, but it would seem likely. It can therefore be reasonably concluded that there must have been a wages bill of over £20 a week. On the usual assumption that every wages bill involves overheads to twice its value, for fuel, lighting, rates, insurance and materials consumed, the regular outgoings must have amounted to approximately £60 a week. Total expenditure on this estimation must have been at least £4,200 a year.

The main source of income was members' subscriptions, which were 3d a week until the end of March and thereafter 4d. During the course of the year 1,715 new members were recruited. To get the simplest calculation, we will assume linear rather than exponential growth. On this basis an average of 34 new members joined each week. The average

1915 number paying 3d a week was 2,156, yielding £50 a week for 39 weeks. Annual income under this head was thus £2,301. If the entrance fees of the new members are included, the figure rises to about £2,600.

There were other sources of income. The two relatively prosperous branches, Sligo and Belfast, made contributions from time to time, but Sligo was inclined to be a bad payer. Branches of less than 500 members were required by rule to remit to the head office all their funds apart from a reserve of £5. Those of over 500 were allowed to keep £10. Sligo with 200 members would have an annual income of about £200. Salary and expenses might absorb about £100 of this, so that approximately £100 might be remitted. The 1915 roll book for Belfast lists only 323 members, but only 29 of these joined in 1915, and moreover, all the names are of men. It seems possible that this is the roll book of the dockers, their numbers being reduced by the lock-out by the Head Line. But on the most optimistic assumptions, Belfast can hardly have contributed more than £400. Perhaps another £100 might come in irregular payments. Against this, however, it would be necessary to set subsidies paid to branches running at a loss, for example Aungier Street, Thomas Street and Inchicore. Perhaps a net £400 might be derived from outside branches.

Social activities at Liberty Hall earned a profit. The most important of these was the game of 'House'. According to one minute, £5 from the 'House' was applied to some urgent purpose. There are other references which suggest a profit of £40 a week, but how consistently this level was maintained is uncertain. Perhaps one could hazard that this category of income might amount to £1,150 a year.

There were a number of rooms in Liberty Hall which had been let to tenants before the lock-out. At the beginning of 1915 most of these were vacant. There were two shops in Eden Quay. One of these was used by the IWWU Co-operative Society: a number of women who had not been re-employed after the lock-out were there engaged in making shirts. They were not good payers. The Citizen Army was charged no rent for its room. Other rooms were occasionally let for jumble sales and other events.

All manner of expedients were tried. One of the shops was

used to sell textiles. It contained a section devoted to literature. In the middle of the year a hairdresser was installed. He barely made his wages. There was a room attached to the Thomas Street premises. A miniature rifle-range was installed there, and for a few weeks it brought in £4 a week. It was then let at £60 a year. Attached to the Emmet Hall, Inchicore, was an apartment and a shop. The apartment was occupied by Michael Mallin of the silkweavers' union; he can only have paid a few shillings a week. The shop was let at 7s a week. It is doubtful if all these assets brought in more than £100 a year. 1915

That activities at Croydon Park did not raise its rent is clear from the decision to relinquish it. It was from time to time let for Gaelic football matches, and on one occasion the union charged £30. The union's own team was not charged. Indeed there was a very liberal policy in encouraging athletics. For a time nine calves were grazed at 6d a week, later a number of horses at 5s. For a time a gardener was employed, and presumably a caretaker.

There were two items of exceptional income, namely £200 compensation for damage done to the Emmet Hall by the military, and a loan of £40 from the Bricklayers' Union. Of the £200 a quarter was paid to the solicitor on account. On quite a favourable computation the total income would thus be about £5,120. That is to say that, leaving aside exceptional items of expenditure, such as arose, for example, from industrial disputes, regular income exceeded regular expenditure by about £1,050. Unfortunately, however, one of the functions of a trade union is to provide exceptional expenditure.

At the first committee meeting of 1915, held on 3 January, Connolly made a special appeal to the members to avoid industrial action that would entail undue expense. The policy of caution and retrenchment was not universally understood. There were expressions of dissatisfaction, and Foran complained of a crusade of antagonism against the leadership.

Wherever the union was strongly entrenched it was practicable to request increases of wages to match the rising cost of living without risking a dispute. The port employers were asked for an advance of 1s a day. It was reported on 24 February that the stevedores had agreed to pay. The coal

1915 firms agreed to pay an increase to the men on the boats, but not to those on the quays. Bairds and McCormicks offered 8d a day, and this was accepted. There was some difficulty in persuading the men working the Silloth boat to accept: they had already gone on strike. In general, as Foran remarked, on the water-front the union had now recovered the bargaining position it had enjoyed before the lock-out.

Before the dockers' claim was settled the committee was reminded that its own employees had pockets too. They discussed a letter from the officials of No. 1 branch asking for a wage increase to meet the rise in the cost of living. Some of the members were favourably inclined; others were as strongly opposed. In the heat of the discussion personalities were raised. Foran persuaded the meeting to await the completion of the negotiations with the employers. Next week he had to report that two delegates, having heard what had been said of them, had offered their resignations. Connolly explained how a similar problem had been solved in Belfast. The general body had agreed to give the officials a wage increase as soon as the men on the quays received theirs. It was in this way that there arose the custom of linking the pay of officials to that of the dockers.

A special committee meeting was held on 3 March, when the pros and cons of the award were again debated. Some thought the staff 'well paid for what they did'. Connolly supported the staff: they were entitled to an increase 'in consideration of the abuse they have to put up with from time to time'.[1] When the general meeting was held on 14 March it was decided to hold a ballot. Only 328 votes were cast: 144 for the increase, 175 against (such are the recorded figures). The officials were nevertheless given an increase of 3s a week by a resolution passed on 14 April. The increased rate of members' contributions came into effect on 3 April.

The union's finances obviously depended on the functioning of its branches. Apart from No. 1 and No. 3, now with difficulty paying its way, the greatest improvement seemed possible at Inchicore. Foran addressed a meeting at the Emmet Hall, and social facilities were improved, for example by accepting a billiard table in lieu of payment by Aungier Street and sending it to the railwaymen. Thanks to the increased income from contributions, Connolly was able to 1915 visit Wexford, Waterford, Cork and Belfast. He reported that the position at Wexford was bad, in Waterford fair, and in Cork improving. He suggested that William Partridge should be appointed travelling organiser to visit country branches and 'work them up'. He then proposed that the union should hold its first National Conference on Whit Sunday. That weekend the Approved Society was to hold its statutory meeting. When Partridge took up his appointment Michael Mallin took over his work at the Emmet Hall.

The General President, Thomas Foran, took the chair at the conference, and Connolly delivered the secretary's report.[2] He explained the financial position, but asked the delegates to keep it to themselves. He spoke of 'extraordinary difficulties'. But he also announced the intention of publishing a new newspaper to replace the *Irish Worker*. He proposed the election of an Executive Committee, to be responsible for the management of the union, but suggested that between its sessions the committee of No. 1 branch should act as a standing committee empowered to do what was necessary. The position of this committee was thus regularised. This was the first time in the history of the union that the rules were implemented. The date was 24 May 1915, and the union had thus been in existence and its rules registered for just over six years.

Delegates reported the position in their areas. James Flanagan explained that his branch had won an increase of 6s a week for the dockers. Their main difficulty was the antagonism of the Head Line. John Lynch tabulated the gains since the establishment of the union in Sligo. It now 'controlled practically the whole work of the town'. His fellow-delegate, however, complained of the difficulty of organising shop assistants and brewery workers. Corish reported that in Wexford the members had 'almost entirely fallen away', Bohan that after the lock-out many members had lapsed, though he had hopes of getting them back. Denis O'Riordan appealed to the EC to try to reorganise Cork because of its first-class fighting material. P. Crimmins said that the Dún Laoire branch was small but solvent.

An Executive Committee was then elected on the basis of one representative each from Munster and Connacht,

1915 two from Ulster and four from Leinster. Denis O'Riordan represented Munster, John Lynch Connacht, Michael Cunningham, John Bohan, John O'Neill and Patrick Stafford Leinster. But Ulster seems to have had only one representative, James Flanagan. It seems possible that in this instance the rules were misinterpreted. The general officers served *ex officio*.

After the meeting Connolly took the delegates into the basement of Liberty Hall to show them the Furnival machine on which he intended to print his newspaper. It had been purchased in February, and its arrival had not passed unchallenged. One of the members had objected to the committee that he feared it might be used for the production of illegal literature. It was indeed used to print the Proclamation of the Irish Republic in 1916, though this, of course, was unforeseen. Connolly was astutely associating the highest authority of the union with his publishing venture.

On 26 May the committee received a report that the conference of the Approved Society had not gone smoothly. A sub-committee was set up to investigate the financial relations between the society and the union. In the sequel the registrar decided to withdraw approval and transfer the members of the AOH. Connolly persuaded him instead to put in a manager.

The communication from the National Health Commissioner has not been preserved. But the report delivered on 24 March 1914 had contained the passage 'I attended personally at the registered office and found no person in charge of the books. The accountant was stated to be in Liverpool for the purpose of recruiting his health.' After describing the registers as 'quite unfit for any kind of audit' he added with a touch of wry humour: 'Payment of benefits. The officials in charge of this department appear to be very careful and energetic.' It is clear that P. T. Daly had not been able to restore order.

It was decided to vacate Croydon Park, and the landlord was given six months' notice.

* * *

The *Workers' Republic* was first published on 24 May.

James Connolly was the editor. It consisted of two folios 1915
of foolscap with three 14-em columns to the page. Some of the display fonts looked a trifle old-fashioned, but the total effect was pleasing enough. Since movable type was used, printers must have been employed. But even if the wage bill amounted to £5 a week, the sale of 1,200 copies at 1d each would be sufficient to provide it. The paper was not a charge on union funds. Indeed its nominal proprietors were the Irish Workers' Co-operative Society, whose committee included William O'Brien and Countess Markiewicz and met from time to time at the Trades Hall. It is possible that it was deliberately kept separate from the union because of the Defence of the Realm Regulations. The title was decorated by a scroll on which was inscribed in Irish the famous aphorism of Camille Desmoulins, 'The great only appear great because we are on our knees – let us rise.' The last word 'Éirdhmis' appeared centrally in large letters. An English translation was printed below.

The second *Workers' Republic* was the product of Connolly's most advanced experience. A man of genius is never fully grown. His last writings show Connolly assimilating the lessons of an unprecedented world crisis and developing entirely novel and original concepts. He formulated fresh policies based on this understanding. His prose, always trenchant, acquired a new depth and precision. Among supporting writers the most prolific was Cathal O'Shannon, who provided the 'Northern Notes' from Belfast. Unfortunately, in accordance with the custom of the day, most contributions were anonymous, but it is possible to identify J. J. Burke, J. J. Hughes, M. J. O'Connor of Tralee, Eamon Lynch of Cork, and Mario Esposito, the Celtic scholar.

The first issue of the paper gave a list of recent wage awards. The stevedores had won 1d a ton on all rates; the deep-sea dockers had won 1s a day. The casual cross-channel men also gained 1s a day, and the constant men 8d. Dublin Dockyard had conceded 3s a week, Ross & Walpole 2s, and General Carriers the same.

But not all employers were easily persuaded. In February the union had written to the Midland Great Western and Dublin South Eastern railway companies asking for wage increases. The employers did not deign to reply. An ultimatum

1915 was sent them on 5 June. Again there was no reply. Strike action followed on the 14th. The companies then informed the press that the men had made no demands but simply walked out. The changed climate of industrial relations was shown by the fact that there were no blacklegs available. Men belonging to other unions refused to do the strikers' work. Had the union possessed greater financial resources, its victory would have been certain. As it was, the strike imposed a severe strain. In the second week of July all branches were requested to send to Liberty Hall their total cash resources. All but Aungier Street complied. But on 21 July Connolly told the committee that he was unable to pay strike benefit and recommended a return to work. Thanks to a loan of £40 from the Bricklayers, the struggle lasted a further week. But thereafter the men returned to work, and some of them left the union.

It was doubtless the exigencies of this struggle that led to the rupture with Delia Larkin. During the prosperous days of 1911-13 the IWWU had been allowed the use of a large front room and had not been pressed to pay for it. After the lock-out she was on the payroll of the Approved Society, but devoted herself mainly to the IWWU and the co-operative shirt factory. Obviously, in view of the inquiry into the affairs of the Insurance Section, this situation could not continue. In 1918 Larkin wrote to Foran of an occasion when he took Connolly's side against Delia. Possibly it was over this issue. On 28 July the committee was told that Delia Larkin had locked up the shirt factory and left Dublin in a huff.

The women blamed Connolly. Some of them demonstrated both inside and outside Liberty Hall, distributing leaflets and even hurling abuse. On 4 August the branch committee decided that they should be excluded from the building. A meeting for the purpose of reorganising the IWWU took place on 10 August. It was decided to convert it into an affiliated branch of the ITGWU. Larkin had held, for what reason is not clear, that women were not eligible for membership of the union. From this time on, however, women's branches could be affiliated. Helena Molony accepted the secretaryship pending a general meeting. The workroom was reopened and arrangements made for the sale of clothing on the instalment system. Three collectors were appointed, Mrs Shannon, Mary MacMahon, and the famous Rosie Hackett, who worked in the shop. But demonstrations continued for a time, and on 25 August the branch committee transferred its sittings to a more secluded room. Two comments are worth making. Firstly, insufficient study has been made of the character and activities of Delia Larkin and her influence on her brother. That she was a significant personality in her own right is not open to question. When in February 1915 a newspaper took a poll to decide who was the most popular woman in the movement, Delia won without difficulty. But there seems to have been a restless, quirky streak in her character, an inability to see anybody's point of view but her own. Secondly, one should note the danger of appointing politicians to work that demands primarily clerical and administrative expertise. The Approved Society suffered from this disadvantage over many years. 1915

Difficulties did not come singly. The Sligo branch secretary joined the British army, and Connolly decided to go to Sligo to make arrangements for a successor. The No. 3 branch membership fell further, and Bohan had to reduce his staff. In Belfast, following a large fire in the docks, ITGWU men were employed in salvage. When they objected to the low rates they were being paid, soldiers were brought in to do the work for nothing. A number of tramwaymen were dismissed and told to enlist in the army. Connolly visited the city twice in August.

At the beginning of September the manager of the Approved Society announced impending dismissals. Connolly advised Foran to resign before the axe fell. It was decided to bring him on to the union payroll with responsibility for the retail shops and the printing. At this time P. T. Daly had charge of the printing. There is no evidence that he resented his supersession by Foran, but in the light of later events it seems likely. He had been ousted by Connolly; now he was ousted by Foran. Many baseless allegations were made against Daly. He was not highly competent and sometimes took the easiest course. But his essential integrity should not be doubted. His was the tragedy of the second-class mind, bright enough to aspire, too dull to achieve. The action he took at this point was to become a member of the Dublin

1915 Fire Brigade Union, which he then for a time represented on the Dublin Trades Council. He continued to work for the Approved Society and remained a member of the Transport Union.[3]

During September a wages movement began simultaneously in several industries. Electricians who were receiving 9½d an hour struck for 11d. There was a shipping strike which (according to William Martin Murphy) showed the 'reign of terror' under which the unhappy employers were once more groaning. The strike of the Crumlin farm labourers must have depressed him still further. In October the union negotiated a 4d a ton minimum when grabs were introduced to replace hand unloading at the gasworks. The dockers of the 'casual' boats (Cardiff, Silloth, Bristol and the Clyde) won 7s a day overtime (to be discussed later). Notices were sent to the 'constant' lines, asking for the same rate. The employers refused the demand in a joint letter, whereupon the 'casual' firms withdrew their offer. The union decided upon a withdrawal of labour, and a mass meeting was held in Beresford Place in protest against the employers' 'conspiracy'.

Unfortunately the union was in no position to finance a lengthy stoppage. On 14 October Connolly wrote to the Executive of the Dublin Trades Council. He explained the financial position and requested the balance of the 1913-14 Dublin relief fund which had just been remitted. A reference in the minutes indicates that it may have amounted to £200. He added: 'We will scarcely be able to pay our first week's strike pay without your aid, and as the men now out have been the backbone of the union all along, we feel that it would be shameful if they were left in the lurch now.'[4]

The strike was settled on 23 October. The aim of achieving a single rate for the whole port was not successful. The 'casual' firms settled for the terms already agreed. The 'constants' made an advance of 3s, bringing the wage up to 37s a week. The settlement was not accepted with good grace, and the meeting of the Dublin and General men was particularly stormy. Some of the dockers, including a member of the branch committee, denounced Connolly as a 'masters' man'. He was so angry that he left the room, but not before inviting them to find somebody who could get them a better offer. Before long he was asked to return, and the offer was accepted. 1915

The City of Dublin Steampacket Company refused to pay the increase agreed by the other firms. Its dockers, who had not been affected by the strike just ended, ceased work on 8 November. On that day a special meeting of the Dublin Master Carriers received a deputation from the Employers' Federation headed by William Martin Murphy. He urged on them the desirability of a general lock-out of all ITGWU members. He thought the government would then be compelled to resort to strong action against the union. It is interesting that he did not now think that action by the employers alone would be sufficient. He was busy at his old game of provocation. But the tirade in which he made his proposal was heard in silence. When one cautious sceptic inquired what would happen if the boot were on the other foot and the government took strong action against the employers instead, the matter was allowed to drop. The City of Dublin Steampacket Company was nevertheless able to continue its operations with the aid of blacklegs, and the dispute dragged on for many months. The Master Carriers granted an application for an increase of 2s a week on 17 November and agreed that no man should be victimised for refusing to go to the City of Dublin Steampacket Company's quay.

The dispute with the shipping company exerted a constant strain on the union's weak finances. Some small relief was afforded by the vacation of Croydon Park and the sale of the cow, calf and furniture, which fetched £50. The sale of the piano was considered, but the sum offered was too small to be of use. Bohan was asked for £20 for strike pay on 7 December. Collections were made. Trade unionists were asked for donations, and a Christmas draw was undertaken.

Apart from this burdensome dispute, however, the affairs of the union were prospering well enough. Important advances were won for the gas workers in October. On the 17th of that month Connolly visited Tralee, where Partridge had been organising. It was hoped that the local branch of the Workers' Union would transfer, and apparently it did so, but the date is uncertain because the press continued to use the old name. The moving spirit of the Tralee Workers' Union

1915 was Michael J. O'Connor, vice-president of the Trades Council. O'Connor was a solicitor's clerk. He was dismissed from his employment on account of his activities with the Irish Volunteers. Partridge addressed a great open-air protest meeting on 30 October. He went to Dublin and secured the consent of the union to the appointment of O'Connor as its Co. Kerry organiser. O'Connor founded the Fenit branch on 5 December.

The choice of Co. Kerry for vigorous organising activity is interesting in view of the selection of Fenit for the arms landing in 1916. Connolly cannot be assumed to have known of the plans of the 'offensivist' faction within the IRB and the Volunteers. There is evidence that as soon as Roger Casement entered upon his mission to Germany plans for the landing of arms were discussed and Fenit was considered. Both Partridge and M. J. O'Connor were IRB men, but it is doubtful whether they were in the confidence of those planning a rising. There is no doubt that the IRB favoured the organisation of the general workers, and there may have been influences specially favouring the south-west. Their ultimate plan, after Fenit had been finally decided upon, was to use a large body of Volunteers to bring the arms to Tralee and then to dispatch them by rail eastwards into Co. Cork and northwards as far as Athenry. The plan would be facilitated if ITGWU branches were established at the two ports of Fenit and Dingle and in the railway towns of Tralee, Killarney and Listowel. On the other hand, there is no direct evidence that this is what the establishment of the union branches implied.

There were favourable developments in Belfast before the year ended. The ITGWU won its members on the docks a rate of 10½d, to apply when the shorter working day began on 1 November. The carters applied for 4s a week, but accepted 2s. Goods men at Grosvenor Street station came out for a 5s claim. In December brewery workers began to join the union.

The roll book records a membership of 3,659 in the Dublin No. 1 branch at the end of 1915. The members were distributed among about 120 undertakings. The largest concentrations were at Morgan Mooneys (164), the Gas Company (150), the City of Dublin Steampacket Company (150),

the Dublin Dockyard (100) and the Dublin and Wicklow 1915
Manure Company (80). There were 442 casual dockers and 211 casual labourers. That is to say 17.6 per cent of the membership consisted of casual workers. There were also 63 agricultural labourers, 47 builders' labourers, and 133 bottlemakers distributed among three establishments.

On 2 January 1916 the Executive Committee met in 1916
Dublin. Those who attended were Foran, Connolly, Bohan, O'Neill, Flanagan and O'Riordan. Connolly reported on the work of the union, which he contrasted with that of the British unions, who had 'sold themselves body and soul to the capitalist class since this war started'. The ITGWU, he said, had lost one branch, Waterford, and gained three in Kerry: Tralee, Fenit and Dingle.

The difficulty in Waterford had been the inadequacy of the secretary. Foran had visited the city and salvaged the Approved Society. After making some gains the dockers had become complacent and failed to keep up their subscriptions, which had then been allowed to lapse. The branches in best shape seem to have been Dublin No. 1, Dublin No. 3, Belfast and Sligo. Little was happening in Cork, though the branch had held a quarterly meeting on 2 October. The Aungier Street branch had been dissolved in November.

A meeting of the committee of No. 1 branch followed on 5 January. A plan to classify the sections was worked out, and it was proposed to secure representatives on the committee from coal-boat men (4), coal-quay men (4), carters (4), grain bushellers (2), grain carters and breasters (4), general labourers (2), casual dockers (2), chemical workers (2), general carters (4), gas workers (1), engineering section (1), railwaymen (1), market section (1), and corporation workers (1). The general officers and trustees served *ex officio*.

The general meeting was held on 9 January. Nominations for sectional representatives were made and voted upon. Where the number of nominations was insufficient, arrangements were made for sectional meetings. The organisation of the union was thus made tighter and more effective. The basis for its future development was laid in this period when it was directed by Connolly. At all these meetings Connolly stressed the gravity of the financial position.

1916 The general meeting of No. 1 branch re-elected Larkin as General Secretary of the union and Foran as General President. A member named Thomas Healy objected to Foran, and it was disclosed that a small group of comparatively new members had been canvassing for Patrick Stafford. But Stafford declined to stand. The elections were contrary to the rule that provided that the General Secretary should be elected every other December by a ballot vote of the members. A General President and General Treasurer ought to have been elected in the same way. Even more remarkable is the fact that there was no move to re-elect Connolly. Perhaps it was held that since Larkin was re-elected unanimously and unopposed, it was not necessary to re-elect the man he had appointed as his deputy. Dangerous doctrines were beginning to show their horns. Were all Larkin's appointments inviolable until his return?

It may be asked why Connolly, who had secured the election of an Executive according to rule (or at any rate nearly according to rule) and held a general meeting on time, did not insist on the carrying out of the rules regarding the election of officers. There are two possible explanations: firstly, the expense of a ballot; secondly, the expectation that Larkin would soon be back in Ireland. Nobody could foresee that Larkin would not return for seven more years, or that Connolly's authority would be lost within five months.

The dispute with the City of Dublin Steampacket Company dragged on. On 17 January there were suggestions of a return to work on the old terms. Father Brady, Parish Priest of St Laurence O'Toole's, discussed with Connolly the possibility of mediating. The delivery of coal to the offending company was reduced to a minimum. No union member would cart anything for it. NSFU members residing in Dublin refused to work its boats. But at the end of March the company offered them an extra 5s a week, which, on advice from London, they accepted. Connolly commented: 'The scab who carries a union card is the scabbiest of all scabs.'[5] Despite this setback, the ITGWU men refused to go back. Finally, on 17 April, the company agreed to dismiss all scabs, and the men returned to work pending arbitration.

A court decision that the playing of 'House' was illegal

deprived the union of a useful source of revenue, and Foran 1916 sought to compensate for the loss by converting the unused room into a small theatre. The barber's shop was another problem. When Foran asked the manager for his accounts he walked out and was not seen again. Connolly was authorised to engage a new man. The Inchicore branch was still unable to pay its way, and No. 1 was compelled to pay the rent of the Emmet Hall.

Progress continued despite all the difficulties. Organisation was extended among the gas workers. The inside men joined the Transport Union, while the outside men remained with the Gasworkers. A new manager brought from England dismissed office staff and caused dissatisfaction by lengthening the hours of work. The union that had won the eight-hour day was supporting the war now. The clerks and outside men began to turn towards the ITGWU, especially when the English union accepted a massive dilution of labour.

The trickle of spontaneous organisation, which was to become a flood in 1918, began early in 1916. On 11 January members of the Tralee Trades Council set up an ITGWU branch in Killarney. On 19 February Partridge and M. J. O'Connor addressed a meeting in Listowel, where a branch of the union was established. Séamus McGowan, the Sligo journalist, wrote to the *Workers' Republic* of stirrings in Galway. A remarkable event was the holding in the Blacksmith's Hall, Gort, of the first recorded trade union recruiting meeting in South Galway. The *Workers' Republic* was on sale in Gort; possibly Liam Mellows had a hand in it.

Wage increases were won by Sligo dockers. Wexford stocking factory workers struck for higher pay and shorter hours. Tralee Workers' Union demanded a 5s a week increase for all skilled and semi-skilled workers; 2s was conceded after two days. Claims on all the employers in a town were unusual in 1916, though they became common later. Fenit dockers won 6s a week. Sligo seamen and firemen went on strike together with the dockers, and P. T. Daly was sent from Dublin. On 20 February the Cork branch held a special meeting which we can assume was concerned with the wages movement.

From the above account it will be clear that there is no justification whatsoever for Seán O'Casey's claim that

1916 'Connolly had left his union to give all he had to the Citizen Army.'[6] On the contrary, it is he who deserves the main credit for the fact that the union survived and recovered. But at the same time Connolly's involvement with ICA resulted in the union's facing another crisis before it had fully recovered from the first.

8

Connolly and Easter Week

> The tree of liberty must be refreshed from time to time with the blood of patriots and tyrants.
>
> THOMAS JEFFERSON

Connolly's disappearance – agreement with the IRB – planning the Rising – Connolly's thinking – role of the union – the Citizen Army – the Rising – execution

1916

Connolly left Liberty Hall at lunchtime on Wednesday 19 January 1916.[1] He was not seen again until he returned to Countess Marckiewicz's house late on Saturday night. He warned nobody of his departure and would tell nobody where he had been or why he had gone. He was tired. He had 'walked forty miles'. He had 'been in hell'. Too much attention must not be paid to the precise words he used to ward off inquiries: he was addicted to the enigmatic joke. The full implications of this strange episode are even now not entirely clear. People die off. Documentation replaces memory and is no more reliable. An uneasy consensus arises, which may be little more than 'a fable agreed on'.

It is generally held that, at a certain point, Patrick Pearse, Eamonn Ceannt and other members of the Irish Republican Brotherhood who were determined on a rising decided to take Connolly into their confidence and invite him to join them. The Supreme Council of the IRB met on Sunday 16 January. According to Denis McCullough, 'That was the meeting at which it was decided that a rising would be held.'[2] According to Leon Ó Broin (condensing or paraphrasing McCullough), 'The next step was to appoint a military committee.... MacDermott and Pearse were accordingly appointed to represent the Supreme Council in the committee, with power to co-opt. The committee took charge of all the arrangements.' In McCullough's own words, 'As far as Tom Clarke and myself were concerned, we abdicated.... The

1916 Supreme Council lost volition and the military committee took over.'[3]

It is a reasonable assumption that an effort to co-opt Connolly was made without delay. That explains his absence. While he was away, rumours flew. Foran, Mallin and O'Brien discussed the matter during Thursday lunch-hour. The Countess talked of starting a putsch by the Citizen Army alone. Fortunately Connolly returned before anything foolish was done, but he agreed in future to carry a whistle with which to summon help if an attempt were made to kidnap him.[4]

To proceed with the rising was the vital policy decision of January 1916. But it has been shown by Diarmuid Lynch[5] and others that considerable preparation had already been made. Lynch claims that a military committee was set up by the Executive of the Supreme Council at his suggestion in May 1915. This was contrary to the constitution of the IRB, but in any case it is clear that by this time the IRB was no monolith. Pressure of events divided it into an offensivist and defensivist wing as it divided the Volunteers.[6] The date of the rising was presumably discussed with Connolly, and Piaras Béaslaí was dispatched to New York, leaving on Sunday 23 January. His task was to inform Clan na Gael.

The *Workers' Republic* was issued on Thursday but bore Saturday's date. The issue of 22 January carried a letter from The O'Rahilly which suggested a conference between representatives of the Citizen Army and Volunteers. Whether this relates to the other conference in any way is not clear. But the issue of 29 January was explicit; its editorial must have been penned within a day or two of Connolly's return:

> The issue is clear, and we have done our part to clear it. Nothing we can say now can add point to the argument we have put before our readers in the past few months; nor shall we continue to labour the point.
>
> In solemn acceptance of our duty and the great responsibilities attached thereto, we have planted the seed in the hope that ere many of us are much older, it will ripen into action. For the moment and hour of that ripening, that fruitful blessed day of days, we are ready. Will it find you ready too?

Without Connolly's account of what happened, we have, of course, only half the story. What would induce the General Secretary of a functioning trade union, where decisions had to be taken all day, to leave his work without informing his colleagues? One can only guess that he did not expect to be away long. Once at his destination and learning what the business was, he presumably decided to see it through.

That business was planning the rising. But what kind of a rising? Many accounts of the period give an impression that Connolly had a hard mental struggle and had considerably to adjust his ideas. He had for several months been calling for action. What sort of action had he in mind? Where did the union stand in his calculations? To arrive at an estimate of these matters it is necessary to examine his calls for action from the time of the outbreak of war.

* * *

From every article he wrote after 4 August 1914 it is clear that the fact of war dominated Connolly's thinking. He regarded it as a monstrous international crime and denounced it repeatedly. His approach to the war was based on the manifesto of the International Socialist Conference at Stuttgart:

> In case war should break out, it should be their duty to intervene in favour of its speedy termination and with all their powers to utilise the economic and political crisis created by the war to rouse the masses and thereby hasten the downfall of capitalist class rule.

This approach was sloganised in the words 'Turn the imperialist war into a civil war' and given the short title 'revolutionary defeatism'. Connolly continuously stressed the desirability of Britain's defeat. By the same token he would expect German socialists to work for Germany's defeat, though this was not his responsibility and is merely implicit.[7]

His first article after the outbreak of war showed that he regarded the Irish struggle as an independent international factor. He visualised 'armed battling in the streets' for the purpose of preventing food exports.

> Starting thus, Ireland may yet set the torch to a European conflagration that will not burn out until the last throne and the last capitalist bond and debenture will be shrivelled on the funeral pyre of the last war-lord.

This vision of the revolution could not be realised by shutting oneself up in buildings, defending them for a week and thus saving Ireland's soul, though Connolly has been accused of seeking this.[8] At the same time he considered the possibility of defeat:

> For some of us the finish may be on the scaffold, for some in the prison cell, for others more fortunate upon the battlefields of an Ireland in arms for a real republican liberty.[9]

At the end of October 1914 he was still thinking in terms of international revolution, but with less confidence:

> If it requires insurrection in Ireland and through all the British dominions to teach the English working class that they cannot hope to prosper permanently by arresting the industrial development of others, then insurrection must come, and barricades will spring up as readily in our streets as public meetings do today.[10]

But who was to do the fighting? In the same article we read:

> Equally true is it that Ireland cannot rise to Freedom except from the shoulders of a working class knowing its rights and daring to take them.
>
> That class of that character we are creating in Ireland. Wherever then in Ireland flies the banner of the Irish Transport and General Workers' Union there flies also to the heavens the flag of the Irish working class, alert, disciplined, intelligent, determined to be free.[11]

On the subject of the threat of conscription he wrote:

> We of the Irish Transport and General Workers' Union, we of the Citizen Army, have our answer ready. We will resist the Militia Ballot Act, or any form of conscription, and we begin now to prepare our resistance. Upon the Volunteers we urge similar resolves, similar preparations. . . .
>
> The resistance to the Militia Ballot Act must of necessity

> take the form of insurrectionary warfare, if the resisters are determined to fight in Ireland for Ireland, instead of on the continent for England. Such insurrectionary warfare would be conducted upon lines and under conditions for which text books made no provision.
>
> In short it means barricades in the streets, guerrilla warfare in the country.[12]

It seems therefore that Connolly had in mind what might be called a 'proletarian revolution' which would free Ireland and establish some form of socialism at one blow. There were two models for such a revolution, and Connolly was familiar with both. In the article of 8 August 1914 he wrote of those who opposed the Russian revolution of 1905:

> Surely the childish intellects that conceived of the pro-Russian [i.e. pro-Tsar] campaign of nine years ago cannot give us light and leading in any campaign for freedom from from the British allies of Russia today.[13]

A year later he quoted Lissagary's *History of the Commune of 1871*, with which, from his early association with the old communard Meillet, he must have been familiar for years.

The 1905 model was the more appropriate, namely industrial stoppages developing into a political general strike and armed insurrection. That this type of development was still in his mind is evident from his editorial of 22 January 1916, which was probably written on the 18th, the day before he met Pearse. The function of the ITGWU is referred to. Should it come to a trial at arms,

> The greatest civil asset in the hand of the Irish nation for use in the struggle would be the control of Irish docks, shipping, railways and production by Unions that gave sole allegiance to Ireland.[14]

This was in keeping with Connolly's view that the reason for the failure of the socialist parties to prevent the war was 'the divorce between the industrial and political movements of labour'.[15] If the socialists had, for example, called for a railway strike, they would not have been obeyed.

But a new note was sounded at the end of 1915: the calls for militant action become ever more insistent, though they are accompanied by a regretful awareness of impotence:

> Had the misguided people of Ireland not stood so callously by when the forces of economic conscription were endeavouring to destroy the Irish Transport and General Workers' Union in 1913, the Irish trade unionists would now be in a better position to fight the economic conscription of Irish nationalists in 1915.[16]

This note is heard again in Connolly's last editorial before his agreement with the republicans:

> We have succeeded in creating an organisation that will willingly do more for Ireland than any trade union in the world has attempted to do for its national government. Had we not been attacked and betrayed by many of our fervent advanced patriots, had they not been so anxious to destroy us, so willing to applaud even the British Government when it attacked us, had they stood by us and pushed our organisation all over Ireland, it would now be in our power at a word to crumple up and demoralise every offensive move of the enemy against the champions of Irish freedom.[17]

The conscription crisis two years later showed just how right Connolly was.

There is little doubt that as the winter drew on Connolly considered the possibility of attempting a rising with the aid of the Irish Citizen Army alone. R. M. Fox in his history of the ICA states that 'a few weeks before the Rising' he called its members one by one into an upper room at Liberty Hall and asked them whether they were prepared to come out without the Volunteers. Diarmuid Lynch rightly objects that by this time Connolly could have no doubt that the Volunteers would act.[18] In his more recently published memoirs Frank Robbins explains that this incident took place in the autumn of 1915.[19]

By January 1916 Connolly had every reason to be a sadly disappointed man. His hopes had suffered successive blows. The European proletariat had not risen. Ireland refused to act as the trigger. And, when he looked realistically at his union, as he scratched around for strike pay for the City of Dublin Steampacket men, he had to recognise that it was not in a condition to play a major part in the revolution. When the military committee approached him his own plans were in ruins. The workers were simply not ready for the rising that would put an end to thrones, debentures and war-lords. But why not one simply to secure Ireland's independence? What if the process as a whole must be broken into two stages, a national and a social? There was every occasion for the severe 'mental struggle' he later referred to.

From that point onwards Liberty Hall functioned at two levels. The normal work of the union continued above ground. It is strange that while Connolly recognised the degree to which war propaganda, together with 'separation allowances', had demoralised sections of the people, he still hoped for a spontaneous rising once the attempt was begun in Dublin. He told Bulmer Hobson that Ireland was a powder magazine that required only a match.

The two levels interacted from time to time. Connolly adopted a policy of deliberate encouragement of every national sentiment. He organised a lecture on Robert Emmet and wrote an editorial on St Patrick's Day.[20] When, however, he decided to hoist the green flag over Liberty Hall there were murmurs of dissent. The decision was announced in the *Workers' Republic* of 8 April. The branch committee met on the 12th. William Fairtlough, one of the trustees, moved 'that a general meeting of members be called in order to decide whether the flag should be hoisted or not'. He found a seconder in William O'Toole, and the committee was almost equally divided, with Andrew Early and John Farrell very much against the exercise. Foran secured the adjournment of the meeting so that Connolly could be present. He was supported by Michael McCarthy, and his motion was carried.

Next evening there was a fuller attendance. Connolly was present. A number of accounts of what took place have been published. The minutes show that Farrell moved that the general body of members should be consulted before the flag was hoisted. Undoubtedly he was anxious not to give the authorities an excuse to raid the hall as they had already raided the shop attached to it. He was supported by Early. Connolly replied that he

> would not appeal to the general body against the decision of the committee as he had worked harmoniously with them since he took up the position he occupied and he

> would hand in his resignation rather than fall out with them or give it to anyone to say there was disunion in the ranks. Personally he had taken up a position from which he was not going to retreat. Nor did he expect any Irishman would do so.

Of course, Connolly was not saying that every Irishman would take up his position. He was saying that having taken it up himself, he would not retreat from it. But Fairtlough had taken up another position. He moved that the motion stand. Connolly then asked permission to speak privately to Farrell, and this was granted. After the discussion Farrell withdrew his motion, and Fairtlough did not persist. What had Connolly said to Farrell? It has been suggested that he told him of the impending rising and appealed to his patriotism. One would think this a line of action fraught with considerable risk unless Connolly knew Farrell very well indeed. It seems intrinsically more likely that an alternative account is correct and that Connolly connected the raising of the flag with the Citizen Army's intention of vacating its premises in Liberty Hall.

The flag was duly hoisted. It had been intended that the ceremony should be performed by Countess Markiewicz, but when she was found to be unavailable, Connolly invited fourteen-year-old Mollie O'Reilly. The event generated great enthusiasm, though some may have felt misgivings. It is quite clear that if Connolly found it so difficult to secure a majority for a demonstration, there could be no question of the union's taking an official part in an insurrection.

* * *

The story of the Easter Rising belongs properly to general Irish history. Yet without the resources of the union it would have been a very limited effort. The union housed the Citizen Army free of charge. It tolerated, to what degree willingly and wittingly is not certain, a host of activities which were completely illegal in British law: the making of bombs and weapons, storage of ammunition, as well as the preparation of medical facilities. From Tuesday 18 April Liberty Hall became the essential headquarters without which a rising would have been impossible. The Proclamation of the Republic was printed by a union member, Christy Brady, in the basement of the hall. 1916

The General Secretary of the Volunteers was Bulmer Hobson. Neither he nor their titular head, Eoin Mac Néill, was informed of the military committee's plan to use Pearse's position as Director of Organisation to convert manoeuvres called for Sunday 23 April into the real thing. But on Monday 17th Hobson's suspicions became aroused. He and Mac Néill confronted Pearse in the early hours of Tuesday morning, and Pearse admitted that he had committed the Volunteers to an insurrection. The Volunteers' premises were thus no longer available, even after Good Friday, when Hobson was abducted. The use of Liberty Hall was vital.

It was in Liberty Hall that the military committee met on Saturday 22 April. Now that Hobson was out of the way, they were wondering how to deal with Mac Néill. There was hope that he might delay decisive action until it was too late. Then came a fresh disappointment. Two messengers arrived from Kerry, the organiser William Partridge and William Mullens of Tralee.[21] They brought news from Austin Stack that the arms landing had failed and that Casement had been arrested. Then came Mac Néill's final countermand, which was not only sent out by couriers but also inserted in the *Sunday Independent.*. At a further meeting, on Sunday morning, it was decided, Clarke dissenting, to postpone the Rising to the following day.

The military plan of the Rising perished with its leaders. It must be inferred from what happened. There seem to have been two components, linked but capable of being activated separately. First there was a general rising based on arms to be landed at Fenit and distributed east and north as far as Athenry. This presumably had the object of immobilising British troops in the interior while the main effort was made in Dublin. The same significance would attach to planned actions in Cork, Wexford, Meath, Monaghan, etc. The failure of the arms landing resulted in there being only a token general rising.

In the same way the countermand reduced the mobilisation in Dublin to less than a thousand men and women. What might have had a sporting chance was converted into a certain loser. As the Irish forces moved off from Liberty

1916 Hall just before noon on the 24th Connolly whispered to William O'Brien: 'We are going out to be slaughtered.' The insurgents seized the GPO and a string of garrisons around the inner city. The effect of this was to cut off the military from the administrative areas of the city. Connolly was in command at the GPO headquarters, outside which the Proclamation was read. It declared an independent republic that would guarantee equal opportunities for all citizens. The revolution was not to be socialist but democratic. But if successful, it would remove all external obstacles to socialist development.

The British had immediately available 2,500 troops. On Monday afternoon 1,600 more were brought from the Curragh. By the time General Maxwell arrived on the Friday 12,000 were in action. The insurgents fought bravely, but outnumbered to this degree they must inevitably lose one outpost after another until the GPO was isolated. The Citizen Army had about 35 members in the GPO. Its main force was in Stephen's Green, 116 strong, with approximately another 30 holding part of the Castle and surrounding buildings. About 20 more were distributed around a number of less important posts. It is clear from this that there was a mobilisation of about 200. (The 1915 list had contained 340 names, though how many of these were still members in 1916 is, of course, not known.)

Among well-known union members in the Stephen's Green garrison were William Partridge, Michael Mallin (commandant) and Rosie Hackett. The second in command was Countess Markiewicz. Another union member, Seán Connolly, who led the action against the Castle and occupied the guard-room and Upper Castle Yard, lost his life in the attack on surrounding buildings.

The insurgent positions at the Castle had fallen by 3 p.m. on Tuesday, and the Crown forces restored communications along the line of the quays. At the same time Michael Mallin was forced to retire from the Shelbourne Hotel to the College of Surgeons. The process of encirclement and compression went on relentlessly. On Wednesday artillery shelled Liberty Hall from Tara Street, and a Royal Navy yacht, the *Helga*, was brought up the Liffey. By Thursday the GPO was isolated, and Connolly, severely wounded in the leg, was directing the defence from a stretcher. By Friday the fire was so intense that it was impossible to put out the incendiary shells that were falling on the roof. It became necessary to evacuate the building. Finally, when it was seen that further resistance would merely lose more life, Pearse surrendered to General Lowe at about 3 p.m. on Saturday. The order to cease fire was countersigned by Connolly.

Then came the savage vengeance which did more to awaken the people to the purpose of the Rising than the Rising itself. According to F. S. L. Lyons, there were 171 courts martial and 170 convictions; in more than half of these cases the death sentence was imposed, though in all but fifteen cases it was commuted to penal servitude. Several thousand men and women were arrested without charge or trial and deported to prisons and internment camps in Britain. The first executions were those of Tom Clarke, Thomas MacDonagh and Patrick Pearse on 3 May. On the 5th Major John MacBride was shot. There were four executions on the 8th, those of Eamonn Ceannt, Con Colbert, Michael Mallin and Seán Heuston, and one on the 9th, that of Thomas Kent. Then at last the protests began, led by Bernard Shaw, who pointed out that 'nothing in heaven or earth' could prevent the shot Irishmen from joining the great martyrology of Ireland alongside Robert Emmet and the Manchester Martyrs. The last to be executed were Seán MacDermott and James Connolly. He was still unable to walk and had to be carried by stretcher to the place of execution, where he paid the supreme penalty propped in a chair. The day was 12 May.

Among those who lost their lives in the Rising were Peadar Macken, Gaelic enthusiast and member of the Socialist Party of Ireland, and Councillor Richard O'Carroll, leader of the Labour Party in Dublin Corporation. Francis Sheehy-Skeffington died in the course of a bizarre incident when three innocent civilians were brought into Portobello barracks and shot out of hand by a young sprig of a Co. Cork landlord family, Captain J. C. Bowen-Colthurst. Sheehy-Skeffington was one of the most remarkable men of his generation. A member of the SPI, he was largely responsible for securing the publication by Maunsel of Connolly's *Labour in Irish History*. He was a well-known feminist and published a life of Michael Davitt. It was a strange irony that with him perished the man who had accused Larkin of being pro-German, P. J. McIntyre.

9

Resurrection

We shall rise again.
JAMES CONNOLLY

The imperial terror – destruction of Liberty Hall – Johnson from Belfast – re-establishing the union – Sligo ITUC – Houston appointed – wages movement resumes – William O'Brien – agricultural workers – rift with Citizen Army – Derry Congress

1916 During the Rising thousands of pounds' worth of property belonging to workers, artisans and small shopkeepers was wantonly destroyed by the soldiery, some of whom acted the part of licensed ruffians. The government undertook to compensate the wealthy merchants of O'Connell Street but had nothing to say to the lesser folk. Members poured into trade union offices in search of relief. But the prohibition of all meetings made organisation difficult and hazardous.

A month passed before the severity of military rule began to relax. The Trades Council Executive met on 25 May. It was a sad little gathering which stood silently in a vote of condolence to the relatives of Connolly, Peadar Macken and Richard O'Carroll. William O'Brien was in Frongoch internment camp. P. T. Daly, who had not lifted a finger, let alone fired a shot, was imprisoned incommunicado, and the TUC was without its secretary. William Martin Murphy's press, which had openly demanded the execution of Connolly, was exulting in the disintegration of the Labour movement. The meeting elected Thomas Farren acting secretary. Thomas Johnson was present on behalf of the ITUC, and his proposal to hold the Annual Meeting in August rather than at Whitsuntide won ready assent.

During Easter Week there was a strict control of railway transport. But as soon as he could safely do so Joe Metcalfe, the assistant secretary of No. 1 branch, came into Dublin

from his house in Bray to find Liberty Hall badly damaged 1916
and occupied by soldiers. John O'Neill had been arrested. He tracked down Peter Ennis, the caretaker, who had escaped into the next building through a hole in the wall when the bombardment began. Finally he assembled Michael McCarthy, Joseph Kelly, Thomas Mills and James Smyth for a meeting in Abbey Street.

The soldiers evacuated the hall during the first week of June, but they left it uninhabitable. The first meeting of the No. 1 branch committee therefore took place at the Trades Hall, where the union was found emergency accommodation. McCarthy took the chair and Metcalfe recorded the minutes. In addition to those who had met in Abbey Street, there were William Fairtlough, Michael Brohoon and Patrick Stafford. The work of repair was undertaken by the unpretentious men who had manned the engine-room while Larkin and Connolly strode the bridge.

The City Engineer had warned that Liberty Hall was in a dangerous condition. One deputation was sent to consult with him, another to find a builder. The barber, who had reopened the shop on 8 May, was instructed to appear before the committee. Michael Cunningham and Michael Brohoon were appointed delegates to the Trades Council to fill the places of Foran and Partridge, who were in jail. Arrangements were made about office hours and the payment of officials. The union's available cash resources amounted to £100. The estimate for making safe Liberty Hall called for £52 10s. The organisation was being rebuilt from ground level.

A special meeting was held on 6 June. Thomas Johnson, who was in correspondence with Downing Street over the seizure of trade union property, was authorised by resolution to receive that belonging to the ITGWU. He recovered a sackful of documents, but all the records of the union had been sent to a paper mill for pulping. Moreover, the military who occupied Liberty Hall destroyed the entire stock of official stationery. The special meeting was attended by Alderman John Lynch. Sligo was thus the second branch, after Dublin No. 3, to make contact with the reconstituted headquarters. Belfast communicated on the 16th, Cork and Killarney on the 18th, and Fenit ten days later. The delegates were re-engaged on 16 June and resumed the collection of

1916 dues. They were authorised to use their discretion in the matter of lost cards. The Insurance Section was rehoused at 29 Eden Quay. Inquiries were begun regarding union property in Thomas Street and Inchicore.

Alderman Lynch remained in Dublin for the meeting of the National Executive Committee of the ITUC on 10 June, when D. R. Campbell was appointed acting secretary. Arrangements were made for the annual meeting in Sligo. It was decided to press strongly for the release of P. T. Daly, Thomas Foran, Michael J. O'Connor of Tralee, William O'Brien and the other trade union prisoners. The first to be released was Foran, who presided at the Dublin No. 1 branch committee meeting on 18 June. William O'Brien's release was delayed: he refused to sign a form of application on the ground that the authorities had no right to ask humiliating questions of an innocent man against whom no charge had been laid. Such demonstrations of lawlessness by the English ruling class had a strong effect on Irish public opinion. If those who made laws had no respect for them, why should those who were governed by them? But, as George Bernard Shaw remarked, something can be done with a tyrannical government, but nothing with a frightened one.

Liberty Hall was discussed again at a meeting held on 28 June. Peter Ennis brought £32 13s which he had taken out of the safe. He reported that the military had looted his apartment and stolen his wife's wedding ring and a sum of money. The coal porters were now on strike for a wage increase, and other disputes were expected. It was desirable to make some part of the premises usable. It was decided to spend something over £3 on reglazing 31 Eden Quay and to open a temporary office at that address. Letterheads were accordingly printed, and the reoccupation began.

* * *

On 5 July the stevedores offered the coalmen an increase of 2d an hour. On the 11th the casual dockers decided to claim a rate of 8s a day. A meeting of the labourers at Inchicore decided to ask for 5s. The City of Dublin Steam-packet dispute was at arbitration in London, but fresh trouble now flared up with the Burns and Laird companies. Foran

handled a difficult situation with considerable skill. He 1916
agreed to make claims on behalf of any section who wished it, but he stated plainly that the union could not support them if the men decided to strike. Moreover, he insisted on their appointing their own negotiators at the final settlement so that it could not be said that he had climbed down out of weakness. Another ingenious device which was soon put into operation was to levy for union funds the first week's payment of any increase awarded.

At the beginning of July a deputation came to Foran with proposals for re-establishing the Women Workers' Union. It was agreed to call a meeting for this purpose and to allow the women a room in Liberty Hall. A sum of £10 was voted for the purpose of repairing the roof. The meeting took place on 18 July. The secretary, Helena Molony, was reappointed pending her release from jail, her duties being performed for the time being by Miss Eden. The meeting was attended by Miss Perolz (a returned deportee), Miss Ffrench-Mullen (captain in the Stephen's Green command) and Thomas Foran.

One of the principal speakers was Michael Connolly, father of the Seán who had lost his life in the action against Dublin Castle. It is only possible to speculate upon the reason for his presence, but as he played a part in later events, it is of interest to do so. He had been employed by the Port and Docks Board for thirty-five years. On the Friday after Easter he was arrested on suspicion, held in Richmond Barracks until the following Monday, and then deported to Stafford. He was released on 1 June. Next day he reported for work. He was told that he could not be re-employed without the sanction of the Board. The union took up six cases of victimisation and received partial satisfaction in all but Connolly's. It is possible that Connolly, being unemployed, helped with the organisation of the women's meeting, and may have received some small consideration for this.

The most rigid economy was practised. No sum of above 10s could be spent without the sanction of the committee. The Corporation was asked to waive one-half of the rates due on Liberty Hall; the ground rent of £73 10s was allowed to stand over. But when young John Rogan applied for a loan of £2 to start the dramatic society again it was granted at once. The shop stewards' commission, which had been cut to 5 per

1916 cent, was restored to 10 per cent. And the entrance fee was reduced to 1s 4d. By the end of July steps were being taken to re-establish the branch at Inchicore. An unsolicited request came for the setting up of a branch at Athlone. The Dublin *Saturday Post* of 5 August commented on the 'well-marked revival of the Labour movement'.

The success which met Foran's efforts to restore the union was favoured by the economic situation. The steady advance of prices made a succession of wage claims inevitable. The government was encouraging employers to make concessions and bringing in legislation to establish boards empowered to fix minimum wages. The employers themselves had learned a little from the events of Easter Week and were learning more as public opinion swung increasingly behind the insurgents. The *Saturday Post* started a series of somewhat inaccurate and sentimental articles about Connolly on 29 July. At the same time employers did not yield to the new mood where there was no evidence of it. In other words, those who wanted more money must join a trade union.

What Foran brought to the union at this time was common sense and immense energy. This he maintained over a long period until his health began to suffer. He had learned much from working with Connolly. But for some time he found it hard to have his authority accepted. He was not an assertive man. He had none of the egotism of Larkin, nor had he the slightly priggish self-confidence of O'Brien. The first revolt was that of Bohan, who was guilty, as the minute put it, of 'bad conduct in the Head Office in abusing the President'. Bohan disliked the satellite position of his branch and had to be reminded of his duty to send in returns. But on 2 August the committee confirmed unanimously that the General President was in charge of the union, though for a short period he described himself as Acting General Secretary.

* * *

The Irish Trade Union Congress met at Sligo on 7 August. The ITGWU sent delegates from Dublin, Cork, Dún Laoire and Sligo.[1] But while the ITGWU was recovering from a setback, those who had met with no setback had gained ground. The National Union of Dock Labourers had made a fresh invasion of Ireland and sent representatives from its branches in Dundalk, Drogheda, Newry, Galway, Derry and Belfast. If the Irish Women Workers' Union is included, the ITGWU paid £13 2s 0d in affiliation fees compared with £6 1s 8d from the NUDL. But its decline relative to other unions can be measured by the fact that the Carpenters paid £22 17s 4d, the Railwaymen £15 6s 7d, and the Drapers' Assistants £12 10s 0d. The ITGWU had fallen to third place. 1916

Congress faced difficult tactical decisions owing to the policy of the British government following the Rising. On 24 May Lloyd George sent Carson proposals for bringing in Home Rule at once, but excluding the six north-eastern counties for a temporary period. He included in his covering letter a private reassurance that temporary meant permanent. 'We must make it clear', he wrote, 'that after the provisional period Ulster does not, whether she wills it or not, merge with the rest of Ireland.'[2] Unaware of the secret proviso, Redmond's party agreed to the proposal, but public opposition forced them into a retreat. Redmond withdrew his assent on 24 July, but Carson kept his letter of acceptance and used it with effect at a later date.

The Sligo meeting felt itself under the shadow of partition. A deputation from the ITUC had waited on Lloyd George, who told them that the alternative was the continuance of martial law indefinitely. There was a resolution against partition, but the delegate from the Belfast Trades Council urged that the question of Home Rule should be deferred until six months after the end of the war. His amendment gained only three votes. The anti-partition resolution was passed.

But Belfast delegates also differed on the question of the war. Thomas Johnson, whose rescue operations immediately after the Rising had earned him a debt of gratitude, personally supported the Allies. He himself was prepared to maintain the unity of the Irish Labour movement, but he feared forces in the North which would be prepared to disrupt it on the issue of the war.[3] He therefore adopted a 'facing both ways' stance which became the Irish Labour movement's strongest precedent. There was a minute's silence in memory of the dead of Easter Week and the dead in the trenches. To the

1916 end of his days Johnson declared that he had no alternative.

In the light of later developments, and without prejudice to Johnson's sincerely held views, it is still surprising that, at this crucial test of Irish Labour, no voice was raised to avow Connolly's programme of revolutionary opposition to the war, not even that of William O'Brien. There was no condemnation of military rule, no demand for the release of the prisoners. The explanation must be that although public opinion had undoubtedly shifted, it had not yet shifted far enough.

It may be asked whether, if the trumpet had given a less uncertain sound, there would have been disaffiliations. If the Ulster unions had disaffiliated, Congress would have lost something over £12 a year. The cross-channel unions were of greater consequence: they contributed £84 of the total income of £148. These men lacked Connolly's tumultuous imagination. They felt he had failed, just when he was about to be justified. They wanted to play safe. And perhaps at a time when Dublin lay in ruins and the jails were full it was understandable.

* * *

While the ITUC was in progress the Inchicore branch was re-established at the Emmet Hall. Almost at once it dispatched emissaries to the rural workers, and meetings were held at Saggart and Rathcoole. A mass meeting at Crumlin on 17 September was addressed by Bohan, John Redmond and Thomas Kennedy of the Socialist Party of Ireland. By trade a leather trunk maker, Kennedy had met Larkin while working in Scotland. He returned to Dublin in 1909 and joined the Dublin No. 3 branch in 1913. The Crumlin meeting was attended by agricultural labourers, brickmakers, carters and roadside workers, many of whom joined the union.

Discontent was not confined to manual workers. In two years the pound had lost 40 per cent of its value. On 19 September the railway clerks held a meeting at the Banba Hall. Their slogan was a sign of the times: 'We must not starve.'

The thought uppermost in Foran's mind was the restoration of the union's finances. He worked hard to bring as

much of Liberty Hall as was possible back into use. He secured 1916
£350 from an American relief fund. The shirt factory was reopened in the first week of October, and Dr Kathleen Lynn established a surgery. The finances of the Insurance Section were still in grave disarray. Foran's remedy was to reduce the pay of P. T. Daly, who had been released at last, and to put Micheál Ó Maoláin on half pay. This decision caused resentment. So did Foran's opposition to increasing the salaries of the officials. Seldom indeed, except after a dockers' increase, did Foran allow a staff claim to pass on the nod.

Partridge and M. J. O'Connor were still imprisoned. Difficulties in Waterford and Tralee led Foran to search desperately for substitutes. On 10 September he suggested that Tom Johnson might spend a month in the south. But early in October he appointed a Donegal man, Denis Houston, on a permanent basis. It is to be guessed that Johnson, himself unable to oblige, suggested his fellow trades councillor. The urgency with which his services were required was shown when, a few days before he took up his duties, the Tralee branch reported internal disagreements which they were unable to resolve. Foran could only reply that nearly all his officials were out of action. To a second appeal, dated 11 November, he replied that Houston was fully occupied in Cork. He hoped they could hold together until O'Connor was free.

Houston proved a highly effective organiser. On 21 November he held a meeting in Cork City Hall in which he was joined by Alderman Kelleher and Tadhg Barry. Barry had republican connections and greatly admired Connolly. When his less socialistically inclined Sinn Féin friends grew maudlin over the dead martyr he used to remind them that they had little time for the living fighter. On one occasion, he recalled, the SPI had booked the Sinn Féin hall for a meeting. When Connolly arrived it was locked up, and though Barry was present, he had no key. He apologised profusely, but Connolly shrugged the matter off. He was used to it.

The two Trades Councils had amalgamated in October, and the Cork Labour movement entered one of its most successful periods. So vigorous was its condition that Houston was soon able to visit Tralee, solve the members' problems, and leave the town almost completely organised. He went on to

1916 Limerick and Galway, but decided to concentrate on the south.

Throughout the autumn the wages movement in Dublin steadily made way. There was a new dimension in industrial relations, namely government intervention, which, though it restricted the unions, restricted the employers more. Under the Munitions Act it was necessary to give three weeks' notice of a stoppage of work. When such notice was given it was usual to inform the Board of Trade and state that the union was prepared to go to arbitration. Under such conditions it was difficult for an employer to retaliate with dismissals. Thus on 29 September the workers at Dublin Dockyard gave the required three weeks' notice in support of a demand for 1d an hour. On 4 October Foran accepted ¾d. The strike of the gas-meter makers, some of them members of the Gasworkers' Union, began in mid-October, and Jack Jones came over from London. The dispute went to arbitration on 22 October, and a rise was awarded on 14 November. Most trade unionists will recognise what is now a very familiar pattern, but in 1916 it was a novelty. While the number of strikes increased, especially where industries were being organised for the first time, in the old hotbeds of contention something of a regular pattern of wage bargaining began to be established. Carters demanded 30s a week, railway workers an increase of 5s, and claims were made on the shipping companies. Even Inchicore saw-mills paid a negotiated increase. On the other hand, the grave-diggers at Glasnevin were compelled to strike for their demands.

In only one field did Foran fail of success. On 14 September he and Fairtlough applied for compensation for damage to Liberty Hall by Crown forces. The amount claimed came to a total of £1,943, of which £752 was for damage to the structure of the building and the remainder related to its contents, furniture, stationery, press, type and pipe-band instruments. The authorities refused to entertain the claim. Foran crossed to London in November and tried to engage the support of British Labour. In this he had no success. J. S. Middleton, secretary of the Labour Party, received him once; thereafter he sent one of his clerks to meet him. He was not permitted to visit Reading or Aylesbury. He returned with the impression that British Labour was

'rotten'. Not a penny of compensation was ever received from 1916
the British for the destruction of Liberty Hall, though the claim was not abandoned until 1925.

On 16 December a Special Conference was held in the City Hall, Dublin, under the auspices of the Irish Trade Union Congress and Labour Party. Its subject was the 'food crisis', and Thomas MacPartlin in opening the proceedings observed that while the cost of living in Ireland had risen by 80 per cent, the highest wage increase had not been more than 10 per cent. The increase in the cost of living was largely due to exceptional exports of food. Thomas Johnson advocated compulsory tillage and state control of shipping, road and rail transport and mining. Food prices should be controlled. Favourable mention was made of the action of the people of Kenmare who had overturned farmers' carts and let the potatoes 'run about the streets for the people'. The ITGWU was represented by Corish, Foran, Brohoon, Michael Lynch and Houston. From the IWWU came Louie Bennett and Miss Ffrench-Mullen.

There were still 600 prisoners in Frongoch and a number at Reading. They had been held for seven months without charge or trial. With a view to impressing American opinion, all of the untried prisoners were released on 22-23 December. They included Helena Molony and M. J. O'Connor. The Citizen Army, under the title of 'The Connolly/Mallin Social and Athletic Club', had returned to its room in Liberty Hall. It had organised the sending of Christmas hampers to the internees. When these returned, bringing their hampers with them, a great Christmas banquet was arranged. Trestle tables were set up in the old 'drill room' and covered with white paper. The galley was manned for the first time since the lock-out. Then there was dancing in the concert room. On
8 January 1917 the IWWU held a meeting to welcome back 1917
Helena Molony. A general meeting was held on the 11th at which she resumed her post as secretary. Rosie Hackett was appointed clerk.

The recovery of the union must have exceeded Foran's most sanguine hopes. At the Annual Meeting of No. 1 branch held on 21 January he was able to declare: 'Never in the whole history of the union was the organisation in a better position, both numerically and financially.' There may have

1917 been a touch of rhetoric here. It is hard to reconcile the claim with the figures. In the return to the Registrar of Friendly Societies the membership claimed at the beginning of 1917 was 14,500 compared with 26,135 at the beginning of 1913. But that there had been a spectacular recovery was not in doubt.

Foran proposed Larkin's re-election as General Secretary. Michael Connolly seconded, and no vote was needed. Foran himself was re-elected unopposed, Laurence Redmond and John Nolan remained the delegates. But Michael Cunningham and Thomas Healy then came forward with the proposal that P. T. Daly should be elected to the position of Acting General Secretary, previously filled by Connolly. Rogan objected that the rules provided for no such appointment. What, then, had been Connolly's status? Had Larkin as General Secretary exceeded his powers when he appointed somebody to act in his place? And had the committee any right to accept his nominee? The difficulty arose, of course, from Larkin's prolonged absence. What is appropriate for a brief emergency can lead to difficulties when another emergency is piled on top of it. It was decided that Foran should carry on, but he ceased to subscribe himself 'Acting General Secretary', though he was precisely that. John O'Neill, who had been inactive since his release in July 1916, resumed the No. 1 branch secretaryship, with Joe Metcalfe as his assistant.

William O'Brien, who had applied for membership on 30 December 1916, was elected vice-chairman of the branch. The Dublin *Saturday Post* did not distinguish this position from that of the vice-presidency of the union. It was natural enough for them to suppose that if No. 1 branch was empowered to elect two general officers, it must be empowered to elect a third. These trivialities, arising from circumstances which were quite unusual, caused untold trouble in later years. Houston was re-elected organiser. He could give a good account of his work in Cork. He had latterly visited Kilkenny and Athy and had established a new branch through the absorption of a local society at Killorglin. He remained in Dublin for a short spell, on 27 January holding a successful meeting of rural workers at Baldoyle.

The early months of 1917 saw the beginning of the union's drive into rural Ireland. There was widespread discontent. The Land League had emancipated the farmers, but the 'fall of feudalism' had not extended to the labourers. Even in Co. Dublin the 'living-in' system still survived, its worst abuses mitigated by the proximity of the city. Here there had been sporadic trade unionism since 1890. At the other extreme, in Co. Donegal, farm servants still lined up at hiring fairs. This system Houston took for granted and had to be persuaded that it lowered the dignity of labour. Throughout the west, however, the most powerful influence in turning the attention of the rural worker towards the question of wages was the virtual cessation of land division. It is interesting to note how the struggle developed under the different conditions in different parts of Ireland. 1917

The winter of 1917 was the most severe since 1895. There were severe food shortages, and prices were on occasion forced up to intolerable levels. Yet on 21 January when a deputation from the Irish Land and Labour Association waited on the Chief Secretary to press for an agricultural minimum wage they said they would be content with 12s 6d a week. Some labourers were earning only 9s. The position regarding prices may be exemplified from a fair held at Athlone during the first week in February. The farmers had formed a 'ring' to engross supplies of potatoes already reduced by bad weather and excessive exports. They demanded 15s a cwt. On this occasion the police intervened and permitted nobody to charge more than 8s.

A meeting of the Land and Labour Associations of Counties Laois and Carlow was held at Portlaoise on 4 February. Its purpose was to discuss 'reorganisation along trade union lines'. Though rents and allotments were discussed as well as wages, the change of emphasis was shown clearly by the wage level demanded. It was 25s a week, twice the minimum requested by the national organisation.

In Tralee, by contrast, the issue of land division came to the fore. On 10 March, the day after the government announced its decision to set up agricultural wages boards throughout the country, about 130 labourers walked into the town three abreast to protest against the sale of a large farm at Ardfert. They carried a banner inscribed 'The Land for

1917 the Poor' and 'We Will Not Starve'. The most proletarian reaction was in North Cork. About fifty labourers who had joined the 'Churchtown Labour League' struck and conducted 'protest route marches' on St Patrick's Day. They paraded the area between Buttevant and Ráthluirc demanding 'fifteen shillings a week plus diet'.

Early in March the ITGWU engaged the services of Thomas Lawlor, a member of the Progressive Branch of the Tailors' Union, to organise in Co. Dublin. On 11 March, accompanied by Foran and O'Brien, he addressed farm workers at Blanchardstown. Their local leader, G. O'Driscoll, took the chair and explained that they had formed a Land and Labour League in hope of securing increased wages, but had been unsuccessful. He invited Foran to explain the advantages of trade union membership. A Blanchardstown branch was founded that day. It was the first instance of a Land and Labour League coming over to the union. Lawlor held meetings at Rathcoole, Clondalkin, and Baldoyle. He did not confine himself to agricultural workers. He organised the handymen of small engineering shops and forges, among them the 'smiths' helpers' and other poorly paid workers. His work was interrupted by a dispute in his own trade, but resumed in May.

By then the union's sights had been raised. On 21 March Foran proposed to the committee of No. 1 branch the objective of 'getting all the agricultural workers of Ireland organised'. His opinion was that if their standard of living on the farms could be raised sufficiently, they would not wish to come into the towns and compete in the streets. It is of considerable interest that this honest, intelligent, energetic and likable, but essentially 'ordinary' man should be the first to tackle so fundamental a problem of Irish society as the antagonism of town and country. The explanation is probably that for the first time there seemed to be a possibility of solving it in practice. What the genius of Davitt had imagined, the common sense of Foran was to attempt in reality.

* * *

The return of the internees at the end of 1916 led to an

immediate revival of the national movement. Six hundred 1917
men had spent eight months undergoing their political education in a rebel university. They now distributed themselves throughout the country. Count Plunkett, whose son Joseph had been executed, defeated Redmond's candidate in the Roscommon by-election on 3 February 1917. William O'Brien was one of his helpers. There was as yet no general agreement on tactics, and some people were thinking of a fresh insurrection. The Citizen Army had recommenced drilling, thereby causing uneasiness among the union officials. On 4 February when the election result was announced the ICA hoisted a tricolour on the roof of Liberty Hall. The caretaker was instructed to take it down. He did so with some difficulty, since the flagstaff was nailed to scaffolding erected by the contractor repairing the hall, himself the leader of the Citizen Army.

The incident marked the beginning of a period of friction between the union and the ICA. One point of dispute was the drilling. Another was the introduction into concerts at Liberty Hall of items which the authorities would certainly regard as seditious. The sober non-belligerents who controlled the union were determined that the organisation was not going to be shattered for a third time. But the young men were impatient of counsels of caution. The swing of public opinion towards militant separatism had infected them with a touch of republican arrogance. Meetings were held and deputations received over several months.

On 17 March Count Plunkett announced a national convention to be held in Dublin on 19 April. The union was invited to send representatives, but there was some hesitation. It was decided to be guided by the Dublin Trades Council, of which William O'Brien had become secretary on John Simmons's retirement. The Council was in a quandary. It was committed to a pledge-bound Labour Party, but since the Sligo conference there was no clear policy on the question of separation from England. O'Brien was deputed to attend the conference in order to state Labour's case. But Labour had no case so far as the terms of reference of the conference were concerned, for its purpose was to seek a policy for national independence. Inevitably O'Brien found himself drawn into the national movement in a personal cap-

1917 acity. But the official Labour movement stood aloof. In the days that followed it was frequently called upon to back up national policies, but was not itself in a position to formulate them.

The rift with the Citizen Army widened. On 6 May one of its members threatened to assault the caretaker when he tried to bar his way. Yet it was their own action, not that of the ICA, that brought on the No. 1 branch committee what they feared, for on 12 May they closed the hall and draped its frontage with a streamer carrying the words 'James Connolly – murdered May 12th, 1916'.

The police insisted that it be taken down, and it was. But women members of the ICA hastily made another of calico, deployed it on the roof and barricaded all access. This time the police made their own way into the building. Three days later they served on Foran, O'Neill and Ennis a notice issued by a magistrate, Mr Drury, ordering the closure of Liberty Hall, 31 Eden Quay and the passage connecting them. Foran at once tried to secure its withdrawal and consulted the Lord Mayor. He was asked to give an undertaking regarding the Citizen Army. He refused to sign the document produced, but gave a verbal assurance that its terms would be observed. Liberty Hall was therefore neither closed nor open. It was decided that no meetings were to be held in the hall without sanction of the committee, the only exceptions being those of the Socialist Party of Ireland, the Connolly Co-operative, the catering staff and sections discussing their routine business. After a few weeks the authorities seem to have felt reassured that the hall was not going to be used a second time as the centre of an insurrection. On 19 June it was agreed to allow the members of the ICA to use the hall 'as ordinary members of the union'. This probably meant that the committee would allow them to hold a business meeting and wink at their collecting subscriptions. But they would have to do their drilling elsewhere.

Understandably the Citizen Army felt that the officials were not maintaining the tradition of Connolly. On the other hand, they were not circumstanced like Connolly. It could be argued that once the republican forces had merged in 1916 they should not have separated. The first function of the ICA had been to protect locked-out workers from

violence. After a period of uncertainty following its separation 1917
from the union in March 1914 it found itself a role as a spur to the 'offensivist' wing of the war party within the Volunteers. Neither of these purposes were relevant in 1917, certainly not after the Sligo decisions. A political organisation of the working class was, on the other hand, a crying need. It is understandable that the officials favoured the SPI.

* * *

The steadily intensifying political activity proceeded against the background of the continuing wages movement and the growth of the union. Despite the demands of the war, there were men idle on the quays. This was especially true of provincial ports. Ocean-going ships were prohibited from calling at Galway or Limerick, and in April fifty dockers left Limerick for England. Some of the cross-channel services were discontinued, for example that between Wexford and Liverpool. There was at first indignation when the Irish town was deprived of its accustomed imports. But the British government seemed determined to propagate the economic principles of Sinn Féin, and alternative sources in Ireland were quickly found. In Dublin a campaign was conducted against undermanning, and a restaurant was opened at Liberty Hall for the convenience of the men who were unemployed.

Wage claims were made on the shipping companies; however, these seldom led to industrial action. At the end of March Foran went to Belfast, where the stiff-necked Head Line was at last brought to arbitration. The exception was the City of Dublin Steampacket Company, which held to the old tactics of dismissals and consistently refused arbitration. It kept up this stand until October 1917, when it was taken over by the shipping controller. All the dismissed men were offered re-employment. The nightmare of 1915 had become reality in 1917.

Outside Dublin the most rapid advances were made in Sligo and Cork. In February Alderman John Lynch established a branch at Ballisodare, based on the flour mills, and at Maugherow among farm workers employed by the Gore-Booths of Lissadell. Building workers struck in Cork at the beginning of April. Houston preferred a claim on behalf of

1917 the labourers, and on 8 April Foran sent £60 from Dublin. A week later work was resumed pending arbitration by the Director of Munitions. For some reason, possibly because he was not consulted, Foran was dissatisfied. He told his colleagues that Houston was 'getting too independent'. By the beginning of May he had set up six branches in Cork city and had won increases for workers in the coal trade, the grist mills and two shipping lines. Foran seems to have feared that Houston, instead of travelling the country setting up new branches, was building up a local empire in Cork.

He suggested sending Cathal O'Shannon, a native of Randalstown, Co. Antrim, who had worked in the Belfast office since 1912, to replace Houston and free him for travelling. After visiting Cork in company with O'Shannon in the middle of July Foran declared himself completely satisfied. He left O'Shannon as Houston's assistant. O'Shannon was an IRB man and while in Cork lodged with the famous Wallace sisters, whose small shop with its secret exit housed so many revolutionaries 'on the run'. The work expanded so rapidly that in August 1917 Cork No. 1 branch leased 'Connolly Hall', their commodious premises on Camden Quay. As Houston could not be spared for travelling, it was decided to appoint new organisers.

In order to create a favourable atmosphere for his Irish Convention, 'a bone thrown to a snarling dog' designed to impress America, Lloyd George decided to release the sentenced prisoners.[4] The men were rapturously received when they reached Dublin on 18 June. Later on that day Countess Markiewicz was brought from Aylesbury prison by her sister Eva Gore-Booth. She stayed two days with Eva in London. Then Máire Perolz and Helena Molony arrived to accompany her to Dublin. On 19 June a deputation from the IWWU waited on the No. 1 branch committee and secured permission to decorate the hall for the Countess's homecoming. She arrived on 21 June and drove in Dr Kathleen Lynn's car to the skirl of pipes to Liberty Hall. After a brief appearance at one of the windows she left for Rathmines. Foran advanced £5 from union funds to meet her immediate necessities and was given permission by the committee to use his discretion if more were needed.

The Inchicore branch, fresh from another tussle with the

GSWR in which all grades stood together, lent the Emmet Hall for the reception of Herbert (Barney) Mellows, brother of Liam. The union premises had become a local cultural centre where a branch of the Gaelic League was established. But one of the giants was missing from the festivities. Partridge had been released on 20 April, but was too sick to travel. He was in touch with Inchicore in May; but although he passed through Dublin on the 13th, he went straight to his brother's home in Ballaghaderreen, Co. Mayo. The Trades Council invited him to speak in Phoenix Park, but his health would not permit it. He died on 26 July. At the immense funeral gathering on the 28th Foran and John O'Neill represented the union, and Countess Markiewicz delivered the oration. 1917

By the late spring of 1917 it seemed as if a frenzy of organisation had seized the people of Ireland. The Land Leaguers seemed reincarnated in their grandchildren. The rise of Sinn Féin was spectacular. *Nationality*, Griffith's weekly paper, listed 27 new clubs in the issue of 19 May; these were widely distributed through the country, in traditional rebel centres like Tipperary town, Clonmel and Kilmallock, but also in Ballyjamesduff, Ballybay, Westport and Letterkenny. The issue of 4 August reported 38 new affiliations, that of the 11th 58, and that of the 28th no fewer than 104. Monster meetings were addressed by de Valera, Cosgrave, Griffith, Eoin Mac Néill and Count Plunkett.

Although the Labour movement had recovered more quickly than the republican movement, it enjoyed nothing like so rapid an expansion. For one thing, fewer people were eligible for membership. For another, industrial organisation usually had to be fought for. Again, the Sligo disclaimer made the legacy of 1916 available for those with the courage to seize it. Nevertheless the progress of the union was notable. Its main strength was in Dublin and Cork, and round each city it was pushing slowly into the country. For example, the Blarney branch was founded on 23 June. In Sligo there were five branches, necessarily smaller than those around the big cities. There was little progress in Belfast. But Co. Kerry was well organised. The Wexford branch was functioning and had taken the initiative in forming a Trades Council. An important achievement was the re-establishment

1917 of a branch in Waterford, where Houston organised the carters and corporation workmen; it began to function on 7 July. While apparently not yet the official secretary, Tom Dunne of the Tailors' Society seems to have managed its affairs.

The union continued to be involved in expensive disputes, of which the most prolonged was that at the Blanchardstown margarine factory. The carters at Boland's flour mills came out, and there were strikes and a brief lock-out on the quays. Nevertheless the organisation was steadily passing from a debtor to a creditor position. A grant made to the Stonecutters, who were facing difficulties, created so much goodwill that an amalgamation took place at the end of the year. The money that Connolly had borrowed from the Bricklayers was paid back in June 1917.

An incident which aroused great indignation was the attack on John Lynch by Laurence Garvey and his two sons on Sligo quay on 18 July. Garvey, a former stevedore, had fired a ship during the 1913 strike and had been unable to get work thereafter. He and his sons emigrated to Glasgow. In July 1917 he returned for a holiday, but made no bones about his intention to 'do for' Lynch. He received one year's imprisonment, and his sons six months. People contrasted this leniency with the five years awarded to Patrick Higgins who, in the heat of a pitched battle, had thrown a policeman into the Liffey.

* * *

When the Irish Trade Union Congress assembled at Derry on 5 August the ITGWU once again paid the highest sum in affiliation fees, that is to say something more than either the Carpenters or the Railwaymen.[5]

The most hotly debated subject was the action of the National Executive in appointing delegates to the conference to be held at Stockholm for the purpose of considering ways of ending the world conflict. The Irish delegates were to be William O'Brien of the ITGWU and D. R. Campbell of the Belfast Trades Council. The influence of the Transport Union was thrown behind the National Executive, opposition coming for the most part from northern and cross-channel unions. The question then arose of mandating the

delegates. The bone of contention was the Russian call for 1917
'peace with no annexations or indemnities'. It is seldom that Foran recorded his position on a political question. His brief intervention is therefore of great historical interest. According to the report,

> Mr Foran said it was the capitalists who would benefit by indemnities. German socialists, like British socialists, were in a minority as regards the war. Mention had been made of the destruction of the German war machine. Were they going to destroy the German war machine and keep the British one intact? Were the workers of this country afraid to meet the workers of the world? Had they so little confidence in the ability of the workers of the world to evolve machinery for the creation of peace for the world?

James Flanagan, on the other hand, reflected Belfast opinion. 'There will have to be indemnities,' he declared, adding inconsequentially that 'Civilisation will have to be saved.' It is clear that the battle that had been shirked in 1916 now had to be fought. The anti-imperialist stand of 1914 was being reaffirmed, but with an important difference: the question of Irish independence remained shelved. The motion against indemnities was carried by 68 votes to 24. The official report records the following dialogue:

> 'I am glad that there are 24 Britishers in the room,' commented Mr Hall.
>
> 'And some are of military age,' rejoined T. Lawlor.
>
> 'I hope they will refuse to take those delegates in the boats and also refuse them passports,' Hall came back.
>
> 'William O'Brien had the last word: 'I hope they will refuse to take scabs too.'

O'Brien then proposed a resolution condemning the proposed partition of Ireland. It was carried unanimously. The Derry Congress thus saw a continuation of the Sligo compromise, but, thanks to the growth of war-weariness, a marked reapproximation to Connolly's position on the war.

10

The One Big Union

All the world over, I will back the masses against the classes.

WILLIAM EWART GLADSTONE

Wages boards – union band – Limerick – organisation spreads – internal disagreements – conscription crisis – Waterford – migratory workers – Carlow – union census – 'one big union'

1917 By the late summer of 1917 the Transport Union was an accepted fact of life both to the employers of the cities and to the government. In Dublin the only trade association that did not recognise it was that of the Master Carriers. But its intrusion into the smaller towns and the countryside often met stern resistance. There were rural capitalists who were living in a past age.

The Agricultural Wages Board was established in September 1917. The union was invited to appoint a representative and chose Foran. The Board's first duty was to fix minimum wages. According to the rates agreed, male workers over nineteen years of age were to be paid not less than 25s a week in Co. Dublin; the corresponding rate in Kildare and Meath was 22s 6d, and in the remainder of the country 20s; women were to be paid not less than 15s, 12s 6d and 10s in the respective areas. When the regulations came into force it was noted that Co. Dublin farmers generally observed them, but regarded the minimum as a maximum. In more remote parts, as yet untouched by trade unionism, there was a temptation to ignore the tariff and rely on the workers' traditional docility. At the same time there was a new motive for trade union organisation, namely to compel an employer to carry out his legal obligations. The organisation of labour was no longer on the footing of a conspiracy against the state.

The growth of the union and the acceptance of delegated responsibilities placed increased pressure on Foran's time.

The question of assistance became urgent. Efforts had been 1917
made to secure the services of R. J. P. Mortished, a civil servant with Labour and socialist sympathies, but the plan fell through. On 14 September it was finally decided to engage J. J. Hughes as chief clerk. He was to have charge of correspondence and leave Foran free for matters of policy. Hughes was an extremely talented person. The son of a trade union official, he was a strong IRB man and had been out during Easter Week and in prison afterwards. He was an able musician and composed the air to Connolly's 'Watchword of Labour', which he sang for the first time at the SPI Connolly commemoration on 5 June 1918. The reorganisation of the union was largely his work.

On 25 September 1917 Thomas Ashe died on hunger-strike as a result of general ill-treatment and forcible feeding in Mountjoy. At his funeral the ITGWU contingent was so big that many people thought it surpassed even that of the Volunteers. But it suffered from one grave deficiency: the union had no band. The old instruments, destroyed by the Crown forces, had not been replaced. It was with some sense of humiliation that the committee discussed alternatives. On 14 October a decision was reached. An organisation of the importance to which the ITGWU had now attained must have a first-class band. Pipes would not do: it must be of brass and reed. The necessary steps were accordingly taken.

The strike at the Blanchardstown margarine factory dragged on until mid-September, when consideration was given to a proposal to 'black' coal supplies. Foran had consultations with the coal merchants, who told him that if the union resorted to sympathetic action, they would lock out all their men as they had done in 1913. Foran decided that he could not afford to call their bluff. The union had not abandoned the sympathetic strike, but appreciated that it must be, as he said, 'used with discretion'. He advised the strikers to return on the basis of the management's last offer.

Throughout the autumn of 1917 there was a strong influx of members. Practically every section secured wage increases, frequently by negotiation with employers' associations. The 900-strong chemical workers' section was offered 5s a week. A 3s 6d increase was won from the Master Carriers, bringing wages up to 36s 6d, or 15s 6d above the pre-war rate. Negot-

1917 iations with the Fishmongers' and Poulterers' Association ended in agreement. Following an influx of drapers' porters a strike at the Army and Navy stores gained 4s a week for men and 2s for boys. A new branch was established at Swords.

Two new organisers took up their duties on September 3rd. They were M. J. O'Connor of Tralee and Connolly's old lieutenant John Dowling of Cóbh. To O'Connor belongs the credit for establishing the organisation in Limerick. After a few weeks in Kerry he moved north and held a meeting in the city on 30 September. He enjoyed the enthusiastic co-operation of the Trades Council and its secretary, B. J. Dineen. Tradition has it that the first members in Limerick were timber-yard workers. While this may well be so, press reports of the meeting mention only munition workers, of whom all present enrolled.

On the following Sunday O'Connor, P. T. Daly and Patrick Walshe of Limerick Trades Council attempted some organising at Bruff, where the local Trade and Labour organisation was considering amalgamating with the Transport Union. An open-air demonstration in the city was arranged for 11 November, but had to be postponed to the following day owing to torrential rain. In those days bands were used to attract audiences, and the employment of two of them ensured a large attendance. Many laundry workers and employees of Cleeve's toffee factory came into the union and formed the basis of the union's first women's branch.

The ITGWU captured Limerick without firing a shot. The local people had already won the battle in the industrial struggles of the spring. Indeed so strong was the movement in Limerick at this time that the Trades Council published a periodical, *Bottom Dog*, which first appeared on 20 October and ran continuously until the following August. During part of this period it was the only Labour journal published in Ireland.

The influx of women workers into the trade union movement created problems which were solved differently in Dublin and Limerick. James Larkin had maintained that the word 'person' meant 'a male human being'. Women were therefore not eligible for membership of the ITGWU, and for this reason his sister Delia was brought to organise the Irish

Women Workers' Union. When, two months after the setting 1917 up of the Limerick women's branch, attempts were made to organise the laundry-girls of Dublin, they were recruited into the IWWU, although the Transport Union helped them. The meeting held at the Central Hall, Exchequer Street, was addressed by Lawlor and MacPartlin as well as by Mary Hayden of the Gaelic League. The union had branches in Dublin, Bray and Cork. Louie Bennett, who, according to her biographer R. M. Fox, was active in the laundry-girls' campaign, was in favour of developing the women's union separately, and from this point the two unions began to drift apart. She had no basis in Limerick, so that in that city the word 'person' had its epicene status restored. The laundry workers were recruited directly into the Transport Union and won a wage increase while the Dublin women were still being organised. The decision to change the word 'person' to 'wage-earner' was made at the Executive meeting of February 1918 and was carried out when the rules were changed at the end of that year.

In December 1917 a fourth Dublin branch, catering for theatrical workers, made its appearance, and just before Christmas the managements of the Royal, Queen's, Tivoli and Abbey received a claim for increases in wages. The branch then organised cinema workers. There were stirrings in Belfast, where 500 dockers struck for a wage increase. Dublin dockers won a further advance of 4s a week.

By the end of 1917, indeed, the union had recovered all the ground lost in 1914 and 1916. The restoration of Liberty Hall was virtually complete, though 31 Eden Quay remained the official address until the end of February 1918. Membership was in excess of 25,000. The load of debt was largely discharged, and the mortgage on the premises was being steadily paid off. The organisation was able as well as willing to sustain such protracted struggles as the Portarlington lock-out, which cost £60 for each of many months. Social activities had been resumed. The band was being reorganised. The charitable work so characteristic of the Larkin era was resumed. In 1917 once more the children of poor parents were given a Christmas dinner. Above all, there was a dynamism which was to carry the organisation throughout the length and breadth of the country.

1917 John Dowling had opened a branch in Tullamore early in October and began organising in the smaller towns. At the end of November he had reached Portarlington and enrolled a number of members in Russell's saw-mill, a large plant exclusively engaged on government contracts. The owners announced that they would not tolerate the ITGWU and locked out all its members. The Board of Trade proved surprisingly unperturbed, though after a time the local Munitions Council went so far as to suggest that the employers had acted illegally.

1918 The lock-out was maintained for eight months with the unintended effect of arousing interest in trade unionism in three counties. On 6 January 1918 a mass demonstration was held in Portarlington market square. A large contingent from the Tullamore branch was present. Michael Whelan took the chair. The meeting was addressed by members of the King's County Land and Labour Association, who declared that the town workers had the support of the agricultural labourers.

On 18 January Dowling was arrested, handcuffed, bound with straps and hustled from the town. He was lodged in Mountjoy and so roughly handled that he required medical attention. The pretext was some technical breach of the defence regulations alleged to have been committed in Co. Kerry. He refused to answer questions and went on hunger-strike. He was released on the 21st and after three days of recuperation in Dublin was back in Portarlington, where he remained until the end of June. During this period he organised branches among the turf workers of Ferbane, and at Clara, Banagher and Edenderry.

During the struggle in Wexford rural workers had shown their solidarity with the townsmen through their own organisations. The same happened at Portarlington, but now these organisations, having been compelled to turn their attention to wages, were considering joining the movement originating in the towns. This process had already taken place in the Dublin area. It was now beginning in the intermediate zone, not dependent on the Dublin market but influenced by it. There were a number of policies available, for example transformation, affiliation or fusion. On 1 January the Meath Labour Union resolved that they would affiliate to the ITUC.

However, between January and April they read of the meetings in Dublin in support of the Russian revolution. They concluded that Irish Labour was heavily infected with socialism – as indeed it was – and on 2 April they reversed their decision, resolving instead to affiliate to a new organisation known as the 'Association of Rural Workers and Workmen's Labour Unions'. The Johnstownbridge branch of the ILLA discussed the establishment of a 'Labour Union' for the whole of Kildare. There was a desire for something intermediate between a land league and a trade union. 1918

Sometimes the decision on affiliation seems to have been determined by nothing more than where the organiser happened to be. On the one day a branch of the ITGWU was set up at Naas and a branch of the ILLA at Rathdowney. The union held meetings at Athy, and during the winter branches were established at Navan, Newbridge and, in the outer Dublin area, Skerries and Balbriggan. These were town branches in agricultural districts. They brought the union out of the city and showed the countrymen how townsmen went about improving their standard of living. At the same time, though the farm worker wished to increase his earnings, the dearest wish of his heart was to work a holding of his own. In this transitional period there was sometimes a strike, at other times a cattle-drive. In an issue of *Liberty* published in 1952 Bill O'Brien, who joined one of the country branches around this period, records that when in 1913 he heard of the strikes in Dublin his boyish mind assimilated them to cattle-drives and he was glad there was still some spunk in Ireland. The way in which other strands of Ireland's revolutionary tradition were being spun into a single thread was shown when Countess Markiewicz visited Portarlington on 20 March to speak at a benefit meeting in aid of the workers at Russells. She was met by the Tullamore and Killenaule pipe bands, and her speech was about Easter Week.

Another protracted struggle took place in Arklow. Workers at Kynoch's explosives factory asked for an organiser in September 1917. Thomas Lawlor visited the town on 6 October. Within a few weeks the branch had 600 members. Application was made for the payment of a 12½ per cent bonus which had been awarded to munitions workers on 15 February 1918. On 22 February Kynochs paid off 700

1918 members of the union and wrote to Foran that they had already informed the local secretary that 'We do not intend under any circumstances to recognise your union.'

Kynochs went so far as to announce their intention of closing the factory. The British government had long been urging them to move their business to England. Their plan was to dismiss their remaining 1,300 workers over a period of weeks. Such an upheaval threatened political consequences. Redmond intervened, and the firm adopted delaying tactics: offers to pay less than the full 12½ per cent, and proposals to replace male by female workers. By this means they staved off the necessity of payment until September 1918. The workforce could then be run down, for the war was drawing to a close.

* * *

Any rapidly growing organisation is liable to suffer internal strains. Some people get on; others are disappointed. As early as September 1917 Foran told the No. 1 branch committee that there was an undercurrent in the organisation which troubled him, and that he intended to call an Executive Committee meeting to discuss it. It must be remembered that even at the beginning of 1918 the union was not administered according to rule. No National Conference had been called since 1915. The general officers were still elected by No. 1 branch, and the EC was not elected by ballot. Foran decided that all irregular procedures must stop. The hostile undercurrent in Dublin No. 1 could not be contained unless the rules were strictly obeyed and the national leadership represented the members as a whole. The size and influence of the organisation demanded that amateurism he replaced by professionalism.

The Annual Meeting of No. 1 branch took place on 13 January. So greatly had the branch grown that it was necessary to hire the Mansion House for the meeting. At the committee meeting of 7 January Foran indicated that he expected opposition. His fear, somewhat exaggerated as it turned out, was that 'it was intended to make a clean sweep of existing officials'.[1] He feared this might be the last committee meeting he presided over. At the same time the factional nature

of the opposition was shown by his efforts to secure the 1918
maximum attendance.

Unfortunately the proceedings of the general meeting were not recorded in any document that has survived. From the report in the *Saturday Post* it appears that the branch did not *elect* general officers or members of the Executive, but proposed names to be included in a ballot, that is to say *made nominations*. Foran was proposed for General President, Larkin for General Secretary, and William Fairtlough, Joseph Metcalfe and Michael Cunningham for trusteeship. They were all accepted unanimously. There were, hosever, four candidates for the branch's one nomination of a member of the Executive. A ballot would therefore have to be held to select one of William O'Brien, Patrick Stafford, Bernard Conway and Michael Brohoon. Foran was unanimously elected branch president, and John O'Neill and Joseph Metcalfe were re-elected unopposed. But the two delegates, Laurence Redmond and John Nolan, were challenged by two would-be delegates, D. Courtney and Michael Connolly.

The ballot took place on 26-28 January. Redmond and Nolan romped home with 823 and 763 votes respectively; Connolly polled 139 and Courtney 77. Joseph Kelly was elected General Treasurer with 638 against Thomas Doyle's 112. Despite the rule, two nominations were made to the EC. Those chosen were O'Brien and Stafford; O'Brien received 548 votes, Stafford 518 and Brohoon 405 (Conway appears to have withdrawn). Connolly and Courtney were already disgruntled, and following their defeat they became more so. These ballots represented the first exchange of shots in a prolonged and damaging internal conflict which dragged on for years before reaching a devastating climax.

Its origins were complex. While Foran's success in rebuilding the union was generally recognised, there were those who looked back nostalgically to the days when they were part of a small family of which Larkin was the father. In 1917, when John Bohan was resisting Foran's leadership and P. T. Daly was neglecting his duties in the Insurance Section, Larkin had backed Foran, told Bohan to 'quit fooling' and Daly to 'do his work'. But when the consequences of the Sligo compromise became apparent Larkin could not understand what had happened. By its inability

1918 to agree on the aim of Irish independence, Labour condemned itself to playing second fiddle, to the Unionists in north-east Ulster and to Sinn Féin in the rest of the country.

Early in 1918 Larkin wrote to Foran complaining that Hannah Sheehy-Skeffington, Patrick McCartan and Nora Connolly had become propagandists for Sinn Féin and were ignoring the contribution of the Labour movement. He was, after three years in exile, out of touch with Irish realities. He had not witnessed the proliferation of Sinn Féin clubs all over the country. He did not understand that this new national movement might retain Griffith's name but was in policy very different. Nor could he understand that while Labour had retained freedom of action in the industrial field, it had tied its hands politically. Larkin might criticise O'Brien for working with Sinn Féin; he failed to realise that if O'Brien did not do so, he was powerless to influence national affairs. Larkin wanted a Labour representative in the USA; indeed he would have liked to have been that representative himself. While Larkin's views were not generally known in detail, sufficient would be known of them to encourage a certain ultra-left current whose representatives believed, or pretended, they were working for Larkin.

On the other hand, it is hard to believe there was not an intrigue against Daly, which he unfortunately met with counter-intrigue, each side making the other worse. Daly and O'Brien had fallen out in September 1917 over the Kilmainham co-option. A vacancy on the City Council had resulted from the death of William Partridge. It was customary to co-opt in place of a deceased member another of his party. On this occasion Sinn Féin insisted on nominating, in opposition to the Labour man, a person named Doyle, who was accepted owing to the support of both Unionists and the UIL. O'Brien was angry with Daly for not pointing out that Kilmainham was a Labour seat and for not referring to Partridge, the Inchicore branch of the union, or the Trades Council. The main part of his indignation should, of course, have been directed against Sinn Féin. It was difficult to see what Daly could do if all the other parties were determined to line up against Labour. But O'Brien was convinced that Daly had not done his best.

Daly was shortly afterwards in hot water with the Trades 1918
Council over another matter. One of the practices which had brought discredit on Dublin municipal politics had been the acceptance of financial 'testimonials' by councillors. These were raised by subscription from the employees of public bodies. The practice had been condemned by the Labour movement, even though from time to time its members succumbed to the temptation to accept an 'unsolicited gift'. At the end of 1917 Daly, who had been critical of others, yielded to temptation himself. He was embarrassed when on 17 December the Trades Council made its position unmistakably clear by passing a resolution condemning the acceptance of testimonials.

But the ugly rumour which swept Dublin in February 1918 must have been started either maliciously or irresponsibly. It was that P. T. Daly was a spy, reporting not to Dublin Castle but direct to London. Rumour is, of course, its own substantiation and is spread even by those who do not believe it. The allegation probably originated in republican or Sinn Féin circles hostile to Labour. In a Dáil Éireann inquiry held in 1919 J. J. Hughes gave evidence that while active in Liberty Hall during the great lock-out he had been 'told' that Daly was a spy. At that time Hughes, though active in the Labour movement, had moved for the most part in IRB circles where Daly was unpopular.

On 9 February Daly applied to No. 1 branch committee for a transfer of his membership from Sligo to Dublin. He had, of course, held membership in Sligo, but it had lapsed. The reality of the matter is that the Sligo branch had reinstated him irregularly by giving him the number in the register that belonged to a deceased soldier called Gordon. Clearly knives were being sharpened for something.

At the Trades Council meeting of 16 February Daly complained that a caucus had met 'not a hundred and fifty miles from Parnell Square' for the purpose of ousting him from the presidency. O'Brien was extremely antagonistic and came near to challenging him to prove his innocence. Micheál Ó Maoláin sprang to Daly's defence in the *Evening Telegraph*. William Richardson attacked Ó Maoláin and referred to a 'recent ballot' which he suggested had been rigged. His suggestion was that the box contained some 200 more voting

1918 papers than were counted. As we have seen, that would not have been sufficient to alter the result, even it it were true (which there is no evidence to suggest). Ó Maoláin denied responsibility for the ballot. Seán O'Casey wrote to declare Daly's friendship with Tom Clarke. Mrs Tom Clarke wrote denying any such thing. The correspondence was still in progress when on 11 March Foran defeated Daly for the presidency of the Trades Council by 46 votes to 40. It would be understandable if Daly suspected the hand of O'Brien, striking at his most dangerous rival in the Labour movement.

Richardson's hare was chased by a 'lover of the Citizen Army', who alleged irregular disqualification of members and cast a slur on 'some ICA gentlemen who went to Fairyhouse and backed Ruddigore'. This was a stroke at Foran. Fairyhouse races were held on Monday 24 April 1916, the day of the Rising – and Foran's passion for racing was well known. Finally, on 8 March the three defeated candidates published a letter in the *Evening Telegraph* protesting against the conduct of the ballot and the election of William O'Brien, the tailor. Other writers enlarged the allegation, 'Ruddigore' adding that whereas the union claimed to possess £3,000, 'gossip says £400 or so'. Gossip! A reputable newspaper printing libellous gossip! Clearly the 'Evening Trolley-wobble' was back to its vomit.

The committee of No. 1 branch summoned the three culprits to appear before them. They refused to come. The committee then suspended them. Under the 1915 rules, whilst the branch could order the suspension, they must invite the Executive Committee to investigate with a view to reinstatement, fine or expulsion. When no investigation followed and the members were in danger of finding themselves out of benefit they engaged E. J. Duggan as their solicitor and threatened to sue. The matter dragged on for a considerable time. Ultimately the union took counsel's opinion. It was that the branch had acted irregularly. They sued the union for reinstatement, and ultimately the court found in their favour and granted the relief sought. The three suspended men were restored to membership, both resented and resenting.

Despite the cross-currents, the work of organising the country went on. The membership almost doubled during the first six months of 1918. Following the absorption of the Stonecutters Thomas Farren was appointed organiser in place of Thomas Lawlor. Foran paid Farren what he received himself, namely £2 10s. The best-paid man in the union was Denis Houston, whose salary was £3 a week. Throughout 1918 Houston was paid more than the General President. 1918

A district committee was established in Cork to co-ordinate the work of the branches, and T. O'Donovan was appointed secretary at the end of January. In April the Cork No. 1 branch won wage increases equivalent to £10,000 a year for tramwaymen, corporation workers and bread-van drivers. Branches sprang up throughout the county. The Cóbh branch was started in January, with Seán O'Connor as secretary. Ráthluirc was organised in February, Youghal and Skibbereen in April, Buttevant and Bishopstown in May.

In March porters, vanmen, carters and general and agricultural labourers were organised at Nenagh. While there was as yet no branch in Kilkenny city, workers in the starch factory at Graiguenamanagh joined the union early in April. There followed a long and bitter dispute at the end of which the branch secretary, Michael O'Doherty, found that no employer in the town was prepared to engage him. He lived to the age of ninety and used to boast that he had outlasted all those who had blacklisted him. In March the Sligo branch organised the timber-yard men and general labourers of Manorhamilton.

In March 1918 the ITGWU acquired a weekly journal. Towards the end of 1917 Thomas Johnson had, with the assistance of colleagues, purchased a defunct magazine, *Irish Opinion.*[2] It was reissued as a 'weekly journal of industrial and political democracy' under the editorship of L. P. Byrne. Its third issue was subtitled *The Irish Labour Journal*, but from 19 January 1918 the subtitle became *The Voice of Labour*. From 30 March it became in effect the official organ of the union under the editorship of Cathal O'Shannon. L. P. Byrne continued to contribute, and W. P. Ryan wrote in Irish about the centenary of Karl Marx.[3]

Additional clerical staff now employed at Liberty Hall

1918 included Ernest Nunan, one of the 'London Brigade' who returned with Collins in 1916, and Eamon O'Brennan. These took up their duties from the beginning of the year. In March W. J. Reilly, a local tailor, became full-time secretary in Sligo, though Lynch remained on the payroll. In April Eamon Hayes was engaged in Cork. There was no expansion in Belfast, where the branch consisted in effect of 500 dockers. In April 1918 they successfully resisted an attempt to lengthen their hours of work which, if implemented, would have resulted in dismissals. Efforts to extend organisation to other sections were unsuccessful.

One result of the general expansion was the down-grading of the committee of Dublin No. 1 branch. The main policy decisions were now made by the regular Executive, whose minutes, though available at the time of a lawsuit in 1924, cannot be traced at present. For a while, however, in virtue of Foran's chairmanship, the committee served as a standing committee to which the President referred matters that arose or claimed his attention between Executive meetings. For example, on 31 March he spoke of the rising discontent among agricultural labourers and local authority employees. The work of organisation was, however, rudely interrupted by a political bombshell.

* * *

On 9 April 1918 the British government announced a Military Service Bill which would enable it to extend conscription to Ireland by Order in Council. The bill passed the Commons on 16 April. The Irish Parliamentary Party, its policy in tatters, left Westminster as a protest and by withdrawing its candidate in the Offaly by-election of the 19th ensured the unopposed return of Dr Patrick McCartan of Sinn Féin.

The Lord Mayor of Dublin invited representatives of organisations opposed to conscription to confer with him at the Mansion House on 18 April. The National Executive of the ITUC sent three delegates, each from a different province: William O'Brien (Dublin), M. J. Egan (Cork) and Thomas Johnson (Belfast). They also called a conference of the Labour movement for the 20th.

At the Lord Mayor's conference Eamon de Valera and 1918
Arthur Griffith represented Sinn Féin, John Dillon and Joseph Devlin the parliamentarians. The famous pledge to resist conscription 'by the most effective means at our disposal' was drafted by de Valera, and it was decided to invite the entire population to sign it on the following Sunday, 21 April. A deputation was sent to Maynooth, where the Catholic bishops were holding their annual meeting, William O'Brien representing Labour. The bishops declared their support.

The Labour conference on Saturday 20 April was attended by 1,500 delegates. Here it was decided to have a general strike on the following Tuesday. The committee of No. 1 branch met on Sunday. While an Executive fund had been established, it seems that the union's main resources were still under the control of the senior branch. Foran arrived late. He gave instructions that £1,000 should be withdrawn from the bank and placed in the hands of some trustworthy person where it would be available for emergency purposes.

The strike of 23 April 1918 was the greatest shut-down in Irish history. Outside the Belfast area all factories closed; trains, ships, trams and hackney carriages were immobilised; shops, offices and even public houses remained shut. Next day the *Irish Times* commented: 'April 23rd will be chiefly remembered as the day on which Irish Labour realised its strength.' As Tom Johnson put it at the Special Conference,

> The Irish Labour movement stands now as the bulwark of free democracy in Western Europe. We are resolved to fight for the freedom of the working classes of Ireland, and we are also fighting for the freedom of the working classes of England.

There was no demonstration in Dublin. Out of an almost superstitious awe of the date 24 April (the anniversary of the Easter Rising) the government had proclaimed all meetings from early April to mid-May, and the ban was not worth breaking. But elsewhere the mood of the people was unmistakably shown. In Limerick all societies affiliated to the Trades Council took part in a procession. M. J. O'Connor spoke on behalf of the ITGWU. Many employers paid wages for the day lost. In Sligo 2,000 people followed bands and

1918 banners to the Town Hall square and listened to the mayor, Alderman John Jinks of the Railway Clerks, and John Lynch of the ITGWU. The stoppage was incomplete in Belfast. Though many Protestant workers were perfectly willing to come out against conscription, their local officials refused to obey the call of the ITUC. But at Ballycastle Orange and Green united, and bands at the demonstration played 'The Boyne Water' and 'A Nation Once Again' alternately. In Belfast Tom Johnson and D. R. Campbell addressed 3,000 people, many of them Protestants, outside the City Hall. When Johnson's London employers heard of his 'disloyalty' they dismissed him from a position he had filled with credit for many years. He was immediately offered employment by the ITUC, but was for the time being seconded to the anti-conscription committee.

The Irish TUC appealed to the British Labour Party and TUC, who responded with a joint statement condemning the proposal to impose conscription on Ireland. Westminster was embarrassed. There was no intention of a reversal of policy, but the expected Order in Council was postponed from week to week as experts discussed means of getting round the opposition of the Irish people. Two great trade unions stood between the government and its objectives, the ITGWU with 40,000 members and the Railwaymen with 20,000.

* * *

As soon as the immediate crisis was over the task of organising the workers of Ireland was resumed. Its immense importance had been demonstrated. By the end of May there were three branches in Limerick. All had won wage increases, for the benefit of workers in munitions, clothing, tanning and furnishing, as well as of builders' labourers and shop porters. Cleeves had agreed to accept a union shop. All labour was recruited through the union. In June the coal porters demanded that the length of the working day should be reduced from eleven to ten hours. This was a move against 'economic conscription'. A similar motive actuated M. J. O'Connor's objection to the midday closing of retail shops.

There were developments in Waterford. A young man

called W. P. Coates, a native of Kinsale, who had been working for the British Socialist Party in Clerkenwell Green, London, returned to Waterford in order to avoid conscription. He was appointed organiser in May. Within a few weeks he had achieved promising results. There were at this time two branches in the city. Tom Dunne was secretary of No. 1. Most of his members were general labourers, but there were also creamery, building, brewery and gas workers among them. Branch No. 2 was composed exclusively of employees at the munitions factory. Coates extended the organisation into the countryside. At a meeting in Mooncoin on 19 May he recruited Michael Holden, who then helped him to set up the large branch at Kilmacow. 1918

The Dungarvan branch had been founded in February. In April all-round increases were won owing to the energy of L. A. Veale, who now became a full-time or 'organising' secretary. He too extended his work into the county, as far east as Portlaw. On 26 May he and Coates were in Kilmacthomas. Pipe bands paraded the streets of the village. A banner inscribed 'Workers, organise and save yourselves' was displayed. Hundreds of farm workers and general labourers, together with operatives from the creamery, flour mill and woollen mill joined the union. The importance of all this activity was not lost on the more experienced employers. On 6 June, following a two-day strike by sawyers, Messrs Pierce of Wexford agreed to recognise the ITGWU unconditionally.

* * *

The most remarkable achievement was the organising of the migratory 'tattie-hokers' of Co. Mayo. In January 1918 Michael Conway went from Belmullet to Geesalia to discuss conditions on the farms of Scotland. Conway appears to have been an official of the Workers' Union, which, he said, had already organised migratory workers in Donegal. A local priest, Father Hugh Durcan, said he would enrol those present as members of the union. It was stated that Conway had already set up an organisation in Achill.

For some reason the Workers' Union did not hold the new recruits, and in April attempts were made in both Erris and

1918 Achill to set up the 'Migratory Labourers' Union'. The leading spirit was Michael Masterson, who seems to have lived in Belmullet. While the Erris organisation was in progress W. J. Reilly of Sligo was engaged in setting up an ITGWU branch in Ballina. This was founded on 10 April. The most probable course of events is that Reilly suggested that, instead of forming a new union, the migratory workers should join the ITGWU and that he reported the situation to Lynch. In those days there was a subsidised steamship service between Sligo and Belmullet, and thanks to this the migratory labourers were attached to the Sligo branch rather than to Ballina, which had in any case only just been formed.

Meetings were held and demands drawn up. Lynch then notified the Scottish Potato Merchants' Association that the workers would not leave Ireland unless these were agreed to. At first the merchants did not take the revolt seriously. But when the harvest was beginning and they had no workers they decided action was necessary: they would go and get them. Accordingly a special train was sent to Achill Sound, then, like Clifden, served by a Congested Districts Board railway. Nobody boarded it, and it had to return empty.

Lynch and Masterson then went to Glasgow to negotiate. The merchants were extremely stubborn, the plain-clothes policemen very attentive. There was little progress. The merchants told the public that the Irishmen were staying at home in order to escape conscription. They appealed to the authorities to supply them with schoolchildren. The Scottish Union of Farm Servants then declared that they would not work with Irishmen who possessed Exemption Certificates. Through the good offices of the Glasgow Trades Council it was agreed to take the dispute to arbitration. The Mayo men hit the Broomielaw, and Masterson remained with them as ITGWU delegate with an office at 28 East Clyde Street. Arbitration was delayed from month to month, and while the men may have won some financial concessions, it is clear that their conditions of work remained the same as before.

* * *

The important Carlow branch was founded on 2 June at

a meeting addressed by William O'Brien. The initiative had been taken by Patrick Gaffney,[4] a young man from Killeshin just over the Laois border. Born in 1895, he attended the Christian Brothers' school until he was eighteen and acquired a good knowledge of Irish. Mr Patrick Bergin suggested in a lecture to the Irish Labour History Society that his national interests may have been encouraged by Michael O'Hanrahan. He was strongly influenced by the events of 1916 and was drawn into the republican movement while serving a five years' apprenticeship at Shackleton's flour mills. According to tradition, he was dismissed just before the end of his apprenticeship for leaving work early, with his foreman's permission, in order to attend a political meeting. 1918

He had committed no industrial breach of discipline. The politics of the meeting must have been highly repugnant to his employer. One of the Shackletons was a member of the Carlow Urban District Council. He was a strong Unionist who would say he was proud to be Irish until 1916, and he was also the only member of the council to vote against the anti-conscription resolution. On Sunday 14 April nearly 10,000 people gathered before the Town Hall, from whose windows priests, councillors and local notabilities addressed them. It seems probable that, from his employer's point of view, Gaffney's real impropriety was in attending this meeting and that the other was merely an excuse. He was a person of outstanding ability and rapidly built up a flourishing branch of which he was chairman.

The Drogheda branch was founded six days after Carlow. The meeting on 8 June was addressed by O'Brien and Farren. Their recruits were almost entirely general labourers.

A new organiser for the Kilkenny/Tipperary area was engaged at the end of June. Daniel Branniff, a Belfast man, had been working in Scotland in 1916 and had crossed to Belfast to join Cathal O'Shannon and his colleagues. He was among those who got as far as Coalisland, where small groups of insurgents from parts of Ulster were assembling with a view to joining Mellows in Connacht.

From now on the ITGWU was regularly absorbing smaller unions. One of the most important of these was the Kilkenny Trade and Labour Union with 1,200 members. William O'Brien and W. P. Coates visited Kilkenny on 7 July, and at

1918 the end of the month amalgamation was agreed upon. Other small societies also came in: the Dublin Mineral Water Operatives, the Castledermot Labour Association and the Kildare Labour Union. Despite a special visit from Ben Tillett, the dockers of Rushbrooke and Passage, Co. Cork, determined to transfer to the ITGWU, but Houston had great difficulty in persuading the English union to recognise the Irish card.

* * *

During the early part of 1918 it became increasingly clear that the union was developing in unforeseen directions and that it was going to be necessary to revise the rules. The first members had been dockers. But apart from those of Dublin, Sligo, New Ross, Ballina, two creeks of the port of Cork and the deep-sea berths in Belfast, the dockers of Ireland were in cross-channel unions. Most of the railwaymen were in the NUR. While many carters, vanmen and porters, as well as railway-shop workers were in the ITGWU, it could still hardly be described as the predominant transport union. It catered for factory workers in a variety of industries, tradesmen and agricultural workers.

There was a corresponding variety of forms of organisation. There were great general branches like Dublin No. 1. But there were also single-industry branches like Inchicore and occupational branches like Dublin No. 4 (theatrical) and the newly established Dublin No. 5 (catering). Waterford No. 2 was based on a single factory, Aghada, on a military base. Around the main population centres there were small branches based either on agriculture or a single local industry, and in some small towns the entire workforce was organised in the union irrespective of occupation. The process of amalgamation added to the diversity.

Foran and O'Brien worked out a system of organisation which was both industrial and occupational and, with a view to applying it, instructed J. J. Hughes to take a census of the membership on 30 June 1918. The members were divided into five categories according to type of work: transport, fuel, food, productive industry, and 'miscellaneous', which in effect meant 'services'.

The census showed that the union consisted of 43,788

members and that they were distributed as follows:

TRANSPORT (docks, railways, tramways, canals, carters and porters)	7,059
FUEL (coal and turf workers)	1,694
FOOD (agriculture, creameries, egg and poultry trade, bacon factories, hatcheries, bakeries, distilleries, corn and flour mills, groceries, hotels and restaurants, breweries and fishing)	16,888
INDUSTRIES (building, timber mills, brickyards, textile mills, laundries, munitions, gas, chemicals and general labourers)	15,339
PUBLIC SERVICES (public board employees, theatres, clerks, shop assistants and trade agents)	2,808

While the classification used was no doubt appropriate for the purpose intended, it is possible to get a clearer picture of the industrial composition of the union by reclassifying so as to remove the confusion between occupation and industry. For this purpose food processing is treated as industry, retailing as a service, and general labourers are distributed over the three non-agricultural categories in proportion to the numbers in these categories. Gas and coal distribution are classified with transport. The picture that then emerges is:

Infrastructure	11,040
Manufacturing industry	17,054
Total industry	28,094
Agriculture	9,634
Services	5,471

The geographical distribution of the membership is of interest. There were 13,960 members in Dublin, including 8,350 in No. 1 branch, 854 at Inchicore, 3,500 in No. 3, 436 in the theatrical branch and 820 in catering. In Cork city there were 4,042 members, including 3,490 in the No. 1

1918 or Connolly Memorial branch. There were 1,718 members in Limerick, of whom 1,000 belonged to the women's branch. There were 1,103 members in Waterford, 1,018 in Wexford, 508 in Sligo town and 500 in Belfast. These 'city' branches contained no agricultural workers, and to their number it is possible to add Drogheda with 350 members. These branches accounted for about three-quarters of the industrial membership.

The following were the remaining branches of over 500 members, the number of agricultural workers being shown in parentheses: Lucan 688 (450), Newbridge 590 (200), Baldoyle 583 (528), Dungarvan 582 (281), Carlow 554 (176), Balbriggan 547 (187), Kilmacthomas 544 (453), Ballina 510 (50) and Tullamore 500 (8). These large branches were almost all of recent foundation and show a tendency towards combining workers of different occupations and industries. The Executive was encouraging development in this direction. On the other hand, it would be natural for the agricultural labourers of Baldoyle to wish to consult those of Lucan or Balbriggan, if only because they were covered by the one Agricultural Wages Board. In the same way the 54 flour-millers of Carlow might wish to consult the 56 at Ballisodare or the 250 in Cork.

The Executive policy statement on organisation appeared on 1 July 1918, that is to say before the results of the census were known. It took the form of a pamphlet under Foran's name entitled *Lines of Progress*. It was broadly syndicalist in tendency and was based to some extent on Connolly's *Axe to the Root*, a product of his IWW period issued in 1908. Foran argued that 'The days of the local society are dead; the day of the craft union is passing; the day of the One Big Union has come.' This should be 'accepted by Irish Labour as the effective instrument it needs to achieve its final emancipation from the bondage of wage-slavery'. The aim was to change the social system.

The ITGWU was to be given the type of organisation that would enable it to become the 'one big union' itself. Any union aiming to fulfil such a purpose must obviously have its headquarters in Ireland. But 'as the problems of the Irish Working Class are merely manifestations in Ireland of the world-wide difficulties confronting the working class in all countries, the Irish union should be federated with the international working-class movement'. 1918

The internal organisation of the 'one big union' (OBU) was to be based on branches covering the whole of a town and the area within about five miles of it. Large towns should have sub-branches. The separate occupations or industries should be organised as sections, and each section should have a representative on the branch committee. There should be provision for the co-ordination of the work of similar sections (for example those engaged in flour-milling or working on the quays) on a national basis. A high degree of local autonomy should be allowed to branches so as to reduce the volume of work at the head office and to avoid the creation of a huge bureaucracy 'dominating, not directing the union'. The system proposed was based on the practice of the Dublin No. 1 branch. The writer drew the final conclusion:

> The OBU opens up a vista of possibilities which no lover of freedom can contemplate without emotion. Here is work for men, constructive and productive work with which all should be proud to associate themselves. With this machine in their possession the workers of Ireland can break all their chains with ease and from the mass rallying cry of political parties turn freedom into a glorious reality.

The form of organisation it was now proposed to apply throughout Ireland quite obviously had plenty to recommend it. On the other hand, perhaps too much was asked of it if the purpose was to change the social system. If an industrial as opposed to a legislative road to social change could be found, it might conceivably overcome the restraints arising from the Sligo compromise. If it could not, then the search for it implied some retreat from the principle of Labour politics. The matter was later put to the test of practice.

By the summer of 1918 the organisational cadre of the ITGWU was virtually complete. There was a strong central fund, and branches were building up local funds. There was a well-staffed head office in a building owned by the union, the mortgage on which could be repaid at any time. Dublin No. 1 branch had acquired a fine new banner on which a portrait

1918 of Connolly was accompanied by his favourite quotation from Desmoulins. There was a functioning Executive working to an understood organisational plan, and a growing body of capable organisers: some, like W. J. Reilly and M. J. O'Connor, members of skilled trades as was the old tradition, others, like Redmond, Metcalfe, O'Neill and Foran himself, men Larkin had recruited from the quays. But in addition, the union was now beginning to recruit young men who were products of the revolutionary age, men such as Cathal O'Shannon, John Dowling, W. P. Coates, Ernest Nunan and Eamon Rooney.

11

The Great Swing to the Left

Most phenomenal of all was the growth of the Irish Transport and General Workers' Union.

J. DUNSMORE CLARKSON

Meetings proscribed — left wins at Waterford — rural workers — a start in Ulster — election policy — armistice day — new rules — new Executive

The First World War was ended not by victory but by mutiny. 1918
Already when the decision was taken to force conscription on the people of Ireland the belligerent governments were in the position of driving unwilling populations to mutual slaughter. In the last three months of full hostilities one million people were killed or wounded. Their objections were registered in a series of strikes, desertions and mutinies on land and sea as governmental authority collapsed and war gave way to revolution. The resistance of the Irish people to conscription was a part of this general process, and this fact was fully realised by the Labour and trade union movement. The continuing spectacular growth of this movement signified a mass awakening of ordinary people to their own interests.

The immediate reaction of the imperial government to the anti-conscription campaign was to get somebody under lock and key. For this purpose the 'German plot' was invented, and on 17 May 1918 the majority of the leaders of Sinn Féin and the Volunteers were arrested, including members of parliament, and seventy-three of them were deported to England. On 15 June thirteen counties were declared 'proclaimed districts', and on the 18th certain districts were proclaimed 'special military areas'. The intention was to flood these areas with Crown forces and bring in conscription county by county. On 4 July Sinn Féin, the Volunteers, Cumann na mBan and the Gaelic League were designated 'dangerous associations' and their meetings were declared illegal. On

1918 the following day Sir Frederick Shaw, the 'competent military authority', prohibited all 'meetings, assemblies or processions' in any public place anywhere in Ireland, making it clear that the ban applied equally to political and non-political gatherings. Six organising meetings of the ITGWU were forbidden under these regulations, one at Dungarvan, another at Carlow. There was some arbitrariness in their application. When M. J. O'Connor tried to hold an organising meeting at Hospital, Co. Limerick, he was told he required a permit. He and B. J. Dineen of the Trades Council immediately drove to Askeaton, where they established a new branch. Union policy was to refuse to apply for permits. After the refusal of the police to allow a union meeting in Drogheda questions were asked in parliament, and the ban was officially restricted to political meetings. By then it was clear that as far as sports were concerned it could not be enforced.

The most important branches set up in July 1918 were at Ballinasloe, Kilmallock and Castlecomer. The Bennetsbridge branch of the Kilkenny Labour Union became a branch of the ITGWU in the middle of the month. There is a local tradition that this was the first branch of the union to be established in Co. Kilkenny. The chronological list, which frequently postdates, records its foundation on 27 August; the *Voice of Labour* gives July. Possibly James Lawlor and Michael Kelly, to whose memory a plaque was unveiled in 1977, were members of the Labour Union before the amalgamation.

The Annual Meeting of the ITUC opened in Waterford on 5 August. Cathal O'Shannon wrote afterwards that the atmosphere was 'electric'. But the printed report gives no record of the debates, 'owing to circumstances beyond the control' of the National Executive. There seem to have been three contentious issues: the policy orientation to 'right' or 'left'; the position of P. T. Daly; and the question of police permits.

The position of Daly can be disposed of first. On 26 May Foran complained to the committee of No. 1 branch that the Insurance Section was in difficulties. He was afraid that if the union did not intervene, it would collapse. Daly was also in trouble with the Trades Council, whose Executive had found that the affairs of the Fire Brigademen's Union were being conducted irregularly. A proposal to suspend it from affiliation was rejected by the full Council on 3 June, Daly making the point that 'certain gentlemen' were trying to prevent him from attending the ITUC. A committee of inquiry reported on 17 July that the affairs of the FBU were not beyond reform. Daly was therefore set for Waterford.[1] 1918

O'Brien had determined to try to remove Daly from the secretaryship of the ITUC. He intended to propose Tom Johnson. When O'Brien found that Daly was canvassing against Johnson on the grounds that he was an Englishman he decided to offer himself for the position, but stipulated that the change must not be made public till the last moment. Before these manoeuvres could be executed O'Brien was in difficulties himself. On 29 July a letter signed by McCarron, Lynch and the London secretary of the Amalgamated Tailors was read to the Trades Council. It stated that O'Brien had been expelled from the union for having attended the committee meetings of an Irish Tailors' Society, which the English union regarded as a breakaway. O'Brien replied, firstly, that he had attended solely in an advisory capacity, and, secondly, that the usual procedure adopted in the event of an expulsion had not been complied with. 'Why did they not go through the usual procedures?' he asked. The reason was obvious enough to O'Brien: 'Well, the Irish Trades Congress is meeting next week.' The Trades Council supported him, and O'Brien was set for Waterford too.

The Congress opened on a contentious note. A demonstration had been called for 4 August. It was discovered that Thomas Dunne, against his own inclinations but on the instructions of the Trades Council, had applied for and accepted a police permit. The majority of the delegates refused to walk. Then there were objections to O'Brien's taking the chair. McCarron claimed that he was not eligible to be a delegate to the Congress. That the 'left' were to sweep all before them was shown by the vote: O'Brien was seated by 159 votes to 38.

The Waterford Congress was visible proof of the vast strides taken by the trade union movement since 1916. There were 233 delegates compared with the 99 who had met at Derry the previous year. Among them were 35 delegates of the ITGWU. The branches represented are not listed in the

1918 report issued, so there are some uncertainties. It is possible that a more centralised method of election had been adopted in conformity with the new professionalism.[2]

Having been elected to the chair, O'Brien delivered a presidential address which was intensely political. He proclaimed James Connolly the inspirer of the Irish Labour movement and commented on the influence his sacrifice had had 'amongst those great men and women who had given us the great Russian revolution'. He condemned the armed intervention of the western powers and the refusal of their governments to allow delegates to travel to a workers' international congress. He spoke of efforts made to interest foreign socialist parties in the Irish struggle against conscription.

Turning to the domestic affairs of the movement, he welcomed the affiliation of the Irish National Teachers' Organisation and the rapid recruitment of agricultural workers into the unions. He spoke favourably of the wages campaign, but insisted that 'the only real and genuine remedy is to be found in the control of industry, in the interest of the community, by the working class'. He wanted the Co-operative Commonwealth, the Workers' Republic. But one thing was missing, a policy by which Ireland could gain independence from England. If anybody noticed the omission, there is no sign of it in the report. It is clear that while O'Brien deeply and sincerely revered Connolly's memory, he did not understand Connolly's thought.

Indeed the direction his mind was taking shows his essentially practical genius. It was revealed in his remarks on the subject of organisation:

> Here now is our opportunity, when we are a growing and expanding movement. Let us get our fully equipped offices, let us man them with the best men and women either money or love can buy; let our officials be highly skilled, well trained, able, and, where necessary, experts and specialists in their particular lines, and let us adopt all the best and most up-to-date methods of conducting business. For the conduct of our movement is, to a certain degree, a great business and we must have it managed on big business lines.

A resolution requesting the International Socialist Bureau to call a conference was proposed by O'Brien and seconded by O'Shannon. McGowan (Drogheda Trades Council), Foran and Coates supported, while the NSFU opposed. It was carried by 193 votes to 6. But J. H. Bennett of the NSFU then informed the delegates that the seamen would refuse to carry anybody to such a conference. 1918

The resolution on real wages was proposed by Foran and seconded by J. J. Hughes. It called for the 'control of industry in the interest of the community by the organised working class'. It is important, for the proper understanding of what happened later, to note that this demand presumed the possibility of the workers' controlling industry while the employers still controlled the state. The resolution was carried unanimously.

A third important resolution was proposed by Tom Johnson. It charged the incoming National Executive with drawing up a revised constitution with a view to political action and convening a Special Congress, to be held not later than 15 November, for the purpose of considering it. This was agreed to without a vote.

O'Brien then proposed that

> This Congress reaffirms its adherence to the principles of freedom, democracy and peace, enunciated by the Russian revolution, the free and absolute self-determination of each and every people, the Irish included, in choosing the sovereignty and form of government under which it shall live, this real self-determination to be by free, equal, adult and secret suffrage, without any military, political or economic pressure from outside, without reservation or restriction imposed by capitalist or imperialist governments and uninfluenced by the power of any force of occupation; calls upon the International and the Socialist and Labour Parties in all the neutral and belligerent countries to make good in the concrete case of Ireland their general promises to this effect; and claims for Poles, Yugoslavs, Serbs, Belgians, Alsatians, Lorrainers, Egyptians, Indians, and other subject peoples no more than for Ireland, and for Ireland no more than for others.

But what if the Socialist and Labour Parties thus appealed

1918 to were unwilling or unable to make good their 'promises'? Was it to be Sinn Féin? In short, there was excellent principle, but no policy. Perhaps this had been half-consciously felt by the draftsman. The clause beginning 'and claims' would mean exactly the same thing if 'less' were substituted for 'more' each time the word occurs. Tom Johnson seconded, and the resolution was carried unanimously.

The issue on which McCarron and his friends concentrated was that of the left-wing tendency of the *Voice of Labour* whose editor, Cathal O'Shannon, described himself as an 'Irish Bolshevik'. Patrick Lynch, the Cork tailor, launched a particularly vigorous attack. The motion in support of the paper was proposed by William O'Brien and seconded by Thomas Boyle, also representing the Dublin Trades Council. The critics fared so badly that they allowed the resolution to pass without dissent. The meeting was equally unanimous in condemning the NSFU for refusing to sign the declaration against conscription.

Congress now turned its attention to such matters as the nationalisation of railways, educational reform, the expected general election, and the wages of agricultural workers, in connection with which Houston proposed a resolution. After discussing a number of practical matters the delegates heard the results of the elections. O'Brien had defeated Daly by 114 votes to 109. The new chairman was Thomas Cassidy, his vice-chairman Thomas Farren, the treasurer Thomas Johnson.[3]

* * *

On 15 August hundreds of political meetings were held with the object of breaking the ban. Many of the speakers were arrested, among them Gaffney, who had read out the Sinn Féin manifesto. Carlow Urban District Council passed a resolution of protest. His simultaneous involvement in trade union and republican activity illustrates an important point. Emigration, which had up to 1914 been removing 30,000 Irish people to the USA every year, had been reduced to a trickle. In 1918, therefore, Ireland held a good 100,000 young men and women, like Gaffney in their early twenties, who but for the war would have been abroad.

They were the prize Lloyd George wished to win for the imperial army. 1918

Many of them were members of the GAA and the Volunteers. Those with a head for politics might belong to Sinn Féin, but for industrial purposes they were organising in the ITGWU. There emerged among them a theory without historical validity, which nevertheless corresponded roughly to the life they were living. It amounted to this: that there existed one 'national movement' with three 'wings': political (Sinn Féin); military (the Volunteers); and industrial (the ITGWU). The union would, of course, have been necessary even if the country had been completely independent. The emergence of the theory was connected with Labour's difficulties and uncertainties in the electoral field. It transcended Sinn Féin in its social aspirations, but had no alternative to its national policy.

Twenty-eight new ITGWU branches were registered in August 1918. Apart from Mallow and Arigna, they were largely agricultural. The main grievance was twofold: the Agricultural Wages Board minimum was too low, and in any case too many of the farmers were not paying it. The first moves to compel them had been taken in Co. Dublin in May, when the union took a Lucan man to court and won £8 in wages arrears. During harvest time the same issue arose at Dungarvan. In this case, since it was not practical to sue a large number of farmers separately, a strike was used to bring them to arbitration, and £78 back pay was awarded. In Carrick-on-Suir direct negotations between the union and the Farmers' Union resulted in a payment of £200. In this case the Farmers' Union brought pressure to bear on its reluctant members. The farmers of Callan refused to negotiate. In the strike which ensued they came near to losing their harvest.

The extent to which farmers could be in contempt of AWB awards was shown in Kiltimagh, Co. Mayo, where a farmer paid a labourer 10s, without food, for a week of 110 hours. Not all strikes were concerned with wages. At Glenfarne near Sligo over 150 men refused to work until their dismissed section secretary was reinstated. In Co. Laois the branches of the union ran a campaign against the provision of drink at harvestings, claiming that the farmers who supplied it made an excessive profit. This constant activity on a variety

1918 of issues continued to attract the surviving Land League organisations. On 15 August the Executive of the South Kildare Labour Union decided to apply for amalgamation with the ITGWU in Athy.

From August 1918 until well into 1919 there was a steady crescendo of industrial protest. On 19 August 18,000 Dublin building workers went on strike. Workers in the shell factory withdrew their labour and were arrested under defence regulations. The Dublin No. 5 branch of the ITGWU called out all hotel and restaurant staff on the 26th. At Baldoyle aerodrome workers downed tools. The carters of Boland's mills, the printers and even the undertakers ceased work. This was in no sense a concerted movement, but its universality made it formidable. The sharp dividing-line between trades and 'unskilled' had disappeared in the common struggle for wages. The whole country was involved, and it is only possible to give examples. Thus there was a bakers' strike in Limerick at the same time as the Cleeves workers won a closed shop and a victory for the principle of recruiting labour through the union. Following this the workers at Cleeves plants in Co. Tipperary came out for the Limerick terms. Flour-millers at Kilrush, Dungarvan gas workers, Foynes timber-yard workers came out for wage demands. Limerick No. 2 branch won improvements for tanning and timber-yard workers. On 12 September Cathal O'Shannon attended arbitration proceedings in London and brought back 12½ per cent for the Kynochs workers. A few days before he arrived the Prime Minister had been compelled to parley with striking policemen. O'Shannon also brought 12½ per cent for the reinforced concrete ship builders of Warrenpoint. But on 28 October there was a general lock-out at Enniscorthy.

M. J. O'Connor resigned his position in September. He accepted an appointment with the Automobile Drivers' Union, but later became an organiser for the Asylum Workers. He was described by members of the Trades Council as a 'brilliant comrade of great ability and tact'. John Dowling was sent to Limerick to replace him. Eamon Rooney was in Drogheda. He was a strong republican and socialist and a friend of Alex Lynn of Belfast. The union continued to attract to its service thoughtful and dedicated members of the younger generation. 1918

In connection with the Arigna strike John Lynch was charged with unlawful assembly as a result of a seditious speech made at Ballyfarnan on 1 September. He called on the miners to refuse to allow non-union men to work with them. He told the court that he was a soldier of the Irish Republic and was sentenced to three months' hard labour, with a further three in default of bail. (The demand for bail was a convenient way of imprisoning a man for his political convictions, for to give it was to deny them.)

As a result of Lynch's imprisonment, the organising of Connacht fell to Councillor W. J. Reilly. He established branches in Ballymote, Carrick-on-Shannon, Westport, Ballygar and Castlebar. In Castlebar the management of the bacon factory locked out all union members on a Monday and invited them back on Wednesday, with all their demands conceded. But in Ballina, where the union had won the concession of a half-day holiday once a week, the members were locked out for refusing to give it up.

In September 1918 Peadar O'Donnell gave up a promising career as a teacher to become a union organiser. After a short spell relieving Reilly in Roscommon and Castlerea he was sent to take charge of all Ulster outside the Belfast and Co. Antrim areas. He founded a branch in Newry on 3 October, thereafter visiting Monaghan, Armagh, Ballyshannon and Derry. Like Rooney, he was a republican and a socialist. But he was in every way remarkable, with a far-reaching intellect and a pithy and paradoxical turn of phrase that made him a captivating speaker, and he had the courage of a lion; he was, moreover, saturated with the earthy culture of the Donegal Gaeltacht where he was born. Like most of the organisers, he did his travelling by bicycle. At Caledon, a village in Co. Tyrone, where he was refused the use of a hall, he climbed a tree and addressed a meeting from one of its branches, descending afterwards to enrol 107 new members.

The loss of the Executive minutes makes it difficult to assess how far the work of organisation was accompanied by reorganisation based on *Lines of Progress*. Branches were encouraged to amalgamate, and some did, for example Turraun and Ferbane in Offaly, Collooney and Riverstown in Sligo, Tramore and Waterford city. But as new branches

1918 were generally established on a local basis, the amalgamation policy does not seem to have gone very far.

In Dublin, on the other hand, radical changes were introduced. On 21 November J. J. Hughes presented the committee of No. 1 branch with a plan of rationalisation. There was much overlapping in the work of No. 1 and No. 3. In their less charitable moments each could accuse the other of poaching on their preserves or, alternatively, accepting their rejects. It was now proposed to hold a conference to decide precisely which categories of workers the two branches would cater for. When this was done there was a substantial interchange of membership.

There was also progress in the co-ordination of sections. Sectional meetings were held by flour-millers and later by textile workers, and national wage policies were formulated.

* * *

If the industrial work of the union was a history of unbroken success, the same could not be said of the political work done in conjunction with other sections of the Labour movement. Friction between O'Brien and Daly continued. Feeling the weakness of his position, Daly had persuaded Delia Larkin to return to Dublin and found her employment in the Insurance Section. This was to run the risk of involving Larkin in his differences with O'Brien, but perhaps this is exactly what Daly was hoping for. From the first the initiative generated ill-will. Neither the Women Workers' Union nor the Irish Clerks' Association wished to have her as a member and she was politely requested not to apply. One of these unions may have relented later, but relations were soured from the start.

This for the moment was a small matter compared with the problems of the political Labour movement. A general election was overdue and could not be long delayed. At the end of September the Irish TUC and Labour Party issued a manifesto. It set forth Labour's ultimate aims, namely 'to recover for the nation complete possession of all the natural physical sources of wealth' and to 'win for the workers of Ireland collectively the ownership and control of the whole produce of their labour'. There was no immediate programme.

capacity for 'evading difficulties'.[5] The discussion was 1918
accompanied by much personal feeling. O'Brien and Foran were for going ahead irrespective of Sinn Féin, but the NUR delegate told them that his members were all for Sinn Féin. MacPartlin was told that his own members would not vote for him. John Lawlor observed plaintively that 'it would clear the air if their men declared definitely whether they would or would not go to Westminster'.

The ITGWU sent out a circular to the effect that the name of the union must not be connected with any but the official Labour candidates. The union stood for self-determination and the Workers' Republic. It was pledged to Labour policy. But as for individual members, they must do as they thought best.

The Special Conference of the Irish TUC and Labour Party opened on 1 November. The start of the proceedings was marked by an act of retribution. Foran on behalf of the ITGWU moved the expulsion from the Congress of the delegates of the NFSU. His complaint was that whereas Congress was 'pledged to the Internationale', the NSFU had refused to carry its secretary Camille Huysmans on ships manned by its members. W. P. Coates seconded. J. H. Bennett explained that their object was to 'boycott the Germans', but the motion was carried by 99 votes to 10.

But before adopting the political constitution, which was to add a new dimension to working-class influence, Congress decided to put it on the long finger. Tom Johnson recommended that Labour should withdraw all candidates. He explained that they had expected to fight a war election. Now they faced a peace election. D. R. Campbell asked somewhat naïvely what was the difference. The manifesto had pledged Labour to abstain from attendance at Westminster during the war, without prejudice to what would be done in peacetime. The protective condition was now swept away. If Labour abstained in peacetime, another reason must be found. What reason could they offer but that of Sinn Féin? And how would that go down in Belfast?

From September onwards there had been private discussions between the ITUC and Sinn Féin. While preferring a position where Labour stood down, Sinn Féin was prepared to concede a small number of constituencies to Labour men

1918 who would undertake to seek re-election if their party changed its policy to one of abstention from Westminster. J. Anthony Gaughan suggests that it was felt that the quid was not worth the quo.[6] On the morning of the Special Conference members of the National Executive Committee discussed the desirability of Labour's taking no part in the election. A majority were in favour of standing aside.[7] William O'Brien and P. T. Daly voted with the majority. Cathal O'Shannon was for taking part.

At the full conference Foran and O'Brien accepted Daly's proposal for Johnson's reasons. The main opposition came from Cathal O'Shannon, who pointed out that in its international relations Labour needed to be represented by independent parliamentarians. He was supported by Denis Houston and W. P. Coates. The union did not seek to impose uniformity on its delegates.

Why did it not do so? The strength of the ITGWU was such that it could probably get its way. On this vitally important question, an issue as divisive and intractable as the issue shelved at Sligo, why had the union no official policy? One possible explanation is that its leadership still regarded the industrial struggle as the primary one, and the political struggle as its reflection. Foran and O'Brien were not imaginative men. O'Shannon and Coates, on the other hand, were possessors of considerable intellectual capacity.[8] They were political as well as industrial leaders. So, indeed, was Johnson, but he took another view. To the pure industrialist it did not matter very much who formed the government; the workers would protect themselves by their industrial strength.

* * *

On 10 November the Executive Committee of the union met in Liberty Hall. There were complaints of lack of attention to Belfast, and it was decided to send Houston there and to replace him in Cork with Thomas O'Donovan. It was agreed to circulate to branches the new rules that had been drafted. The appointment of four new organisers was approved.

Armistice day was 11 November. Separatists celebrated because there was peace; Unionists because the Allies had

won. Drink flowed freely. There was nothing easier than for 1918
the high spirited young officers in mufti to supply it to members of the less disciplined sections of society and set them attacking the premises of national organisations. The Sinn Féin headquarters in Harcourt Street was first selected for attention. After breaking all the windows and trying to set fire to the building the mob descended on Liberty Hall. The Citizen Army manned the roof and kept the rioters at stone-throwing range by firing over their heads. But the windows were smashed and damage done to the value of over £200 before military police arrived, dispersed the mob, and took the young bloods into custody.

The wages campaign continued uninterruptedly. Agricultural workers were indignant when the AWB awarded them only 3s 6d. In a typical week, that ending on 16 November, there were strikes at Perry's mills in Belmont and among the men constructing the Castlecomer railway. Carters in Waterford and Newbridge demanded an extra 10s a week, and Waterford farm workers secured the recognition of the union. At this time the influenza epidemic was raging; its severity can be judged from the fact that at Arigna only one miner was fit for work. Organising work was interrupted by sickness, and Joseph Gaule, secretary of the Arklow branch, died.

A number of new organisers were appointed before the end of the year. Michael Healy worked from Boyle, Co. Roscommon. Francis McCabe, a captain in the Volunteers, was engaged in Dublin. Séamus Dempsey, who had accompanied Daniel Branniff to Coalisland in 1916, worked first in Belfast, then in Cork. Nora Connolly spent a brief spell in Cork before joining the head office clerical staff. She acted as Dublin correspondent of Sylvia Pankhurst's *Workers' Dreadnought*. At the end of 1918 the union had 67,827 members, a head office staff of 13, and 17 organisers working from offices in Dublin, Belfast, Boyle, Cork, Derry, Kilkenny, Limerick, Sligo and Waterford. The more important branches had paid secretaries and office staff.

* * *

The new rules were registered with O'Connell Miley on

1918 20 December. They were accompanied by an entirely new preface which differs from that of 1909 in placing the main emphasis on the establishment of 'one big union', divided into industrial sections, for all the workers of Ireland. This is stated precisely, whereas it was merely implicit in 1909. On the other hand, the ends to be achieved by means of organisation in 'one big union' are stated somewhat loosely. The political demands such as the eight-hour day, full employment, pensions, nationalisation and land division have disappeared. Instead of the 'Industrial Commonwealth', itself vague enough, we read of 'human rights', 'the rule of the people' and, in another passage, 'natural rights'. The abolition of 'wage-slavery and the control of the means of life and government by one section of the community' seems meaty enough at first glance. But what does it mean? What is wage-slavery? — the wages system, or a level of wages so low that the workers' condition amounts to slavery? And who or what is the 'one section' which is here referred to? It is stated that 'There is no measure of freedom to which our union may not aspire.' But nothing is said of the immediate if modest freedoms it aspired to there and then. The preface seems to advocate the building up of a huge organisation on general principles. How is this curious emphasis to be explained? It may well be that it reflects the confusion in the Irish TUC and Labour Party in face of the election, when all that could be agreed upon was a general objective and all candidates were withdrawn when it became necessary to state an immediate policy.

The objects of the union stated in the 1909 rules were the 'raising of the standard of social life of the workers' and the raising of funds for dispute pay, legal assistance and funeral allowances. The three financial provisions were retained, and a fourth added, namely 'Labour representation', but 'the standard of social life' was deleted. Instead a new general object was declared, based on the ITGWU resolution at the Waterford Congress: 'the building up of an organisation for the purpose of securing the democratic control of industry by the working class in the interest of the community'. Two additional immediate objects were inserted: the 'adjustment of the relations between employers and employed' and the 'affiliation of the union to the Labour and Trade Union

movement, locally, nationally and internationally'. The rules 1918
were thus more precise than the preface.

In the body of the rules the status of the General Treasurer was raised. He joined the General President and General Secretary in charge of the affairs of the union. The independent trustees were abolished, and the assets of the union were vested in the Executive. The supporters of P. T. Daly professed to see in these changes an attempt to 'control' Larkin. But the 1912 rules laid down that the General Secretary must 'act under the instructions of the General Executive'. The signatories to the 1918 rules were Thomas Foran, William O'Brien, Thomas Kennedy, J. J. Hughes, Patrick Stafford and Seán O'Connor.

A new executive was elected in February 1919. The new 1919
rules abolished the old representation by provinces. Six electoral districts were designated. These returned eight representatives, who together with the general officers formed the EC. There were three city districts, Dublin No. 1, Dublin No. 3 plus Lucan, and Cork city. The others were mixed. Belfast was grouped with Inchicore, Bray and the remainder of Co. Dublin. A south-eastern district was bounded by the south-east coast from Arklow to Dungarvan and extended as far west as Roscrea and as far north as Portarlington. A western district covered the counties of Cork, Kerry, Limerick, Clare, Mayo, Roscommon and Sligo.

Dublin No. 1 branch returned three members. The rules provided that branches having more than 3,000 members might *nominate* one additional member for each additional 2,000 members; there is no reference to *electing* them. Dublin No. 1 made only two nominations, but returned unopposed a member nominated by Dublin No. 3. The member returned for No. 3 was nominated by Lucan and Leixlip. There is a hint in the 1918 report that Dublin No. 1 required a solatium in view of the loss of its executive functions.

The new EC consisted of Joseph Kelly, Patrick Stafford and Michael McCarthy of Dublin No. 1, Thomas Kennedy of No. 3, William Kenneally of Cork city, Patrick Kelly of Belfast and James Connor of Tullamore. All these were returned unopposed. In the western group Michael Ryan of

1919 Limerick defeated James Hart of Sligo. O'Brien was returned unopposed to the position of General Treasurer. He took up full-time work for the union on 3 February at a salary of £6 a week.

12

Under the Red Flag

Then raise the scarlet banner high.
Within its shade we'll live and die.

JIM CONNELL

Dáil Éireann – state of the union – Belfast engineers – Monaghan asylum – wages movement – Berne – Limerick 'Soviet' – May Day 1919 – dissension irrupts – rural workers.

When the war ended it was as if a dam burst. Constraint was 1919
at an end, and throughout Europe governments faced the threat of drowning in a sea of turbulent popular activity. James Connolly's prophecy came true, though, as always happens, under conditions which the prophet could not visualise. Crowns toppled. Bonds and debentures became as insecure as their owners. In Ireland the unassuageable thirst for a new order expressed itself in the virtual annihilation of the historic party in which two generations had reposed their confidence. Redmondism was no more. When the results of the general election were announced the Irish Parliamentary Party was left with six seats; Sinn Féin won 73; and there were 26 Unionists. The revolutionary assembly, Dáil Éireann, was established on 21 January. It issued a declaration of independence, and a 'Democratic Programme' drawn up in consultation with Labour.

The majority of the Irish people gave explicit or tacit allegiance to the new institution, and for the next two and a half years British government policy was directed towards the destruction of that allegiance. The ensuing struggle affected the whole of Irish society. More than ever the history of the union depended on the history of Ireland. If we look back from this point, we can see that from 1909 to 1913 the ITGWU played a part not radically different from that of any militant trade union in England. Political overtones obtruded increasingly, in 1913, 1916 and 1918,

1919 but still as interruptions of the normal course of trade union work. From the beginning of 1919 politics were dominant and constantly dictated the course of trade union action.

This was the more so from the central position the union now occupied. The report of the 1919 ITUC credits the ITGWU with 47 per cent of its total affiliated membership, 66,000 against 75,500 for all the rest. Its rank and file were also the rank and file of Sinn Féin and the Volunteers, even the IRB. Its General Treasurer was secretary of the Trade Union Congress until he exchanged positions with the treasurer, Tom Johnson. He continued to occupy a commanding position in Congress counsels. He had access to the leadership of the national movement and could avail of Labour's international connections. It was inconceivable that Irish Labour would take any action without reference to the Transport Union.

The financial position had been transformed. By the end of 1918 the mortgage on Liberty Hall had been cleared, together with all other debts of any consequence. There was a credit bank balance of £18,000 after nearly £8,500 had been paid out in dispute pay during the year.[1] The union had effective ownership and control of the weekly *Voice of Labour*, which Cathal O'Shannon edited from Liberty Hall. In addition, it provided the essential cadre of the Socialist Party of Ireland.[2] This had its own connections abroad. But despite the wide area of its participations, the union's main thrust was industrial. It sought to build the structure of workers' control within the framework of the state. But there was an important new factor: there were now two states, each struggling for supremacy over the other. The union's approach was pragmatic: it did business with whichever of the two rivals was in control of the business. There seems to have been little, if any, pressure on the union to withdraw, for example, from wages boards.

The first major industrial action of the year did not involve the union directly. Belfast engineers took unofficial action for a 44-hour week. The strike spread from industry to industry. Gas and electricity undertakings closed down. Tramwaymen, textile workers and finally the building trade ceased work in succession. Obviously there were deep-seated social discontents which Dáil Éireann would have been wise to scrutinise.

With the authority of Liberty Hall, Houston, now working in Belfast with a capable assistant, Charles Ridgway, offered to bring out the deep-sea dockers in sympathy. This was a turning-point. The engineers declined to accept. The ITUC wired support and offered to impose a 1s a week levy on all affiliated members. This might have produced £5,000 a week. This also was declined. Yet when after a month the strike committee were reduced to advising a return to work on the employers' terms, they put the blame for their defeat on the collapse of the movement across the channel, not on their own refusal of help from their fellow-countrymen. There was some criticism of them for this.

One must, of course, bear in mind the intense parochialism of Belfast. When Jack Hedley, using the name Seán O'Hagan, gathered together a small band of Socialist Labour Party supporters and held an open-air meeting in support of the engineers there was a mixed response. Hedley was challenged and compelled to admit that he was 'not an Ulsterman'. Some shouted: 'Let him speak!' Others declared that they wanted 'no Bolshevism or Sinn Féinism in Belfast'. At the same time the hope was cherished in nationalist quarters that possibly Labourism could do what separatism could not do. Sinn Féin held a special Ard-Fheis on 8 April. A Co. Antrim delegate suggested that the Northern workers were better approached from Liberty Hall than from Harcourt Street. It is possible that some such thinking lay behind the decision to transfer Houston to Belfast.

* * *

While the Belfast strike was in progress there were stoppages in many parts of Ireland. Donegal road workers (probably of the National Amalgamated Union of Labour) ceased work in support of a 50 per cent increase. Portlaoise gas workers, who received 36s a week, struck for 48s. Dundalk docks were idle. Platers were on strike in Derry. In Limerick women laundry workers walked out when a 6s wage demand was turned down.

Then the first 'occupation' took place, not in the south but in Ulster.

1919 The staff of Monaghan asylum were organised in the Irish Asylum Workers' Union. As a result of a week's strike in March 1918, they had won an extra 4s. In September they were still demanding payment for the lost week. In January 1919 they consulted Peadar O'Donnell, who devised an ingenious way of securing payment for one week without losing it for another. His method was to seize the asylum, lock out the governor, barricade all entrances and, for good measure, fly the red flag on the roof of the main building. As a hundred RIC men waited outside, the staff and patients jointly managed the hospital under the direction of 'Governor O'Donnell'. After a few days a local priest, Father McNamee, was allowed in with the management's terms, and agreement was reached. It should be noted that this 'occupation', despite the flamboyant gesture with the red flag, had nothing in common with the 'take and hold' of syndicalist theory. It was simply a means of taking industrial action without withdrawing labour. It was warmly applauded in the Belfast strike bulletin.

In the asylum strike O'Donnell was helping out a weaker union. This was part of the ITGWU tradition, and he would readily get permission from Dublin. In the event he established a branch in Monaghan and later in the year spent several months there. He did not confine himself to Catholic workers. In Caledon, where he established a branch in February, a mill-owner dismissed the union members, beat hard and long on the sectarian drum and waited for the Orangemen to attack the pickets. O'Donnell enrolled a citizen police force to protect his pickets, and then astonished the mill-owner by hiring the Orange band for his demonstration. The Derry branch, founded on 8 January, was first composed of cinema workers. O'Donnell staged demonstrations in the middle of performances. For a time he was assisted by his brother Frank, later O/C 1st Northern Division, IRA. Cathal O'Shannon wrote that O'Donnell 'blazed a trail of glory across Ulster'.

* * *

The ITUC called a Special Conference in Dublin on 8 February. Over a hundred delegates attended. It was decided

to press strongly for a shorter working week and such wage 1919
improvements as would provide workers with a standard of living higher than that they had accepted before the war. It was not, however, found possible to find a formula which would fit all industries. Unions were therefore urged to press their existing claims in the light of the principle agreed at the conference. The result was a great variety of industrial actions widely dispersed throughout the country.

Within days of the conference Sligo Trades Council, of which W. J. Reilly was chairman, discussed the woollen mills and carbide factory at Collooney. The mills employed female labour. Each girl had to make sixty yards of tweed in a week, which was sold at 27s 6d a yard. She received 6s 8d, which would hardly provide food.

The organising of the carbide factory was undertaken by the Collooney secretary, Joseph Connolly. On 7 March he was by himself at the Midland Great Western Railway station when he was viciously assaulted by a foreman named Evans. He was badly hurt and unable to work for some time. Evans explained to a magistrate's court that Connolly had been 'interfering with his men'. He was immediately granted bail.

There was also trouble at Boyle, where Reilly had established a branch just before Christmas 1918. He visited the town again on 6 March and requested the traders to increase his members' wages from 26s to 36s a week. He also asked that shops should close at 7 p.m. except on Saturdays. Getting no response, he threatened strike action. He was told that this would be ineffective in a town where there was no sizeable industry: the merchants would man their own shops and the farmers would bring their own carts. A strike nevertheless began on 25 March. In the absence of any large undertaking whose workers could lead the way, a trumpet was sounded in the Crescent, and all work ceased. A serious riot broke out when a trader's son struck a picket. For the first time since 1913 police broke into houses and attacked people in their own homes. At Boyle petty sessions seventy-eight persons were tried under the Conspiracy and Protection of Property Act, 1875.

The strike dragged on for some weeks and finally went to arbitration. The arbitrator was Count Plunkett. He awarded a wage rate of 32s for a nine-hour day, with a weekly half-

1919 holiday. The employers undertook, however, to take back into immediate employment only 20 out of 150 strikers, the remainder not to be refused future work on account of the stoppage. The men were compelled to agree to work with non-union labour. There was much dissatisfaction, and Reilly was blamed.

The wages movement affected all parts of Ireland. The Waterford branch held its AGM at the beginning of March and elected Thomas Dunne secretary. It was agreed to press for a minimum wage of 50s for a 44-hour week. Dublin butchers, Clonmel carters, part-time teachers in Cork city, labourers in Fermoy and Tubbercurry, all took action and gained concessions during March.

* * *

On 12 March Cathal O'Shannon and Thomas Johnson returned to Ireland from an international assignment. The Irish TUC had decided to be represented at the Socialist Conference in Berne, and of the four delegates appointed two were leading members of the Transport Union. William O'Brien and MacPartlin decided to stay at home. The British authorities had held up the delegates' passports, so that they reached Berne four days late. But they were accepted as a distinct national delegation and were awarded a seat on the Permanent Commission. O'Shannon had spoken in the debate on territorial questions, making it clear that the Irish Labour movement wanted self-determination, that is to say the acceptance of the verdict delivered at the polls. Ramsay MacDonald talked confusedly of liberation within the British Empire.

The Irish delegates had protested against the general attack on the Bolsheviks and signed the Adler/Longuet resolution supporting the dictatorship of the proletariat. This received the backing of the Dutch, Norwegian, Spanish and a majority of the French. At a meeting in the Mansion House O'Shannon declared that 'the Soviet idea was the only one that would confer freedom on Ireland'. Asked to send a message to the reissued *Daily Herald*, he urged them to establish an 'English Soviet Republic'.

It might be thought that the Irish delegates had gone far

enough. But it was not possible to satisfy everybody. One of 1919
the Belfast SLP group was Kitty Coyle, a small intense woman who dressed in red and black and used the pseudonym Selma Sigerson. In articles in the *Scottish Socialist* she singled out Johnson for attack. Firstly, as an Englishman he should not be speaking for Ireland at Berne. Secondly he was a 'moderate' when what was needed was a 'revolutionary'. She presented these views at a general meeting of the SPI on 27 March, when O'Shannon indignantly denounced her attack on Johnson and Johnson described her views as 'insane'. Hedley's group shortly established themselves as the 'Revolutionary Socialist Party of Ireland'. Their hero was the Limerick organiser, John Dowling, whom they described as a 'revolutionary' and a 'direct actionist'. Later they claimed that seven ITGWU organisers were members of their group.

All this may at first sight seem a storm in a teacup. But its implications were far-reaching. Johnson and O'Shannon had gone to Berne for the purpose of promoting the self-determination of Ireland in accordance with the Waterford resolution. On all vital issues they found themselves part of a 'left' minority. But in January invitations had been issued to socialist organisations to attend a conference in Moscow at which a 'left' international was to be set up. This would not have had an immediate effect on the national position, for the Irish TUC would not have been eligible for affiliation. But in an undated letter, presumably written early in 1919, Larkin wrote to Foran: 'Our advice to you and those to be relied on is no conciliation with the Huysmans gang. We have opened up relations with Moscow officially.' The 'we' were presumably the group within the Socialist Party of America with whom Larkin founded his 'Communist Labour Party'. Larkin, like many others at this time, thought a great revolutionary wave was about to engulf the whole of capitalist society. So indeed did O'Shannon. But their immediate preoccupations differed. The fateful fact was that a political rift had appeared between Larkin and his old comrades. Every day Larkin remained in the USA brought an added danger that some second misunderstanding would attach itself to the first and the estrangement become confirmed.

1919 The Limerick branches had been progressing steadily. Early in March the Harbour Workers' Society had amalgamated. But the industrial action known as the 'Limerick Soviet' arose out of the national struggle. According to Hedley (who was, however, in Belfast at the time), its philosophical begetter was the organiser John Dowling.[3] On 6 April a prisoner, Robert Byrne, who had gone on hunger-strike, and had been removed from Limerick jail to hospital, was rescued by a party of armed Volunteers. A policeman was shot dead, and indeed Byrne died shortly afterwards of a wound inflicted by the police. At Byrne's funeral the authorities seemed determined on maximum provocation. Tanks and armoured cars rattled through the streets while aeroplanes roared overhead. The people remained calm.

On 9 April Limerick was declared a military area. Nobody was allowed to pass in or out of it without a military permit. An ingenious means was invented to make the effects of this order as inconvenient as possible: the city 'boundary' was placed near its centre. Every morning thousands of workers crossed the Shannon to work in Cleeve's condensed milk factory, a butter factory and a distillery. These were now declared to be outside the city. Faced with the prospect that the workers would be four times a day stopped and examined by soldiers, the Trades Council called a general strike, and 14,000 men and women accordingly ceased work. The Trades Council took over the entire administration of the city with the concurrence of the mayor and the Sinn Féin councillors. Even the Chamber of Commerce was sympathetic. Milk brought in for Cleeves was sold to the general public at 3d a pint. Profiteering was prevented, and the strike committee even went so far as to print token money which was accepted by shopkeepers. The authorities climbed down, and normal life was resumed after the interval.[4]

In the midst of the Limerick events Alderman John Lynch was released from Belfast jail. He arrived back in Sligo on 9 April. A crowd of 2,000 greeted him at the station, among them the local TD, J. J. Clancy, who had been released before him. The crowd formed a procession and paraded the town headed by a red flag, tar-barrels blazing, a fife and drum band playing, and finally held a public meeting in the Town Hall Square. The Trades Council had adopted the plan of making wage demands on all employers, and the new rates were settled by arbitration at the end of April, the workers' representatives being Lynch, Reilly, and Thomas Foran from Dublin. 1919

The highest point in this first exuberant phase of post-war working-class activity was reached on May Day 1919. Following upon a decision taken at Berne, the Irish Labour Party and TUC[5] called a general strike on 1 May. The call was obeyed everywhere outside the Belfast area, where local officials organised demonstrations on Saturday 3 May. For the second year running all processions were banned in Dublin, but elsewhere there were demonstrations of record proportions. In Cork city 8,000 workers assembled outside the ITGWU offices at Camden Quay, 6,000 from the city, 2,000 from the county. The ITGWU contingent, 4,000 strong, was led by its own Connolly Memorial Band and was divided into six sections, viz:

(1) Dockers, quay workers, Corporation employees, tramwaymen.
(2) Mill workers, Gouldings employees, seed and manure workers, gardeners.
(3) Coal and general carriers, steamship men, bread-van men, undertakers' drivers, coffin-makers, general carpenters.
(4) Provision trade workers.
(5) Printers, insurance agents, pawnbrokers' assistants, harness-makers, barbers' assistants, clerical workers.
(6) Warehousemen, drapers' porters, mineral-water workers, grocers' assistants.

Other unions taking part in the procession included the Electrical Trades Union, the Gasworkers' Union, the NSFU, the NUDL, the NUR and the National Federation of Women Workers.

In Sligo contingents came into the town from surrounding districts, despite torrential rain. The banner, made for the occasion by Street & Farrell, still survives. In Galway the demonstrations, organised on the initiative of the local NUR, had something of a Sinn Féin flavour. Dr Brian Cusack, TD, and the republican solicitor George Nicholls were the main speakers. But in the smaller towns, where the main or even

1919 only trade union was the ITGWU, the red flag was everywhere in evidence: at Monaghan, Portlaoise, Drogheda and Mallow. At Kilmacthomas workers carried a red banner inscribed 'A Workers' Republic'. At Killarney girls were arrested for taking a collection without a permit. They chose to go to prison rather than give bail.

In many of the towns of the midlands and west the ITGWU was the only trade union; in these areas it catered for craftsmen too few in numbers to form an organisation of their own. To branches organising demonstrations Foran sent model resolutions in favour of world peace, the self-determination of nations and making May Day a public holiday. As the 1919 Annual Report put it,

> Over more than three-fourths of Ireland the cessation was complete and meetings were held at convenient centres at which the Labour propaganda was zealously pushed and the red flag of the workers' cause displayed despite police interference. It was very generally admitted that nothing like the completeness of this stoppage could have been affected were it not for the far-flung battalions of the ITGWU.[6]

One of the first strikes to merit the title 'industrial' took place the following week. It affected creameries in Clonmel, Mallow and Tipperary town. There is a local tradition that a branch of the ITGWU was founded in Tipperary in 1915; it is said to have recruited girls working in a glove factory. This seems very doubtful. The year 1915 is comparatively well documented, but no record of the alleged branch seems to have survived. The recorded date of foundation of the Tipperary branch is 31 December 1918. But that the first members were women is likely. The men were organised in the Tipperary Workingmen's Protective and Benefit Society, founded in 1911 by Michael O'Callaghan (a Volunteer who had shot two policemen in 1916 and then escaped to the USA) and William Bourke. The male workers at Cleeve's creamery belonged to this society, but the women had their own branch of the ITGWU. Their secretary was Miss Kathleen Cleary. It would probably be the women's branch that took action in conjunction with members in the other creameries. The strike was of brief duration, and wage increases were won.

The growth of the union during the first six months of 1919 1919 was spectacular. In January 19 new branches were founded, in February 27, and in March 36, the total up to the end of June being 161. So rapid was the growth of Dublin No. 1 that the committee had not time to deal with the applications, and branch officials were permitted to enrol at their discretion those to whom there seemed no obvious objection. Measures were taken to establish a co-operative retail store. The old O'Connell banner was repaired. Members were levied 1s for the purchase of musical instruments, and these were delivered in June. The most important industrial action in Dublin was a hotel workers' strike, which lasted from April to June.

The expansion of the union necessitated the engagement of additional staff at all levels. A women's organiser, Mary Mullen, was recruited in January. Next month Michael O'Donohoe started work in Limerick. From March a former schoolteacher, Maurice Neligan, worked from Tralee, and Archibald Heron, a Portadown Protestant republican who had married James Connolly's daughter Ina, worked in Edenderry and Portlaoise. Joseph Metcalfe left the Dublin No. 1 branch and went to organise Co. Wicklow from his native Bray. John Rogan became a full-time worker in his place. Michael Murphy acted as organising secretary in Mullingar, where a branch was set up on 11 March. At the beginning of April W. P. Coates returned to London and became an organiser for the BSP;[7] he later became secretary of the 'Hands Off Russia' movement and the Anglo-Russian Parliamentary Committee. He was replaced in Waterford by Thomas Nagle, who had been active in the SPI in Dublin. At the union's head office Nora Connolly was joined by her friend Margaret Skinnider, who had been wounded in 1916. It is interesting to note that from this time onward one member after another of the head office staff elected to write his name in Irish. The leading enthusiast was Cathal O'Shannon. Tadhg Barry, released from internment in March, started work at Camden Quay, Cork, in April. Finally the Limerick staff was strengthened by the addition of Séamus O'Brien in May and John McGrath in June. There were two organisers called Séamus O'Brien. The one who worked in Dublin and Limerick was a huge man, formerly

1919 a member of the Western Miners in Denver, Colorado. He was famed for having on one occasion, while emphasising a point at a meeting, put his fist through the lid of a wooden desk.

*   *   *

In the midst of all this dazzling success suddenly there was dissension. The mutual ill-feeling between William O'Brien and P. T. Daly showed itself again at the beginning of May when Daly threatened to sue O'Brien for libel. The libel presumably related to the old affair of the missing IRB funds, for O'Brien wrote to P. S. O'Hegarty, who confirmed the defalcation and added that Daniel Braniff had been present when the Supreme Council had discussed the matter, but that Fred Allan had refused to give evidence against Daly. The Supreme Council had voted Daly an honorarium equivalent to the sum misappropriated. They had thus in a sense wiped the slate clean, and the matter should not have been brought up again, least of all by a third party. Indeed it seems to have been dropped after O'Brien heard from O'Hegarty early in July.

In the meantime there was fresh trouble at the Trades Council. It came to Foran's knowledge that Thomas Lawlor had received a financial testimonial from the employees of the Poor Law Board. Foran reported the fact to the Executive Committee, and at a meeting of the full Council they proposed that Lawlor be requested to resign from the Asylum Board. He loudly protested against the 'devilish attempt to put him out of the Labour movement' and excused himself by saying that his wife had accepted the money without his knowledge. A large number of visitors occupied the back of the hall, and these became more vociferous than the delegates. Foran was a special target of abuse. He was sneered at for not being out in 1916. He received no credit for building up the greatest trade union in Irish history, and whether influenced by the gallery or not, the delegates rejected his motion by 30 to 20. This was on 19 May.

The next meeting took place on 2 June. The chairman informed the delegates that the EC could not accept the decision of the Trades Council and had circulated it to affiliated unions for their consideration. When their action

was denied endorsement they tendered their resignations. 1919
Foran, O'Brien, Thomas Farren (secretary), John Farren (treasurer) and others then walked out.

On Whit Sunday, 8 June, the AGM of the Approved Society was held in Dublin. Foran complained that the administrative fund was deeply in debt. The deficiency was £1,400, of which £500 was due to the union's general fund. He charged Daly with incompetence and was supported by Joseph McGrath, who had been manager of the fund during 1916 and 1917. Daly's contention was that the government did not allow an adequate deduction for administrative expenses. A corroboration of this argument is found in the fact that several years after Daly had ceased to be secretary the complaints continued. Foran's great strength was his diligent concern for union funds. He proposed to undertake the secretaryship of the Insurance Section himself. Perhaps it was with this in prospect that J. J. Hughes had the previous month been appointed assistant secretary. When the vote took place Daly was defeated, and no time seems to have been lost before he was displaced.

The result was a storm that can scarcely have been foreseen. Delia Larkin, Micheál Ó Maoláin and a temporary clerk, Norbury, declared themselves on strike against the 'victimisation' of Daly. They picketed the union offices and on Wednesday 11 June held a protest meeting at Delia's social centre in Langrishe Place. On the 15th a further meeting, presided over by Barney Conway, was held at the Mansion House. Delia Larkin read telegrams of support and denounced the 'shameful campaign' against Daly. A resolution was passed calling upon the union Executive to 'abide by the instructions of Jim Larkin' and to request Foran to retire from the secretaryship of the Approved Society. A statement issued from Liberty Hall replied that the society was quite entitled to elect a new committee and had in fact done so; Foran would act as secretary without salary. But the fateful thing had happened: Larkin was involved in the controversy, and there was war on two fronts.

The Trades Council met again on 16 June. There had been 50 delegates on the 2nd; this time there were 75. And in the 'gallery' were Delia Larkin, Micheál Ó Maoláin and

1919 many of their supporters. Speaking from beyond the barrier, Ó Maoláin objected to the presence of Thomas Foran. There were frequent interruptions, cries of 'Up Larkin!' and 'Up Daly!' At one point there was a call for the singing of 'The Red Flag'. One of the delegates, M. J. Lord, wrote in the *Evening Herald* that the audience 'by yells, calls, abuse, and even threats, succeeded in obtaining the result required'. The acceptance of the resignation of the Executive was carried by 40 votes to 35. When a delegate complained of 'mob rule' the visitors cried: 'Put him out!' At one point Delia Larkin mounted a chair to urge her supporters to 'keep cool'. New officers were then elected. The meeting had lasted three hours.

Two days later Foran, Joseph Farrell and Joseph Doyle wrote to the Trades Council and the press announcing their resignation from the Board of Guardians in view of the Trades Council's approval of the acceptance of testimonials.

The disruptive genius was undoubtedly Micheál Ó Maoláin. Daly at least disclaimed the intention of starting a new union, and Delia Larkin could curb enthusiasm if it too far outran discretion, but Ó Maoláin felt not the slightest responsibility. He went to Waterford on 20 June to rally support for Daly. Meetings were held at Waterford, Wexford and Sligo. At the Sligo meeting Alderman John Lynch complained that he had been prevented from voting at the conference of the Approved Society. He believed it was because he was a 'Larkinite, a Connollyite and a Dalyite'.

A factor in the alienation of some of the old members was undoubtedly the rapid growth of the union. The easy familiar relations which are appropriate for small organisations had had to give way. But the change had been so sudden that it could appear to have been imposed from above. In April 1919 the committee of No. 1 branch was anxious to pay benefit to a member called Kavanagh and was displeased when the General Treasurer refused to sanction payment. On this occasion Foran attended the committee meeting and begged the members not to break the rules. He suggested a way round their difficulty. To deal with a paid official who had power to obstruct but none to decide seemed chilly and inhuman to those who only five years previously had been able to drop in and see Jim and receive an immediate answer whether in accordance with rule or not. One can be quite sure that if Lynch was not allowed to vote, then he was in some way out of compliance. But that would not lessen his dissatisfaction. If the union had grown gradually over a number of years, this difficulty would not have arisen. 1919

Another factor which must not be overlooked is the inexperience of the Executive in mass leadership. In this Daly had the advantage. O'Brien was a man for the committee room, not for the hustings. Foran, moreover, seems to have lacked that savage ruthlessness which a successful leader must possess, however seldom he displays it. He had either to oust Daly and stand on the legality of his position, or he must wait until it was obvious to everybody that Daly must go. As it was, the General President, who ought not to have been taking sides, was made a partisan. If the Executive minutes are ever discovered, they may reveal some unexpected explanation for his action, but on the present evidence it appears hard to avoid the conclusion that Foran made an error of judgment in allowing the presidency into the cockpit. But why should a man as shrewd as Foran have done this? Perhaps it was regard for Larkin.

The difficulty of Foran's position was apparent when the general meeting was held in the Mansion House on 22 June. There was nothing in the rules giving any power of decision to members attending a general meeting. If Foran was not properly elected, it was for the members of the Approved Society to say so. The only person in the room with power to decide whether Foran should remain secretary or not was Foran himself. The sole objective of his opponents must therefore be to break Foran's nerve and induce him to resign. If the calling of the meeting was a concession to the clamour which had been aroused by Ó Maoláin and Delia Larkin, then it is likely that the EC had worked out no clear tactics. There was only one point at issue: whether Daly was capable of managing the Insurance Section so as to maintain its solvency. If there was any dispute, then the matter could be referred to government auditors.

But one irregularity followed another. Foran took the chair. He was thus debarred from ruling out of order any matter which his opponents chose to throw at him. Some-

1919 body asked if Daly's personal character was in question. It was replied that the charges against him were political. Once that was admitted, it was open to J. J. Hughes to present the IRB view of Daly, and to Nora Connolly to say what her father had thought of him. Delia Larkin too sprang to his defence. Foran soon found himself under attack, with no protection from the most irrelevant and extraneous allegations. Somebody proposed that the matter should go for arbitration by Dáil Éireann. But Dáil Éireann had no authority in the internal affairs of the ITGWU; neither, for that matter, had the general meeting. Foran was ultimately overcome. He offered to stand down from the secretaryship of the Approved Society. Ó Maoláin, who seems to have fancied himself in the role of prosecuting counsel, demanded: 'Did you say you will withdraw from the Insurance?' To cries of 'Never!' he replied: 'I will withdraw from everything.' John O'Neill, he added, could run the union. Of course, the complete impracticability of this line of action became apparent to him as soon as he got back to Liberty Hall.

To add to the difficulties of the situation, on 4 July Michael Connolly's suit came up for hearing. He had Gore-Grimes as solicitor and T. M. Healy as counsel. Judgment was given against the union with costs. Daly telegraphed the result to J. Byrne, one of his supporters in Limerick who fancied himself the scourge of the 'moderates' – the moderates being Johnson and O'Shannon. His complaint against them had been that the Limerick Soviet had not been extended to the whole of Ireland. Daly's telegram was delivered to the wrong J. Byrne, who took it in all innocence to Séamus O'Brien, who in turn communicated its contents to Dublin.

It seems that part of the dispute between O'Brien and Daly was considered by Dáil Éireann. The finding was that Daly had defalcated, but that there were extenuating circumstances. The allegations of spying were firmly rejected. It is doubtful if a tenth of J. J. Hughes's statement would be allowed as evidence in any court of law. When the month's truce – if it can be called truce – was up, another general meeting, equally irregular, was held in the Mansion House. Once again every issue but the real one was thrown into the melting-pot. For, whatever else Daly had done or was doing, the only valid point at issue was whether he could run an insurance business.

If he could not, he was rightly dismissed; if he could, he was unfairly but not illegally dismissed.

According to the *Irish Independent*, 'pandemonium reigned'. Its reporter wrote: 'To describe the proceedings as a regular bear-garden would convey a poor idea of the disturbances created.' While J. J. Hughes was attacking Daly, Colgan, the young Citizen Army man who later married Delia Larkin, produced a revolver. When later taken to task for this by the Army Council he stated that it was not loaded. Nevertheless it produced an immediate effect, a stampede in which at least 200 people fled into Dawson Street. The meeting broke up when some of Ó Maoláin's henchmen stormed the platform. William O'Brien was knocked off his chair, and Joseph McGrath showed his skill as a pugilist. All this happened not because Foran had acted the part of a soulless bureaucrat, but because he had not. The division created in the Dublin Labour movement was not healed for years.

* * *

In the industrial field the main disputes of mid-1919 were on the farms. Following the eclipse of the UIL the EC of the ITGWU decided to try to absorb the Land and Labour Associations. On 2 February Thomas Farren agreed on the principle of amalgamation with their officials in Co. Laois and thereafter visited local branches. The result was that the associations in Ballybrittas, Castletown, Borris-in-Ossory, Mountrath and Mountmellick fused with the ITGWU. Attention was next paid to Co. Wexford, the result of which was the Bunclody agreement which safeguarded the benefits of those who transferred. This arrangement became a standard procedure under which Taghmon, Camross, Clologue, Boulavogue, The Harrow, Monamolin and Kilteely amalgamated during the course of the year.[8]

The rural workers' wages movement began in April 1919. In the north of Ireland members of the National Amalgamated Union of Labour struck for wage increases at Carrigans and Manorcunningham in East Donegal. Non-strikers were assulted by pickets, and shots were fired. These developments accorded with a general tendency for the struggles of 1919 to be more bitterly fought than those of the preceding year. Farmers

1919 were joining the Irish Farmers' Union and offering organised resistance. In Kildare the union asked for a weekly wage of 50s and only ITGWU members to be employed. There were sporadic strikes in Carlow, Kerry, Offaly and Co. Dublin. With regard to the last, on 6 May the IFU called on its members to lock out all members of the ITGWU unless the strikes at Lucan, Palmerstown and Clondalkin were called off.

Wage claims in the south were very much more modest than those in Co. Dublin. But they were not received with better grace. Early in June serious strikes broke out in the Buttevant district of North Cork, where farmers refused to pay 35s without diet and 27s with it. At Churchtown shots were fired at a farmer's son. The men at Buttevant creamery joined the stoppage on 9 June and two days later paraded surrounding villages with a red banner inscribed 'Workers of the World Unite'. A man who brought his own milk into Churchtown creamery was fired on, and a jennet was killed. This struggle coincided with strikes in the building trade, timber yards and laundries of Limerick, which were closely followed by a strike of tailors.

The policy of the EC was to fight in as many districts as possible. That at least is known from a surviving letter from William O'Brien to the Carlow branch secretary dated 2 July. The letter explains that the 'war is already on' in Meath and Kildare. It requests the names of a small number of large farmers close to Carlow town upon whom individual demands could be made following the rejection of the county claim by the IFU.[9] The agricultural workers' strikes dragged on until 25 August, when a settlement was reached because farmers were anxious to get animals to the Dublin Horse Show. Many years afterwards, speaking of this lengthy series of agricultural strikes, O'Brien stated his recollection that in 1919 'for every one pound of income there were two pounds paid out'. The balance sheet, however, does not show this. It shows a surplus of income over expenditure of over £11,000. But it also shows that out of a total expenditure of £74,726, £40,571 was paid out in strike benefit.

The Annual Meeting of the ITUC (now officially designated the Irish Labour Party and Trade Union Congress) opened at Drogheda on 4 August. The ITGWU affiliated on the basis of 66,000 members and paid fees of £550. The number of delegates was 68, of whom 21 came from Dublin, 7 from Cork, 6 from Limerick, and two each from Belfast and Swords. The old centres, Sligo, Wexford, Waterford and Tralee, had one delegate apiece, as had such more recently established branches as Carlow, Kilkenny, Tullamore, Dungarvan and Mallow. The newly established branches of Newry, Derry and Dundalk were not represented. But the union's strong rural base was shown by the presence of delegates from Lucan, Swords, Skerries, Athy, Naas, Newbridge, Drumree (Co. Meath), Newcastle West, Kilmacthomas and Thomastown, as well as from small towns like Bray, Blackrock, Castlecomer, New Ross and Castlebar.[10] 1919

The effect of this great ITGWU delegation on the composition of the conference can be appreciated when it is noted that only seven other delegates were members of organisations of 'unskilled' workers. The NUDL sent delegates from Cork, Derry and Newry. The Agricultural and General Workers' Union sent two delegates, one of them James Everitt, subsequently a Labour TD. This organisation was strongest in the south-east and had decided to affiliate to the ITUC following the strike against conscription. One of its leading figures was Seán Etchingham of Courtown, a strong IRB man, who led the Rising in Wexford in 1916. The Meath Labour Union (Duleek) and the NAUL (Branch 190, Derry) sent one delegate each. All these organisations subsequently merged in whole or in part with the ITGWU.

As requested at Waterford, the National Executive Committee had drawn up proposals for the amalgamation of unions. Their membership pointed out that of 700,000 adult wage-earners in Ireland, something over 250,000 were organised, and that of these about 220,000 were affiliated to the ITUC. There were seventy trade union bodies, some of them very small and local. The problem was to secure 100 per cent trade union organisation and to fuse the existing bodies into one all-inclusive Irish Workers' Union. This should be divided into self-governing industrial sections organised both nationally and locally. The Trades Councils would then become councils of local industrial sections.

The central organisation should be finally responsible

1919 for financing and controlling 'all the larger movements'. Its subsidiary sections would be ten in number, covering the following:

(1) Agriculture, land, quarries, roads.
(2) Transport and mechanical communications.
(3) Building and construction.
(4) Food processing.
(5) Distributive trades (including carting).
(6) Engineering and metal work.
(7) Clothing and textiles.
(8) Painting, paper and allied trades.
(9) Public services.
(10) Miscellaneous.

M. J. O'Lehane proposed a motion to the effect that a Special Congress should consider the subject. He was supported by J. J. Hughes, who emphasised that the reorganisation and amalgamation to the Irish trade union movement along the proposed lines was essential to achieving workers' control of industry. Eamon Rooney proposed that a start should be made with the transport industry by calling a conference of dockers and others. Foran, O'Shannon and others supported the principle of the 'one big union' while recognising the difficulties. The principle was opposed by members of craft and cross-channel unions, but these did not object to a conference and amalgamations industry by industry. Generally speaking, the supporters of the motion gave voice to the syndicalist concepts contained in Connolly's pamphlet *The Axe to the Root*. They were concerned with building up 'an industrial republic inside the shell of the political state'. In *Old Wine in New Bottles* Connolly had suggested that the form of its organisation was not the only factor making for the success of a trade union. His second pamphlet had been written in the dark days of 1914. It did not seem relevant amid the enthusiasm of 1919, when the movement was filled with a sense of universal purpose and the secretary, William O'Brien, refused to take a salary because he received all he needed from the ITGWU. There was, of course, another pathway to 'workers' control' which was mooted by those who believed that the Limerick Soviet should have been extended to the whole country, but it was generally accepted that the time was not opportune for such action. The resolution on amalgamation was carried. 1919

Several ITGWU delegates addressed the Congress. Houston spoke of the failure of the Belfast strike committee to accept help from the ITUC and called for the maintenance of compulsory tillage. J. J. Hughes urged the establishment of a Labour College. Thomas Farren proposed a resolution on housing. Cathal O'Shannon moved, and Rooney seconded, two motions, one of fraternal greetings to the workers of Russia, the other condemning the League of Nations and the Treaty of Versailles. Both were carried without dissent. Country delegates spoke. N. T. Phelan of Kilmacthomas moved that agricultural workers should be paid a weekly wage 'at least equal in purchasing power to a pre-war wage of 20s a week'. He was supported by Patrick Ryan of Thomastown.

Finally Thomas Foran told the meeting that he had received a cable from Larkin stating that the British and American governments had refused him a passport to return to Ireland. He could, of course, have returned to England. It is hard to believe that if he had appeared on the Mersey, he could have been prevented from coming ashore. Efforts would probably have been made to keep him out of Ireland, and perhaps he felt doubt of his ability to disguise himself. His biographer records that when, a few months later, he was arrested he had a forged passport in his possession. It was probably around this time that O'Brien told a meeting of organisers that he doubted Larkin's ability to lead the union.[11]

The union's first Annual Report was published, it appears from internal evidence, in August 1919. The year under review is 1918, but a general outline history of the union is included by way of introduction. The list of branches includes those registered up to April 1919. But a check with the wages book shows that the locations of organisers were those of August 1919. It is possible that the preparation of the report was begun after the election of the EC, that the body of it was duplicated in April, and that printing was delayed until the nearest thing to a union conference was held when the delegates to the ITUC got together in August. Though they cannot compensate for the loss of the EC minutes, the Annual

1919 Reports, published regularly from 1919 onwards, are an invaluable source of union history.

On 15 September Foran heard from Larkin. The dissidents had been in touch with the General Secretary. The letter was brought by a young man called Eamon MacAlpine, who described himself as 'Larkin's ambassador' and became active in the SPI in that role. The tone of the letter is exasperated. In content it is an attempt to put the clock back. Larkin asks Foran why he did not 'allow this fire to smoulder' until he could return to Ireland.[12] Though there is reason to suspect that Foran acted prematurely against Daly, there is no reason to be sure that the fire, as Larkin called it, would have been content to smoulder indefinitely. There was too much inflammable material around, the general nature of which has been indicated. Larkin asked that Daly should be restored to his position pending his return, that all reference to the dispute should be excluded from the *Voice of Labour*, and that Delia should discontinue publishing the *Red Hand*, in which she was attacking the Executive. Larkin also condemned Michael Connolly for taking the union to court. If Larkin had been able to appear, possibly he might have been able to re-establish the position as before. But it was too much to ask the Executive to set aside the votes of the members of the Approved Society. The union might have found itself in court a second time.

Foran sent Larkin a reasoned reply. He blamed himself not for taking action but for delaying so long and allowing a bad situation to build up. Larkin seems to have accepted his explanations, and the matter dropped.

13

With Victory in Sight

So spake the Fiend and with necessity,
The tyrant's plea, excus'd his devilish deeds.

JOHN MILTON

Raids on Liberty Hall — 'one big union' — Voice *banned* — Watchword *published — Larkin arrested — three strikes — Galway — local elections — rural workers — arrests and hunger-strikes — food exports — Knocklong 'Soviet' — Dáil arbitration courts — agrarian question*

Liberty Hall was raided three times in August 1919. On the first occasion, on 2 August, a revolver was found. Peter Ennis, the caretaker, was arrested but soon released. There were two raids on 22 August. This time the police removed 'strike literature', possibly mainly the leaflet *Fifty Points on Industrial Unionism*. These events marked the beginning of a crescendo of repression which continued for nearly two years. During this period the British authorities showed that they regarded the ITGWU as one of the revolutionary agencies it was their business to put down. And if they were not already disposed to regard Sinn Féin as closely allied to Bolshevism, the statements of Cathal O'Shannon would, at the least, have aroused their suspicions. Moreover, in Ireland at this period it was not possible to define 'legitimate trade union activities' and hold aloof from all else. 1919

In the wave of repression which began with the proclamation of Dáil Éireann as an illegal institution (10 September) the *Voice of Labour* was suppressed on the 21st. The editor remained in his office, but his printers, Messrs Cahill & Co. of Dawson Street, were told by the authorities that if they wished to keep their business, they had better stop printing it. O'Shannon was at his parents' home in Randalstown when the blow fell. His assistant, Joseph MacDonnell, wired him: 'Foran instructs that union issue weekly paper.' Although

1919 O'Shannon was on the union's payroll, the *Voice of Labour* was not in theory a union publication. At first Cahills were favourably inclined towards printing an entirely new paper owned and controlled by the union. But they must have decided, on reflection, that a horse of another colour was still a horse, and accordingly resolved to take no risks. The new paper was therefore printed in Manchester by the *National Labour Press*. Another illustration of the impossibility of placing union and national history in separate compartments arose from the proclamation of large areas under the Criminal Law and Procedure Act. Sinn Féin halls were closed down, and in a number of towns (for example Castledermot, Ballina and Kilmallock) the ITGWU branches lost their meeting-places.

The new paper, the *Watchword of Labour*, appeared on 27 September. O'Shannon was editor. The front page of the first issue carried a tonic sol-fa version of Connolly's 'Watchword of Labour'. It was made clear that its aim was to promote the principles of Connolly, who regarded the Labour movement as an essential part of the struggle for national independence. His main article consisted of an appeal to the Irish workers in Britain. Presumably it was hoped to secure circulation among the Irish exiles. The paper was available at the 'Reformers' Bookstall' and other rebel bookshops. Johnson had toured Scotland and the north of England after having been approached by Irish workers who wished to form branches of the Irish Labour Party. He had encouraged them to organise, but urged them to maintain their connection with British Labour. Now O'Shannon told them not only to do this, but to use their organised strength to compel British Labour to live up to the promises of 'self-determination' which had been so freely dispensed. Their slogan should be 'Hands off Ireland'. He declared: 'We ask not for money but for action.' Among contributors to the paper were J. J. Hughes, Tadhg Barry, and Robert Barton, who, mindful of the union's rural membership, seems to have kept in touch with O'Shannon on behalf of the Dáil Department of Agriculture.

On 6 October Foran attended a meeting of the Dublin Trades Council to discuss the possibility of a one-day strike to demand the restoration of Larkin's passport. Larkin advised against it unless there was action in Britain too.

When on 11 November a deputation from the Council, consisting of P. T. Daly and Eamon MacAlpine, was enabled, through the good offices of the British Labour Party, to meet the Chief Secretary, he told them that Larkin had been arrested on the 8th and faced a charge of 'criminal anarchy'. A huge bail had been demanded, and there was little that could be done. 1919

The charge arose out of Larkin's signing the manifesto published in *Revolutionary Age* on 5 July. Its object was to call delegates to a convention at which a Communist Party was to be launched. In the event Larkin did not attend. Differences had arisen among the language groups which were to make up the new party, and his main concern was now to find means of returning to Ireland. The $15,000 bail was raised with the help of John Devoy and members of the American Labour movement. At this period the United States was in the grip of anti-socialist hysteria. Both the Dublin Trades Council and the ITUC offered to raise funds, but the ITGWU announced that it would accept responsibility for Larkin's costs.

* * *

Despite the obstacles placed by the government in the way of organising, the wages movement continued. Shortages were still acute, and prices of food and clothing were soaring. The union continued to expand, and the number of small towns it monopolised increased. More emphasis was placed on the concept of the 'one big union'. The Drogheda conference had accepted the principle of transforming the ITUC into one big union, though it was obvious that the craft unions would drag their feet. Increasingly the ITGWU referred to itself as the 'one big union'. A picture of the *Voice* office in the 1919 report shows a pennant displaying a scarcely distinguishable design beside the letters OBU. The aim of the movement was to win higher wages to meet the increasing cost of living, and shorter hours in order to provide employment.

There was a strike of the Dublin dockers on 1 September, and on 8 September Limerick dockers refused to work after 8 p.m. A strike in the bacon factories was narrowly averted,

1919 but gas workers, now in the Transport Union, plunged the city into partial darkness when they came out for double pay for overtime.

Three important disputes opened at the beginning of December, one in Ballina, another in Limerick, and a third nation-wide. On 1 December members of the ITGWU were locked out by Ballina traders, who added to the lock-out a 'blockade' which applied even to those employed by farmers. Four hundred families were told: 'No transport men served.' They had asked for the restoration of a 50-hour week won at the end of 1918 but later increased to 55 in return for a modest wage concession. The farmers were sympathetic and supplied food to their own workers. The store employees reported the boycott to Liberty Hall, where immediate action was taken. The Dublin Co-operative Society agreed to bake extra bread, which was dispatched by passenger train. Other necessaries followed, and finally the Society opened a temporary branch in the town. It withdrew when agreement was reached upon a 50-hour week without loss of earnings.

The Limerick dock strike affected 400 members of the ITGWU. Negotiations regarding a wage increase began on 2 December, and Foran paid a visit on the 5th. The union was requesting 54s a week for constant men working a 46-hour week and 16s a day for casuals. The aim was parity with Dublin. The coal firms refused, and strike action followed on 8 December. The Bishop of Limerick, Dr Hallinan, called a meeting in the Town Hall at which he explained a conciliation procedure that was working well in Cork. The employers were not favourably inclined. By the end of January 1,000 factory workers were idle as a result of the shortage of coal. The gasworks were reduced to a three weeks' supply, but the union offered to pass their deliveries. Mr O'Hanlon of the Ministry of Labour met the men, who agreed to his arbitrating. The employers, however, refused. The dispute went to arbitration at the beginning of February as a result of action by the Corporation, which appointed a deputation to interview both sides. The casuals increased their pay from 12s to 13s 6d a day, and the constant men from 44s to 48s 6d a week.

The motor permits dispute arose from a decision by the

government that all drivers of automobiles must hold military permits. Members of several unions were affected, in particular those of the ITGWU, the Stationary Engine Drivers, and the Irish Automobile Drivers and Mechanics. The Irish Automobile Drivers' Union, of which M. J. O'Connor was now General Secretary, decided to call a strike on 29 November. The other unions preferred the more prudent action of refusing to apply for permits but taking out any load the employers were prepared to risk on the road. A Special TUC was called and met to consider the question on 16 December.

A strike committee was appointed, but difficulties arose with the Irish Automobile Drivers' Union because of the unresolved disagreement over tactics. Foran thought the IADU leaders too ardent and inexperienced; they wanted to take the initiative and expected others to fall in with their decisions even when they were not consulted. There may also have been little love lost between Foran and M. J. O'Connor, though what records survive give no more than a hint of this. After an aggregate meeting on 6 February, when Foran described the remarks of the IADU spokesman, James Mitchell, as 'hogwash', the drivers called off their strike unilaterally. The members of other unions who had become involved must make what arrangements they could. If it had not been for threats by the ITGWU to take action in support of them, many of them would have been victimised. At the following Annual Meeting of the ITUC only five delegates supported the action of the motor-drivers. At the same time in calling off the strike they succeeded in having some of the worst features of the permit system withdrawn.

* * *

During the second half of 1919 forty-four new branches of the ITGWU were registered. The most important of these was in Galway. It was officially established at a large public meeting in the Town Hall on 18 November. Stephen Cremen presided, and it was he who became the first secretary. He was appointed organising secretary on 8 December. The speakers were Cathal O'Shannon, Séamus O'Brien and Michael

1919 Healy. This Séamus O'Brien was not the huge man from Colorado, but the one who figures in the wages books as Séamus O'Brien II. He later married James Connolly's daughter Nora. He had been appointed organiser at the beginning of October and was allocated to Athlone. He arrived in Galway later in the month, but his headquarters were still at Athlone. At the meeting he launched a sharp attack upon Sexton, who, when the NUDL held its annual conference in Galway, had declared that the separation of Ireland from England would be disastrous.

A few firm facts can perhaps be combined with local tradition in seeking the pre-history of the Galway branch.[1] One of the early activists was Seán O'Healy, a dynamic character with views like Cathal O'Shannon's. He is credited with displaying a red flag at a meeting that was broken up. It is just possible that this incident took place on 1 May 1919. There was on that day a demonstration by the ITGWU at Gort, when, refused the use of the Town Hall, the members held a meeting outside it, flying the red flag, much to Father Cassidy's disapproval, and ending by singing the song of the same name. In Tuam the ITGWU and NUR held a similar meeting, but the police prevented them from flying the flag.

It seems unlikely that no effort would be made in Galway city. But in what was then a strongly pro-British garrison town, the authorities may have felt able to prevent it. According to the Sinn Féin *Galway Express*, clerks to Galway County Council ceased work on 1 May and the Council decided to pay them. The *Express* was favourable to the ITGWU, while the *Connaught Tribune* supported the NUDL.

There is a local tradition that the first premises of the ITGWU in Mary Street, Galway, were used by Sinn Féin and the Fianna Éireann. The first ITGWU members are said to have been Thomas and James Foran from the woollen mills and Thomas Hynes and Thomas Ray, who worked at University College. Since the first workers to join as a body were in the catering trade, which was previously unorganised, the inference seems to be that members of Sinn Féin, dissatisfied with the anti-national influences of the NUDL, joined the union themselves and invited the nearest organiser to form a branch. The IRB solicitor, George Nicholls, who had been in touch with Liam Mellows in 1916, was favourably inclined.

Just before Christmas 1919 he was representing a man whose allotments, which he had improved, had been made over to others. The chairman quoted the parable of the vineyard, remarking that the man who started in the evening got just as much as the man who worked all day. 'Your worship,' said Nicholls, 'that was because they hadn't the Irish Transport and General Workers' Union with them at that time.' 1919

* * *

The union had about eighty employees on the head office payroll at the end of 1919, as well as those paid by the larger branches. The general policy was to merge branches until they reached a size at which they could maintain a full-time secretary. The prospect of having to engage still more staff led the EC to consider their recruitment policy. In December they advertised examinations for applicants for junior clerkships. The compulsory subjects were arithmetic, geography and English composition. The voluntary subjects were Irish, shorthand, elementary book-keeping and modern Irish history.

The long-delayed municipal elections took place on 15 1920
January 1920. On this occasion the ITGWU emerged as an independent political force. The circumstances were unusual by reason of the position in the Dublin Trades Council. On 24 and 25 October the Irish Labour Party and TUC had called a conference of Trades Councils. It was attended by representatives of twenty-two of them and by eleven members of the National Executive Committee, including Farren, Bohan, O'Shannon and O'Brien. It decided that only persons 'nominated and financed by legitimate Labour bodies' should be recognised as Labour candidates and that 'candidates to be nominated by Trades Councils and Trades Unions must be *bona fide* members of Trade Unions selected by a recognised Labour Conference'.[2]

A programme was adopted which was concerned with housing, rents, feeding of schoolchildren, education, direct labour, municipal restaurants, allotments, municipal industries and food supplies. Emphasis was laid on 'the development of all the natural resources for supplying the people's needs on a non-profit-making basis'.

1920 Throughout the country candidates were selected by the Trades Councils in accordance with the decisions of the conference. But at the Dublin Trades Council the ITGWU delegates failed to secure agreeement that persons not in compliance with the resolution on testimonials were ineligible. The Trades Council nominated candidates in accordance with conference decisions. But three unions, the ITGWU, the bricklayers and the painters, offered their own, eight in all, plus Walter Carpenter, who stood for the Socialist Party of Ireland. The ITGWU candidates were Thomas O'Reilly, John Bohan, John O'Connor, Michael Brohoon, Thomas Kennedy and William O'Brien. They were all successful.

These six, plus Joseph Farrell, Owen Hynes and Walter Carpenter, were described by the *Watchword of Labour* as Workers' Republicans, that is to say people who wanted a Workers' Republic. How far they subscribed to O'Shannon's 'Bolshevism' and how far he was permitting himself a degree of journalistic licence is not clear. They cannot have been outraged at what he ascribed to them, although it went far beyond ITUC policy, which was largely formulated by Johnson. The *Watchword of Labour* wrote:

> They stand for the freeing of Ireland from the bondage of English and every other foreign rule and from the slavery imposed by a sweating employing class upon the workers. They stand for the international recognition of the duly elected Parliament and Government of Ireland in as full and complete a sense as the international recognition they helped to secure last year for the independent national working-class movement organised as the Irish Labour Party and Trades Union Congress. . . . They stand for the Republic; and that Republic the Irish Republic; and that again the Workers' Republic.[3]

O'Shannon was president of the Socialist Party of Ireland and a leading figure in the James Connolly Labour College. His enthusiasm was understandable when, out of a total of 1,470 successful candidates, 334 represented Labour. But whether this and the return of 422 Sinn Féin candidates implied that 'the Empire is in danger and with it the whole capitalist system' is a question that history has resolved.

The swing to the left was nevertheless remarkable. The 1920
number of ITGWU councillors in O'Shannon's (incomplete) list of 7 February was 137 returned as Labour, and a further six as Sinn Féin. In Cork city the ITGWU and Sinn Féin offered a joint list, and the Trades Council nominated only three candidates. Denis Houston was returned in Belfast, Joseph Metcalfe in Bray, Charles Gaule in Arklow, Richard Corish in Wexford, Thomas Dunne in Waterford, and John Lynch in Sligo. In the early part of 1920 Irish Labour reached its zenith. It was completely identified with the national cause.

* * *

The question of elections to the ITGWU Executive was raised in January, and the absence of a representative from Ulster was discussed. The Executive wrote to all branches in group 8, pointing out the desirability of Ulster representation, but the only nominations were from Drumree and Killeshandra, a place admittedly in Ulster but ninety miles from industrial Belfast. The new Executive consisted of the three general officers, who were unopposed, together with Michael Duffy (Drumree, Co. Meath), Patrick Gaffney (Carlow), Michael Hill (Cork), Michael Ryan (Limerick), Thomas Ryan (Waterford), Thomas Kennedy, Patrick Stafford and Michael McCarthy (Dublin).

A second census of the union membership was taken on 31 January. The total strength was now 102,823. Of these 40,439 were in agriculture, mining and fishing. There were 16,063 in food production, and 15,109 in transport and distribution. In manufacturing industry there were 12,126, in construction 8,527 and in public services 10,609. The largest single category was that of agricultural labourers, of whom there were 30,292. The next two largest groups were those of carters with 5,877 and road workers with 4,548. The dockers had fallen to fourth place, with 4,387. In 1918 only 24 per cent of the union members had been employed in agriculture. In 1920 the proportion had risen to 37.5 per cent. The decennial census that should have been taken in 1921 was postponed until 1926, by which time long-term trends had reasserted themselves. The relative numbers of

1920 rural and urban population did not, however, change rapidly until later in the century. According to the 1926 figures, 72 per cent of the population of the twenty-six-county area lived outside towns of 1,500 inhabitants. The union was thus still twice as urban as the population.

If we bear in mind that the organisation of agricultural labourers was for the most part confined to twelve counties,[4] conclusions can be drawn. Table 22 of *Agricultural Statistics*, (Department of Industry and Commerce, 1928) gives some interesting particulars of persons employed in agriculture on 1 June 1912, classifying them by county and according to their social status. According to these figures, the total number of persons engaged in agriculture in the twelve counties at this date was 356,607, of which 225,147 were members of farmers' families, and 131,460 permanent or temporary wage-earners. The wage-earners were thus outnumbered by nearly two to one. And members of the union were outnumbered by nearly ten to one, although this figure will seem less daunting when the distribution of workers over farms of different sizes is taken into account. The total number of persons employed in farms of over fifty acres was about 160,000. We can assume that 120,000 of these were wage-earners, so that the union had organised about 25 per cent of the workforce. There is no point in refining these figures further at this stage. If they are 10 per cent out, the argument is not affected. Trade union organisation in the countryside was not as impressive as it appears at first sight of the high figures. Outside the Dublin area it had developed against a background of state intervention, in effect because without it the government's pay awards, a matter of policy in a period of food shortage, could not be enforced. Once government policy changed, it could be in jeopardy.

Before dealing with the struggle of the farm workers in 1920 we must note their influence on the composition of the new Executive. For Dublin lost a man to the south-east constituency which was represented by Gaffney of Carlow and Thomas Ryan of Waterford. Michael Ryan held the western constituency for Limerick, and Michael Hill replaced William Kenneally in Cork city. But nobody came from Belfast. Despite the rapid growth of the branch, which reached a strength of 3,500 members under Houston's management,

the northern city was swamped by the votes of the country 1920
districts to which it was attached.

* * *

In industry it was comparatively easy to enforce a closed shop by refusing to work with those who refused to join the union. In agriculture it was difficult. In some cases special branch meetings were convened in order to persuade workers that it was necessary. The issue had arisen very sharply when on 22 November 1919 a farmer at Fenor, Co. Waterford, locked out all members when they objected to working with non-union labour. Presumably the work was threshing, for on the 24th a force of locked-out men blocked the road between Ballinaclough and Ballydermody to prevent the bringing in of a threshing machine. It was protected by police armed with rifles and bayonets. The workers routed the police, though not without the expense of a few bayonet wounds, and then dug up the road. When ultimately the machine was brought as far as Fenor church it was seen that the farmer's outhouses were ablaze. His corn and hay was a total loss. On the 28th large forces of RIC men scoured the countryside on all sides of Fenor and took into custody Nicholas Phelan (ITGWU branch secretary), Patrick Hanley and Patrick Dalton. They were lodged in Waterford jail, even though the union had condemned this reversion to the tactics of the Ribbonmen. At the end of December corn and hay belonging to a Mrs Walshe was set on fire. The branch chairman condemned the arson and contradicted rumours that the union was to blame.

During the early months of 1920 efforts were made to increase the proportion of the agricultural workforce belonging to the union. From the beginning of March, when the demand for labour began to increase, a series of organising meetings was held. One of these was addressed by John Dowling at Abbeyfeale, Co. Limerick, in the extreme southwest of the zone of mixed farming. The speech of M. O'Connor of Templeglantine shows clearly what was in mind. He said that this was one of a series of meetings being held through Ireland. It reminded him of the days of the Land League. The driving force behind that had been the labourers,

1920 who drove out the landlords for the farming class. But now they were organising in the ITGWU for a substantial wage and a decent living. The chairman, J. O'Connor, spoke of the superiority of the present union over the old ILLA, but warned that the farmers were now organising against them.

The last remark was a reference to the increasing activities of the Irish Farmers' Union, which was showing signs of becoming a well-organised and vigorous employers' association. There was as yet no concerted attack. Two factors operated to postpone this. On the one hand, the government still retained its wartime agricultural wages policy. On the other, there was reason for all nationally minded people to stand together against repression; those who broke the front courted unpopularity. The farmers therefore held their hands while building up their organisation.

The twelve counties that have been referred to as the best organised by the union formed an extensive area of which the heartland was Wexford, Waterford and Kilkenny. In terms of the development of wage labour, apart from the cities, it constituted the most advanced part of Ireland. It was therefore no accident that it was in Wexford and Kilkenny that the Farmers' Freedom Force was established in the spring of 1920. It was in part political, a kind of electoral arm of the IFU. But there were ample signs that it might become a strike-breaking force, offering violence to pickets in the name of a crusade against Bolshevism. On the other hand, there were also moves towards conciliation. Following a series of strikes in May 1920 Limerick farmers decided to invite the ITGWU to appoint six representatives to a committee, to which they would appoint a like number. An improving level of organisation paved the way for settlements on a county basis. One such was made after a fortnight's stike in Co. Dublin in March.

The 1920 Annual Report contains no ascertained membership figures, but gives an estimate of 120,000. The continued recruitment of rural workers is emphasised. They were joining in 'ever-increasing numbers'. From the statement that 'south of the Ballina/Newry line, the men on the land, save for a few black spots, owed allegiance to the OBU' it would appear that organisation had been extended to the sparsely populated midlands with their predominantly cattle-raising economy.

The 'congested districts' were, however, another matter. Here there was a greater element of subsistence farming, and the regular employment of permanent wage labourers was not yet established. The cry was for land, and seizures were beginning as early as March. 1920

*   *   *

The activity of the Crown forces sharply increased in 1920. In January over a thousand raids were reported, in February over four thousand. After 20 February, when a constable was shot dead in Dublin, a curfew was imposed, and no civilian was permitted in the streets between midnight and 5 a.m. A graphic description was given by Erskine Childers in the London *Daily News*: 'As the citizens go to bed, the barracks spring to life. Lorries, tanks and armoured search-light cars, muster in fleets. . . . A thunder of knocks; no time to dress (even for a woman alone) or the door will crash in. On opening, in charge the soldiers – literally charge – with fixed bayonets and full war kit.'[5]

The difficulty of running a trade union under such circumstances was described by Cathal O'Shannon:

> For the past 8 or 9 weeks, the *Watchword of Labour* has been seized every publication day by orders of Dublin Castle. For over a month, its editor has been on the run, evading arrest. Over a dozen of its officials and organisers have been arrested and deported to England without charge or trial, or prospect of either. Its branch meetings up and down the country have been broken up at the point of the bayonet. Its offices have been entered and raided, and its headquarters, Liberty Hall, raided and searched again and again, from top to bottom.[6]

Among those arrested in one of the raids was Joseph McGrath, TD, manager of the Insurance Section. He was deported to England and imprisoned without charge or trial. William O'Brien was deputed to make representations for his release and approached the chairman of the Health Insurance Commission, who wrote on his behalf to the Chief Secretary, Ian Macpherson. The result seems to have been merely to remind that anti-Irish Scot that O'Brien

1920 was still at large. He was arrested at 1 a.m. on 3 March, held for a while in Mountjoy, then deported and lodged in Wormwood Scrubs. When he arrived there he had had no food for over twenty-four hours. Having waited a fortnight during which no information was forthcoming as to the reason for his imprisonment, he began a hunger-strike on 18 March.[7]

His imprisonment drew an immediate protest from the Irish Labour Party and TUC, who communicated with corresponding organisations in Britain. A by-election was pending in Stockport, a town with a large Irish population a few miles south of Manchester. Polling day was to be 27 March. After receiving no satisfaction from Conservative, Liberal and Labour candidates, a group of Irish trade unionists conceived the notion of nominating O'Brien. Before doing so they elected a deputation consisting of George Clancy and Gilbert Lynch, who on 9 and 10 March met the Labour and TUC leaders in London. They were coldly received, Ramsay MacDonald delivering himself of one of those judgments that made him famous. Reminded that he had himself voted for a resolution on self-determination at Amsterdam, he protested that 'It was passed only out of sympathy and was not intended as practical policy.'[8] O'Brien's supporters returned to Stockport and nominated their man. A vigorous campaign was fought, W. P. Coates coming from London and Alex Lynn from Belfast.

On the sixth day of O'Brien's hunger-strike news came out that his condition was serious. Foran and Johnson visited him in jail and induced W. Adamson of the Labour Party to ask a question in parliament. He was told by Bonar Law that O'Brien had been 'arrested on suspicion of being implicated in a murderous conspiracy that has resulted in the death of so many loyal servants of the Crown in Ireland'. He refused to release him. But on 26 March, the day before the election, he changed his mind, and O'Brien was removed to a nursing home. It was stated that the release was temporary. The last day of O'Brien's hunger-strike, 25 March, saw the arrival in Ireland of the first of the special constables known as the Black and Tans.

While O'Brien was in the nursing home Cathal O'Shannon attended an international Labour meeting in London. On 11

April he was taken up from 'under the eyes of the British 1920
Labour leaders, some of whom were his colleagues at Berne and Amsterdam'. He was interrogated at Scotland Yard, then deported to Ireland and charged at Kells with making a seditious speech. He was lodged in Mountjoy.

While O'Shannon was in transit there were other developments. There were now in Mountjoy over a hundred prisoners held without charge or trial. On 5 April sixty of these began a hunger-strike. On 12 April the Irish Labour Party and TUC decided to call a general strike for their release. The strike was called for the following day, the participating unions sending out their own telegrams. It was an immense triumph for Foran, whose two principal lieutenants were in jail. His 'Notice to Members' ran:

> All members are instructed to note and obey the order of the National Executive of Irish Labour Party and Trades Union Congress calling a general strike of Irish Workers for Tuesday April 13th as a protest against the inhuman treatment of political prisoners and to demand their immediate release. For full particulars and exceptions see Labour Party appeal in press.

Outside the Belfast area the shut-down was virtually complete. As the authorities did not move on the Tuesday, the strike was continued on the Wednesday, and in some places till Thursday, when news of the prisoners' release reached remote areas. This great event, which marked the highest point in the Irish national liberation struggle, and pointed to how it might have been finally and decisively won, deserves a volume to itself, and it is to be hoped that some student with working-class sympathies will one day provide it. There were, of course, great demonstrations in such fully organised centres as Cork, Limerick and Sligo, but what is especially interesting is the spirit of the people in the smaller towns, as quotations from reports to Liberty Hall illustrate.

From Virginia, Co. Cavan, came news that 'We got on to the business houses first, got them all closed, with which we had not much trouble. We then held a meeting and put a picket on all roads leading to town and stopped all people pending [*sic*] special business.' From Kenmare the secretary reported: 'We got all businesses closed down on Wednesday

1920 and had a grand procession through the town and on to the chapel where one of our members recited the Rosary in Irish for the release of prisoners.' The message shows the bewilderment of ordinary people. It concludes: 'It is terrible the way the government are treating us.' The *Watchword of Labour* described their methods as 'tyrannical'. At Portlaoise stockowners were given ten minutes to close down the fair, and the branch committee availed of the free time to tackle all members who were in arrears. 'There is a divil of a lot of them,' wrote the secretary, 'but before I give up I am going to have them good members or fired out. They are not going to wear badges and shout and still be scabs.'

Unable to make contact with officials of the Workers' Council, the secretary of the Kilkenny branch acted on his own initiative. The result was a complete stoppage which was spread throughout the county by means of telegrams. At Tralee 'The Trades Council was turned into a Workers' Council who took full control of everything. We had our own police who kept order, saw that all business was suspended, issued permits for everything required, pickets patrolled the streets, in fact the workers controlled all.' At Naas a 'picket of "red guards" brought to their senses' shops that refused to close. Kilkenny carpenters, working on the grandstand at Punchestown, joined in enthusiastically. A procession a thousand strong was supported by Sinn Féin. In Killala all business stopped, and the ITGWU led a torchlight procession in which they were followed by Sinn Féin and Canon O'Reilly, the parish priest.

A postscript to the Muine Bheag report ran:

> On the second day of the strike we held a public meeting on the Market Square and publicly proclaimed the establishment of a Provisional Soviet Government, policed the town to keep order and ration out food supplies and appealed to all not to molest in any way any member of the forces of the army of occupation, and on last night when all was over it was publicly made known that we were withdrawing all and would allow business to be carried on as usual.

The small country branch at Castletown, Co. Laois, was unable to stop work on the scattered farms, but brought out the road workers. The secretary concluded his letter: 'I see that the Editor of the *Watchword of Labour* is in the claws of these hellish barbarians.' 1920

Séamus O'Brien wrote from Galway:

> How quickly those sturdy sons of the 'city of the tribes' and the hardy clean-cut manly boys from Connemara jumped into the fray, took control of the foodstuffs of the city, which they divided equally, regardless of wealth; how with lightning agility they tracked down the profiteer, took possession of the butchers' shops, allowed no more than two pounds of meat to any one family and every other necessity in proportion.

Farmers who came seeking inflated prices for turf and potatoes were pounced upon by pickets. Their prices were hastily reduced. In Waterford maximum retail prices were fixed, and it was laid down that no charge must be made for cutting bacon into rashers.

The stoppage was complete in every town and village in the counties of Cork and Limerick. In Kilmallock the Town Hall was commandeered, 'red-flaggers manned the castle entrances, tree-trunks and carts were used to compel compliance with the order to halt, cars not driven under permit were turned back. . . . One was struck by the absolute recognition of the Soviet system.'

It was, of course, 'Soviet system' without state power. Why, then, did the state tolerate it? For one thing, it was conditional and could be ended by climbing down in a field where climbing down was common enough to entail no loss of face. For another, it was proclaimedly temporary. Séamus O'Brien might write: 'God speed the day when such councils shall be established all over Erin and the world, control the natural resources of the country, the means of production and distribution, run them as the worker knows how to run them, for the good and welfare of the whole community, and not for the profits of a few bloated parasites' – but he recognised that what the workers had seized was merely the local government. And doubtless the British authorities appreciated that any attempt to dislodge them by force might provoke a struggle in which O'Brien's dreams might acquire unintended reality. For the middle classes, now completely alienated

1920 from the paramount power, were debarred from exercising a restraining influence. There were two alternatives: to recognise the Republic and bring that restraining influence into effect, successfully or otherwise; or to give way temporarily, pour in the Black and Tans, and attempt a 'military solution'. The authorities chose the latter policy. But the prisoners were released on 15 April.

The man selected to carry out the government's heavy-handed policy was Sir Nevil Macready, who arrived at the North Wall on 14 April. He had been brought into Scotland Yard to break the police union and had succeeded. He combined mountainous arrogance with cavernous ignorance. His great joy was dressing up in military uniforms, and his autobiography is interspersed with pictures of himself in various senatorial poses. His opinion of the situation in Ireland was that 'Red murder stalked through the length and breadth of the land.' He regarded the Irish as a 'people characterised through past centuries by lack of discipline, intolerance of restraint, and with no common standard of public morality [who] can only be governed and held in check under the protection of a strong military garrison'. Clearly Sir Nevil Macready was the right man for the job.

Arrests continued. Ernest Nunan was the next of the Liberty Hall staff to find his way into Mountjoy. He was taken from his bed at midnight on Thursday 15 April by a platoon of soldiers who could offer no explanation as they drove him to the prison. O'Shannon went on hunger-strike on the 27th and was released with others on 5 May. He remained in the Mater Hospital for a further week. In the meantime on 16 April Larkin's trial had closed. He was sentenced to 'from five to ten years' imprisonment' on 3 May.

* * *

While in the nursing home O'Brien kept in touch with union affairs by correspondence. The EC met on 24 and 25 April, and J. J. Hughes sent an account of its deliberations on the 29th. There had been disagreements in Limerick, where a resolution had been passed requesting the transference of Dowling to another area. 'Both sides' were summoned to

Liberty Hall. The subject of a full-time EC was not discussed. 1920
The subjects of 'land' and 'area industrial councils' were also held over. The 'Wicklow and Wexford job' was reported to be 'ripening rapidly'. (This is a reference to amalgamation discussions with the Agricultural and General Workers' Union in Enniscorthy.) There was no demand for a No. 1 branch meeting. (Presumably large meetings were impracticable owing to the disturbed conditions.) The general strike had galvanised sleeping branches into life. One gets the impression that the EC relied heavily on O'Brien's experience and was disinclined to make innovations in his absence. According to the ITUC report, O'Brien was released on 6 May, but the date deducible from his own reminiscences, 12 May, seems more likely. He arrived back in Dublin on the 15th, in the company of Thomas Kennedy, and was greeted by cheering crowds at Westland Row.

Another subject referred to in Hughes's letter was the decision to limit the export of food. Lloyd George's government was dedicated to free enterprise and, contrary to the advice of the trade, removed price controls from bacon and butter on 31 March 1920. The Irish Council of the NUDL decided to refuse to load foodstuffs for export. They were supported by the ITUC and the ITGWU. Hughes remarked that in certain ports, notably Belfast and Derry, there were refusals to load commodities like eggs, of which there was a glut. On 15 April the ITUC gave instructions that the embargo should be confined to butter, bacon and live pigs. In an open letter to the bacon-curers the ITUC offered them two alternatives: either they would meet and devise means of governing the industry with the primary object of supplying the Irish people with bacon at a reasonable price, or 'the organised workers themselves would take the task in hands'. The letter continued: 'A protest may be raised that it will be illegal to enter into possession of a factory without the proprietor's sanction, that such act would be prevented by the armed forces of the British Crown. We answer: perhaps, perhaps not! We shall take the risk.'[9] In the event conferences were arranged with manufacturers and farmers, who agreed to earmark a proportion of their production for home consumption at unchanged prices.

The first and most famous factory seizure took place on

1920 17 May at Limerick Junction, the armed forces of the British Crown being conspicuous by their absence. Knocklong creamery, the property of Messrs Cleeve, was a large central factory fed by a number of separating stations which in turn were supplied with milk by farmers. It manufactured butter, condensed milk and other by-products. The complex contained one of the largest ice-making plants in Ireland. The workers in the creamery and separating stations were members of the ITGWU. For some time past there had been attempts to win improved wages, but these had been frustrated by the action of the works manager, who had made himself unpopular in a number of ways.

According to the *Watchword of Labour*, 'The workers and the union decided to take things into their own hands. They decided to cease work for the company on Saturday 15 May, and to go back to work immediately and run the factories for themselves.' On Monday morning they invaded the manager's office, saw him off the premises and installed in his place Séan O'Hagan, or, to give him his legal name, Jack Hedley. With him was the local branch secretary, an employee called John O'Dwyer, and 'Jack Dowling and John McGrath to watch progress on behalf of the union'. The Cleeves nameplate was removed from the door, and the billheads were changed. Streamers were affixed to the frontage inscribed 'Knocklong Soviet Creamery' and 'We make butter, not profits'. The red flag was hoisted above the roof together with the tricolour. Farmers brought in 97 per cent of the usual milk supply. In addition to fulfilling existing contracts, the workers secured orders from co-operative societies, for example Belfast. At the end of five days the factory was handed back in return for substantial wage increases, dated back to 24 March, and the removal of the works manager.

The above account, apart from O'Hagan's real name, is taken entirely from the union journal. It contains particulars which seem at first sight somewhat improbable, or at least to require an explanation. What was Hedley doing in Limerick? Why make him manager and not one of the workers? Strike actions required the sanction of the union's head office. Was this obtained? If so from whom, and in what form?

As regards Hedley's background, he was arrested in Belfast

in June 1918 and brought before the notorious Alan Bell. His cause was scarcely helped when Kitty Coyle of the Socialist Labour Party produced a large crimson handkerchief on which she proceeded to blow her nose. 'No red-flagging in here!' snapped the magistrate. Hedley was imprisoned and immediately went on hunger-strike. He was released under the 'Cat and Mouse' Act and left for England. Rearrested in England, he was brought back to Ireland and imprisoned in Mountjoy, where he was one of the hunger-strikers released by the two-day general strike. From the account in the *Watchword*, it is clear that he was well known to the editorial staff and recognised as *persona grata*.

His own explanation of his presence in Limerick is that when he was released from Mountjoy he had a conversation with Thomas Kennedy, who told him that there were disagreements among the officials in Limerick and that allegations of excessive drinking were being made against one of them. He asked Hedley to go there, presumably as a socialist friend of Dowling, form a private opinion on this matter, and report back to him. Hedley stated that in the same conversation Kennedy told him that the union was considering organising small farmers. The first statement is corroborated by the fact that on 30 April the Limerick organisers were called to Liberty Hall and their differences thrashed out. As we have seen, the land question was on the agenda of the April EC. Hedley also said that he was in Limerick on 1 May and that he addressed a meeting at Glin.[10]

From these circumstances it would seem that permission for the strike must have been given. The spotlight was shining down on the Limerick organisation. The same argument applies to the seizure. But the officials were also aware that it would be 'illegal to enter into possession of a factory'. It may have been thought expedient to allow the attempt to be made by a man who was not legally the agent of the union, though he became a local hero. Another curious coincidence is that on Tuesday 18 May a special conference of the IFU met at Galway, and one very large pig producer assured the gathering, as if expecting to be contradicted, that Dublin dockers absolutely insisted on eating only the very best rashers. Was Knocklong also a shot across the bows of

1920 the food industry? The prestige of the ITGWU was greatly enhanced in East Limerick and South Tipperary, and the Tipperary Workingmen's Protection and Benefit Society decided to amalgamate.

* * *

During the evening of 21 May Michael Donnelly, a member of the dockers' section of No. 1 branch who had fought with the Citizen Army in 1916, called at Liberty Hall with important information. A ship bringing military supplies for the Crown forces had tied up and would be discharged on the following day. Less than a fortnight earlier the London dockers had refused to load the *Jolly George* with a cargo of military supplies for the armies of intervention in eastern Europe. O'Brien and Foran decided to call upon ITGWU members to refuse to unload this ship. It was unloaded by the military. The next military cargo was taken to Dún Laoire, where once again the dockers refused to touch it. In this instance the railwaymen refused to work a train until they were satisfied that it carried no war material. The process was repeated at Cork and Cóbh.

The ensuing struggle lasted seven months. The brunt was borne by the railwaymen, 400 of whom were locked out at the North Wall. Their maintenance demanded the raising of £1,000 a week. Throughout the course of the dispute individual railwaymen were being suspended, and the number without work constantly increased. The dockers' position was not so difficult: the regular vessels did not bring military supplies, and the 'casual' men could work more or less where they chose.

* * *

Despite increasing violence on the part of the military authorities, the wages movement slackened only very slowly. Limerick city, for example, was 'shot up' by police on 27 April and 1 May. That in no way deterred the gas workers from striking on 9 May. There was a greater readiness for accommodation among employers, due in part to their recognition of the workers' power which had been so spectacularly

demonstrated. There was also a disinclination to harm the 1920
national cause. When on 18 April the Agricultural Wages Board awarded 34s a week to men aged over twenty, many farmers preferred to pay it rather than risk strike action at a time when the common enemy was threatening both themselves and their workers. But as British civil administration either crumbled or became unacceptable there was an increasing inclination to turn to arbitrators appointed by the Dáil Ministry of Labour, for which the only socialist in Dáil Éireann, Countess Markiewicz, was responsible. But the union did not withdraw its representation from wages boards.

Strikes continued, especially of newly organised workers. The first strike of domestic servants took place at Kilrush in June. It was successful and established standard rates for nursery maids and domestics of various grades. Waterford gas workers had to strike to win Cork rates. The first dispute in which the union went to arbitration before Dáil assessors was that between Cork city carters and the Master Carriers. Terence MacSwiney was one of the arbitrators who awarded the men a minimum wage of 62s 6d for a 48-hour week. This was in early June, and later in the month a six-week-old strike of general labourers in Kinsale was settled by Dáil arbitration. A threatened strike of farm workers at Buttevant was averted altogether.

It was not always easy to bring employers to arbitration. On 17 June a Ráthluirc employer dismissed two men. The others walked out. On the following day a general strike of all the workers in the town began at 11 a.m. All business stopped. This was the 'one big union' in action. William O'Brien was in Limerick and arrived at Ráthluirc at midday in company with Dowling. They found the entire working population waiting at the railway station. Headed by a cyclist carrying a red flag, they marched in procession to the main street, where they were addressed by William O'Brien, John McGrath, Dowling and Hedley. The employer then agreed to arbitration, and work resumed at 2 p.m. On the following day Dowling and O'Brien went to Tipperary to arrange the transfer terms for the Workingmen's Protection and Benefit Society. A demonstration to launch the new branch was organised on 29 June. It was addressed by John Dowling and Nora Connolly. Here was another town where the entire

1920 working class was in one union.

The tendency to turn to the Dáil was encouraged by the Agricultural Wages Board's poor award, namely 34s for male workers aged over twenty. The union regularly negotiated 37s, and sometimes even more. But there were cases where strong Sinn Féiners tried to compel acceptance of the AWB standard. In such cases the ministry would arbitrate between the parties, but it would not lay down standards of its own. It developed its policy along legal and adminstrative, not along social lines. Some have blamed this deficiency upon the lack of labour representation.

* * *

The relation between the social and political aspects of the revolution were raised in an important letter published in the *Watchword of Labour* on 1 May. An anonymous author, presumably a rural worker, wrote:

> All through the Sinn Féin portion of the country there are large tracts of land in the hands of a few, so that if a fair divide of the land were made there would be plenty to secure a decent living for all rural workers. If the Sinn Féin strong farmers are sincere in their loud-voiced, sky-scraping, fire-proof patriotism [a reference follows to the men who gave their lives in 1916]... can they not prove their patriotism, not by giving their lives, but part of their surplus property to the workers of Ireland as a whole?

After more in the same vein and a demand for nationalisation of the land, the writer concluded:

> Connolly's war-cry in life was 'You must throw off England's yoke before you can throw off the yoke of the capitalist.' Is it possible that by his death . . . the situation has been reversed and that the war-cry of the future will be 'We have scrapped capitalism at home in order to be stronger in our fight to make scrap iron of the chains that bind our nation'?

In this fascinating glimpse of the outlook of an advanced rural worker we can see general and special influences at work. There is the old-established land-hunger and the revival of Davitt's demand for land nationalisation. There is envy of the farmer and distrust of his patriotism. There is impatience with the Dáil policy of seeking sovereignty through foreign recognition rather than by direct popular action. From this comes the fallacy that a nation can alter its social system without controlling its own institutions. 1920

After the statement that Connolly held the view that national independence took precedence over socialism, the editor (not O'Shannon) inserted: 'He did not.' He thus appears to share the writer's opinions. On the other hand, he may merely have had in mind Connolly's belief, embodied in the Proclamation, that no struggle for independence against a powerful enemy can be successful without the involvement of the mass of the people.

Within weeks the issue was up for trial in the court of practical experience. A mighty wave of land seizures swept the country, particularly the west. It was directed for the most part against landlords and ranchers, though if any 'strong farmers' had read the *Watchword* article, they too may have felt misgivings. The British authorities were powerless. The traditional enemies of the people flocked to Dublin to ask Dáil Éireann for protection. But this was seen not as the last desperate effort of a reactionary class to escape what it had brought upon itself; it was seen as recognition of the Republic. These people must be succoured to avoid splitting the nation. The feelings of the writer of the *Watchword* article can be guessed: 'I told you so.' The hopes of the small farmers and landless men had been dashed when victory was in sight.

Though Griffith had his way in this matter, things might have been different had Labour been represented in the Dáil. The union accepted the accomplished fact and merely reported its decision on the land question. But what a worker/farmer alliance might have meant was shown at a meeting on 17 April at Killeshin. This was Gaffney's birthplace, but his presence was not reported. The speakers were Séamus Lennon, TD, and Archibald Heron. Lennon told how Sinn Féin had raised £6,500 to buy Kilcumney farm. It had been handed over to six labourers to work co-operatively, stock being purchased at Kilkenny fair. The labourers drew standard wages, but would divide any profits at the end

1920 of the first year. Heron remarked that some people laboured under the delusion that the object of trade unionism was merely to increase the weekly wage of the members. There were loud cheers when he declared that 'The intention of the IT and GW Union was to support any organisation in the fight for freedom of every kind.'[11]

The number of new branches established in the first six months of 1920 was 70, 36 in the first quarter, 34 in the second. There was no sudden advance after the two-day strike, but growth did not cease. The estimated membership had grown to 130,000, covering every county in Ireland. The head office wages book lists 90 employees, organisers, office staff, maintenance workers, a charwoman and a caretaker. Amalgamations were taking place. On 13 June, a few days before the Tipperary meeting, William O'Brien and Thomas Kennedy visited Enniscorthy, where the Executive of the Agricultural and General Workers' Union agreed to wind up their organisation and join the ITGWU. Its Wicklow secretary, James Everitt, became a union organiser. In Dublin the Portmanteau Makers' and Leatherworkers' Trade Union also sought amalgamation.

The main work of the union was concerned, of course, with wages movements. Its largest single item of expenditure was dispute pay. But it made itself the backbone of a political strike for national objectives. In Limerick it took up the issue of housing. In Waterford it succeeded in preventing the auction of a farm for grazing. Instead there took place a sale 'by permission of the ITGWU'. Despite the rural workers' appeal, the union took no attitude to the land war and published the Dáil's injunction 'Register your claims and they'll be looked at when Ireland is free' without comment. This was a new political issue, and only Eamon Rooney grasped its importance. In the practical field the union gave constant support to the Socialist Party of Ireland and fielded candidates on the programme of a Workers' Republic. In the social field the brass and reed band had made a name for itself, giving a concert in the Abbey Theatre on 9 May and playing selections at the Fianna Aeriocht in Croke Park in the following week. But the central conception of the leadership was their objective of bringing all the workers of Ireland into one trade union. There was indignation when, after the

ITGWU had organised workers in a town where organisation 1920
had been previously unknown, English craft unions came in to poach the tradesmen. This reaction was not one of jealousy. It was believed that national independence would be won by the Dáil and that industrial action by the workers of Ireland, once they were united, would establish the Workers' Republic.

For four years the union had gone from strength to strength. The story was one of unbroken progress. We must now look into the factors by which that progress was brought to a halt.

14

The Wind from the North

Assassination is the extreme form of censorship.
GEORGE BERNARD SHAW

Threat to Unionism – Belfast pogroms – Dáil Courts – events in Cork – Black and Tans – munitions strike – Tadhg Barry arrested – end of the post-war boom – staff discontents

1920 On 12 June 1920 the results of the county, rural district and Poor Law elections were published. Once again Labour did well and Sinn Féin better. But the importance of the result was that it completed the picture first sketched in January, that of the growing isolation of Unionism. There were 33 administrative counties in Ireland; the unionists controlled only four of them. There were 206 rural districts; the Unionists controlled 34. Republicans held five out of Ulster's nine counties. Extensive areas of Down, Derry and Armagh returned Republican rural district councils. In the very citadel of Belfast a swing of eight seats to Labour would destroy the Unionist majority.

Apart from one county, Antrim, whose nationalist fringe was of small weight, there was no area that could be certified homogeneously Unionist. Appreciation of this fact led to the renewal of a plan that had been discussed since partition was first mooted, and which was indeed used as a veiled threat at the Buckingham Palace Conference of July 1914. This was to create a 'homogeneous Ulster' by forcibly expelling all who possessed nationalist convictions. It was likely to be as disastrous in failure as in success.

There was no time to be lost. The Unionist position was being too rapidly eroded. Protestant workers in transport, milling, malting and timber working, were benefiting from national settlements in which the ITGWU was the driving force. In Monaghan town Catholics and Protestants had united under the red flag and after a five-day strike won all-round increases of 6s a week. Their example was followed within a month by the shop assistants of Carrickmacross. 1920

The ITGWU officials in Ulster were men of considerable ability. Houston's record of success we have noted. At the beginning of 1920 the Belfast branch secretary was Charles Ridgway, who so pleased Liberty Hall that O'Brien urged the branch to increase his salary. While the branch hesitated Ridgway was offered work by another union, and in order not to lose his services, the EC appointed him organiser in Dundalk. In June 1920 his place in Belfast was taken by William McMullen. At first the dockers were reluctant to accept him, but he too was recommended for a salary increase and within a year had silenced all his critics. Peadar O'Donnell was concentrating on Derry, where the branch secretary was James Houston, one judges, from his correspondence with Denis, no relation. Eamon Rooney in Drogheda would sometimes oblige by visiting Newry.

The effectiveness of the organisation can be illustrated by the case of a North Mayo flax-grower who declined to employ union men. The Ballina and Killala branches sent, in a message to Belfast, the numbers of the railway wagons carrying his crop to the spinners, and Houston saw that it was not unloaded. Workers from cross-channel unions transferred in a steady trickle, 150 flour-millers from the NAUL in February, flax-dressers in April. A start was made in the organisation of laundry-girls and pork butchers. There were catering workers and a flourishing branch in Harland & Wolff's shipyard, where contractor's men were laying a new slipway. Organisation was proceeding among nurses, cinema workers and lorry-drivers. It was even proposed to organise taxi-men.

The effect of this work was to galvanise other unions into action. When a shirt-cutters' strike took place in Derry and the leadership proved ineffective the workers turned to Peadar O'Donnell. Sectarianism was at an ebb and Labour morale was at its highest since 1907. For the first time for years a Labour paper was published, the *Northern Democrat*. At a May Day demonstration Samuel Porter, one of Connolly's members in the old Belfast ISRP, foresaw the eclipse of Unionism by insurgent Labour, and at this point the reactionaries took alarm.

1920 They found their example in Caledon. After O'Donnell's initial successes Fulton, the blanket manufacturer, locked out his workers, who were Protestant and Catholic in approximately equal numbers, and brought in scabs who were Orangemen to a man. He then took the precaution of inviting a gentleman called Turkington from Belfast to organise them in the Ulster Workers' Union, a successor of the 'yellow' union established on the quays in 1907. He was also a landlord and began the systematic eviction of all locked-out workers, and these, as notices fell due one by one, for the most part lost heart and emigrated to Scotland. Two of them appealed from the judgment of the petty sessions, and in this case Fulton, fearing unfavourable publicity for his blankets, climbed down. But his plan had worked. There was talk of countering it with a boycott of Ulster goods. But this O'Shannon opposed, making the case that goods could be 'black' or 'white' irrespective of their place of origin. These events took place in the latter part of 1919, though the appeal to the High Court was put down for May 1920.

Turkington's organisation published a remarkable balance sheet which seemed to indicate that it lived rent free and that somebody paid its telephone bills. It acknowledged donations from people whose names were decorated with such symbols as MBE. On several occasions the *Watchword* exposed its sectarian activities. Running parallel with the UWU was a 'yellow' Labour Party. It was called the Ulster Protestant and Unionist Workers' Association. In the elections its candidates, Turkington included, received derisory votes.

The *Watchword* of 12 June reported three significant events. The ITGWU organised the grist-mill workers of Belfast. The textile unions published a plan of amalgamation. The Belfast City Council refused to receive a deputation of unemployed ex-servicemen. The following week O'Shannon wrote a leading article pointing out how little people in Belfast knew about the rest of Ireland, and how little they were known by their fellow-countrymen. 'Has the time not come', he asked, 'when more attention should be given by Republicans . . . to the several burning Ulster questions?' In fact it was too late.

Within a few days sectarian riots turned the city of Derry into a shambles. The orgy of rioting and murder, which put a stop to all business for nearly a week, was instigated by the 'yellow' Labour Party under the pretext of defending Protestant ex-servicemen from the Catholics who had taken their jobs. 1920

O'Shannon's first reaction was to put the blame equally on the two sides. The instigators were, of course, only identified later. But he made what he thought a constructive suggestion. There should be a 'Red Army' which would defend all workers impartially. His next issue contained a letter from a Derry trade unionist who said that in anticipation of some such provocation this had actually been done. A non-sectarian Citizen Army had been established. But once the violence began it had disintegrated, each man flying to his sectarian camp. There was every reason for apprehension.

For a time there was uneasy peace. More violence before 12 July might invite a government ban. And there were passions to be inflamed. At Finaghy Field Carson's demagogy reached unsurpassable heights. He drew a lurid picture of the Fenian hordes massed for the attack on 'Ulster' while using insidious methods to destroy it from within. What he found particularly insidious was the combination of the Republican question with the Labour question. A voice interrupted: 'Ireland is the most Labour centre in the United Kingdom.' 'I know that,' said Carson without enthusiasm, but insisted: 'We in Ulster will tolerate no Sinn Féin.' In other words, it was vital to the interests that he served that Ulster Labour should be Orange Labour. Let it become Republican and there was a danger that it might prove too successful. He declared he was tired of words without action and warned the government that action would be taken.

It was. On the morning of Wednesday 21 July leaflets were handed out in the shipyards advertising a meeting called by the Ulster Protestant and Unionist Workers on private property, a wharf beside Workman Clarke's shipyard. It started at 1.30 p.m. and was attended by some shipyard workers, mostly from Workman Clarkes but a few from Harland & Wolffs. There seem to have been a number of unemployed men and boys. The chairman worked in the shipyard. One speaker was a 'Labour' councillor from Bangor. The other, McKay, was a member of the 'yellow' Labour organisation and was credited with provoking the riots in Derry.

1920 The disturbance began when an Orangeman asked for the speaker's credentials. He was set upon and badly beaten. The meeting became a mob. 'Crowds of boys and young men', as an eye-witness put it, 'armed with sticks, iron bars, pipe tubes, etc.' rushed headlong into Harland & Wolff's yard. The Catholics working on the slipway contract were driven out. Some were thrown fully clothed into the river and had to swim to safety under a hail of bolts and rivets. Then came the socialists, Protestant or Catholic, and the Catholic tradesmen. Needless to say, all the members of the ITGWU branch were incontinently hurled out.[1]

News of what had taken place flashed through the town. When shipyard workers passed through Cromac Square on their way home they were challenged by angry Catholics. But for the prompt action of the IRA there would not have been a Protestant shop left in the Falls Road. There was less compunction in the Orange districts, though there were instances where Ulster Volunteers tried to calm down the rioters and protect property.

In the following days the pogrom spread. Protestants drove Catholics out of mixed factories. The union and the IRA opposed retaliation, but it was bound to happen. Then came evictions. Those who would not move were 'burned out'. Sometimes Catholics and Protestants agreed to exchange houses, thus showing their fundamental community of interest in a crazy perverted way. The Lord Mayor refused to call together the City Council; instead he enrolled a special police force composed of Protestants only. In certain parts of the city it was an advantage to be seen carrying a Union Jack. The *Watchword of Labour* accused the authorities of trying to create a politically homogeneous six counties and criticised the NUDL for tamely accepting the dismissal of its Catholic members. The ITGWU declared that *its card was sacrosanct.* A large number of the expelled workers were carpenters, and their reinstatement was demanded by the Amalgamated Society of Woodworkers. The companies could not comply. The EC called a strike, but only a third of their members came out. Those who did not do so were expelled. The ITGWU complimented the Woodworkers' EC, but deplored the blow to trade unionism. When the dust settled 5,000 Catholics were on the streets, penniless, many

of them homeless. Large numbers of them went to Glasgow. 1920
The union sent Houston to Scotland, where he spent several weeks on relief work and £250 was sent to the relief fund.

What was considered most deplorable was the inaction of the officials of some of the cross-channel craft unions. They would deplore the pogrom in private, but were afraid to call on their executives to take action. The result was a tendency for the general workers' unions to fall apart, the Catholics joining the ITGWU and the Protestants following Turkington. Two officials who had the courage of their Labour convictions were Midgley and Donaldson.

The ITGWU was singled out for attention by all the forces of reaction. On 1 September Workman Clarke employees who assembled at the yard each morning, not for work but to organise blackguardism, attacked deep-sea dockers on board the *Ballygawley Head* and shot dead a member of the union, James Cromie, who had served five years in the Royal Navy. On the same day Black and Tans were saving the hay and running the saw-mill of R. M. Saunders of Aherlow, whose men had joined the union and gone on strike for the British government award. An advertisement placed in the Derry edition of the *Belfast Telegraph* by the Ulster Unionist Labour Association urged all Protestant workers to refuse to have anything to do with the ITGWU, 'which preaches republicanism', and to join their amalgamated unions.

In the South there was a widespread demand for a boycott of Belfast goods which Cathal O'Shannon was strong-minded enough to resist. His international experience had taught him that imperialism was standing in the wings, only waiting to come on stage and play a very decisive part. Nevil Macready was told to prepare to hand over the north-east of Ireland to the force of special constables which the Lord Mayor was now recruiting from within the Protestant community. It was hoped that this would free British troops for service elsewhere in Ireland or, in the event of Labour troubles, in Britain. This counter-revolution was to be sealed by partition.[2]

The pogrom resulted in wage reductions. The Protestants who took the places of Catholics were sometimes paid £1 a week less. When employers found that workers had left their trade unions and joined the UWU they immediately took a few shillings from them. Needless to say, that organisation

1920 did not long prosper. The 'document' was reintroduced. Somebody printed forms headed *Great Northern Railway* which Catholic employees were compelled to sign. They undertook not to have anything to do with Sinn Féin. The essentially political character of the pogrom was shown by the fact that in many cases Catholics who were prepared to swear an oath of allegiance to the King of England were allowed to remain at work, while Protestants who would not were sent packing. But the religious cloak that was thrown over what was in essence a quasi-Fascist operation prevented the British working class from seeing their duty. O'Shannon hoped for action across the channel. Disappointed, he acquiesced in the Belfast boycott, but with grave misgivings. It would only harm those who wished to trade with the rest of Ireland. It was the beginning of the recognition of partition. From now on Dáil Éireann was taking decisions which it had no hope of enforcing over the whole country.

* * *

A James Larkin Defence Committee had been set up in New York and, after the sentence, was considering an appeal. Frank P. Walsh was prepared to act without fee. After the verdict the trial judge had read out a cablegram stating that Larkin was born in Liverpool and had a criminal record, having been convicted on three charges of larceny of union funds. This information was doubtless obtained through the consular service. A birth certificate had indeed been included, but it belonged to the wrong man. Foran did, however, cable his complete confidence in Larkin's innocence and his conviction that the Simon Punch larceny case was a frame-up. The New York committee was in correspondence with the union throughout its existence. It consisted of members of the Irish Progressive League, together with friends of Connolly and Con O'Lyhane. O'Lyhane himself had died as a result of prison experiences, having been turned out of jail with double pneumonia in the depth of winter.

It was, of course, natural that Larkin's sister should wish for an agitation in Ireland, and it would be a safe assumption that Delia was the moving spirit behind the Larkin Defence Committee which was now set up in Dublin with Trades

Council support.[3] It contained all those elements surrounding 1920
P. T. Daly from which the Transport and General Workers' Union, and particularly O'Brien, were most estranged. Members of this Defence Committee sold stamps for the benefit of the 'Larkin Sustentation Fund', although the union had undertaken to bear all expenses. They decided to call a national one-day strike for 21 July. There was no stoppage outside Dublin, where a few hundred dockers acted out of loyalty to their old chief. But the cry was raised, very unjustly, that the union was not prepared to stand by its General Secretary.

* * *

In July 1920 Dáil Éireann took what the historian Dorothy Macardle called a 'momentous decision'. It decreed the establishment of Courts of Justice and Equity. The arbitration courts that had been set up in June 1919 and which had won such acceptance that the Crown courts frequently had not a single litigant were, strictly speaking, perfectly legal in English law. They acted in accordance with the Arbitration Act, 1886, while assuming judicial trimmings not implied in it. Indeed Sinn Féin 'courts' had arbitrated before the Dáil existed. The new development was unequivocal. It was an assertion of separate sovereignty.

The new system operated at three levels: a Supreme Court, district courts and parish courts. The union recognised these courts. It undertook litigation before them on issues of demarcation, and indeed lost money when the Free State declined to enforce their judgments. Members of the union Executive served as justices, for example Thomas Kennedy in South Dublin. At the same time the union could not overlook the fact that there are two sides in a dual power, and more than one class in a nation. It was obviously not practical to withdraw from the Agricultural Wages Board and other British state organisations until the Dáil had extended its social policy. Moreover, these bodies covered the whole of Ireland, and the union had to serve the interests of its members wherever they were.

1920 The Irish Labour Party and TUC met in Cork city on 2 August. On the previous night police and military had raided and wrecked the ITGWU premises in Camden Quay. Soldiers and Black and Tans roamed the streets after 10 o'clock curfew, shooting at any lights they could see. The NEC had to finish the evening in a darkened hotel. A defensive note was sounded. In Cork there was no gay talk of sweeping tumultuously forward to the Workers' Republic. There was satisfaction with the electoral successes, but this meant little enough at a time when, in the words of the President, 'The country has been turned into an armed camp. The soldiers of a foreign power are billeted all over the country with all the paraphernalia of war. The country is being governed by naked force.'[4]

Of all meetings of the Irish Labour Party and TUC, that held in 1920 was the most strongly national. There was warm support for the railwaymen who were refusing to carry war material. On the key constitutional question, however, the position taken up was self-contradictory. A resolution, carried almost unanimously, called for 'the withdrawal of all the British military and other executive forces from Ireland, leaving the people of Ireland, through their authorised and elected representatives, the responsibility and power to maintain public order and fulfil all the functions of government'. This was in effect to give allegiance to Dáil Éireann. The resolution then affirmed the right of the people of Ireland, as a single national entity, to decide their form of government by plebiscite 'even though their choice may be complete separation from or complete unity with Great Britain'.[5] This was to withdraw it again. Something treated as settled in the first paragraph was treated as unsettled in the second. Some delegates accepted this as statesmanlike avoidance of a difficult issue. Others, O'Shannon among them, thought the plebiscite would afford the opportunity to establish a Workers' Republic by political means.

A deputation of expelled workers from Belfast was permitted to address the meeting. It was made clear that, far from consisting primarily of Republicans, the men driven from their work were the 'backbone of Trade Unionism in the North'.[6] The number of Protestants expelled from the shipyards was 400. Cathal O'Shannon drew a parallel with the white terror in Hungary.

The total number of delegates was 248. Thirty of these represented Trades Councils; these included Rooney, Metcalfe and Peadar O'Donnell. The ITGWU sent 70 delegates; these included the entire Executive, and there were also 21 from Dublin, 10 from Cork, three from Limerick and one from Waterford. The development of the union in the rural areas was shown by the presence of delegates from Newbridge, Naas, Castlebar, Birr, Fermoy and Knocklong. In two respects the ITUC in 1920 differed from that organisation today: there was an almost complete absence of Northern delegates, and the influence of the ITGWU was greater. Only twelve delegates had addresses in the six-county area that was being annexed. The second largest delegation was that of the Tailors. It numbered only ten. By contrast, at the 1974 Congress of the ICTU, out of 405 delegates, 91 came from Northern Ireland. The ITGWU sent 65 delegates compared with 30 from the Workers' Union of Ireland and 35 from the ATGWU. Its proportion of the whole had fallen from 28 per cent to 14 per cent.

The ITGWU delegates remained in Cork for a union conference. The 1919 Annual Report was discussed and accepted; it was printed and published in September. The conference was told of the reorganisation of the Approved Society in June when new rules were adopted. It was stated that the Executive had drafted a policy document on the subject of land holding and purchase. If, as one assumes, it was on the lines of a resolution adopted at the ITUC, then it advocated co-operative farming and 'direct ownership and cultivation by local and national administrative bodies' – in other words, the co-operative, collective and state farm combination later adopted in Soviet Russia. This resolution had been seconded by Houston. It is significant that it came from Offaly Trades Council and was directed against the graziers. There was nothing to satisfy the land-hunger in congested districts.

Questions were asked about the Larkin Release Committee (i.e. the committee organised by Delia Larkin). During the discussion members were assured that Larkin's wife was on the union payroll. She was indeed in receipt of £3 10s a week. But this was on 17 August increased to £8, the salary of a general officer. A suggestion was made that financial assistance

1920 should be given to Connolly's widow, and apparently an offer was made immediately. It was rejected somewhat indignantly by Nora, but very diplomatically by her mother, who explained that Connolly had died for the whole Irish nation, not for one section of it. Later the union assisted Máire Connolly with her medical studies.

The delegates left Cork highly impressed with the growth of the organisation in the south. A number of smaller societies had amalgamated, including the brewery workers and the gas workers, this making the ITGWU even more fully the heir of the NUGGL. The dockers in Tillett's union in Cork, Passage West and Midleton had come over, together with the Vintners' Assistants.

On 12 August the Lord Mayor of Cork, Terence MacSwiney, was arrested in a military raid on the City Hall. He went on hunger-strike at once. He was tried by court martial on the 16th, sentenced to two years' imprisonment on the charge of possessing seditious literature, put on board ship, landed at Pembroke Dock and lodged in Brixton jail at 4 a.m. on 18 August. That evening Michael Hill, one of the local officials, telephoned to Liberty Hall the information that as soon as it was known that the Lord Mayor had been deported, union shop stewards had unanimously resolved to ask Mr Foran to take action. The *Watchword of Labour* published a protest and a two-page defence of MacSwiney.

* * *

The work of the union was now conducted with increasing difficulty. From burning down creameries the Black and Tans now turned to sacking whole towns. On 20 September police, military and Black and Tans wrecked houses in Carrick-on-Shannon and Tuam. At Tuam J. Higgins, secretary of the ITGWU branch, was arrested. Stephen Keane, secretary of the Trades Council, was taken out and 'horribly beaten' because he refused to resign from the union. The forces of legalised terrorism burned down the greater part of Balbriggan, including a hosiery factory which employed 200 members of the ITGWU. The attackers decamped with lorry-loads of loot.

The president of the Aherlow branch was arrested and held

for two weeks, during which time he was tortured with bayonets. Organiser W. J. Reilly was dragged from his car at Dromahair by drunken policemen and put up against a wall. He was saved by the arrival of an officer more sober than the rest. Yet despite such conditions, the Sligo branch organised a day of sports at Manorhamilton. A few days later Tomás Connole, secretary of the Ennistymon branch, was shot dead in cold blood. The Black and Tans who murdered him in the course of 'reprisals' set his house on fire and flung his body into the flames. At that time the holding of inquests was illegal in Co. Clare. 1920

Richard Corish, mayor of Wexford, was arrested in his own Town Hall. The Enniscorthy organiser, Michael O'Donoghue, was arrested in his hotel on a visit to Dublin. The records of the Ardee and Louth branches were destroyed when their secretaries' houses were raided. O'Brien, whose article in *Liberty* has already been quoted, described the life of a country branch at this time. The Black and Tans singled out the ITGWU members for physical attack. Meetings were held at night in inaccessible cattle-sheds. A number of the members were Volunteers, and these would watch at crossroads while the committee was in session.

On 25 October, the day MacSwiney died on hunger-strike, a 'ring of steel' was fixed round Dublin, and what the *Independent* described as an 'amazing series of raids' took place. Even the Gresham Hotel was not immune. Pedestrians were searched in the streets and bloodhounds employed. The union sent a substantial contingent to Cork for the funeral, the local members turning out *en masse* in the procession. On the night of 12-13 November Black and Tans raided the Connolly Memorial Hall in Camden Quay, set fire to it, and almost completely destroyed it. This was not on the occasion of the general burning of the main buildings of the city, but was a selective raid on a limited target. The branch was soon meeting again in the room over the bar in Oliver Plunkett Street where it first met after reorganisation. Its secretary was Tadhg Barry, and among its most prominent members were William Kenneally and Bob Day, who reported that though many books and records were lost, ledgers, shop stewards' books and cash had been kept at a place of safety. It was decided to sell off a branch property at South Terrace

1920 and hold a public meeting to inaugurate a rebuilding fund.

At the next meeting Hill reported on an Executive meeting, probably that held on 17 November. Foran had stated that eight branch premises had been destroyed and their books burned. Three branch secretaries had been shot, and thirty-two were in jail. He also reported on his visit to the USA accompanied by James Larkin junior. This must have taken place after 25 September, when young Larkin relinquished his employment as a junior clerk in Liberty Hall. He also reported that the expansion of the union had made necessary the acquisition of new offices at 35 Parnell Square. In future Liberty Hall would be the headquarters of No. 1 branch. Limerick was luckier than Cork. On 22 November the union's rooms were entered by an armed man in mufti while the military waited outside. He was seeking a man called O'Dwyer. He returned the next day and made a detailed examination of books and membership lists.

In Galway the police and military, having made it clear that they preferred workers to join amalgamated unions, began a campaign of harassment against the ITGWU members which culminated in November 1920 when the premises were burned down and the branch secretary, Stephen Cremen, was driven out of the city. The wearing of the union badge was forbidden, and the branch, then numbering 1,500 members, was effectively broken up. Veale from Dungarvan and Houston from Belfast made exploratory visits. Then Gilbert Lynch, a new organiser, was sent from Dundalk. He was taken out of his bed in the small hours and expected to be shot. He was, however, handed over to some soldiers, who recognised his strong Lancashire accent and let him go. He did not remain in Galway.

The Bunclody branch also was broken up. A strike was in progress, and the military believed themselves obliged to assist the employers. They arrested the strikers, scrubbed them with cane brushes, threw water on them in cold weather, and threatened to shoot their secretary if he did not return to work. The secretary himself was stripped naked and chased round a barrack square by soldiers with fixed bayonets. They then released him, telling him that he would be shot if he did not secure a return to work. He advised the men to stand firm. But they were cowed and signed a document undertaking to work with non-union men. The secretary's name was Ignatius Redmond, and he remained a member of the union. 1920

Liberty Hall was the subject of a serious raid on 24 November, during the reign of terror immediately following 'Bloody Sunday'. At 12 noon the area between Marlborough Street and Butt Bridge was isolated, and two armoured cars appeared at the entrance of Eden Quay. The building was attacked by Auxiliaries with loaded revolvers, who burst in and remained for five hours. These ex-officers considered themselves a cut above the Black and Tans. They were commanded by Brigadier-General Crozier, who resigned because he was not allowed to maintain discipline among them. He described them as mostly 'hoy di hoy lah di dahs'. They showed class as well as national bias. Farren and Johnson were taken out at once and put in a lorry where they remained for two hours. During this time, the greater part of the male staff were arrested.[7] Some fifteen or twenty builders' labourers who were on strike were bundled into lorries and driven off. The prisoners were taken to the Auxiliaries' quarters in Dublin Castle.

Meanwhile a destructive search was made from the foundations to the roof. Floors were ripped up; window frames and fireplaces were pulled out; furniture was smashed. Correspondence, records and books that yielded no information were piled in the street and set ablaze. Typewriters, stationery and petty cash were looted. In the cellars the wall separating 29 Eden Quay from the Butt Bar was knocked down with sledges, and the foreman, whom this unusual intrusion surprised, was arrested. The instruments and band equipment were wrecked. O'Brien, Johnson and Farren were soon released, others at intervals. Nobody was charged with any offence. O'Brien estimated that the Auxiliaries' spree caused £5,000 worth of damage; a claim was later made, but not a penny was ever recovered. The EC re-established the head office in Parnell Square.

The minutes of the Cork branch have survived. An entry for 22 December reads:

> At this stage three Black and Tan police rushed into the room armed with Webley revolvers and hand grenades and shouted 'Hands up.' One stood on the desk and two soldiers,

1920 not Black and Tans, were ordered to search members. After about ten minutes' search the Black and Tans, who though under the influence of drink were not unduly aggressive, left.

At the beginning of December the *Morning Post* announced its discovery that the *Watchword of Labour* was financed by 'Moscow gold'. This was doubtless an invitation to suppress it. But in any case it was found impossible to continue it. The London and North Western Railway Company refused to accept parcels consigned to Dublin. Recourse was had to the Post Office, but after a few weeks this organisation imposed a similar ban. The paper was then dispatched in bulk to Belfast. Here Winifred Carney collected the parcels at Donegall Quay and sent them on to Dublin from Great Victoria Street. Sometimes they arrived in whole, sometimes in part. When they ultimately reached the retailers, shops were raided, stocks were seized. The decision to close down the paper was taken reluctantly. The last issue appeared on 4 December.

The military encampment at Ballykinlar was converted into a concentration camp, the first prisoners being sent there in November. Protests in England began to mount. Huge meetings were held. Arrests were extended to British citizens like Sylvia Pankhurst and Colonel L'Estrange Malone, MP. Asquith spoke of Lloyd George's 'hellish policy'. The Prime Minister had the Government of Ireland Act on the statute book by the end of the year, but he had to keep up the pressure until the six-county parliament had been set up. Under these circumstances some of the younger organisers of the ITGWU felt that they should be in the field and joined the newly established Active Service Units. Peadar O'Donnell resigned at the end of October. Arthur Mitchell suggests that Eamon Rooney went to the IRA at the same time,[8] but the wages book shows that he was with the union until after the truce. Archibald Heron's last pay-packet was dated 28 May 1921. Patrick Gaffney drew expenses to attend a conference in November 1920, but none in 1921. One imagines that he went 'on the run' early in 1921 and formed the Co. Carlow Active Service Unit in the spring.

It speedily became clear that it would be dangerous to

hold general meetings or to attempt the election of a new EC. 1920
The 1921 EC is identical with that of 1920, with the omission of Michael Ryan. Increasingly the work of the union was conducted by committees. Outrages were of continual occurrence, a particularly shocking example being the murder of the secretary of the Skerries branch, Thomas Hand, who was shot dead in the family home in the presence of his mother, sisters and brother.

* * *

All this time the dockers and railwaymen had been refusing to load or convey military supplies. A crisis came early in November when the railway companies threatened to withdraw all services if the men did not return to work. A special meeting of the Irish Labour Party and TUC was called and met on 16 November, with Foran in the chair. It was decided to defy the threat. But shortly afterwards negotiations were begun, and it was agreed to carry whatever the companies were prepared to risk on the trains. There was no victimisation, except for about fifteen men on the GNR(I).

The conference dealt with one other matter. William O'Brien moved a resolution which had been agreed by the NEC and the British Labour Party. It had been urged in the House of Commons by W. Adamson. Its proposals were:

(1) The withdrawal of the British armed forces from Ireland.
(2) The calling of a Constituent Assembly elected on the basis of proportional representation by a free, equal and secret vote.
(3) That such assembly should draw up a Constitution for Ireland, on the understanding that such Constitution should be made operative subject only to two conditions; namely that it affords protection to minorities; and that the Constitution shall prevent Ireland from becoming a military or naval menace.

This is not the place to analyse these proposals, except to remark that they might mean one thing to the Irish and another to the English.

1921 The Cork branch, unlike Dublin No. 1, decided to hold its Annual Meeting. This took place on 23 January at the Father Mathew Hall. William Kenneally took the chair and gave a general report. He suggested a voluntary levy of 10s per member for the rebuilding of the hall. The secretary, Tadhg Barry, reported discussions with the British Labour delegation. It was disclosed that the Cork branch had, out of its local fund, given as much as £1,319 in donations to worthy causes. During 1920 Kinsale strikers received £50, brewery workers on strike £150, the memorial to the murdered Lord Mayor, Tomás MacCurtain, £146, the railway munition fund £750, the city distress fund £100, and the butter workers £323. The rapid spread of unemployment was referred to. It was stated that the branch policy was only to fight when fighting was forced upon them. The members pledged themselves once more to struggle for the Workers' Republic.

On 30 January Tadhg Barry was arrested at a meeting of the City Council. He was taken to Spike Island by the military and subsequently lodged in the concentration camp at Ballykinlar. Eamon Lynch and Michael Hill were arrested about a week later. Lynch had come to Cork to attempt to settle a tramway strike which now dragged on until April. Much of Hill's work was now undertaken by Kenneally, who was so well appreciated by the Tramwaymen that they sent a resolution to Dublin asking that he should be appointed to Lynch's post as organiser for the duration of Lynch's imprisonment. The branch also asked that Kenneally take Hill's place on the EC, but it was decided that this would be contrary to rule. Galvin, a leading member of the branch, was the next to be arrested, but he was not held. The head office notified branches that the arrears of imprisoned members would be disregarded. The minutes of the meeting at which this was announced ended as follows:

> At this stage, curfew drawing near, it was agreed that the meeting stand adjourned until the next evening, Thursday, at 7.30 p.m.

The wages movement now ceased. It was becoming a matter of resisting wage reductions. For weeks on end all sections in Cork were closed to new members. Those who had dreamed of organising all the workers of Ireland and seizing industrial power had now to learn the sad lesson of 1891. Industrial power depends on employment. The spread of organisation must be restricted in order to protect the interests of those who were organised already. It was back to the days of limiting the number of apprentices. 1921

* * *

While no minutes of the Belfast branch covering the first half of 1921 have survived, a certain amount of inward correspondence has recently been found.[9] It shows the union holding its own, but finding difficulty in competing with the cross-channel unions who had strong social insurance departments. Denis Houston sent to the head office a copy of a Workers' Union leaflet showing the sick and unemployment benefits payable to its members and suggested that similar schemes might win members for the ITGWU.

O'Brien was fairly sharp in his reply. He thought Houston had forgotten the amount paid out in dispute pay, over £81,000 between 1 January 1919 and 31 December 1920. He added that the union had paid thousands of members not in benefit, and he knew of no other union that would do this. He concluded:

> We are certainly not going to turn the union into a friendly benefit institution and neglect the main purpose for which it was formed.[10]

In Britain there was proceeding that series of amalgamations which created the (Amalgamated) Transport and General Workers' Union. There were suggestions that the Irish branches of the NUDL should be transferred to the ITGWU, and Foran visited London to press this demand. When he returned Cathal O'Shannon replaced him. Although he waited till the end of April, he did not secure a decision. After 'Black Friday' (17 April) Robert Williams of the Transport Workers' Federation told him that the British movement was likely to be busy with its own problems for the foreseeable future, and the matter was not decided until the autumn.

While in London Cathal O'Shannon, awaiting events from day to day, appears to have occupied himself with research

1921 into Irish working-class history. Now that the wages movement was a thing of the past, O'Brien was wondering by what means he could hold the union together. The 1920 Annual Report refers to the demoralising effect of unemployment. But unemployment did not begin to assume serious proportions until November of that year. The report was not published until December 1921, and it may be that its generalisations derive more from 1921 than 1920. The report suggests that the 'rot' was countered by the amalgamation of branches. But that O'Brien had additional plans is shown by his correspondence with O'Shannon. He wanted to embark on an ambitious programme of education, the centre of which would be the publication of James Connolly's writings.

Political events supervened. The terror was intensified. Massive searches in which whole blocks were cordoned off became commonplace. The Black and Tans and Auxiliaries were encouraged to retaliate to attacks on themselves by executing reprisals on the property of completely innocent people. Sir Henry Wilson, no lover of Republicanism, but at last fearing for the discipline of his army, told Lord George: 'If these people ought to be murdered, then the government ought to murder them.'[11] Indeed the government was doing its bit. On 14 March six men were hanged in pairs while 40,000 people kept vigil outside Mountjoy Prison. Four of them were said to be trade union branch officials. They died protesting their innocence to the last. A deputation consisting of Mrs Desmond FitzGerald and Miss Louise Gavan Duffy waited on the committee of No. 1 branch, who agreed unanimously that a protest should be made. The result was a half-day general strike.

Unemployment soared, reaching 100,000 by the end of March 1921. This was no local crisis caused by military disruption, but a world recession. The post-war boom had finally collapsed. The problem now was not keeping Irish food at home; it was keeping foreign food out.

The Irish Labour Party and TUC issued a manifesto at Easter containing proposals for meeting the crisis. It was an appeal for national unity based on the 'Democratic Programme' of Dáil Éireann. It proposed national economic planning, a moratorium on rents and land annuities, voluntary conscription of wealth, a maximum rate of profit and compulsory tillage. The 1921 Annual Report recorded the response: 1921

> How did the employers answer the demand for unity? It would be ungenerous not to acknowledge and untrue to deny that some of them had sufficient patriotism to restrain them from identifying themselves with their confrères in other countries in the wage-reduction campaign, which at this period raged throughout the world, but truth compels the remark that, if the Irish employers in general did not provoke industrial strife during the January-July period, their abstention must in the main be written down, not to the promptings of patriotism, not because the will was absent, but because the way was, and because they full well appreciated that wage reductions in organised Ireland would be met by weapons which had been steeled in shape and in effectiveness, in the grim forge of experience, and which would be wielded with all the more fierceness on anyone menacing the essential unity of the Nation.[12]

On 19 April the Government of Ireland Act came into force. A general election was held on 19 May in twenty-six counties only. There was no poll: all candidates were returned unopposed. But in practice the Republic had been reduced to twenty-six counties. The six-county election took place on 24 May under conditions of unparalleled terror, as effective against Protestants who fell out of line as against Catholics who were never in line. Once the six-county parliament was established, Britain's minimum objective was achieved. The main aim having been achieved by force, the secondary aims could be referred to the arbitrament of fraud. Lloyd George opened discussions with de Valera, and a truce was declared on 11 July.

* * *

Beginning in the autumn of 1920 there was considerable discontent among the union staff. To some extent this would reflect the constant strain and anxiety of living under the terror. It may also have reflected the unanalysed feeling of malaise that afflicts a movement when it begins to suffer defeats. The Belfast pogroms had destroyed for the time being the prospect that the workers could unite Ireland. That the Belfast events would prove as fateful as the similar events of 1797 was shown in the fact that the initiative was passing to reaction. It is also of interest that the discontent arose during a period when Foran was frequently absent, either sick or travelling.

On 25 October 1920 a memorandum to the EC was signed by D. O'Leary, E. Ua Nunan [*sic*], H. M. Hoyne, M. Skinnider, Nora Connolly, A. Heron, Cathal O'Shannon and George Spain. Who were these? Four of them were 'Young Republicans', the 'don't-care-a-damn brigade' of 1914. The memorial was strongly worded. It arose from the imprisonment of Bernard McMahon, a clerk first engaged in July 1918. The request ran:

> It is the custom of capitalist Republican employers to pay their servants in jail, and sometimes in full, in similar circumstances. The same course has been adopted by the TU in the case of other officers and officials. It will not be denied that the fortunes of the union are to a great extent interwoven with those of the Republican Movement. . . . We therefore trust that the EC will now give this matter immediate and sympathetic consideration.[13]

The reply came on 11 November 1920 and was resentful. It was addressed to O'Leary and 'members of the staffs of the HO, National Health and No. 1 branch' and declared that 'No official or employee of the union who has been imprisoned ever had any just cause for complaint as to his treatment.' The EC thought the memorial uncalled for.

But the EC had a further complaint before it at the same meeting. It was sent on 28 October 1920. It was signed by E. ua Nunáin [*sic*] and thirteen others; all signed their names in Irish. They included Margaret Skinnider and D. O'Leary, but not Nora Connolly or Cathal O'Shannon. They wanted a more generous scale of sick pay. The aggrieved party was Michael Hickey, who had worked for the Cork branch in 1918 but transferred to Dublin in March 1919. The memorial complained that the Finance Committee had decided to pay him during sickness on a low scale 'said to be introduced only as a safeguard', and pointed out that 'Capitalist employers pay clerical staff full wages for a considerable time. So does No. 1 branch.' It seems that Hickey was receiving half pay. The EC replied on the same day that it declined to make a change. Then came the dismissal of Miss Hoyne. Memorials were presented calling for her reinstatement.

From this time on there was a constant stream of complaints, and it would probably not be far wrong to regard the fundamental issue as one of pay. The basic salary was £3 10s a week. A request for an increase was made early in November. About this time J. J. Hughes ceased to attend EC meetings. O'Brien engaged a 'confidential clerk'. The head office was moved to Parnell Square. Foran was sick or travelling. The organic links between the officials and their staff were weakened. To meet somebody on the stairs is one thing; to send a memorandum in triplicate is another. The officers and the EC were beset with difficulties. One day a branch official must be got out of military custody. Another day the chief finance clerk is arrested with the keys of the safe in his pocket. A collapse takes place in Athlone. An organiser flatly refuses to travel into the 'war zone'. The first six months of 1921 were full of frustration and inconvenience.

The staff were, moreover, not for the most part career employees. Some of them were dedicated revolutionaries. The swift growth of the union had resulted in the substitution of management for leadership. At first, like the journeymen in the guilds, they clung to the past, sending memorials against capitalism and appealing to Republican solidarity by writing their names in Irish. When they realised that management had come to stay they did the inevitable thing: they started an officials' organisation. Its secretary, Michael Sheppard, notified J. J. Hughes of its formation on 23 April 1921. Perhaps the last straw was the sudden withdrawal of the customary holiday on Easter Saturday morning.

There were signs, moreover, that O'Brien in particular was beginning to enjoy the exercise of administrative authority. J. J. Hughes as chief clerk and assistant secretary had the privilege of an office of his own at the top of the building. O'Brien instructed him to move into the general office with the other clerks. Doubtless he felt that he was being demoted a second time. He refused to go. O'Brien then appealed to the

1921 EC, to whom Hughes put his case. The decision went against him. The EC resolved 'that the General Treasurer was within his right in ordering the Assistant Secretary, Mr Hughes, to give up his room . . . and he is to comply with it'. This was on 30 April. On 25 June Hughes tendered his resignation, which was accepted in a formal note. He was not thanked for his past services.

Things went differently when O'Brien clashed with the committee of No. 1 branch. On 30 June Frank Robbins of the Citizen Army made the suggestion that the EC should issue a monthly financial report to each branch, and it was agreed to invite the General Treasurer to attend. At the next committee meeting the secretary read out O'Brien's reply. The members 'expressed surprise at the tone of the reply . . . and instructed the secretary to write a further letter'. On 10 July a special committee meeting was held for the purpose of electing delegates to the ITUC. Foran attended. On 14 July O'Brien put in an appearance, said he had every sympathy with Comrade Robbins's views, but knew from experience that his suggestion would not be a paying proposition. 'He then gave a detailed account of the finances of the union for the year 1920 and also for the current year up to the first of July.' The committee were highly gratified and thanked him, whereupon he replied most graciously that both the EC and he himself 'would be only too happy at any time to supply any information the members of No. 1 branch committee required'. Even if he was now becoming a hard disciplinarian, he remained no mean diplomat.

Another staff problem was that of organising the organisers. After a brief schooling by Foran they were largely left to their own initiative. If a directive was sent out from the head office urging, for example, that an attempt should be made to organise the workers in some specific industry, there would be a response. But all would not respond with equal alacrity, and there was no machinery for checking. It was decided to ask the Cork branch to agree to the transfer to Dublin of the organiser Eamon Lynch, since it was felt that his abilities were being wasted in a restricted field. The Cork branch agreed, and Lynch came to Dublin in January 1921 to act as organiser of organisers. He was not in charge

long. At the beginning of February he and Michael Hill were 1921
arrested in Cork. Hill was interned, but Lynch was released. However, he did not take up his duties in Dublin. He drew one week's salary and was behind bars once more.

On 25 May, following the burning of the Custom House, Liberty Hall was raided twice. Executive member Patrick Gaffney, his death sentence, imposed for his part in the Ballymurphy ambush, commuted to life imprisonment, was lodged in Mountjoy at the beginning of July. Arrests and harassment continued until the hour of the truce of 11 July. Then suddenly all changed. Bonfires blazed. Fairs and festivals resumed. A sense of relief, relaxation, even exhilaration, swept the country – except in the six north-eastern counties: there the pogrom was renewed.

Modern Ireland was born. England recognised that she could not rule all Ireland, but sought means of ruling a part and preserving the maximum influence in the remainder. Irish Republicans recognised that they in turn could not win all Ireland by military force. Fighting was replaced by bargaining, and the quality of the bargain struck is not the concern of this work.

15

The Birth of the New Regime

For each man kills the thing he loves.

OSCAR WILDE

Reorganisation – Articles of Agreement – defensive struggles – electoral policy – two armed camps – staff problems – civil war – Larkin's return – the split – the Waterford farm strike – the end of Larkinism

1921 As soon as the truce was in operation no time was lost in summoning the union's 'Resident Executive', which met on 13 July. From now on minutes are available, and it is possible to follow the management of the union on a regular basis. But the minutes record only facts, and the historian must imagine the hopes, expectations and intentions evoked by a dramatically transformed situation. The first decision was to call a meeting of the union's delegates at the Annual Meeting of the Irish Labour Party and TUC, which was to convene in Dublin in August.

This Congress was a sober affair. The soaring hopes and boundless confidence, not to say revolutionary euphoria, of past gatherings had disappeared. The economic climate was chilly. The wages movement was virtually at an end, though advances were still being made here and there. The system of wartime controls was already partly dismantled. It was a matter of resisting ever more pressing demands for wage reductions as the 'universal laws of economics' took over from fallible human contrivance. In his presidential address Foran reported that very few employers had been able to impose cuts. He contrasted the position in Ireland with that in Britain where 'the workers went down like corn before the reapers'.

There were signs of malaise. Unemployment was threatening some unions with falling membership, and some of them had resorted to 'poaching'. Painters objected when the

ITGWU organised the men who coated agricultural machinery, even though it had won them a rate above that of the house-painters and even though all the other employees in the factory belonged to the Transport Union. The plasterers took another view: it was their practice to refuse applicants permission to establish branches in towns completely organised by the ITGWU. The NUDL organiser attacked the concept of the 'one big union'. In view of potential divisions, the ITUC decided to set up arbitration machinery. The affiliation of the newly established Dublin Workers' Council was accepted, though this was to thrust P. T. Daly further into the cold and nourish his resentment. 1921

It was obvious that big political moves were afoot. When we look back from the present the broad trend of events is only too clear. Britain and America were resolving their last differences within the Versailles system and moving to an accord on naval parity and an Irish settlement. Britain had successfully ensured her future presence in Ireland by establishing Stormont. It remained to get the best bargain she could in the twenty-six counties. But bargainers do not usually disclose their full position.

The Irish national leaders were also preparing to compromise. If this were not so, as Frank Robbins argued, 'the only discussions would be for making arrangements for the evacuation of the British forces from Ireland'.[1] De Valera too kept his cards close to his chest; but what was unhappily plain was that whatever was his sticking position, the interests of Labour were irrelevant to it. Alexander Stewart of the Belfast Trades Council declared himself 'humiliated' by the fact that the working-class movement was not consulted. Johnson was confident that Labour would make its presence felt, but could not say in what way. Foran repudiated the principle of partition, but offered no means by which it could be undone. Indeed the fact had not been accepted. Something had happened, but nobody would admit it.[2] There was no question of demanding a voice in the negotiations. The mood was one of falling back on Labour's fundamental strength, its industrial organisation. This must be remembered in assessing what ensued.

1921 Perhaps a certain sense of frustration and loss of direction may be read into the brief wave of factory seizures that took place. On 26 August the red flag was unfurled over the Bruree bakery of Messrs Cleeve. A streamer announced: 'We make bread, not profits'. But the workers' demands were simply the reinstatement of five men who had been dismissed in the previous November. At a later stage Cleeves demanded compensation from the union, but liability was disclaimed. The offices of the Cork Harbour Board were taken over by Bob Day and William Kenneally. Here the claim was a £3 10s weekly wage. Day installed himself as Harbour Commissioner under the red flag. The Castleconnell fishery takeover was also prompted by a wage claim.

The cross-channel unions and the smaller Irish unions were in the worst position to resist wage reductions. Many of their members, indeed whole unions, sought entry into the ITGWU. In October there was an influx of railwaymen who worked for the LNWR on the North Wall. Though classified as railwaymen, they did dockers' work, and the settlement reached by the NUR for Holyhead and other British ports left them the worst-paid dockers in Dublin. Farriers, steel-erectors and mosaic tilers sought amalgamation.[3] In both Dublin and Belfast seamen deserted the NFSU, and mutuality arrangements were made with the breakaway Seafarers' Union in Southampton.

The extent of the disorganisation caused by the Anglo-Irish war and the Black and Tan terror was not fully assessed until October. Out of a total of 583 branches on the roll, 115 had totally collapsed. Others were weakened by shortage of funds and the imprisonment of officials. The task of reorganisation was put in hand at once, the opportunity being taken to create large branches in accordance with *Lines of Progress*. There was indeed fresh recruitment in agriculture. The dissolution of the Agricultural Wages Board on 1 October left rural workers with the alternatives of wage reductions or union membership. The refusal of farmers to pay harvest bonus led to an increase in organisation in Limerick.

The important Galway branch was re-registered on 18 November. Stephen Cremen had returned to the city and took the chair at a public meeting. J. A. Henderson, an organiser appointed in June 1921, represented the Executive. 1921 When Cremen had gone on the run enemies had whispered that he was less afraid of the Black and Tans than of discrepancies in his books; however, the EC satisfied itself that the funds were intact and agreed to his reappointment. The slow work of restoration and reinstatement went on throughout the autumn and winter. Skibbereen was revived on New Year's Day, Ráthluirc not till 27 January.

The process accelerated as prisoners were released. On 11 September there were still 3,200 in jail, 1,700 of them untried. On 11 October O'Brien was permitted to visit Gaffney on union business. He had been elected O/C prisoners and was not released until the general amnesty following the Treaty. When told he was free, he declined to leave until all other prisoners had gone home. There were bonfires on the Carlow hills when he returned to Killeshin. Tadhg Barry died in Ballykinlar on 15 November, shot (possibly by mistake) while waving to some departing friends. His death was a grievous loss to Cork. Eamon Lynch and Michael Hill was released at the end of the month. Slowly the old routine was restored.

Even in Belfast, described in the Annual Report as 'a city racked, torn, shot up with dissensions', the ITGWU was able to 'keep the rates of its docker, flour-mill and other members abreast with those of other union men similarly engaged elsewhere in Ireland'. This was in spite of 'having to contend . . . with the weak-kneed attitude of other unions in servilely submitting to wage-clips'. Attempts were made to break fresh ground in the North. Organisation was begun among the miners of Coalisland.

Perhaps the most important sign of recovery was the republication of the *Voice of Labour* on 22 October. Its editor, Cathal O'Shannon, in no way moderated its 'Bolshevik' tone, though its rival, R. J. Connolly's *Workers' Republic*, hinted that its leftism was mere demagogy. It gave the hospitality of its columns to Walton Newbold, the first British Communist MP, and later to Harry Pollitt. It was contemptuous of the British Labour leaders. Its great strength was in its weekly record of struggles actually taking place in Ireland. Where it differed from the *Workers' Republic* was in its implicit belief that the national struggle in Ireland was now over and that the time of class war was at hand.

1921 In this connection it is worth tracing briefly the relations between the union and the Republicans. Michael Collins had always taken the greatest care never to appear to be interfering in the union's internal affairs. After the truce there were signs of a change. Dan Breen approached William O'Brien with the statement that the secretary of the Ballingarry branch in South Tipperary was a spy. He asked O'Brien to remove him. O'Brien told him that the branch had the right to change its secretary if its members wished. A meeting was indeed held, and a new candidate was proposed. The voting was performed in a very strange manner: the two candidates were told to stand at the door facing outward, and at a word of command they both marched down to the village; each member of the branch then followed the one he thought should be secretary. All of them, even those who had verbally supported the old secretary, marched behind his opponent. O'Brien later learned that the new secretary could neither read nor write. Somebody else was then appointed, and in a short time the alleged spy was back at work.[4] Later the Dublin Brigade protested to Parnell Square at the refusal of No. 1 branch to accept a man into membership. This time there was a protest against the interference.

A more serious action took place in Co. Kilkenny, where Republican police compelled striking workers to repair a water main. After the signing of the Treaty but before the split in the IRA the workers occupied Mallow mills. They were forcibly removed by the IRA under Commandant Liam Lynch. On 24 February 1922 T. D. Hallinan of Messrs Webb, flour-millers, Mallow, wrote to the Minister of Defence, Dáil Éireann, Dublin, thanking him 'for the protection afforded us during the recent Labour trouble here' and enclosing a cheque for £50 for IRA funds.[5]

After the army split the anti-Treaty section moved uneasily in the direction of the working class. But until the civil war began it is not always possible at once to identify those responsible for a particular incident, though a guess can be made. In the strongly Republican county of Waterford, at the end of February 1922, mysterious fires destroyed several farm-houses. Masked men carried out reprisals, taking care to select ITGWU officials. In this case a large force of IRA men was moved into the district, martial law was declared, and the outrages, aimed at driving the union organisers out of the district, ceased. The *Voice of Labour* congratulated the IRA. 1921

Two months later there was a contretemps at Birr, in the area of the pro-Treaty 3rd Southern Division. The IRA had commandeered lorries. They apparently believed themselves entitled to commandeer the drivers as well, and when some of these objected they were held in custody. The ITGWU branch to which the drivers belonged resolved that their members be instructed to refuse to drive armed men of either party. By this time the unions were in the midst of a campaign against 'militarism'. Quite apart from the political events that accompanied it, it is possible to see this succession of incidents as demonstrating workers' reactions to the attempts of a new ruling class to establish a state machinery.

* * *

The Articles of Agreement, which led to the evacuation by the British army of twenty-six counties and the subsequent establishment of the Irish Free State, were signed in the small hours of 6 December 1921. They contained partition and an oath of allegiance to the British Crown. So much appeared in the early editions of the Dublin *Evening Mail*. The *Voice of Labour* of 10 December ignored this shattering event, a fact which may imply disagreement in high places. In the following week the editor wrote: 'This week Ireland is passing through the most terrible trial of our modern history.' He appreciated that 'Unanimity either for or against the Treaty or Agreement is impossible from the very nature of things.' But he went on:

> At this stage and until Dáil Éireann has had an opportunity of debating the question, the *Voice* does not propose to intervene. . . . The Dáil and not Labour has been entrusted and invested by the Irish people with the authority and responsibility. In that, the people may have done well or ill – it is for none of us to say now.

What was the explanation of this extraordinary act of abdication? Here is the one that was offered:

> 1921 But to the Unions, the branches of the Unions, the Trades and Workers' Councils, we give this advice at this most critical moment in Ireland's storm-tossed story: whatever the provocation, whatever the depth of feeling, let no Union, Branch or Council as such take sides, by resolution or otherwise, with either party to the division of opinion in the Dáil. To take such foolish action will be to split and rend in twain the Unions and the whole Labour movement on the very eve of its most crucial trial, the general offensive of the Irish employing class timed for next January.[6]

The *Workers' Republic* went to press on 6 December, possibly before the terms of the Treaty were known.[7] But the next issue contained a blistering attack on its terms: 'If this shameful treaty is ratified, the Republicans have forgotten the centuries-old cry of all Irish rebels . . . betrayed the cause of Tone and Emmet.' And the writer added, perhaps a trifle optimistically: 'No compromise will be tolerated by the Irish working class.' The editor also commented adversely on the 'bureaucrats of Liberty Hall', whom his English friends regarded as 'Bolshies' because of their leftist talk. The *Workers' Republic* would be prepared to accept a capitalist republic, as the winning of this would equip the workers for setting up their own.

Other articles that appeared in R. J. Connolly's paper show that at this stage he expected the imminent downfall of the British Empire, possibly as a result of a war with America, and a great universal upsurge of the world proletariat. O'Brien, at any rate, was old enough and shrewd enough to doubt the validity of this perspective. He preferred to conserve union funds in expectation of a capitalist counter-attack. There is no evidence that it struck anybody in the camp of official Labour that the offensive might come in a *political* form from a reactionary *government*.

1922 On 7 January 1922 the *Voice of Labour* published a statement issued on 10 September from Comstock jail by James Larkin. It attacked not only the Treaty but also those who signed it:

> We stand for the dead. We entered into a compact with them when living. We will not fail them. Clarke, Pearse,

> Connolly and our other comrades did not die for a phrase. 1922
> They did not die that unscrupulous, ambitious creatures that have climbed to power over the dead bodies of our comrades should be permitted to seal, sign and deliver in a written hand the soul of our race.

Now, though Larkin did not get on well with Connolly, he could be described as his 'comrade' in the union. Pearse had accepted young James at his school; but Pearse and Larkin shared no enterprise. For mentioning Clarke there was no basis whatsoever. One can imagine the annoyance this statement caused to men like O'Brien who had been immeasurably closer to Connolly than Larkin. Larkin had apparently persuaded himself that he had been a Republican all the time, and he was claiming 1916 as part of his mnemonic empire.

O'Shannon accompanied the statement with a disclaimer:

> The *Voice* is in duty bound to say that, while agreeing heartily with the anti-Imperial and anti-monarchical position set forth in the statement, both the Irish Transport and General Workers' Union and the *Voice* dissociate themselves from much that is in the document, and in particular from the personal charges of cowardice, treachery and aggrandisement made therein.

An open political rift had appeared between the union and its General Secretary. Larkin was speaking, of course, the language of a man with nothing to lose. But to cry treachery is to strike a match in the dark; one needs a nose for gas.[8]

* * *

The expected employers' offensive did not materialise – partly, no doubt, because of the political uncertainties that followed the Treaty settlement. Not, of course, that there was sweet industrial peace; but industrial conflict took the form of individual struggles rather than a concerted class war. The dockers had conceded a reduction of 1s a day in September 1921, but though the employers regularly demanded further reductions, these were constantly postponed. According to the Annual Report,

> 1922 Although having to contend with the wobbly line pursued by the cross-channel unions catering for a minority of the dockers in some ports, [the men] won clean out by their vigorous resistance and uncompromising attitude, and the bosses retired from the fray, so much dishevelled and worsted that they did not renew their offensive till the end of the year.[9]

There were more reductions than this sanguine narrative would imply. Workers lost 1s 6d at Pierces in Wexford. Reductions were agreed in Tullamore on a town basis. The expulsion of the occupiers of Mallow flour mills was followed by the acceptance of a cut. But about half the union membership retained their maximum wage to the end of 1922. Union membership, which reached the 100,000 mark in 1920, remained near that figure to the end of 1922. The fighting spirit of previous years remained unimpaired among the rank and file, even in the provincial towns. For example, on 4 March the *Voice of Labour* reported a demonstration of 1,000 workers, complete with red flags, which concluded with a mass meeting in Mullingar Town Hall. When the owners of Tipperary gasworks decided on wage reductions and dismissals the workers seized the plant and operated it themselves under the red flag. This was, of course, only possible because of the weakness of the central administration of the country.

The rural struggle was resumed in March 1922 at the conclusion of two years of relative calm. A weekly wage of 43s had been agreed in North Co. Dublin and Meath after a four-day strike in 1920. This was maintained in 1921. The farmers demanded a reduction of 6s, and on 4 March the workers struck, 2,000 in Dublin and 1,000 in Meath. Again peak rates were maintained. The Annual Report added:

> A novel feat was subsequently accomplished by the unemployed men in Meath, who demanded work on the ranches on the basis of one man, at least, to fifty acres. This demand was vigorously pressed and largely succeeded.[10]

At the same time the employers were chipping at the union position. Lusk and Donabate were not included in the

43s agreement. There were strikes in a number of counties, in general successful, but invariably defensive.

The most important stoppage was that of the LNWR dockers on the North Wall in Dublin. This began in February. The object was parity with non-railway dockers. The outcome was successful, and in July 111 members gained an increase of 26s a week.

*   *   *

Under the Articles of Agreement there was to be an election in the twenty-six counties for an assembly which would ultimately control the Irish Free State. The Irish Labour Party and TUC called a Special Conference on 21 February. The question was whether Labour should offer independent candidates. Cathal O'Shannon took the chair. The proposal that Labour should participate was made by Tom Johnson. Transport Union delegates were divided, and the Executive minutes throw no light on the reason. A proposal by Helena Molony that Labour should take no part was seconded by Thomas Kennedy, who made some pointed remarks about Labour's lack of a policy on the constitutional question:

> It was all right talking about the Workers' Republic, but when they went before the working-class electors, the question they would have to decide was 'whether you are for peace or war, and whether you are prepared to carry the Treaty into effect, or oppose it, and put up with the consequences'. Could the National Executive inform them why they had not given an opinion on the issue itself? They must have an opinion on it, and why not the National Executive? Every voter must have an opinion on it, and they might as well face the issue as it existed. . . . He thought it unfair to put forward a programme which did not definitely set out their position on the Treaty issue.[11]

By contrast, William O'Brien strongly supported participation, and the decision to take part was carried by 104 votes to 69.

1922 By now the country was visibly separating into two armed camps. These confronted each other directly in Dublin, but in the rest of the country they held separate territories, depending on who won the first skirmishes. Labour did not see in this development the preparation of real interests to contest the issue of state power, but rather the growth of the principle of 'militarism'.

When the extremer Republicans seized the Four Courts and other buildings in central Dublin repeated efforts at mediation were made by William O'Brien and others. But each side had what seemed to it unanswerable arguments. It grew ever clearer that force alone could decide.

The Irish Labour Party and TUC called a general strike 'against militarism' on 24 April. Efforts were made to ensure the neutrality of the Citizen Army by incorporating it in a 'Workers' Army' that would cover the whole country. William O'Brien was the moving spirit and supplied two sums of £100 each for the project. But no army can fight for neutrality, and the project soon fell through. The most spectacular of all factory seizures took place on 13 May while the Republicans and the supporters of the Provisional Government were alternatively sparring and negotiating, each hoping to win without fighting. Messrs Cleeve had threatened to close all their creameries unless the workers accepted a wage reduction of 33⅓ per cent. Dowling and Hedley organised the seizure of factories at Carrick-on-Suir, Bansha, Clonmel, Kilmallock, Knocklong, Bruree, Dromen, Athlacca, Tankardstown, Balingaddy and Aherlow. But whereas in 1920 the Knocklong Soviet had enjoyed the support of the farmers, who had brought in their milk as usual, in 1922 the class struggle had supervened, and the farmers were demanding that the Provisional Government should 'govern or get out'. At the same time the first skirmishes of the land war in Co. Waterford were fought, for the moment to the workers' satisfaction.

The attack on the Four Courts made work impossible at Parnell Square. O'Brien took some of the staff to his home, but no work could be done. Postal services were disrupted. Transport became irregular. Unemployment increased. Union affairs were conducted under grave difficulties for many months. But that the hearts of the people were not with the civil war was shown by the results of the election held just before its commencement. Seventeen Labour candidates were returned, some of them with big majorities, fourteen of them members of the ITGWU. There was a strong popular sentiment for peace. But unfortunately peace does not come from wishing. 1922

* * *

The most difficult task for any general is to maintain the morale of a retreating army. There is a danger that every discontent will be magnified. There must be no favouritism or injustice. Unfortunately these maxims were not cogitated by the union leadership. Michael Sheppard was asked to do accountant's work at clerk's wages, and when he refused he received 'instant dismissal'. Early in April four clerks in the finance department put in a claim for £4 a week on the grounds that a new clerk had been engaged at that figure, whereas their wages remained £3 10s. The EC turned them down. They therefore declared themselves to be on strike, and inserted an advertisement in the *Irish Independent* urging all union branches to withhold payments to the head office until their claim was satisfied. The four were Ernest Nunan, Margaret Skinnider, Una Garvey and Sheila Bowen (Ní Bhóin), Republicans who had been recruited during the 'four glorious years'.

The EC replied that there was no strike. But the *Workers' Republic* published an editorial denouncing the 'bureaucrats' of Liberty Hall, lauding the principle of the 'rate for the job' and calling for the overthrow of the leadership.[12] The Women Workers' Union seems to have interested itself in the case, though to little effect. A number of branches made representations in favour of the 'girls'. Clifden decided to hold back cash, and support for the strikers came from Campile, New Ross, Carlow, Corbally, Kanturk and Monaghan. The Monaghan secretary wrote that if the EC sent out 'any more circulars like the last' they would have 'the lot of us on strike'. More significantly, Bohan and Dublin No. 3 branch seem to have sided with them.

The EC at first replied that the four employees had dismissed themselves. Later, although supported by the greater

1922 part of the union's membership, the EC felt it necessary to justify their position. They said the four had not discussed their grievance with other employees, sought an opportunity for discussion with the EC, or raised the matter at their own branch. To the last the four replied that they were members of Dublin No. 1 branch, of which their employer, Foran, was chairman.

It would be wrong to read too much into this series of events. That there was no question of eliminating Republicans is clear from the fact that the union invited Patrick Gaffney to become an organiser in Co. Carlow. He was a member of R. J. Connolly's party. He seems to have declined, as he was not present at the meeting of full-time officials held on 4 April 1922.

Nevertheless there is evidence of a deterioration of the 'atmosphere' within the union. As well as dismissals, there were resignations, for example that of Nora Connolly. Gradually the dedicated revolutionaries were replaced by career staff. It would be a fair speculation that the strong disciplinarianism which was associated with William O'Brien, and which made him unpopular in some quarters, was distasteful to those who had come to work for the union in the flush of idealism at the prospect of the 'Workers' Republic'. The result of the efflux was that at times there was a shortage of staff.

After the outbreak of the civil war a new type of personnel problem beset the Executive. In late July Charles Ridgway was arrested in Monaghan where the subsequently well-known Eoin O'Duffy was installed as military governor. He was subjected to insults and threats and lodged in Dundalk jail. The Republicans were pressing hard on the town, and when one of their bombs blew a hole in the prison wall the organiser walked out to freedom. A strike was in progress at Lucan. What more likely to conduce to industrial peace than to arrest Frank Purcell, the organiser? He too was thrown into Dundalk jail. He does not seem to have spent long there, and presumably he was released when the Republicans took Dundalk on 13 August. There were doubtless numerous cases of petty harassment but the other important arrest was
1923 that of the Athy secretary, Supple, early in 1923. A strike was in progress at the time. He was taken to Carlow and held

there several months, at one time being offered his freedom 1923
if he would instruct the members to return to work. He refused. A particularly tragic event occurred when his mother, acting on a rumour that he was about to be released, visited Carlow to join him. When told that the rumour was false, she collapsed and died in the branch rooms. These three had no Republican connections that can be ascertained. But some union members fought with the Republicans, one example being Ignatius Redmond in Wexford, whose subsequent tragic end illustrates the evils of civil war.[13]

* * *

Throughout the autumn and winter, signs multiplied of a maturing employers' offensive. They were anxious to wound, but, in the highly uncertain political climate, hesitated about striking. In December the shipping companies demanded a wage reduction of 2s a day, to come into effect on 1 January 1923. This was resisted and postponed. There had been a marginal rise in the cost of living, partly as a result of interruption of production and dislocation of transport. The mid-1922 index, taken against a pre-war base, stood at 185. In January 1923 it was 190. Waterford farmers demanded wage cuts, but were still unable to enforce them. The *Voice of Labour* recorded with alarm the increasing activity of the Farmers' Freedom Force, a paramilitary organisation which it likened to the Italian Fascists and the Ku-Klux-Klan. In the Athy area members of this body intimidated farmers who paid the old wages; they also threatened to shoot union officials. Demands were made for a reduction of 20 per cent by Dublin carters. Although the line was held, there was an uneasiness among the membership, even pessimism and apathy. When in January the No. 1 branch held its general meeting only thirty-six of the thousand present bought the *Voice of Labour*, and Thomas Foran criticised the rank-and-file members from the chair. A lock-out in Belfast was followed by a general lock-out of thirty-five flour mills throughout Ireland, beginning on 20 January. In those unimaginably dark days of civil war, governmental repression and economic stress, some demoralisation was understandable. Some blamed the leaders of the union, and his old cronies

1923 like Barney Conway used to sigh: 'There'll nothing happen till Jim gets home.'

* * *

The *Voice of Labour* of 27 January announced Larkin's release. While some union officials may have felt that they had enough trouble without Larkin, allegations that they had been backward in procuring his release would be unfair. Foran had kept up a continuous correspondence with the Larkin Release Committee in the USA. Its secretary was Emmet O'Reilly, who was later succeeded by T. J. O'Flaherty. It had the support of the Irish Progressive League and the American Association for the Recognition of the Irish Republic. Members of the Connolly Clubs, founded by Con O'Lyhane, provided its most active core, together with Connolly's old supporter John Lyng and Peadar Nunan.[14] In 1922 Peter Larkin, now in Liverpool, grew increasingly restive. He accompanied his letters to Foran with strictures on the supporters of the Treaty. Among his diatribes was one on the subject of 'cunning careerists', which Foran seems to have believed was directed against himself, for he wrote a somewhat resentful reply. At the same time he suggested that something spectacular should be done to secure Larkin's release. The result was Peter Larkin's visit to America.[15]

While on bail pending appeal Larkin had interested himself in the project of the Ulster defence alliance of sending a relief ship to Belfast. It was a worthy project, but now that it seemed he was free to return, Larkin seems to have pictured himself sailing up the Lagan as redeemer. Together with Jack Carney and Hannah Sheehy-Skeffington, he spoke at public meetings and raised a considerable sum of money including $1,500 at one meeting in Chicago. He inspected some ships at Long Island, then cabled Foran requesting £5,000 to complete the purchase and load for a voyage with a volunteer crew.

Larkin was addicted to what Dostoyevsky called 'double thoughts'. Good was to be done, and Larkin was to be seen doing it. The General Treasurer, on the other side of the Atlantic, living in a totally different physical and political environment, saw no more in the proposal than a raid on his hard-earned funds for the aggrandisement of a General Secretary who had been paid his salary for nothing for close on a decade. Foran cabled back a negative and asked when Larkin proposed to return. O'Brien in the meantime busied himself with securing the adoption and registration of new rules, the effect of which was to vest control of the union in the hands of an Annual Conference and to give the General President precedence over the General Secretary in the policy and management of the union.[16] A delegate conference discussed the rules on 24 and 25 April. It was admitted that there had been insufficient time for their full consideration, but they were unanimously recommended to the branches. O'Brien breathed easily as he waited for Larkin. 1923

But others were also waiting for Larkin. Like fallen angels holding their synod in the abyss, the delegates to the Dublin Trades Council discussed the implications of Larkin's impending return. P. T. Daly urged the necessity of meeting Larkin before he could come under the influence of others. Accordingly, when he stepped off the *Majestic* at Southampton the first people he met were the dissident deputation. He proceeded to London, where a Communist Party delegation met him at a venue in Bloomsbury.[17] They impressed upon him the changed character of the Ireland he was returning to. There had been a war and a revolution. The entire movement had been transformed. Some people had matured, others aged. Larkin must bide his time and get his bearings. Perhaps after a brief spell doing this he might care to make a visit to Moscow. After three days in London he left for Holyhead.

According to William O'Brien, the Executive learned of his expected arrival in Dublin from a newspaper advertisement. O'Brien refused to go to Westland Row to meet him when he arrived on 30 April. But Foran went, and that evening Larkin spoke as of old, from the window of Liberty Hall, and the 'old spot by the river' resounded with rhetoric and applause. The Republicans had ceased hostilities a few hours before Larkin arrived. His message was peace and reconstruction – but a nation, one and indivisible. That is to say he maintained his anti-Treaty position.

He met O'Brien on 2 May, and relations were strained from the start. At the EC meeting on the 6th he complained

1923 of the refusal to send the £5,000 and offered his resignation, saying he would become an ordinary member of the union. O'Brien would have allowed him to go his way, but Larkin was not yet estranged from the others, and Foran suggested that he should go on a speaking tour as soon as it could be arranged, in order to get to know the members of the country branches. He agreed to this, and a working arrangement appeared to have been established.

At the Connolly commemoration meeting on 13 May he appealed to Republicans to cease all hostilities and to give up their arms. They must continue the struggle for 'Ireland a nation, one and indivisible' by other means. This last was in fact excellent advice, and wisely timed. The counter-revolution had triumphed and now dictated the conditions under which further opposition could be conducted. A few days later, whether influenced by Larkin's statement or not, de Valera issued his famous 'dump arms' order to the 'legion of the rearguard'. There was nothing else to be done.

Professor Larkin points out that 'Only a man with a profound sense of duty and enormous moral courage could have burdened himself with so thankless a responsibility. Larkin was so affected by what he was going to say that he took the unprecedented action of sitting up during the previous night *preparing his speech.*'[18] An unruly crowd in which Republicans heckled the earlier speakers received him with cheers and listened to him in silence.

A week later he began his tour. In the meantime there had been a union conference at which he was the soul of sweetness and light. He spoke at Wexford, New Ross, Waterford, Dungarvan, Clonmel, Mallow and Cork. He was to go on through Ráthluirc and Tipperary to Thurles. He was not scheduled to speak in Limerick, but it was in Limerick that he suddenly decided to abandon the tour and return to Dublin. He arranged that Jack Carney, who was accompanying him, should send him a telegram purporting to call him back.[19] He had determined to try to drive O'Brien out of the union.

Why? Was it because he disliked O'Brien? Professor Larkin suggests that he was surprised at the extent of O'Brien's influence in the union.[20] But a few pages later he suggests that Larkin *overestimated* that influence, which, he says, was

largely dependent on Foran's.[21] It would perhaps be better 1923
to seek an explanation in terms of Larkin's own perspectives for the future. He had formed the opinion that the national revolution was over and that the Republicans must turn to constitutional methods. But he could not see that the world socialist revolution was also, for the time being, over. He announced his intention of going to Moscow, and, when he did go, explained the setbacks the working-class movement had suffered in terms of the treachery of individuals.[22] This union, which he had once believed the outward sign of his own revolutionary conviction, flaunting defiance of all principalities and powers, even of reality itself, now seemed to him nothing more than a humdrum protection society. He did not stop to consider whether in existing circumstances it could be anything else. He tore off to Dublin to wreak vengeance on the 'traitor'.

He had quarrelled with O'Brien almost as soon as he had arrived, and over an absurd triviality. Larkin made the preposterous claim that he had been sent to the USA on the instructions of Pearse, Clarke and Connolly. O'Brien knew he had not. Larkin, with a dream of rebuilding Labour/Republican unity against the Free State, was trying to assume the mantle of the martyrs. A friend would have passed it off as a harmless foible; his enemy contradicted him flat. When he told Foran that O'Brien must leave the union he gave as his reason the fact that 'he called me a liar'.[23] The disastrous course of action he now took may be explained in various ways, of which one has been suggested. It cannot be excused on any grounds whatsoever.

On 3 June he addressed a meeting of Dublin No. 1 branch and poured forth denunciations of O'Brien and, by implication, all who would not join in the witch-hunt. He seems to have worked on the principle that all is fair in what he believed to be the class war. He claimed to have instructed Connolly to leave the Irish Neutrality League, and to have founded the Friends of Irish Freedom. He complained about the withholding of £7,500 in 1913. But above all he objected to the new rules. At the EC meeting on the following Tuesday he moved that O'Brien was not a valid member, but was overruled. On the following Sunday he held a meeting of No. 3 branch in which he moved the suspension of Thomas Kennedy,

1923 insisting that Kennedy should not have a hearing, and finally moving the chairman out of the chair and putting the question himself. The following morning Larkin and a small group of loyal supporters seized the headquarters at Parnell Square and also occupied Liberty Hall. They were put out when the union secured an injunction. Larkin was thereupon suspended from his position as General Secretary, but the union was now irremediably split.

The majority of the Dublin membership backed Larkin, and it is necessary to ask why. Many of them had joined while he was in the city, and his heroic status was not diminished. Again, there was the Daly faction and others who felt themselves aggrieved by O'Brien. O'Brien had broken no rule, but he had moved knowingly within the rules and had allowed himself to lose contact with the rank and file. Finally there was Larkin's rumbustious oratory, which seemed to express every discontent, frustration, disappointment and suspicion which the ordinary man felt at the machinations of authority. Larkin won little support in the country. The issues he raised in the meetings were tried in the courts, which found for the union with costs. Larkin was a bankrupt once more.

* * *

Larkin's impetuous egoism had created a position in which the employers could launch their general offensive with the certainty of success. The employers announced that from 13 July they would pay dockers 2s less per day. On the 16th 1,500 men ceased work, with Larkin as their leader. Once again he was in command at Liberty Hall and stood at the window thundering against social wrongs. The union Executive were in a difficulty. If they were to hold the dockers, they must pay strike pay. Yet Larkin must win credit for any measure of success. In the event there was none. On 26 October they accepted a compromise, a reduction of 1s a day. Larkin denounced them for it, but advised the men to accept. From then on the key sections of the Dublin working class went down like ninepins — coal porters, carters, granary workers, seamen and firemen. Emmet Larkin points out that working-class organisation was pushed back to its pre-war position – but, one should add, not to that of 1891. The 1923 latest gains were lost, the penultimate preserved.

In 1924, while Larkin was in Moscow, his brother Peter founded the Workers' Union of Ireland. James claimed that this was done against his instructions. Who can say? A deep fissure opened up in Irish working-class organisation which was not filled for many years. As would be expected, the bulk of the union's Dublin membership went over; the country membership did not. At the same time the general confusion was favourable to the establishment of the Amalgamated union, derived from the old NUDL. The ITGWU took legal action against the ATGWU to prevent its using the initials TGWU.

The effect on union membership was disastrous. In 1922 the figure was 100,000. In 1923 it dropped to 87,000. The census taken in 1925 showed a membership of only 51,000. In 1926 the union affiliated to the ITUC on the basis of 40,000 members. The 1929 membership was down to 15,453. It did not begin to climb again until a new generation was compelled to face new problems.

There is no doubt that the leadership placed the main blame for the union's decline on Larkin. The bitterness was intense and long-lasting. He was like Shakespeare's glorious warrior famoused for fight 'after a thousand victories once foiled'. Any good that he had done was denied or forgotten. That his disastrous misjudgment of the situation played a large part cannot be denied. But unions uninfluenced by the Larkin split were affected also. The employers' offensive would have come anyway. The purpose of a union is to keep up the price of labour by engrossing it. This is, inevitably extremely difficult in a buyer's market.

The last long bitter struggle of the period under review was that of the farm workers, and it was defeat in this, even more than the breakaway of the WUI, that reduced union membership. Reference has been made to the Farmers' Freedom Force and their containment by the Republicans. The victory of the pro-Treaty forces deprived the farm workers of this protection, and W. T. Cosgrave's government decided that the prosperity of the country depended on the prosperity of the farmers, which the farmers in their turn thought depended on wage reductions, and proceeded to demand them.

1923 Mr Emmet O'Connor, in his excellent memoir of the course of the farm workers' struggle in Co. Waterford, shows that preparations for the 1923 employers' offensive were more elaborate than in previous years and that something of an alliance between different classes of farmers was built up. The alliance included both landowners and unpurchased tenants, classes whose interests were usually thought to be antagonistic. At a wages conference the union held out for the maintenance of the 1920 rates. The farmers refused, and the strike began on 17 May, during the brief honeymoon period after Larkin's return. During the first phase of the strike considerable success was registered. Sympathetic action was taken by dockers, railwaymen, shop assistants, carters, creamery workers and others.[24] It was when the military were used to disperse pickets and protect the movement of farm supplies that things changed for the worse. Mr O'Connor writes:

> On 1st June, in fulfilment of an undertaking given to the IFU by the Minister for Home Affairs, 250 troops arrived in Waterford from Dublin. They were members of a unit known as the Special Infantry Corps, which was specifically raised to maintain order during the strike. The Specials immediately began to relieve the regulars. They manned a chain of outposts through the affected area; guarded farmers' property from attack by arsonists and saboteurs; protected scabs from union vengeance; provided escorts for all convoys as intermittent sniping was continuing; and conducted arms and ammunition searches.[25]

In other words, it was a second civil war, with the class that had fought for the Republic now fighting for itself. On 4 July Major-General Prout, who had distinguished himself in the Kilkenny area during the civil war, imposed a curfew on the whole of East Waterford, with the exception of the city, and declared martial law within the curfew zone. Union rooms were raided. Flags and banners were confiscated. In August and September the farmers formed vigilantes who harassed strikers and burned down the cottages of union activists. The strike was still in progress in November. But in view of the drain on union funds, finally on 8 December

William O'Brien and Foran went down to Waterford to throw in the sponge. 1923

The union organiser, a Belfast man named Baird, objected 'that his union, the Boilermakers, had unsuccessful strikes and they went so far as to mortgage their head offices to pay for their members'. William O'Brien pointed out that only a small number of ITGWU members were agricultural workers. It was not strictly speaking true; and if it had been true, it would have been a reason for standing the expense.[26] The wheel had now come full circle. The union had stood aside while the Free State was established. Now the forces of that state destroyed the rural organisation, which rapidly fell to pieces, and drove the final wedge between town and country workers.

Mr O'Connor acutely remarks that the Waterford farm strike marked the end of 'Larkin-style' trade unionism. It did so because the new government, having consolidated its political position, then proceeded to reorganise the economy in the interests of the class it represented. Larkinism, a product of the great unrest that developed from 1907 onwards, as the clouds of world crisis gathered, had little theoretical basis. Larkin had a deep fellow-feeling with the deprived masses and had a vision of their rising in their might. His was the voice, the call, that was to galvanise them. Therefore he felt himself above rules. He was engaged in a holy war.

The ITGWU in its early days flourished under the influence of some of the most dynamic characters of western European Labour history. Larkin was the most spectacular of these, and Larkinism is the name of the ill-defined syndicalist tendency that died at the hands of its creator, after which the union suffered its third great historical setback.

While not fully recognised in his lifetime, today Connolly is seen as the greatest, from nourishing an intellectual flame which burns to this day. Yet the central figure, the man who was there all the time, quiet, persistent and unflamboyant, lacking any of the charisma of his more brilliant colleagues, was Thomas Foran. It was he who tried to prevent the final disastrous quarrel between Larkin and O'Brien. Time and again he foresaw danger and moved to protect the union. Perhaps so novel a venture as the ITGWU was in its youth required the intervention of giants. It was nevertheless

1923 the creation of ordinary men and women who applied their will and muscle to the common task; and, as John Kells Ingram put it,

> True men, like you men,
> Are plenty here today.

Appendices

APPENDIX A

Nomenclature and Synonyms

Many trade unions have unwieldy names which are seldom used in full and provide a variety of abbreviations. Those with which difficulty is likely to be encountered are fortunately few, and the synonyms are set out below. The official name is given first.

Irish Transport and General Workers' Union. Irish Transport Workers' Union. Transport Union. ITGWU.

National Union of Gasworkers and General Labourers (Webb, 420). NUGGL. Gasworkers' and General Labourers' Union (Webb, 402). Gasworkers' Union. GWGLU.

National Union of Dock Labourers. NUDL. Dockers' union. This was the west-coast union that became a part of the Amalgamated Transport and General Workers' Union. ATGWU (TGWU in England).

Dock, Wharf and Riverside Labourers' Union of Great Britain, Ireland and the Netherlands. Dock, Wharf and Riverside Labourers' Union (Webb, 405). This was the east-coast union which made little attempt to organise in Ireland. Dock labourers' union.

Dublin (later *Irish*) *United Labour Union.* Bricklayers' Labourers.

Amalgamated Society of Railway Servants. ASRS. Originally confined to skilled grades. Later amalgamated with National Union of Railwaymen. NUR.

National Union of Sailors and Firemen. Sometimes National Union of Seamen and Firemen. Seamen's and Firemen's Union. NUSF.

Workers' Union. WU.

National Amalgamated Union of Shop Assistants, Warehousemen and Clerks. NAUSAWC. This was the British-based union.

Clerical and Allied Workers' Union. (Irish. Not to be confused with British union of same name.) Irish Clerks.
Irish Land and Labour Association. ILLA.
Irish Labour Party and Trade Union Congress. Before 1918 Irish Trade Union Congress and Labour Party. Irish TUC. ITUC. The trade union function dominated the political. Note that the British TUC is written Trades Union Congress.
Dublin United Trades Council and Labour League. Dublin Trades Council. DTC.
National Amalgamated Union of Labour. NAUL.

There are variations in the literature which may arise from the process of amalgamation, for example 'National Amalgamated Union of Sailors and Firemen'. The Webbs make no effort to record which forms are original, and minutes of trade union bodies show little consistency.

APPENDIX B

Rules

No copy of the original rules appears to have survived in Ireland. Mr Berresford Ellis in his *History of the Irish Working Class* (London 1972, p.183) quotes from these. He recalls being shown a tattered copy annotated with uncomplimentary comments, but he cannot remember where he saw it. (Could it possibly have been Sexton's copy?) The rules here reproduced are those registered with D. O'Connell Miley on 10 October 1912. From extracts from the first rules kindly supplied to me by Professor Emmet Larkin it is quite clear that there is virtually no difference, and I thought it best to reproduce the earliest rules of which a printed copy is available in Ireland. They are reproduced here exactly as they appear in the original.

PREFACE

Trade Unionism in Ireland has arrived at a certain stage of growth when this question confronts us – What is to be our next step in fostering its future development? Are we going to continue the policy of grafting ourselves on the English Trades Union movement, losing our own identity as a nation in the great world of organised labour? We say emphatically, No. Ireland has politically reached her manhood; industrially she is in swaddling clothes. And it is our purpose, come weal or woe, to cherish the infant with the milk of economic truth; clothe her in the school of experience; educate her in the solidarity of the workers of Ireland with their fellows the world over; in the hope that in the near future she may become sensible of her dignity and powerful enough to voice her own demands. The workers in Ireland must realise that society is changing rapidly, the capitalist class in Ireland is being reinforced by the influx of foreign capitalists, with their soulless, sordid, money-grubbing propensities. It behoves the Irish workers to realise the power of the employing class, who are not only well organised industrially but practically monopolise the political power in this country as they do in all other countries at present. The old system of sectional unionism amongst unskilled workers is practically useless for modern conditions (this also applies to the skilled workers). When you consider that there are at least 800,000 so called unskilled workers unorganised, surely it must be recognised that the necessity for such an organisation as this we invite you to enrol in is self-evident. The Irish Transport and General Workers' Union offer to you a medium whereby you may combine with your fellows to adjust wages and regulate hours and conditions of labour, wherever and whenever possible and desirable by negotiation, arbitration, or, if the conditions demand it, by withholding our labour until amelioration is granted. Further, we demand political recognition for the enforcement of our demands. Our immediate programme being a legal eight hours' day; provision of work for all unemployed, and pensions for all workers at 60 years of age; adult suffrage; nationalisation of canals, railways and all means of transport; the land of Ireland for the people of Ireland. Our ultimate ideal: the realisation of an Industrial Commonwealth.

By the advocacy of such principles and the carrying out of such a policy, we believe we shall be ultimately enabled to obliterate poverty, and help to realise the glorious time spoken of and sung by the Thinkers, the Prophets, and the Poets, when all children, all women, and all men shall work and rejoice in the deeds of their hand, and thereby become entitled to the fulness of the earth and the abundance thereof.

RULES

Rule I. – Name of Union and Registered Office.

Irish Transport and General Workers' Union.

Rule II. – Objects of the Union.

The organisation is for the purpose of raising the standard of social life of the workers, and the raising of funds to provide for:—

(*a*) Dispute Pay in the case of Strike or Lock-out, or as the result of obeying the lawful demands of the Union at the rate of 10s. per week;

(*b*) Legal assistance for the purpose of enforcing the application of industrial laws and the recovery of wages;

(*c*) A Funeral Allowance for members;

And generally to regulate the relations between employers and employed, to encourage co-operation and enterprise amongst its members.

Rule III. – Who May Join.

The Union shall consist of any number of persons, of not less than 16 years of age, who accept the principles and methods of the Union, and who are not eligible to join a skilled Trade Union; or skilled workmen who desire to help the Union may become members providing they show that they are members of their own Trade Union; or whenever any body of members believe that the interest of their occupation require special technical organisation such body may be affiliated upon accepting the principles of the Union and conforming to its rules.

Rule IV. – Entrance Fee.

The Entrance Fee from any district or locality shall be fixed by the General Secretary and Executive in consultation with the local branch, who may raise or lower the fee as they deem necessary for the betterment of the Union. Penny each shall be charged for contribution card and rule book, and 3d. for badge.

Rule V. – Union Contributions.

Clause A. — *General Fund and Legal Assistance.* — Section 1.

– Those who wish to provide for dispute pay, funeral, labour representation, and legal assistance, shall pay the sum of 4s. 8d. per quarter. Such payments to be made in the following manner:– 4d. per week and a quarterly levy of 4d.

Section 2. – 3s. 7d. per quarter, such payments to be made as follows:– 3d. per week and 4d. quarterly levy.

Section 3. – 2s. 6d. per quarter payments to be made as follows:– 2d. per week and 4d. quarterly levy.

The benefits for such payments to be in proportion to contributions paid (See Rules IX and XI).

No person shall be allowed to qualify under lower rate of contributions and benefits, who in the opinion of the Executive is receiving a weekly wage sufficient to pay higher rate of contributions.

Clause B. – *Honorary Members* (approved by the General E.C.) who shall pay a minimum of one guinea per annum.

Such Honorary Members will have no vote or any power to interfere with policy of Union.

Rule VI. – When Entitled to Benefit.

Members shall be entitled to legal assistance after paying six consecutive weeks' contributions, and dispute pay after paying 52 weeks' consecutive contributions. Members shall be entitled to half funeral benefits after paying twenty-six consecutive weeks' contributions, and full benefit after paying fifty-two consecutive weeks' contributions.

Rule VII. – Arrears of Contributions.

(*a*) Members more than eight weeks in arrears shall be fined 6d. – such fine to be considered arrears – and be out of benefit until such arrears be paid, and forfeit all claim to benefits of Union.

(*b*) All arrears owing by any member when claiming benefit from the funds shall be deducted from any payment made to such member.

Rule VIII. – Clearance Card for Members Transferring to another Branch.

Members removing from the neighbourhood in which their Branch is situated must obtain from the Secretary of their Branch a Clearance Card, stating date of entry, class to which member belongs, amount of benefits during current fifty-two weeks, and arrears at the time of transfer. Such Clearance Card must be deposited with the Secretary of the Branch nearest the member's new place of residence within fourteen days of the date of clearance.

Rule IX. – Disputes.

Members paying under Section 2, Rule V., 3d. per week will receive in case of dispute, lock-out, or victimisation, subject to E.C.'s ruling, 8s. for ten weeks, 4s. for ten weeks, 2s. for ten weeks.

Members paying under Section 3, Rule V., 2d. per week will receive in cases of dispute, lock-out, or victimisation, subject to ruling of E.C., 5s. for twelve weeks, 2s. 6d. for twelve weeks.

Every member of the Union paying full subscriptions, in benefit, who may be locked-out by an employer, or withdrawn from employment by the Union in consequence of any trade dispute, on satisfying the Branch and the General E.C., as to the *bona fide* nature of the dispute, shall receive the sum of 10s. per week for ten weeks, 6s. for ten weeks, 3s. for ten weeks. Any member claiming strike or lock-out pay must sign the Vacant Book each day. Members failing to sign shall forfeit benefit for such days.

Should any member obtain employment for three days in any one week he shall not be entitled to any dispute pay for that week.

For each day under three days that the member obtains employment the day or days so worked shall be deducted from the dispute pay.

No dispute pay shall be paid until six days after ceasing work and the members have signed the book for that period.

After the first week odd days may be paid.

Dispute benefit to cease on the day employment is resumed.

Any member on the dispute or lock-out fund having employment offered and refusing the same shall not be entitled to any further benefit during such dispute or lock-out.

No notices to cease work shall be recognised by the General Executive unless their consent has been obtained prior to such action, provided time for consideration has been given by the firm employing our members.

In sudden and unavoidable disputes the General Executive shall have discretionary power to grant or withhold dispute pay.

The General Secretary shall have power to negotiate when our members are in dispute, and the General Executive may close any dispute when they consider it advisable in the interests of the Union.

When a dispute occurs a Strike Committee must be elected by the members in such dispute. Such Strike Committee shall be subject to the control of the General Executive.

With every request to the General Executive to serve notices to cease work the Branch Secretary must forward to Chief Office:—

The number of members who voted for and the number who voted against the dispute;

The number of workmen directly affected by the dispute;

The number of members entitled to benefit, with their Chief Office number;

The number of members not entitled to benefit; and

The number of non-members, if any, and the position of similar workmen in the district.

The Branch, subject to the General Executive, shall have power to fine or expel any member acting in these or any other matters against the interests or well-being of the Union.

Any member working four weeks consecutively shall be ineligible to resume on dispute pay for that dispute.

Any member working during a dispute after having received instructions not to do so shall be fined a sum not exceeding £1, or is liable to be expelled.

A Strike is a stoppage of work caused by members refusing to work for any particular employer, but such stoppage must have received the sanction of the General Executive before any benefit can be paid.

A Lock-out is where members are laid idle by an employer attempting to impose or introduce conditions on his workmen which the General Executive has authority to resist.

In cases where members are prevented from following their usual employment in consequence of a labour dispute over which the Union has no control, such case may be brought to the notice of the General Executive, and they may decide whether such be supported, and, if so, to what extent.

Rule X. – Legal Assistance and Accidents.

Every member of the Union, in benefit, who desires to take legal action for compensation in case of accident, of recovery of wages, or for enforcing the application of any Industrial law which may have for its object the protection of the members, must report the case, through the Branch, to the Central Office, and, if approved by the General Executive, the case shall receive the legal assistance of the Union.

A member who sustains an accident whilst following his usual employment shall at once send details of the accident, together with the name and address of his employer and foreman, along with a doctor's note, to the Branch Secretary. Should a member be killed, or too seriously injured to send in a report to the Branch Secretary, notice may be given by any other member or any other person to the Branch Secretary. In each case such information shall be immediately sent on, along with the doctor's note, by the Branch Secretary to the Chief Office on the form provided for the purpose.

Rule XI. – Funeral Benefit or Benefits.

At the death of a member in benefit the wife, nominee, or next-of-kin, shall receive in accordance with the following scale:—

Members of twelve months' standing, and who shall have paid twelve months' contributions, shall be entitled to funeral benefit as follows:—

At 4d. per week – Member, £6; wife, £3. 3d. per week – Member, £4; wife, £2. 2d. per week – Member only (male or female), £2 after twelve months' membership.

Members of six months' standing, and who shall have paid six months' contributions, shall be entitled to half benefits.

Death Certificate – Every application for death allowance must be accompanied by a certificate, signed by a registrar of deaths. The above-mentioned certificate shall be given to the Branch Secretary, who shall forward them to the Chief Office within 24 hours of its receipt by the Branch Secretary.

Rule XII. – Financial Assistance to Labour Members.

The General E.C. is empowered to grant sums of money

in aid of the support of any Labour member on any public elective body, provided the said Labour member is not connected with any political party.

Rule XIII. – Branch Meetings, Trades Councils, and Branch Funds.

A Branch shall consist of not less than twenty members and as many as may be approved by the District Committee, where one exists, or by the General Executive in cases where there is no District Committee.

Each Branch may hold weekly meeting.

Branches are empowered to levy their members not more than one halfpenny per week to allow of affiliation with local Trades Councils and other Labour bodies, and for benevolent purposes towards members.

Rule XIV. – Issuing Circulars or Attempting to Injure the Union.

No address or circular shall be issued by any Branch excepting where such address or circular has been approved by the General Executive. Any member or members of a Branch violating this rule shall be fined 2s. 6d. each, and shall also be immediately suspended from all benefits of this Union for one month after fine has been paid. But if the General Executive of the Union so decide, such member or members may be excluded from membership of the Union.

Should a member be found guilty of attempting to injure the Union, the Branch shall have power to suspend him and report his conduct to the District Committee, where one exists; or, in case the Branch is not included in any district, to the General E.C., who shall investigate the nature of his or her offence, and the D.C. or General E.C. shall then have power to fine the member an amount not exceeding 10s. for a first offence and £1 for a second offence; or, if the nature of the offence is such as to constitute a grave injury to the Union, the member may be expelled without the option of a fine. The member, in case of being fined or expelled by the District Committee, shall have the right of appeal to the General Executive Committee. When any member is expelled by the District Committee or General Executive he shall forfeit all claims to the benefits of the Union.

Rule XV. – Branch Officers.

The Branch Officers shall be Chairman and Secretary (who shall also act as Treasurer), and shall be nominated at a general meeting of the members of the Branch elected by ballot, and hold office during the pleasure of the Branch. No person to be elected to any Branch office until he has been a member of the Union for twelve months. This is not to apply to new Branches. No member to be eligible to hold office, or continue to hold office, who is more than eight weeks in arrears.

Rule XVI. – Branch Committees.

A Branch Committee of not less than four members shall be formed, who, along with the Branch President and Secretary, shall transact all business referred to them by the Branch, and see to the due observance of the rules of the Union. All officers and members of committee shall be elected by ballot.

XVII. – Duties of Branch Chairman.

Every Branch Chairman shall preside at all meetings of his Branch. He shall see that the business is conducted in accordance with the rules, he shall decide points of order; he shall take and (after confirmation by the Branch) sign all minutes. The Chairman shall preside at all meetings; during a dispute see to proper payment of benefits, and also the due observance of all rules, and shall aid in the efforts to secure a settlement.

XVIII. – Duties of the Branch Secretary and Salary.

Every Branch Secretary shall attend all meetings of his Branch at the time on which the Branch may decide. He shall keep an account of the contributions of the members in a book provided for that purpose, and sign members' contribution cards for each contribution. He shall keep the accounts of the Branch in a clear and intelligible manner, and keep all documents, accounts, receipts, books, and papers in such manner as the Branch may appoint. He shall pay all benefits in accordance with the rules, taking an official receipt for each payment made on behalf of the Branch. He shall make application to the chief Office for such monies as are needed to meet all legal claims. He shall conduct such correspondence as belongs to his office, and forward a weekly return of all income and expenditure and forward all monies in hand with the exception of £5 in case of Branches under 500 and £10 in case of Branches of 500 members and over. He shall also furnish the Central Office with such detailed information on matters pertaining to the Union as may be required by the General E.C. from time to time. All fines and levies incurred by members of the Union must be accounted for by the Secretary. In cases of dispute or lock-out the Secretary must see to the members affected signing the book daily. He shall check such record, keep a correct amount of all monies received and paid out. No money to be paid without a duly signed receipt on the Dispute Pay Sheet. He shall report to the General Secretary, and communicate any information tending to be helpful in settling the dispute.

Branch Secretary's wages shall be such as fixed by Branch, subject to endorsement of Executive Committee.

XIX. – The Duties of Branch Collectors and Salary.

Collectors shall be appointed by Branches for the purpose of collecting the weekly contributions of members where a number are employed together. The Collectors shall sign all members' cards, and enter all monies received thereon. No amount paid by a member and not so entered can be accredited by the Union. Collectors shall pay over to Branch Secretary all monies received by them at the meeting of the Branch following after the date on which such monies are collected. Collectors shall receive as remuneration for their services 5 per cent of the amount they collect.

XX. – District Committees.

Where a number of Branches consider it advisable for the better organisation or improvement of the Union, a District Committee may be formed and they shall have local autonomy within the rules, and, where the rules are silent, under the instruction of the General Executive. They may meet when circumstances and conditions require, and shall receive the cost of travelling to and from the place of meeting.

XXI. – Officers of District Committees' Duties.

The Officers of the District Committee shall be:—

(*a*) Chairman, who shall preside at all meetings of the District Committee, and sign all minutes after confirmation;

(*b*) Secretary, who shall keep the District Accounts and minutes, conduct all correspondence appertaining to his office, and generally carry out the instructions of his committee.

The Chairman and Secretary shall be elected at and from a meeting of the District Committee, and shall receive such remuneration as may be recommended by the D.C. and endorsed by the General E.C.

Rule XXII. – General Executive Committee.

The General Executive shall be composed of one delegate from Munster, one from Connaught, two from Ulster, four from Leinster (and General President and General Secretary), and shall be elected each year in November, and take office on January 1st following. They shall meet at least four times in each year quarterly and such other times as occasion may require. Each member of the General E.C. shall receive 12s. 6d. per day whilst attending the E.C. meetings with third-class fares to and from the place of meeting.

Each Branch of Union can nominate one, and not more than one, candidate for Executive; but all members are entitled to be nominated for the office of General President and General Secretary.

Any paid official having to travel to the E.C. meeting shall receive the sum of 6s. per day and third-class fare to and from place of meeting.

Rule XXIII. – Duties of the General Executive Committee.

The General Executive shall have the management and control of the Union in accordance with the rules. It shall have the power to order a levy for any Trade Union purpose or for Labour representation after giving seven days' notice to Branches and a majority vote of the members being in favour of the same; the votes to be taken at the next Branch meeting following the one on which the notice is received. It shall have power to federate the Union nationally or internationally subject to a majority vote of the members. The General Executive shall have power to decide on questions where the rules are silent and to interpret any doubtful rule, and its decision shall be binding, unless an appeal is made by the Referendum to the whole body of members. The General Executive shall have the power to veto any strike, and order members to return to work after any trade dispute. It shall have the sole control of all funds.

Rule XXIV. – General Executive Committee and Organisation.

The General Executive shall supervise all arrangements at the Central Office and control the Executive Officers. It shall superintend the work of organisation, and, if required, appoint special organisers for special work.

Rule XXV. – Election and Duties of General President.

There shall be a General President elected every two years, in December, by a ballot vote of the members, and take office on January 1st following. The General President shall, in conjunction with the General Secretary, be responsible for the organisation and extension of the Union. He shall be allowed such assistance by the General Executive as may be necessary, and receive such remuneration as may be decided upon from time to time by the members on the recommendation of the General E.C.

Rule XXVI. – Election and Duties of General Secretary.

There shall be a General Secretary elected every two years, in December, by a ballot vote of the members, and take office on January 1st following. He shall, in conjunction with the General President, conduct the business of the Union in accordance with the rules, and act under the instructions of the General Executive. He shall be allowed such assistance at the Central Office as may be necessary, in order that the business of the Union may be conducted in a proper manner, and receive such remuneration as may be decided from time to time by the members on the recommendation of the General E.C. He shall send a report of each General E.C. meeting to the Branch Secretaries within one month of such meeting. An Assistant Secretary shall be appointed by the Executive.

Rule XXVII. – Election of Union Trustees.

There shall be three trustees, who shall be elected every two years, in December, by a ballot vote of the members, and take office on January 1st following. The President and General Secretary shall be *ex-officio* Trustees.

Rule XXVIII. – General Treasurer.

The Treasurer of the General Fund shall be elected every two years in December by a ballot vote of the members, and take office on January 1st following, and receive such salary as fixed by the Executive (not exceeding the sum of £20 per year). He shall see that all monies of the Union (excepting £20 to be left in the hands of the General Secretary) received shall be banked according to rule, and shall, when required by the Executive, deliver to whoever may be appointed all monies or properties belonging to the Union that he may have in his custody or possession.

Rule XXIX. – Duties of Union Trustees.

The Trustees shall have the general control of the finances of the Union, and shall have the power to refuse to sign any cheques for payment which are not in accordance with the rules; but shall not refuse to make payments or sign cheques for payments which are in accordance with the rules.

Rule XXX. – Banking of Union Funds.

The funds of the Union shall be banked in a Joint Stock Bank in the names of the three Trustees. Each cheque for the withdrawal of money from the bank shall be signed by the General President and one Trustee, or by three Trustees, and each cheque shall be countersigned by the General Secretary. When the funds at the bank have reached such a sum as is considered sufficient by the General E.C. of the Union all amounts above such sum shall be invested by the Trustees in Co-operative Securities or Municipal Corporation Stock.

Rule XXXI. – Inspection of Books

Every member having an interest in the funds of the Union

shall, at any reasonable time and on giving due notice, have the right to inspect the books of the Union and the list of members at the Registered Office.

Rule XXXI. – Nominee for Funeral Benefit.

A member may by writing under his hand, delivered at or sent to the Registered Office or Branch Secretary's address, or made in a book kept for the purpose, nominate a person to whom any sum of money payable by the Union on the death of such member at his decease shall be paid: provided the person so nominated, and not being husband, wife, brother, sister, nephew or niece of the nominator, is not an officer of the Branch where the nominator is a member.

For each such nomination one shilling shall be paid, and sixpence for each revocation or variation, which money shall go to the General Fund of the Union.

A payment made to a person who at the time appears to the majority of the Committee to be entitled thereto on the death of a member, shall be valid and effectual against any demand made upon the Union. Recovery of the money to rest with the next-of-kin or lawful representative from the person receiving the same.

When the Union has paid money to a nominee in ignorance of a marriage subsequent to the nomination, the receipt of the nominee shall be a valid discharge to the Union.

Rule XXXIII. – Alteration of Rules.

The Rules shall only be altered by the General E.C. after amendments have been asked for and sent in by the Branches, such amended Rules to be finally voted on by the members.

XXXIV. – Dissolution of Union.

The Union may be dissolved, and its funds divided, with the sanction of five-sixths of the votes of the financial members.

Rule XXXV. – National Convention.

A National Convention of the Union shall be summoned every year. Summonses for the Convention shall be sent out to Branches three months before the date of meeting. Notices of motion for the Convention must reach the General Secretary two months before the date, and an agenda paper of Convention business must be sent to Branches one month before the date of its assembling. Secretaries of Branches are required to summon a general meeting of their members for the purpose of electing delegates and considering the agenda as soon as possible after the necessary papers reach them. Except where a general meeting is ordered the decision of the Convention so summoned shall constitute and be construed as the ruling of the Union. Such Convention to be held in the same town as, and on the day following, the Irish Trades Congress, if possible.

Rule XXXVI. – Annual Audit and Election of Auditors.

The accounts of the Union shall be audited in January of each year by two members elected by ballot in the preceding December, such Auditors to receive remuneration at the same rate as members of the General E.C., or by a registered accountant.

The Registered Office is in Ireland, at No. 18 Beresford Place, Dublin, in the City of the County of Dublin. In the event of any change in the situation of the Registered Office notice of change shall be sent within fourteen days to the Registrar in the form prescribed by the Treasury Regulations in that behalf.

Peter Ennis
Stephen Clarke
John Bohan
Joseph Kelly
John O'Neill
Thomas Hewson
Thomas Foran
James Larkin

Notes

INTRODUCTION
(pp. 1-9)

1. *Irish Worker*, Jun. 1893.
2. Michael Davitt, *Fall of Feudalism in Ireland*, London 1904, 406.
3. According to the 1891 census, out of a total of 936,759 persons engaged in agriculture, 118,980 were classified as 'general labourers'. The corresponding figure for 1901 was 117,863, showing a reduction of only 1,117 in a decade during which 60,697 left the land.
4. Sidney and Beatrice Webb, *The History of Trade Unionism*, New York 1965, 406.
5. *Commonweal*, 5 Apr. 1890.
6. *Labour World*, 6 Dec. 1890.
7. *Weekly Freeman*, 3 May 1890.
8. *Justice*, 21 Mar. 1891.
9. Desmond Ryan, *Remembering Sion*, London 1934, 57.
10. Webb, 600ff.
11. W. J. Lowe, 'Lancashire Fenianism', *Transactions of the Historical Society of Lancashire and Cheshire*, Vol. 126 (1977).
12. Information supplied by Mr J. L. Jones.

Chapter 1
LARKIN'S IRISH BREAKAWAY
(pp. 11-25)

1. J. Anthony Gaughan in his life of Thomas Johnson notes with surprise that Larkin first met Johnson at an ILP meeting when their birthplaces were not a quarter of a mile apart. This arises from placing Larkin's birth in Berry Street. Combermere Street is at a much greater distance.
2. James Connolly, *The Reconquest of Ireland*, Dublin 1934, 310.
3. McMullen's memoir is compiled from newspaper reports. The author was living in Belfast in 1907 and knew Larkin for many years.
4. Emmet Larkin, *James Larkin*, London 1965, 31.
5. *Ibid.*, 37.
6. R. M. Fox, *Jim Larkin*, New York 1957, 69.
7. Webb, 498.
8. William O'Brien, *Forth the Banners Go*, Dublin 1969, 55.
9. *Irish Times*, 1 Dec. 1908.
10. See *Dundalk Democrat*, 2 Jan. 1909, for Dobbins's reply.
11. Diary of William O'Brien, 4 Jan. 1909 (NLI, MS. 15675).

Chapter 2
FOUNDATION AND CONSOLIDATION
(pp. 26-50)

1. O'Brien, 56.
2. Dublin Trades Council Minutes, 15 Mar. 1909 (NLI, MS.12782)
3. *Waterford News*, 7 May 1909.
4. Each generation has its vogue words. In 1896 Connolly spoke of a 'Socialist Republic', then of a 'Workers' Republic'. An earlier phrase had been 'Co-operative Commonwealth'. One guesses that 'Industrial Commonwealth' was a modification of this expression under syndicalist influence. People were often as vague about the meaning of these terms as they are today when talking of 'socialism'.
5. *Cork Examiner*, 13 Aug. 1909.
6. See *Irish Times*, 6 Sep. 1909.

Chapter 3
ENTER THE GIANTS
(pp. 51-75)

1. Diary of William O'Brien, 2 Aug. 1911.
2. Connolly, in the foreword to *Labour in Irish History*, wrote: 'The capitalist system is the most foreign thing in Ireland.'
3. Diary of William O'Brien, 16 Nov. 1911.
4. The sole surviving Roll Book of the early Belfast branch gives the date of Connolly's entry as 22 July 1911. This implies that after moving to Belfast he retained his Dublin membership until he was appointed northern organiser. See J. Anthony Gaughan, *Thomas Johnson*, Dublin 1980, 20-1, for Mrs Johnson's account of the move. I had my information from Daniel McDevitt many years ago.
5. The first *Irish Worker* had been published in the 1890s by Bernard Doyle. It was very much the organ of the skilled trades. The *People's Advocate* was started in 1891 by the National Union of Gasworkers and General Labourers. It expressed the alliance between the organised 'unskilled' workers and the socialists and republicans. It would be interesting to know whether Larkin was aiming consciously at uniting two traditions.
6. Tom Mann, *Memoirs*, London 1923, 259.
7. *Irish Worker*, 26 Aug. 1911.
8. The involvement of Socialist Party of Ireland activists, like Lyng and Carpenter, in the ITGWU doubtless contributed to the movement for merging the SPI and the Independent Labour Party. The merged organisations adopted the name Independent Labour Party of Ireland in 1912.
9. O'Brien to Connolly, 28 Sep. 1911 (NLI, MS.13908(iii)).
10. I have not been able to ascertain who gave the title Liberty Hall to the ITGWU headquarters. The expression occurs in Goldsmith's *She Stoops to Conquer* in an English context. It was later used by the writer of stories for boys, Captain Marryat, in *Midshipman Easy* in order to satirise radicalism. It is a tale of the sea, and prob-

ably Larkin read it like most other Victorian schoolboys.

11. Dublin 1 (Liberty Hall), Dublin 2 (James Street), Dublin 3 (High Street), Belfast, Dundalk, Newry, Sligo, Dún Laoire, Bray, Kill o' the Grange, Wexford, Waterford, New Ross, Enniscorthy, and Dublin (Jacobs).
12. *Irish Worker*, 8 Jun. 1912.
13. James Connolly, *Socialism Made Easy*, New York 1905, 13-17. Attempts have been made to attribute this conception to Marx. See Bernard Ransom, *Connolly's Marxism*, London 1980, 42. The passage is in *Capital*, III, 455 (Kerr Edition, Chicago 1909; cf. *Das Kapital*, III, Dietz Verlag, Berlin, n.d., 423). These attempts are based on a misunderstanding. '. . . sie die kapitalistische Hülle gesprengt hat', translated 'has burst its capitalist shell', refers not to industry in general, still less to trade union organisation, but to 'Arbeit der Oberaufsicht und Leitung' (labour of superintendence and management), which would be necessary even when capitalist ownership had ceased to exist. This is clearer if 'Hülle' is simply translated as 'covering'. Its being covered by capitalist ownership conceals the fact that management is work. Marx (through the agency of Engels) was making a theoretical point. Those who seized factories on the strength of this passage did so not because their theory was strong, but because the 'political state' was weak.
14. James Connolly, *The Axe to the Root*, Dublin 1934, 16.
15. *ITUC Report, 1912*, 12-13.
16. *Ibid.*, 61.
17. *Ibid.*, 45.
18. J. D. Clarkson, *Labour and Nationalism in Ireland*, New York 1925, 249.

Chapter 4
HOME RULE IS CHEAP RULE
(pp. 76-94)

1. O'Brien to Connolly, 1 Oct. 1912 (NLI, MS.13908(iii)).
2. *Irish Worker*, 14 Dec. 1912.
3. *Ibid.*, 22 Nov. 1912.
4. The signatories were Larkin, Foran, Bohan, John O'Neill, Peter Ennis, Joseph Kelly, Stephen Clarke and Thomas Hewson.
5. Arnold Wright, *Disturbed Dublin*, London 1914; see Connolly's review in *Irish Worker*, 8 Nov. 1914.
6. See Connolly in *Daily Herald*, 6 Dec. 1913.
7. *Ibid.*
8. Emmet Larkin, 115.
9. O'Brien to Connolly, 22 Mar. 1913 (NLI, MS.13908(iii).
10. O'Brien to Connolly, 5 Jun. 1913 (*ibid.*).
11. The full list is Larkin, Metcalfe, Brohoon, Michael McCarthy, Bernard Conway and William Fairtlough from Dublin No. 1; John Bohan and Thomas Burke from Dublin No. 3; and Edward Gibson from No. 16 branch (the Aungier Street branch). Connolly represented Belfast, James Byrne Dún Laoire, and James Stanford and P. T. Daly Sligo.

12. In the columns of the *Irish Worker* he appears as plain Michael Mullen, but he was known to Gaelic enthusiasts as Micheál Ó Maoláin *as Árainn*. Seán O'Casey lodged with him for a time in Mountjoy Square, and he has been suggested as an inspirer of the character Séamus Shields in *The Shadow of a Gunman*.
13. Webb, 104.
14. Connolly to O'Brien, 29 Jul. 1913, in *The Attempt to Smash the Irish Transport and General Workers' Union*, Dublin 1924, 163.
15. *Irish Worker*, 26 Jul. 1913.

Chapter 5
WAR ON THE WORKERS
(pp. 95-121)

1. See James Connolly, 'The Dublin Lock-out and its Sequel' in Desmond Ryan, ed., *The Workers' Republic*, Dublin 1951, 176.
2. A special edition of the *Irish Worker*, published on Wednesday 27 August, give an account of the events leading up to the tram strike.
3. *Daily Herald*, 6 Sep. 1913.
4. See O'Brien, 83-92. On p. 85 O'Brien records his feeling that Larkin was displeased at his sending for Connolly, thereby usurping Larkin's authority. On the other hand, he transferred the demonstration to Croydon Park in his capacity as secretary of the strike committee. It is possible to see here the earliest sign of the future rift between Larkin and O'Brien. The strike committee seems to have been established in the first place because of the involvement of several unions in the Easons dispute. It widened as the dispute widened and grew steadily in authority. A dual control involving the meticulous O'Brien and the impetuous Larkin could scarcely work without friction. In general at this time O'Brien was 'pro-Larkin'. Connolly had been openly critical of Larkin from an earlier period, O'Brien joining him in the summer of 1914.
5. *Report of British TUC, 1913*, 192.
6. It has been said that Connolly was driven to the Countess's house in the viceregal car. The late Mr Eamon Martin assured me that this was not the case. The viceregal car brought the release order to his sister's house, and Connolly was collected in a taxi.
7. Connolly in Ryan, ed., *The Workers' Republic*, 122-6.
8. Webb, 104.
9. Reproduced in *Irish Worker*, 11 Oct. 1913.
10. Connolly in Ryan, ed., *The Workers' Republic*, 143-4.
11. *Ibid.*, 144-5.
12. *Ibid.*, 146.
13. Here is a specimen: 'Shaun Casey, head of Larkin's souper pipers' band, Seville Place. Well, Shaun, my Irish-speaking bowsie, you were afraid of the Toiler scout to bring the band to the runaway army's Swords march out. How much of the collection did you collar? Or did you hand it over to Delia for the cause? Keep enough to pay the rent on the bandroom. If not, they will have to

play outside churches again. But mind the blues do not see you, or you will have to start telling them where you were baptised.' There are references here to several incidents in which O'Casey was involved, for example the police interference with the St Laurence O'Toole Pipe Band on the occasion of its performing outside a Protestant church, when O'Casey averted trouble by explaining that he had been baptised there. The trusting will think McIntyre had a remarkable intelligence service; the suspicious will wonder if he had semi-official communicators.

14. R. W. Postgate, *Builders' History*, London 1923, 417.

Chapter 6
DOWN BUT NOT OUT
(pp.122-138)

1. The other members present were James Gannon, James Byrne, Michael Cunningham, John Cunningham, Bernard Conway, Andrew Early, James Smith, Michael Brohoon, D. Heffernan, P. White and P. Doyle.
2. Glasgow *Forward*, 7 Feb. 1914, quoted in Ryan, ed., *The Workers' Republic*, 142 (where the date is incorrectly given).
3. Glasgow *Forward*, 14 Mar. 1914, quoted in Ryan, ed., *The Workers' Republic*, 146.
4. Connolly in Ryan, ed., *The Workers' Republic*, 149.
5. James Connolly, *The Axe to the Root*, Dublin 1921, 38.
6. *Ibid.*, 41.
7. See V. I. Lenin, 'Imperialism' in *Collected Works*, London 1942, 177; also Clarkson, 181.
8. Dublin *Saturday Post*, 21 Mar. 1914.
9. Connolly in Desmond Ryan, ed., *Socialism and Nationalism*, Dublin 1948, 111.
10. The ITGWU delegates numbered 17, viz: James Larkin, Bernard Conway, John O'Neill, Michael Cunningham, Thomas Foran, P. T. Daly, James Connolly, Daniel Coveney and Daniel Carey (Cork), John Bohan, Thomas Burke and Thomas Kennedy (Dublin No. 3), W. P. Partridge (Inchicore), John Lynch and P. Kealey (Sligo), Richard Corish (Wexford) and Frank Moss (Agricultural Labourers' Branch.)
11. Connolly in Ryan, ed., *Socialism and Nationalism*, 130.
12. Arthur Mitchell, *Labour in Irish Politics*, Dublin 1974, 60.
13. Larkin to Quinlan, 18 Aug. 1914, in *Attempt to Smash*, 166. In 1948 I discussed with Seán O'Casey Larkin's reason for going to America. He said that Larkin had used funds belonging to the Insurance Section of the union for paying strike benefit and was afraid of a second misappropriation prosecution. The matter seemed to me so important that I made a note which I still have. Years later I learned that Joseph Casey, described by Martin Margulies (*Early Life of Sean O'Casey*, Dublin 1970, 35) as a 'clerk and salesman for the health insurance division of the ITGWU' was in fact Seán O'Casey's brother, whose legal name was Isaac. He

left for Liverpool under a financial cloud. The 'faked audit' referred to in *Attempt to Smash*, 82, bore his signature. These facts may help to explain Larkin's anxiety to go to America as early as November 1913. (O'Brien, 61-2).

14. *Western News* (Ballinasloe), 17 Aug. 1915, quoted in *Workers' Republic*, 4 Sep. 1915.

Chapter 7
ORDEAL BY DEBT
(pp. 139-156)

1. Minutes of Special Committee of No. 1 branch, 5 Mar. 1915.
2. Dublin No. 1 was represented by Connolly, O'Farrell, Michael Cunningham, Patrick Stafford, P. Forde, Joseph Metcalfe, and John O'Neill; No. 3 sent John Bohan and Thomas Burke; Aungier Street sent Robert de Coeur, and Inchicore Michael Mallin. Dún Laoire sent P. Crimmins, Bray S. Mulvey, Waterford John Power and John Murphy, Cork Denis O'Riordan, Sligo Alderman John Lynch and Councillor Kelly, Wexford Alderman Richard Corish, and Belfast James Flanagan (sometimes spelt Flannagan).
3. The dispute between O'Brien and Daly resulted in a Dáil inquiry and a lawsuit. Much of the relevant information can be found in NLI, MS.15657 (folder containing letters, telegrams, newspaper cuttings, etc.).
4. *Attempt to Smash*, 137.
5. *Workers' Republic*, 1 Apr. 1916.
6. Séan O'Casey, *Drums under the Window*, New York 1950, 399.

Chapter 8
CONNOLLY AND EASTER WEEK
(pp. 157-167)

1. William O'Brien, Preface to Desmond Ryan, ed., *Labour and Easter Week*, Dublin 1949, 9. Samuel Levenson, *James Connolly*, London 1973, 282, says that Connolly's disappearance was about a week earlier, but does not give his reasons for thinking so. It is a bold man who tries to upset an O'Brien date. Further evidence, though indirect, is provided by Frank Robbins, *Under the Starry Plough*, Dublin 1977, 73. Pearse gave Connolly an autographed copy of *An Mhathair* dated 21 January 1916.
2. McCullough told me this around 1969, and it is confirmed in Leon Ó Broin, *Revolutionary Underground*, Dublin 1976, 167. The existence of conspiracy within conspiracy is documented in Pádraig Ó Snodaigh, *Comhghuaille na Réabhloide, 1913-16*, Dublin 1966. The point is that the offensivist policy became official in January 1916; that is the political turning-point.
3. Ó Broin, 167.
4. Connolly's youngest daughter, Mrs Fiona Connolly Edwards, confirmed this detail in 1961.
5. Diarmuid Lynch, *The IRB and the 1916 Insurrection*, Cork 1957, 25.

6. See Maureen Wall's contribution in K. B. Nowlan, ed., *The Making of 1916*, Dublin 1969.
7. See 'On German Militarism', *Irish Worker*, 22 Aug. 1914.
8. Maureen Wall in Nowlan, ed., 190, n.15.
9. *Irish Worker*, 3 Oct. 1914.
10. *Ibid.*, 31 Oct. 1914.
11. *Ibid.*
12. *Ibid.*, 24 Oct. 1914.
13. *Ibid.*, 8 Aug. 1914, quoted in Ryan, ed., *Socialism and Nationalism*, 131.
14. *Workers' Republic*, 22 Jan. 1916, quoted in Ryan, ed., *Labour and Easter Week*, 137.
15. *International Socialist Review*, Mar. 1915, quoted in Ryan, ed., *Labour and Easter Week*, 60.
16. *Workers' Republic*, 18 Dec. 1915.
17. *Ibid.*, 22 Jan. 1916.
18. Lynch, 60.
19. See Robbins, 55-6. The 1915 dating disposes of some of Diarmuid Lynch's sceptical remarks.
20. *Workers' Republic*, 18 Mar. 1916.
21. Mullens told me that he did not belong to the Transport Union and that both he and Partridge were acting for the IRB. They took different railway routes to Kingsbridge, one travelling via Limerick, the other via Mallow.

Chapter 9
RESURRECTION
(pp. 168-187)

1. The ITGWU delegates were Foran, Metcalfe, Brohoon, Bohan, Lawrence Prior (Cork), James Flanagan (Belfast), James Nolan (Dún Laoire), together with John Lynch, Michael Lynch and John MacLaughlin from Sligo.
2. Quoted in Dorothy Macardle, *The Irish Republic*, London 1937, 20.
3. I discussed this question with Johnson over a number of years and am confident that I express his opinion accurately. J. Anthony Gaughan in his life of Johnson (pp 69-85) does not seem to get to grips with this vitally important question.
4. Ronald McNeill, *Ulster's Stand for Union*, London 1923, 259, quoted in Macardle, 227.
5. No. 1 branch sent Metcalfe, Foran and Brohoon, No. 3 Bohan and Thomas Kennedy. Belfast sent James Flanagan, Cork Denis Houston and Daniel Carey, Sligo Alderman John Lynch and Michael Lynch. Wexford would have sent a delegate but for 'financial difficulties'. M. J. O'Connor represented Tralee Trades Council, and William O'Brien Dublin Trades Council.

Chapter 10
THE ONE BIG UNION
(pp. 188-210)

1. Minutes of Committee of No. 1 branch, 7 Jan. 1918.
2. In order to launch it he accepted financial aid from a wealthy Englishman, Malcolm Lyon, anxious to encourage socialist-oriented criticism of Sinn Féin. When the hoped-for anti-nationalist tendency did not materialise he asked that a cheque should be returned to him. See Gaughan, 82-4.
3. The committee that managed the paper consisted of Foran, O'Brien, J. J. Hughes, Johnson, MacPartlin, L. P. Byrne and Desmond Ryan.
4. Union records use the anglicised Gaffney. His earliest surviving signature has the form MGamhna.

Chapter 11
THE GREAT SWING TO THE LEFT
(pp. 211-228)

1. See NLI, MS.15657 for many notes and cuttings on this period.
2. Eight delegates gave their address as Liberty Hall: Thomas Foran, J. J. Hughes, Michael McCarthy, William Vickers, Joseph Metcalfe, Joseph O'Neill, John Dillon and James Gannon. These presumably represented No. 1 branch. Thomas Kennedy and J. Walsh probably represented No. 3. James Lawlor of Tallaght possibly represented Inchicore. Denis Houston, Cathal O'Shannon, P. Nagle and John Brew of 8 Camden Quay would represent Cork No. 1. The other Cork delegates were Daniel Barrett and Richard Hawkins. Limerick sent M. J. O'Connor, Edward Walsh and John Flood; Sligo, John Lynch and Michael Lynch. From Waterford came W. P. Coates, M. Holland and Patrick Wilson. Richard Corish represented Wexford, James Flanagan Belfast, and Jeremiah Murphy Tralee. But in addition, there were activists from newly formed branches: L. A. Veale from Dungarvan, Michael Smyth from Newbridge, Joseph Gaule from Arklow, James Moore from Lucan, Michael Nolan from Baldoyle, and E. Kelly from Bray. The union paid £100 in delegates' fees, its nearest rival, the NUR paying only £70 19s 3d.
3. The Executive consisted of Miss Rose Timmons, Thomas MacPartlin, Cathal O'Shannon, M. J. O'Lehane, J. T. O'Farrell, T. C. Daly, Joseph Mitchell and M. J. Egan.
4. Dublin *Saturday Post*, 19 Oct. 1918.
5. Connolly to O'Brien, received Dublin, 6 Oct. 1914, in *Attempt to Smash*, 164.
6. Gaughan, 120.
7. *Ibid.*, 121.
8. Peadar O'Donnell once expressed the opinion to me that Cathal O'Shannon was an 'intellectual giant' frustrated by the greater strength of character of the more humdrum O'Brien. There is no question that he conducted considerable research into Irish Labour history, but lacked the application to make anything of it. W. P.

Coates achieved fame as the secretary of the Anglo-Russian Parliamentary Committee and wrote on political subjects in collaboration with his gifted wife Zelda Kahan.

Chapter 12
UNDER THE RED FLAG
(pp. 229-250)

1. *ITGWU Annual Report, 1918*, 26.
2. At a meeting of the Socialist Party of Ireland at the Trades Hall on 14 December 1918 the subject under discussion was that of the revolutions in Russia and Germany. Those present included Thomas Foran, William O'Brien, J. J. Hughes and Thomas Kennedy.
3. I had many conversations with Hedley over the years, and everything he told that I could check proved correct.
4. The word 'soviet' (Russian for 'council') was thereafter applied to a variety of actions thought to resemble what had occurred in the Russian revolution.
5. The Irish Trade Union Congress became the Irish Trade Union Congress and Labour Party in 1912. The report of the Waterford Congress in 1918 reversed the two parts of the title, and thereafter the organisation became known as the Irish Labour Party and Trade Union Congress.
6. *ITGWU Annual Report, 1919*, 8.
7. The attraction was probably less London than Zelda Kahan to whom Coates was engaged.
8. That similar processes took place elsewhere is shown by a police report of July 1919 quoted by David Fitzpatrick in his monograph on Co. Clare, which indicates that in that county also the LLA had fused with the ITGWU. In some cases, as for example that of Newtown, Drogheda, a Land and Labour Association attempted to organise a strike, realised its lack of experience and amalgamated with the union.
9. This important letter addressed to P. O'Toole at the Carlow office is among the uncatalogued MSS in the National Library of Ireland.
10. Four Trades Councils were represented by identifiable members of the ITGWU: Bray (Alf Metcalfe), Cavan (Peadar O'Donnell), Limerick (Michael Redden) and Sligo (Alderman John Lynch). The Edward Lynch of Cóbh was presumably the union member of that name. Of 211 delegates, 71 belonged to the Transport Union. M. J. O'Connor, the former Kerry organiser, came from Limerick and represented the Asylum Workers' Union.
11. Information from Mr Peadar O'Donnell.
12. This letter is given in full in *Attempt to Smash*, 135.

Chapter 13
WITH VICTORY IN SIGHT
(pp. 251-277)

1. For Galway 'folklore' I am particularly indebted to Mr Bartley Keane.

2. *Watchword of Labour*, 1 Nov. 1919.
3. *Ibid.*, 17 Jan. 1920. The candidates are also referred to as 'Transport' candidates.
4. Carlow, Cork, Dublin, Kildare, Kilkenny, Laois, Limerick, Meath, Tipperary, Waterford, Wexford and Wicklow. This south-eastern area in 1918 contained 91 per cent of the union membership.
5. Quoted in Macardle, 245.
6. *Watchword of Labour*, 13 Mar. 1920.
7. O'Brien, 176ff.
8. *Watchword of Labour*, 20 Mar. 1920.
9. *ILP & TUC Report, 1920*, 28.
10. I only once made notes after a conversation with Hedley, and must to some degree draw on memory. When Dowling died Hedley was given his papers. I have not yet been able to trace them.
11. *Watchword of Labour*, 1 May 1920.

Chapter 14
THE WIND FROM THE NORTH
(pp. 278-301)

1. An account of the Belfast pogrom is to be found in *Watchword of Labour*, 31 Jul. 1920. See also *ILP & TUC Report, 1920*, 100ff.
2. See Nevil Macready, *Annals of an Active Life*, London 1924, II, 487ff.
3. The *Watchword of Labour* refers to this as the 'rump' of the Trades Council.
4. *ILP & TUC Report, 1920*, 70.
5. *Ibid.*, 130.
6. *Ibid.*, 100-3.
7. Those taken in included William O'Brien, J. J. Hughes, George Spain, Michael Sheppard, Ernest Nunan, Archibald Heron, Peter Ennis and Thomas Johnson.
8. Mitchell, 106.
9. This was made available to me through the kindness of Mr Paddy Devlin.
10. O'Brien to Houston, 21 Mar. 1921 (in private ownership).
11. Sir C. E. Callwell, *Field-Marshal Sir Henry Wilson: His Life and Diaries*, London 1927, II, 263.
12. *ITUC Report, 1921*.
13. NLI, uncatalogued MS.

Chapter 15
THE BIRTH OF THE NEW REGIME
(pp. 302-324)

1. Robbins, 227.
2. This *fait accompli* was Britain's trump card in the ensuing negotiations.
3. The following further amalgamations and transfers took place: *Irish Independent* printing-shop workers (Oct. 1921), chemical workers (from WU Nov. 1921), Silkweavers (Feb. 1922), Wood-

cutting Machinists (Apr. 1922), Meath Herds' Union (Aug. 1922), Automobile Drivers (Sep. 1922), Asylum Workers (Oct. 1922), Cork seamen (Apr. 1923), Limerick Pork Butchers (Sep. 1923).

4. See O'Brien, 217-18.
5. Hallinan to Mulcahy, 24 Feb 1922 (NLI, MS.13955).
6. *Voice of Labour*, 17 Dec. 1921.
7. It is possible that the *Voice of Labour* was similarly circumstanced, though, printing with a subsidiary of Thoms, it could be expected to have a more speedy service.
8. I discussed the differences between his father and William O'Brien with James Larkin junior on several occasions. Each time he referred to acceptance of the Treaty as the fundamental issue and accused O'Brien of consciously working for it. But if Cathal O'Shannon was voicing a collective opinion in the *Voice* of 10 December, it would seem that they were prepared to let the two factions fight it out, and then to do business with the winner. When it became clear that the odds were on the pro-Treaty party, that became the legitimised government. After the breach Larkin attacked his former colleagues from an extreme nationalist position, and it may be that James Larkin junior formed his opinion during this period.
9. *ITGWU Annual Report, 1922*, 8.
10. *Ibid.*
11. *ILP & TUC Report, 1922*, 69.
12. *Workers' Republic*, 22 Apr. 1922.
13. Redmond, who was an intelligence officer with the Republican forces, later went over to the Free State. He was found murdered, it was believed as a reprisal for possible passing of information.
14. For this correspondence see NLI, MS.15678. Peadar Nunan was a brother of the secretary of the INTO.
15. There was a plan to 'break Larkin out', and I am inclined to identify it with Peter's mission and Foran's 'spectacular' action. Escape from Comstock, an open prison, would probably not have been difficult, but Larkin declined to accept the plan, possibly because he was considering alternative action. The difficulties of dealing with Peter Larkin are illustrated by his accusing Frank P. Walsh, the Labour lawyer who was prepared to give his services free, of evil intentions when, as a result of his entering an appeal, a movement for a pardon was frustrated.
16. The 1918 rules read: 'The General President, in conjunction with the General Secretary, and General Treasurer, shall be responsible for the organisation, extension and efficient management of the union.' The 1923 rules read: 'Their primary responsibilities shall be as follows: General President and Vice-president – General Policy of the union and conduct of industrial movements, disputes, strikes etc. General Secretary – Recruitment, organisation, education, propaganda and general administration.' All major decisions were to be considered by the five general officers, but if the General President insisted, the matter could be referred to the full Executive.

17. To the best of my recollection, I was told that this consisted of William Gallacher, Arthur MacManus and Robert Stewart.
18. Emmet Larkin, 259.
19. O'Brien, 78.
20. Emmet Larkin, 267.
21. *Ibid.*, 271.
22. Stewart described to me the meeting at which Zinoviev asked Larkin his opinion of one Labour leader after another, Larkin dismissing them with such epithets as 'lily-livered rats', etc. Zinoviev then asked him if there might not be some general political reason for this apparent mass renegacy. Larkin could only argue to the person.
23. O'Brien, 81.
24. Emmet O'Connor in *Saothar: Journal of the Irish Labour History Society* (1980), 40.
25. *Ibid.*, 49.
26. O'Brien, 113.

Index